AF876962

Supporting Users and Troubleshooting a Microsoft® Windows® XP Operating System

Project Lab Manual

Exam 70-271

Supporting Users and Troubleshooting a Microsoft® Windows® XP Operating System

Project Lab Manual
Exam 70-271

First Edition

Kenneth C. Laudon, Series Designer
Frank Miller, MCSE, MCSA
Seth Greenberg

The Azimuth Interactive MCSE/MCSA Team
Carol G. Traver, Series Editor
Kenneth Rosenblatt
Robin L. Pickering
Russell Polo
David Langley
Megan Miller
Brian Hill, MCSE, MCSA
Stacey McBrine, MCSE, MCSA
Richard Watson, MCSE
Brien Posey, MCSE
Tim Oliwiak, MCSE, MCT
David Lundell, MCSE, MCT
L. Ward Ulmer, MCSE, MCT
Wale Soyinka, MCP
Simon Sykes-Wright, MCSE
David W. Tschanz, MCSE
Russell Jones, MCSE
Pete Grondin, MCSA
Lenny Bailes
Mark Maxwell

PEARSON
Prentice Hall
Upper Saddle River, New Jersey, 07458

Senior Vice President/Publisher: Natalie Anderson
Executive Acquisitions Editor: Stephanie Wall
Marketing Manager: Sarah Davis
Project Manager, Editorial: Laura Burgess
Manager, Print Production: Christy Mahon
Production Editor & Buyer: Carol O'Rourke
Production Editor & Buyer: Wanda Rockwell
Manager, Multimedia: Christy Mahon
Composition: Azimuth Interactive, Inc.
Quality Assurance: Specialized Composition, Inc.
Printer/Binder: Courier, Stoughton

PEARSON
Prentice
Hall

10 9 8 7 6 5 4 3 2 1
ISBN 0-13-185237-X

To our families,
for their love, patience,
and inspiration.

Brief Contents

Contents

Preface

The purpose of this Project Lab Manual is to provide you, the student, with another opportunity to review Windows XP concepts and skills, and to apply them to situations that you are likely to encounter on the job. The Prentice Hall Certification Series textbooks contain a great deal of conceptual and hands-on material. The Prentice Hall Certification Series Project Lab Manuals are designed to give you an opportunity to put those concepts and skills to work in a variety of different real-world on-the-job situations, and to understand the textbook contents in greater depth.

The Project Lab Manuals are organized in the same two-page highly illustrated format with conceptual material and instructions on the left-hand page, and screenshots and conceptual diagrams on the right-hand page. The Lessons in the Project Lab Manuals follow the Lessons in the textbook. Each Project Lab Manual Lesson is composed of a number of projects that reinforce the concepts and skills taught in the accompanying textbooks.

Project Lab Manual Lesson Contents

The Project Lab Manual Lessons have a number of elements designed to speed your learning and help you understand key concepts and skills.

Introductory Page: Each Lesson begins with an introductory page that reviews the key concepts and skills that you will be asked to apply in the lesson.

Scenario: Each Lesson has a brief scenario that describes the setting in which the projects take place. These scenarios provide you with a sense of how the concepts and skills that you have learned in the book are used in realistic business settings.

Project/Objective Table: Each Lesson includes a table that lists the Lesson projects and the corresponding exam objective supported. Where the project relates to a basic understanding of the subject matter, this is referred to as "Basic knowledge." You will always know how a project relates to MCDST exam requirements.

General Requirements: At the beginning of each Lesson, there is a description of the hardware and software that you will need to complete the projects in the Lesson.

Project's Exam Objective: For each project there is a description of the specific MCDST exam objective supported by the project.

Overview: Each project presents a specific assignment that builds on the Lesson's main scenario.

Learning Objective: Each project includes a specific learning objective that describes what you will be able to do after completing the project.

Specific Requirements: A list of specific requirements for each project is provided.

Estimated Completion Time: For each project, there is an estimated time for completion based on the experience of MCDST professionals and instructors in colleges and training institutes. You should use these estimates only as a guide because your actual completion times will depend on your prior experience with Windows XP.

Project Steps: Each project includes a set of step-by-step instructions for completing the project. These instructions are similar to those in the main textbook, but often differ because new options and pathways may be explored in the Project Lab Manuals.

Tips: Throughout the Project Lab Manuals you will find Tips and Cautions that offer you suggestions or comments about completing the project and working with Windows XP.

Graphics and Illustrations: As you can expect from the Prentice Hall Certification Series, there are many screenshots and conceptual graphics provided that show you how the software should look at various points in the project. These are intended to familiarize you with the Windows XP environment and assure you that you are on the right track.

Quality Assurance

We have made every effort to ensure that the Project Lab Manuals are written to the same quality standards as the main textbook. The Project Lab Manuals are written by MCDST professionals with many years of real-world experience. The initial instructions and scenarios are then reviewed by independent technical editors who test each project, and each step. These results are then verified by the MCSE/MCSA/MCDST team at Azimuth and the Series Designer and Editor. The end result is a product that students and instructors can understand and trust.

Notice

The projects in the Project Lab Manuals have been built using the most recent release of Windows XP Professional software. Your school or other institution may be using an earlier release of the software, or its environment may differ in some respects from the environment in which the projects were built. At times, these variations in environment and service packs can cause variations in the progression of steps and screenshots so that a screenshot in the book does not precisely match the screen you may be looking at. If this should occur, please report this to the authors at the Web site for this book.

LESSON

1 Developing a Troubleshooting Strategy

Windows XP provides a variety of tools designed to help you troubleshoot and diagnose hardware and software problems. Using these tools, you will be able to isolate and fix a broad range of problems.

Being a successful troubleshooter requires logic, creativity, and confidence. You will gain confidence by practicing troubleshooting exercises and by remembering that problems usually do not arise from random events. Problems are often caused by hardware malfunctions or incompatibility, or software configuration errors, as well as damage to hardware or software. As you work to solve problems, you will need to gather information, develop hypotheses, and test these hypotheses. To work efficiently, you must develop a troubleshooting strategy to help guide you through the steps to evaluate symptoms and resolve problems.

You will typically use the PHO hierarchy—evaluate Physical problems first, tackle Hardware next, and finally, analyze Operating system issues.

As you troubleshoot, you can identify the source of a problem by analyzing the symptoms. To be successful, you must analyze whether:

- Problems occur randomly or as part of a pattern, such as when a user executes a command
- Problems occur after a system update or a software installation
- Any non-Plug and Play devices have been installed
- Differences exist between the Basic Input/Output System (BIOS) or Extensible Firmware Interface (EFI) versions of working and non-working systems

To help identify problems, Windows XP provides you with logs detailing:

- Error messages
- Event view logs
- Performance logs

When you need to solve problems and get a user's system up and running, you can use several utilities that enable you to:

- Create system configuration files
- Return to a restore point

This lesson contains projects that will help you to practice your skills at developing, analyzing, and solving common troubleshooting problems. In this lesson, you will learn basic troubleshooting concepts and how to develop an effective strategy. You will also learn about sources of troubleshooting information and some basic tools to help you solve problems.

Scenario

You have recently been promoted to a project manager position in an IT Help Desk support group at the Ads R Us advertising agency. As part of your new job, you must not only help individual users but also develop guidelines for hardware and software troubleshooting. In the coming weeks, you will be faced with a major challenge: Your company is merging with a smaller agency. All of the computers at the smaller agency require hardware and software upgrades, and they must be connected to the Ads R Us network.

Lesson 1 Developing a Troubleshooting Strategy

Project	Exam 70-298 Objective
1.1 Developing a Troubleshooting Strategy	Basic knowledge
1.2 Discovering the Problem	Basic knowledge
1.3 Evaluating System Configuration	Basic knowledge
1.4 Tracking Possible Solutions	Basic knowledge
1.5 Executing a Plan	Basic knowledge
1.6 Taking a Proactive Approach	Basic knowledge

General Requirements

To complete the projects in this lesson, you will need administrative rights on a Windows XP Professional computer that can access the Internet. You may also find it helpful to refer to Lesson 1 in your Prentice Hall Certification Series Exam 70-271 textbook for further information about the projects covered in this lesson.

project 1.1

Developing a Troubleshooting Strategy

exam objective

Basic knowledge

overview

In order to help provide consistent technical support, you will prepare a troubleshooting strategy for your company. You will use the Microsoft six-step troubleshooting model, which is called the detect method (**Figure 1-1**). Answer the questions to describe how you would implement each step.

learning objective

After completing this project, you will know how to develop a troubleshooting strategy.

specific requirements

See General Requirements.

estimated completion time

60 minutes

project steps

1. **Document the problem:** Describe how you would identify the problem and document it using logs or a database.
2. **Assess the system configuration:** What questions would you ask to assess changes in the system configuration? What tools would you use to assess changes in the system configuration?
3. **Pursue possible solutions:** How would you pursue solutions to problems? Which Web sites would you visit to find troubleshooting information? How would you change software or hardware installations?
4. **Implement a plan:** What steps would you take before implementing a plan of action? What would your plan of action be when faced with specific problems?
5. **Test the results:** How would you test the results of your troubleshooting actions?
6. **Use a proactive method:** What procedures and guidelines would you put in place to work proactively to prevent future problems?

Figure 1-1 The Microsoft detect model troubleshooting flowchart

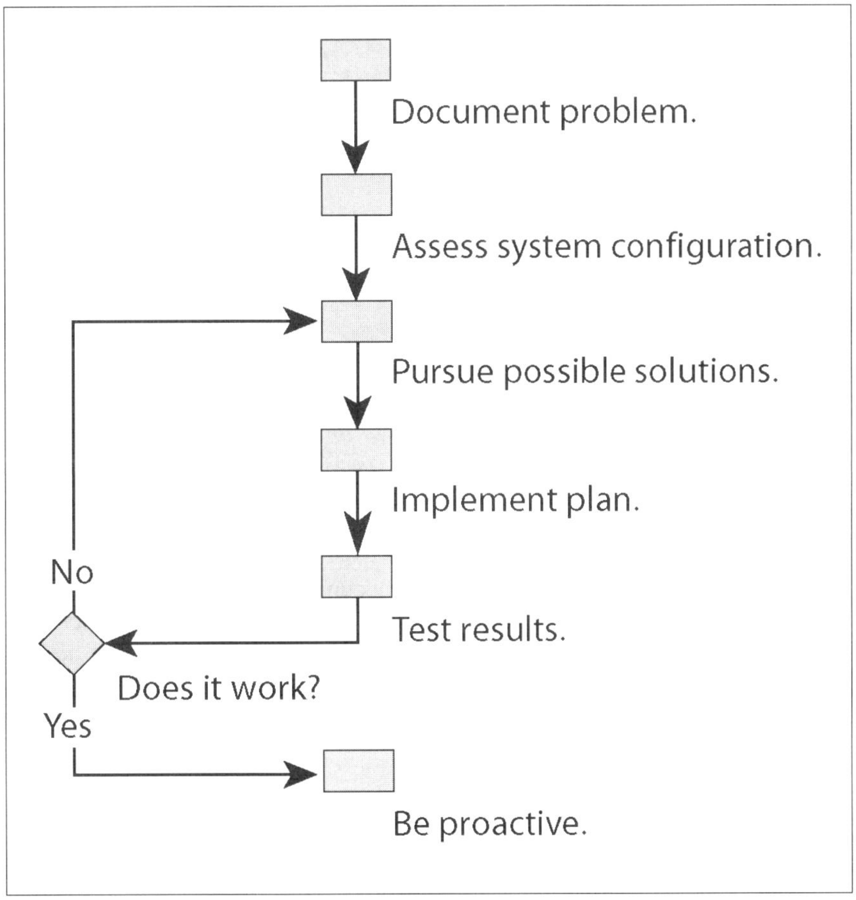

project 1.2 Discovering the Problem

exam objective

Basic knowledge

overview

Today you have not had any complaints about the ad agency's network, but in the past, users have sometimes lost their network connection when attempting to connect to a database or to send e-mail. You decide to check the System log on one of the computers that has lost its network connection.

learning objective

After completing this project, you will know how to check the Windows XP System log in the Event Viewer.

specific requirements

See General Requirements.

estimated completion time

15 minutes

project steps

1. Click **Start** and then click **Control Panel**.
2. In the left pane, click **Switch to Classic View**, if necessary.
3. Double-click **Administrative Tools**.
4. Double-click **Event Viewer**.
5. In the left pane of the **Event Viewer**, double-click **System** to view the **System log** **(Figure 1-2)**.
6. Scroll down the list of events until you see the **tcpip** listing in the **Source** column.
7. Double-click the **tcpip** listing to open the **Event Properties** dialog box **(Figure 1-3)**.
8. Note whether the system successfully connected to the network.
9. Regardless of whether an error has occurred, click the **http** link and read the troubleshooting information on the resulting Web page **(Figure 1-4)**.

Figure 1-2 The System log

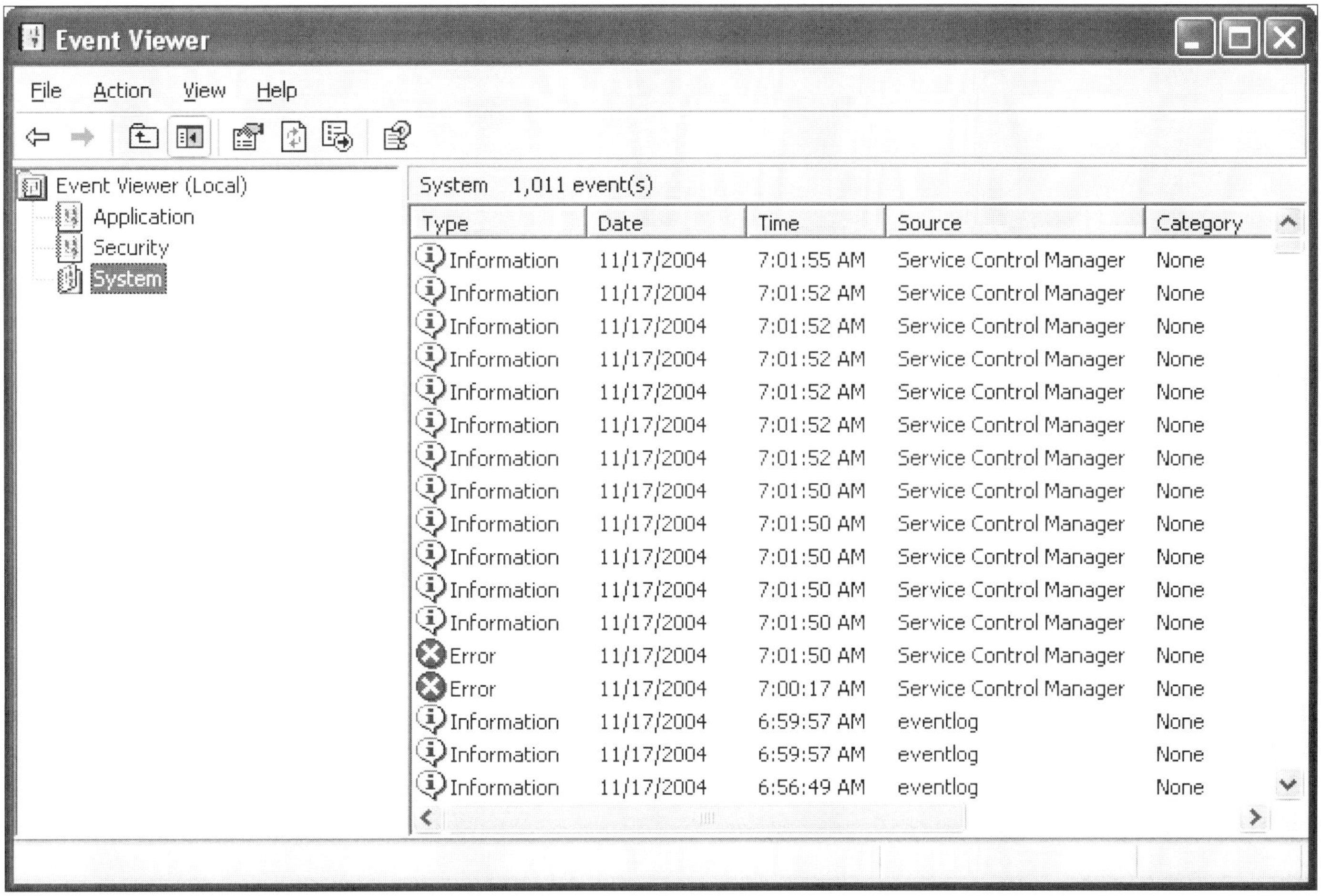

Figure 1-3 The Event Properties dialog box

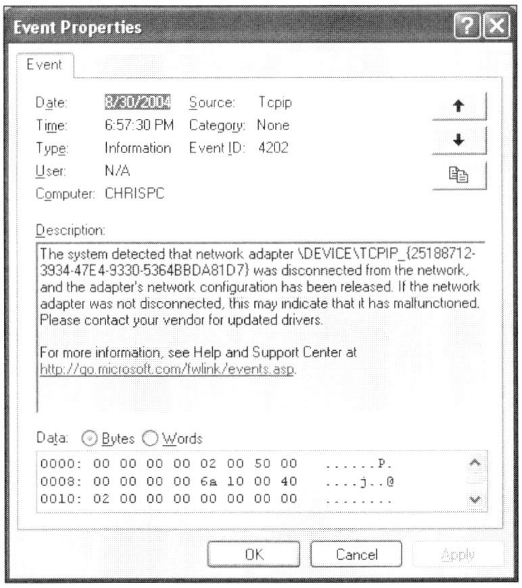

Figure 1-4 Help and Support Center Event ID information

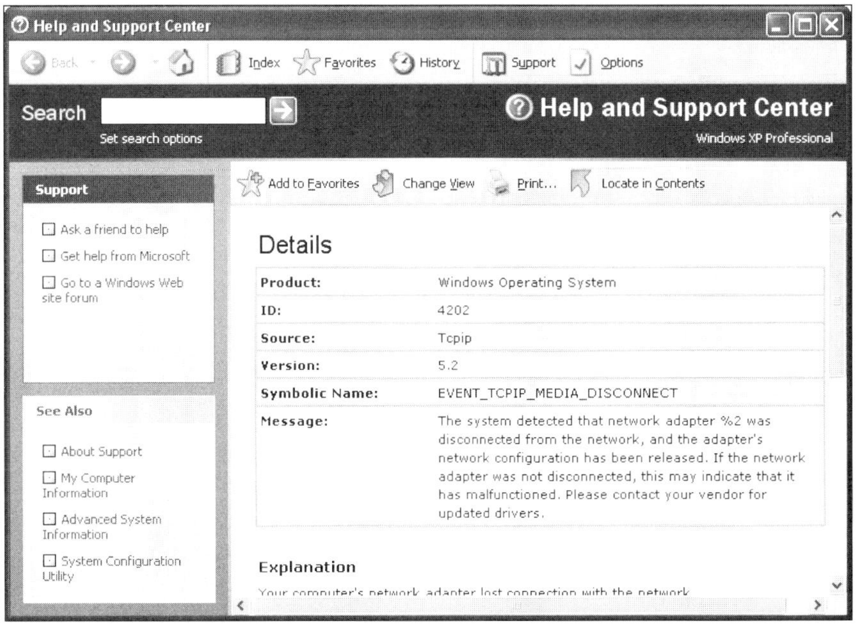

project 1.3

Evaluating System Configuration

exam objective

Basic knowledge

overview

Several programmers at your company have been moved to a new department where they are using old computers. They have reported to Help Desk personnel that CD-ROMs run very slowly on these computers and that some macros no longer run in Microsoft Excel. You decide to compare the system information from a user's old computer to his new workstation to find out if the CD-ROM drive is the same model number as one that is installed on a computer that is not exhibiting any problems. You also want to find out if the drive will read DVDs.

learning objective

After completing this project, you will know how to view hardware and software system information.

specific requirements

See General Requirements.

estimated completion time

15 minutes

project steps

1. Click **Start**, point to **All Programs**, point to **Accessories**, point to **System Tools**, and click **System Information** to open the **System Information** console.
2. In the **System Summary** screen, review the **OS Name** and **Version**, and the **Total Physical Memory (Figure 1-5)**.
3. Expand the **Components** section.
4. Click **CD-ROM** and note the manufacturer and whether the CD-ROM drive can read DVDs **(Figure 1-6)**.
5. Expand the **Office Applications** section.
6. Expand the **Microsoft Excel** section.
7. Click **Summary** to determine which version of Excel is installed **(Figure 1-7)**.
8. Close the System Information console.

Figure 1-5 The System Information console-System Summary

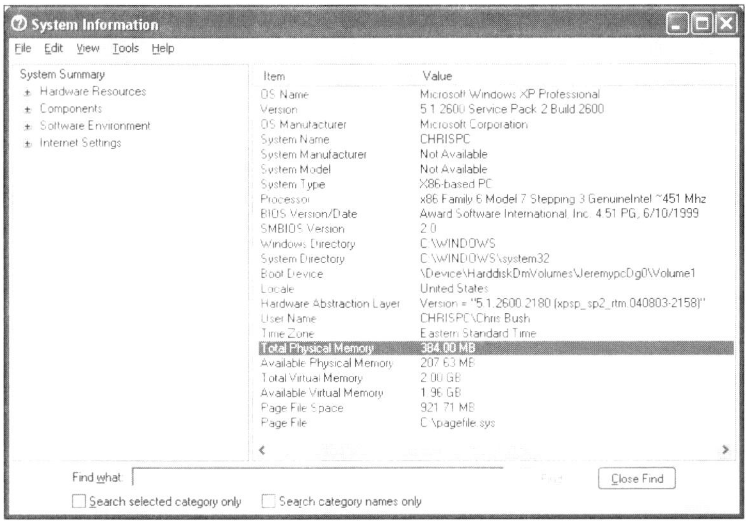

Figure 1-6 Checking the CD-ROM drive

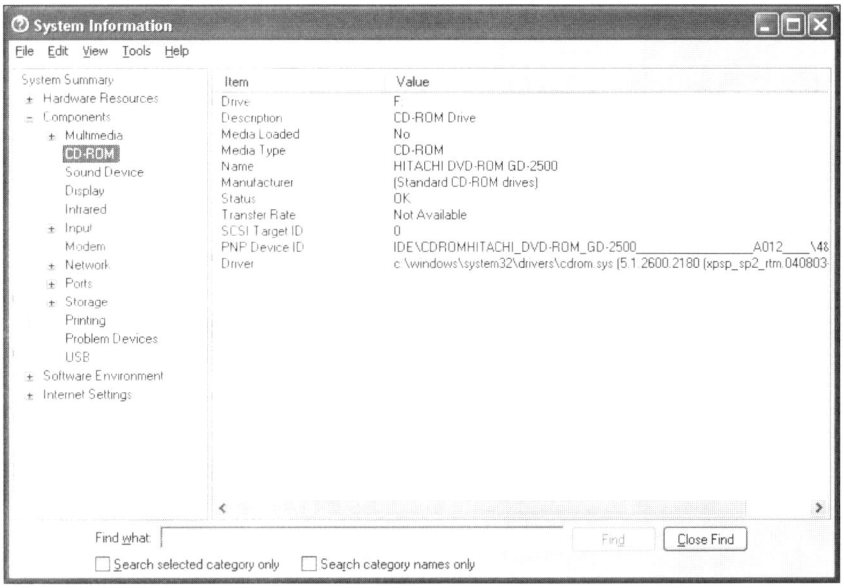

Figure 1-7 Checking the application version

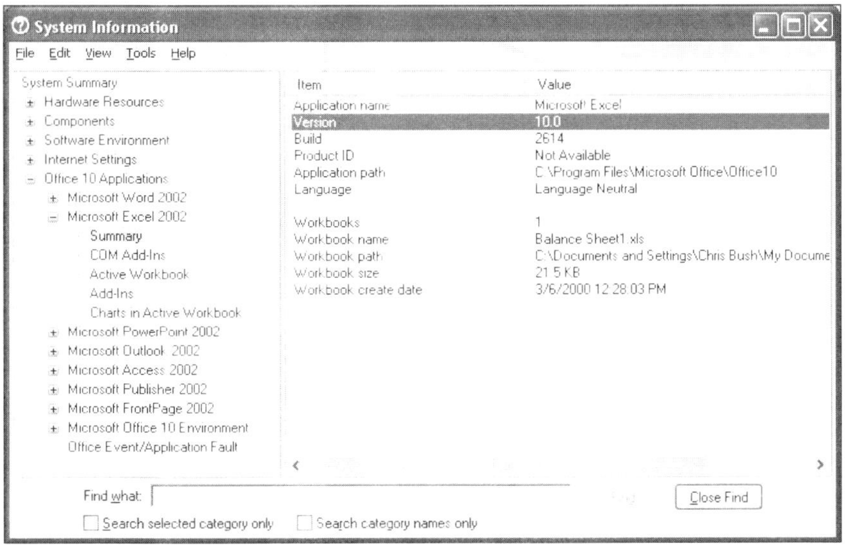

project 1.4 Tracking Possible Solutions

exam objective

Basic knowledge

overview

You receive an e-mail from a user at the company who contends that her laptop mouse touch pad is behaving erratically. She explains that the mouse seems to have "a mind of its own." As she types, the cursor sometimes jumps to different areas of the screen as if she clicked the mouse, but she isn't clicking—she's typing. You decide to check the mouse touch pad device and use the Troubleshoot option in the Device Manager.

learning objective

After completing this project, you will know how to troubleshoot a device.

specific requirements

See General Requirements.

estimated completion time

15 minutes

project steps

1. Click **Start** and then click **Control Panel**.
2. In the left pane, click **Switch to Classic View**, if necessary.
3. Double-click **Administrative Tools**.
4. Double-click **Computer Management** to display the Computer Management console.
5. In the left pane, click **Device Manager**.
6. Expand the **Mice and other pointing devices** section **(Figure 1-8)**.
7. Double-click the mouse or touch pad icon to open the **Properties** dialog box for the device **(Figure 1-9)**.
8. In the **Device status** section, note whether the message states "This device is working properly."
9. To further troubleshoot, click the **Troubleshoot** button.
10. Follow the instruction in the Help and Support Center to troubleshoot the pointing device problem **(Figure 1-10)**.

tip

Some laptop touchpad software installs its own applet in the Control Panel rather than extending the built-in mouse applet. In such a situation, you must open the applet from the Control Panel to troubleshoot the mouse touch pad.

Figure 1-8 Device Manager node in the Computer Management console

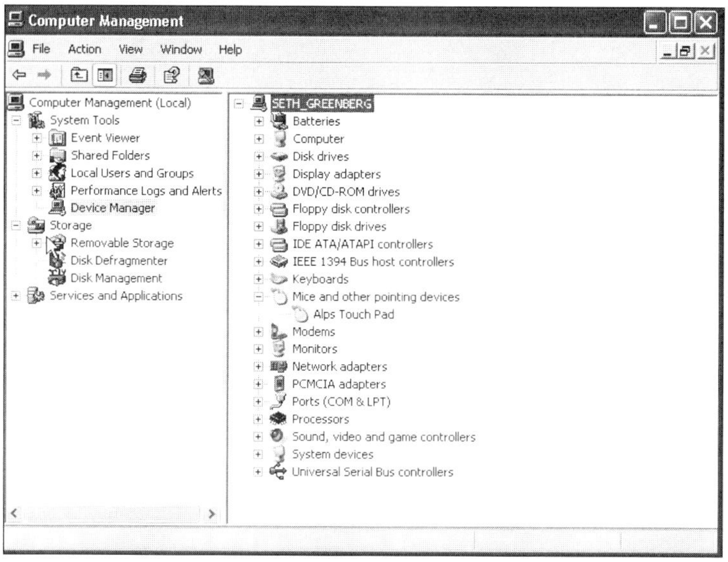

Figure 1-9 Properties dialog box for a mouse touch pad

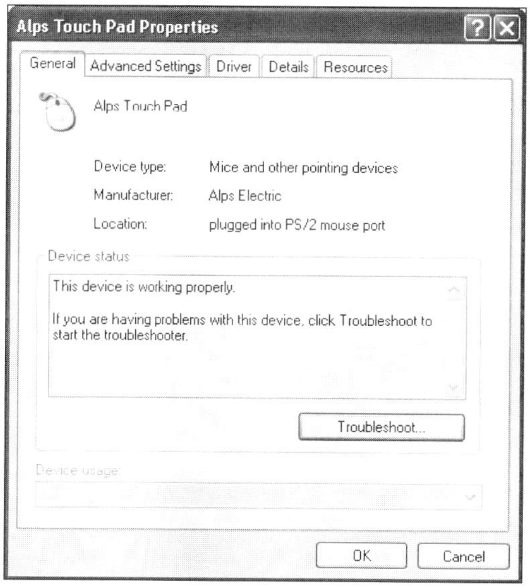

Figure 1-10 Mouse Troubleshooter page in the Help and Support Center

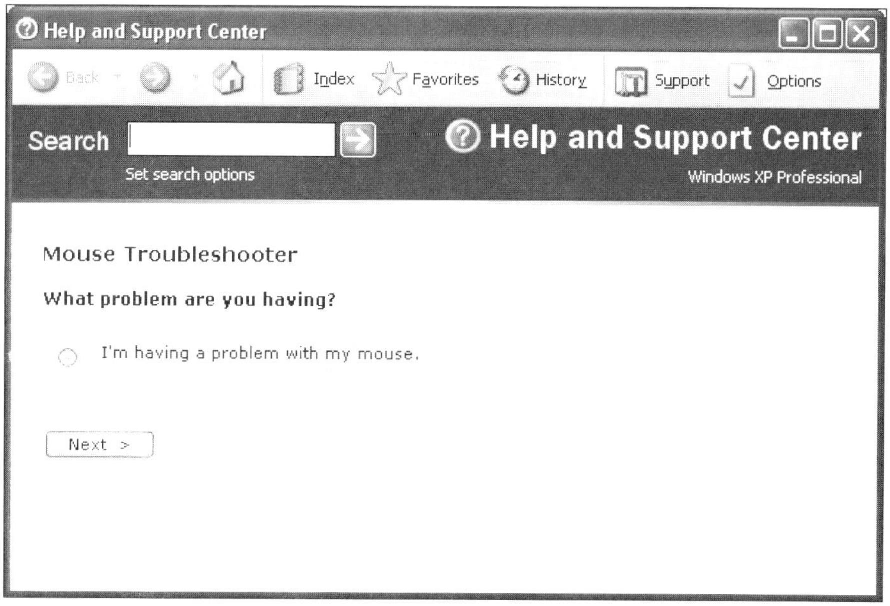

project 1.5 Executing a Plan

exam objective

Basic knowledge

overview

A user sends an e-mail help request in which he reports that his computer is "creeping like a snail." When you quiz him about the problem, you discover that the problem began after he downloaded music from the Internet. You decide that the fastest way to get his computer up and running is to execute a System Restore using a restore point that was created in the previous week before he downloaded the music.

learning objective

After completing this project, you will know how to perform a System Restore.

specific requirements

See General Requirements.

estimated completion time

15 minutes

project steps

1. Click **Start**, point to **All Programs**, point to **Accessories**, point to **System Tools**, and then click **System Restore** to open the **System Restore** window.
2. Notice that the default setting in the System Restore window is set to **Restore my computer to an earlier time**.
3. Click **Next** to open the **Select a Restore Point** screen. On the calendar, a bold date indicates an available restore point.
4. Click a bold date and then click a restore point (**Figure 1-11**).
5. Click **Next** to open the **Confirm Restore Point Selection** screen (**Figure 1-12**).
6. If you want to proceed with the System Restore, click **Next**. Otherwise, click **Cancel**.

Figure 1-11 Selecting a restore point

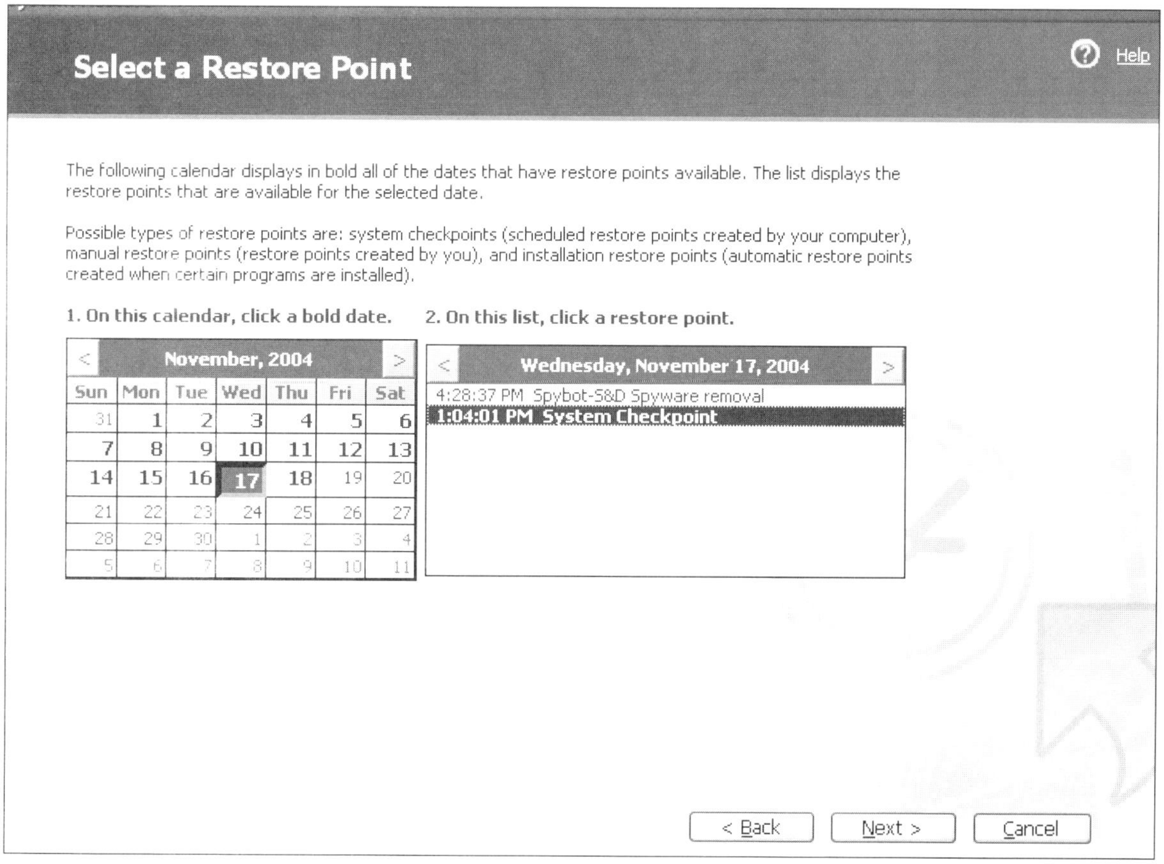

Figure 1-12 The Confirm Restore Point Selection screen

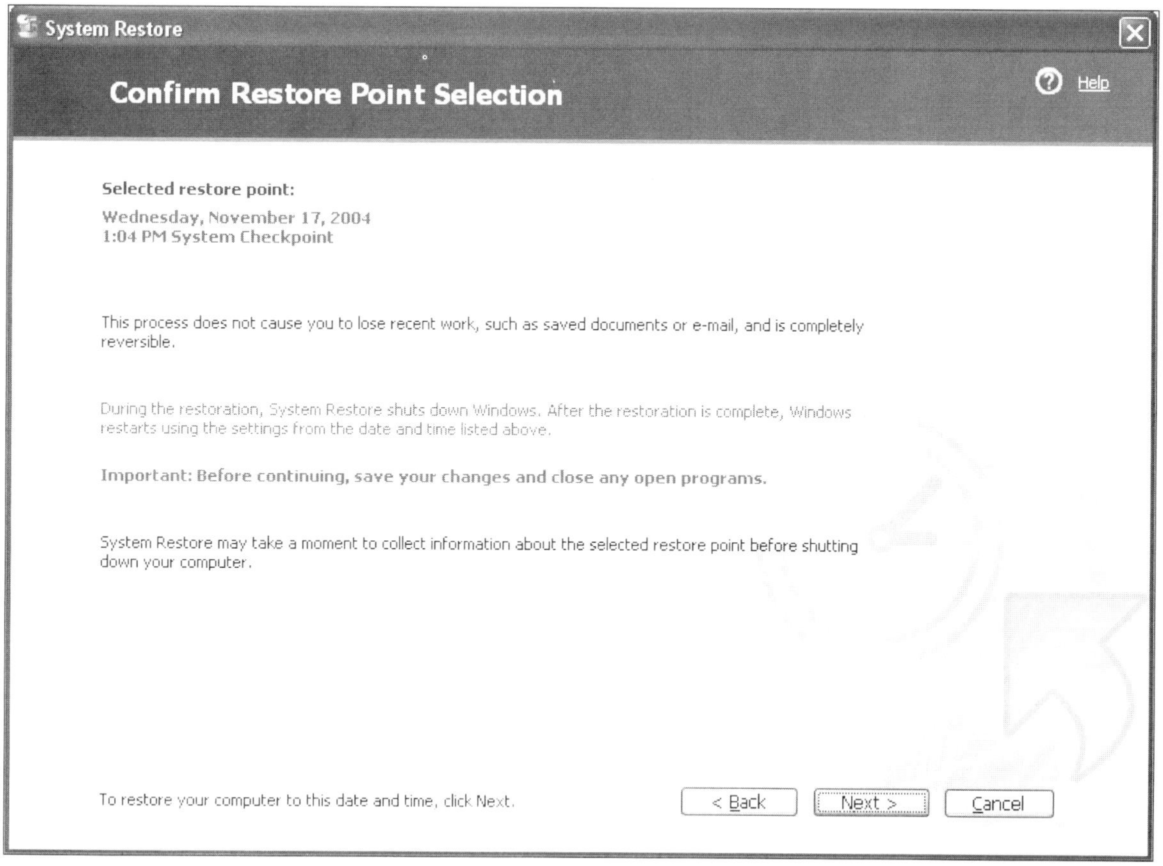

project 1.6 Taking a Proactive Stance

exam objective

Basic knowledge

overview

You want to take a proactive approach to troubleshooting and decide to create a troubleshooting database. You would like to track all hardware and software problems that occur at your company in the database. You also want your Help Desk co-workers to be able to quickly look up past problems and find out what actions were taken to solve the problem. Using reports from the database, you would like to create charts that indicate the most common problems, which departments are reporting the problems, and what type of hardware and software is causing the problems. You want to use the data to predict which future problems are most likely to occur. Finally, you want to use the data to help prevent future problems.

learning objective

After completing this project, you will be familiar with how record-keeping can facilitate future troubleshooting efforts.

specific requirements

See General Requirements

estimated completion time

30 minutes

project steps

1. Create sample input screens on paper for a database that keeps track of hardware and software problems.
2. Create the categories or fields in the database that will help you to create reports showing the history of hardware and software problems, as well as what hardware, software, and user actions caused these problems.
3. To help you complete Steps 1 and 2, review **Figures 1-13** and **1-14**, which depict the process of creating a troubleshooting database.

Figure 1-13 Creating database fields

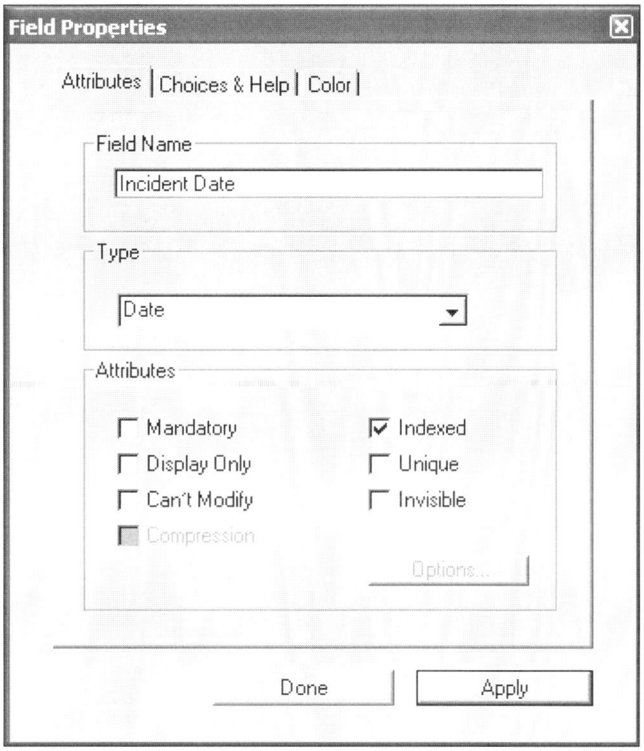

Figure 1-14 A troubleshooting database

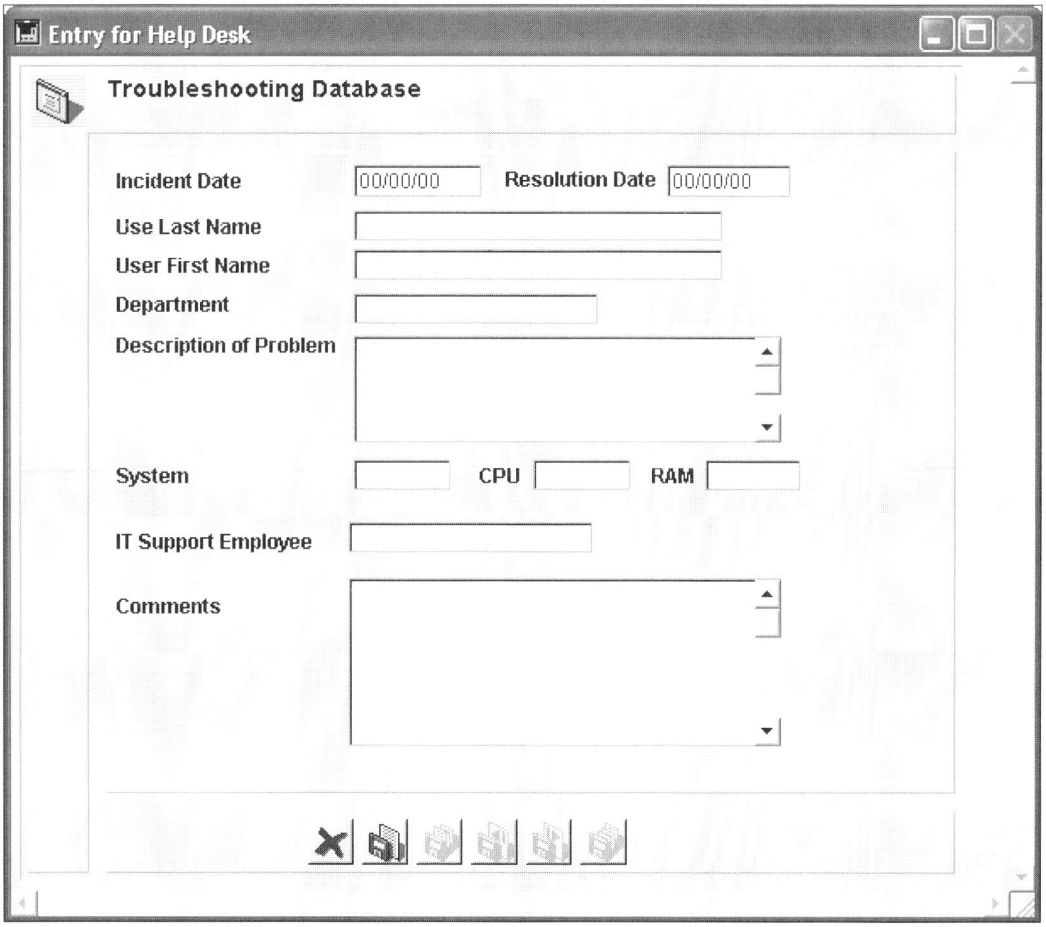

LESSON

2 Introducing Windows XP

Windows XP is available in two main editions, Windows XP Home Edition and Windows XP Professional. Windows XP Home Edition is appropriate for use in a non-business setting. Most businesses require the more robust security and management features provided by Windows XP Professional.

Both editions of Windows XP offer a number of features that enhance user productivity. Windows XP supports a wide range of hardware devices and makes it easy to securely connect to a network and to the Internet. Part of your job as an administrator is to understand the features of Windows XP and how they are best implemented to meet business requirements. Some important features you must understand include:

- Plug and Play
- Power management
- Management utilities, such as the Microsoft Management Console (MMC)
- Encrypting File System
- Automatic Updates
- Disk management utilities
- Fault tolerance utilities, such as Backup and Automatic System Restore
- Networking capabilities

In this lesson, you will examine some of the features of Windows XP and learn how they can be used to meet the business requirements of network users.

Scenario

You have recently been promoted to a project manager position in an IT help desk support group at the Ads R Us advertising agency. The company is planning to update the client computers from Windows 98 to Windows XP. The company has 20 desktop computers and 10 laptop computers. The laptop computers are used by designers who telecommute three days a week. The Ads R Us network is currently configured as a workgroup, although the company is considering a move to a domain in the near future.

You have been asked to help provide documentation to help decision-makers understand the impact of the upgrade. Your documentation will include a discussion of the two editions of Windows XP and a demonstration of some key Windows XP features.

Lesson 2 Introducing Windows XP

Project	Exam 70-271 Objective
2.1 Introducing Windows XP Home Edition and Windows XP Professional	Basic knowledge
2.2 Introducing Windows XP Features and Enhancements	Basic knowledge
2.3 Identifying the Range of Supported Hardware	Basic knowledge
2.4 Introducing Windows XP Enhanced File Management Features	Basic knowledge
2.5 Introducing Windows XP Security Features	Basic knowledge
2.6 Introducing Windows XP Troubleshooting Features	Basic knowledge
2.7 Introducing Workgroups and Domains	Basic knowledge

General Requirements

To complete the projects in this lesson, you will need administrative rights on a Windows XP Professional computer. You may also find it helpful to refer to Lesson 2 in your Prentice Hall Certification Series Exam 70-271 textbook for further information about the projects covered in this lesson.

project 2.1

Introducing Windows XP Home Edition and Windows XP Professional

exam objective

Basic knowledge

overview

Ads R Us is in the process of choosing an edition of Windows XP for various types of client computers. The differences between the two editions are described in **Table 2-1**. You must prepare a document that discusses the two editions and recommend which edition should be purchased for the laptop computers and for the desktop computers. Make your recommendation and support it by answering the following questions.

learning objective

After completing this project, you will know how to recommend an edition of Windows XP based on business requirements.

specific requirements

See General Requirements.

estimated completion time

30 minutes

project steps

1. Which edition of Windows XP is the best choice for supporting both the current and future network infrastructure? Why?
2. How does Windows XP Professional differ from Windows XP Home with respect to recoverability?
3. Describe the differences between Windows XP Professional and Windows XP Home with regards to centrally implementing a standard desktop configuration across all desktop computers on the network.
4. The Web advertising team must be able to test their Web pages. Which edition includes Internet Information Services?

Table 2-1 Key feature differences between Windows XP Home Edition and Windows XP Professional

General Features	Home Edition	Professional
Automated System Recovery (ASR)	No	Yes
Backup utility	Optional	Default
Domain membership in Active Directory	No	Yes
Dynamic disk support	No	Yes
Encrypting File System (EFS)	No	Yes
Enhanced access controls for shared folders and files	No	Yes
Fax services	Optional	Default
Group Policy	No	Yes
Kerberos V5	No	Yes
IntelliMirror capabilities	No	Yes
Internet Information Services (IIS)	No	Yes
Multi-language User Interface Pack (MUIP)	No	Yes
Multi-processor support	No; only one processor supported	Yes; supports two processors
Offline Files	No	Yes
Remote Desktop	Client only	Client and server
Remote Installation Services (RIS)	No	Yes
Roaming user profiles	No	Yes
Networking features		
Client Service for NetWare	No	Yes
IPSecurity (IPSec) user interface	No	Yes
Network Monitor	No	Yes
Simple Network Management Protocol (SNMP)	No	Yes

project 2.2

Introducing Windows XP Features and Enhancements

exam objective

Basic knowledge

overview

Windows XP Professional offers a number of key features to maintain or increase user productivity. You have installed Windows XP Professional on a test computer and must now become familiar with its features so that you can train users after Windows XP Professional has been deployed. You will take a tour of several key user interface components.

learning objective

After completing this project, you will be more familiar with the Start menu, taskbar, and several management utilities in Windows XP Professional.

specific requirements

See General Requirements. You should be logged on as Administrator, the default administrator account created during Windows XP installation.

estimated completion time

20 minutes

project steps

1. Click **Start** and point to **All Programs** to display a list of installed programs.
2. Point to **Accessories** to display the installed accessories.
3. Click **WordPad** to open the **WordPad** program.
4. Type a few words. Open the **File** menu and select **Save** to open the **Save As** dialog box.
5. Type a name for the document in the **File name** list box and click the **Save** button.
6. Close WordPad.
7. Click **Start** to display the **Start menu**. Notice that WordPad is now displayed on the Start menu.
8. Right-click **WordPad** and select **Remove from This List** to remove the program from the Start menu.
9. Click **Start** and select **Control Panel** to open the **Control Panel** (**Figure 2-1**).
10. Click the **Switch to Classic View** link to display the Control Panel applets in the more familiar Classic View (**Figure 2-2**).
11. Click **Switch to Category View** to change it back.
12. Close the Control Panel.
13. Click **Start**, point to **All Programs**, point to **Accessories**, and finally, point to **System Tools** to display a list of system tools.
14. Click anywhere on the desktop to close the Start menu.
15. Click **Start** and then click **Run** to open the **Run** dialog box.
16. Type **mmc** in the **Open** text box and click **OK** to open an empty Microsoft Management Console.
17. Open the **File** menu and select **Add/Remove Snap-in** to open the **Add/Remove Snap-in** dialog box.
18. Click the **Add** button to open the **Add Standalone Snap-in** dialog box.
19. Select **Device Manager** and click **Add** to add the Device Manager to the console.
20. In the **Device Manager** dialog box, leave the **Local computer: [the computer this console is running on]** option button selected and click **Finish** to keep the default selection and have the snap-in manage the local computer.
21. Click **Close** to close the Add Standalone Snap-in dialog box.
22. Click **OK** to close the Add/Remove Snap-in dialog box.
23. Select **Device Manager on local computer** to display a list of device types (**Figure 2-3**).
24. Open the **File** menu and select **Exit** to close the MMC console.
25. Click **No** when prompted to save the changes.

Figure 2-1 Control Panel in Category View

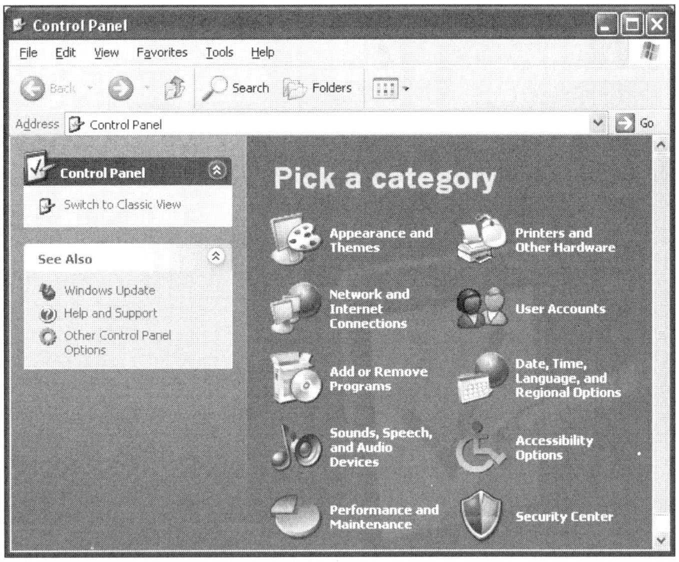

Figure 2-2 Control Panel in Classic View

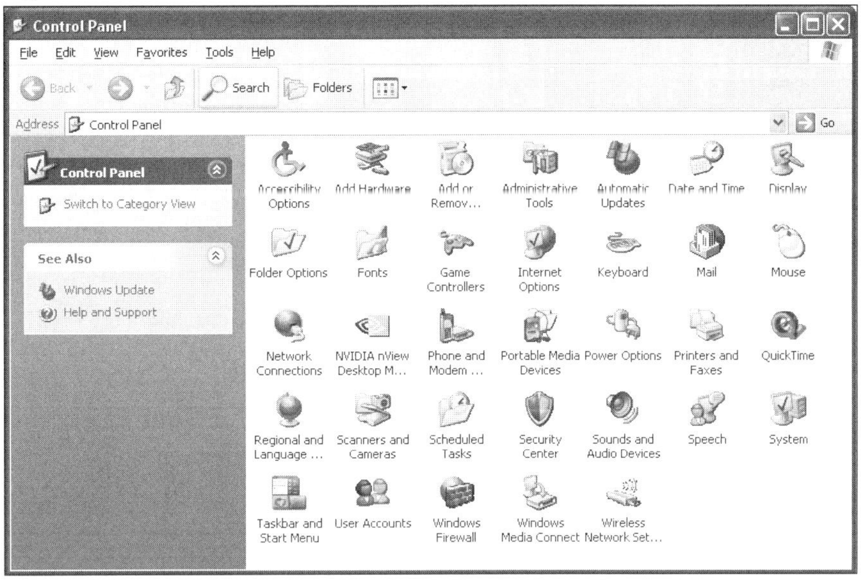

Figure 2-3 Device Manager added to console

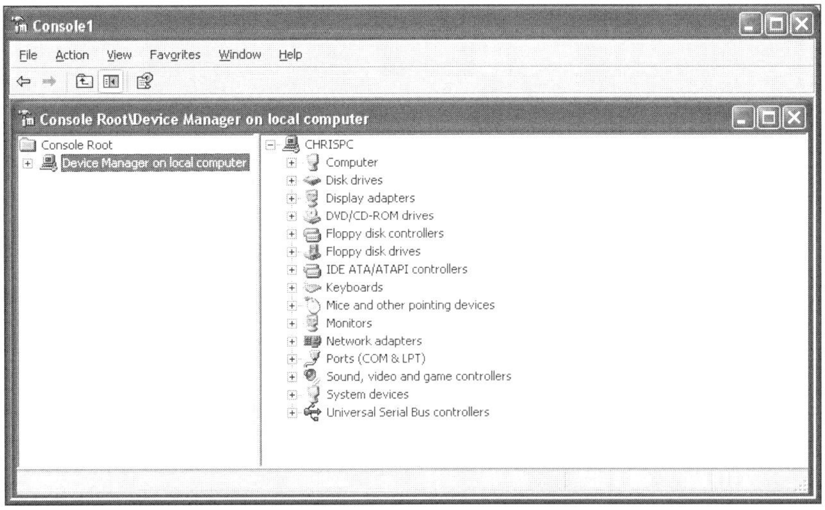

project 2.3

Identifying the Range of Supported Hardware

exam objective

Basic knowledge

overview

You are testing various power management features to determine how the laptop computers should be configured. You are going to explore the default Power Schemes to determine whether they will meet the users' needs. You will also verify that the computer requires the user to enter his or her password when resuming from standby.

learning objective

After completing this project, you will be able to configure power management.

specific requirements

See General Requirements.

estimated completion time

10 minutes

project steps

1. Click **Start** and then click **Control Panel** to open the **Control Panel**.
2. Click **Performance and Maintenance** to open the **Performance and Maintenance** window (**Figure 2-4**).
3. Click **Power Options** to open the **Power Options Properties** dialog box.
4. Record the settings supported by the **Home/Office Desk** power scheme.
5. Select **Portable/Laptop** in the **Power schemes** list box (**Figure 2-5**).
6. Record the settings supported by the **Portable/Laptop** power scheme.
7. Repeat for each of the default power schemes.
8. Click the **Advanced** tab to display the advanced options.
9. Verify that the **Prompt for password when computer resumes from standby** check box is selected.
10. Click **Cancel** to close the Power Options dialog box without making any changes.
11. Close the Performance and Maintenance window.

Figure 2-4 The Performance and Maintenance window

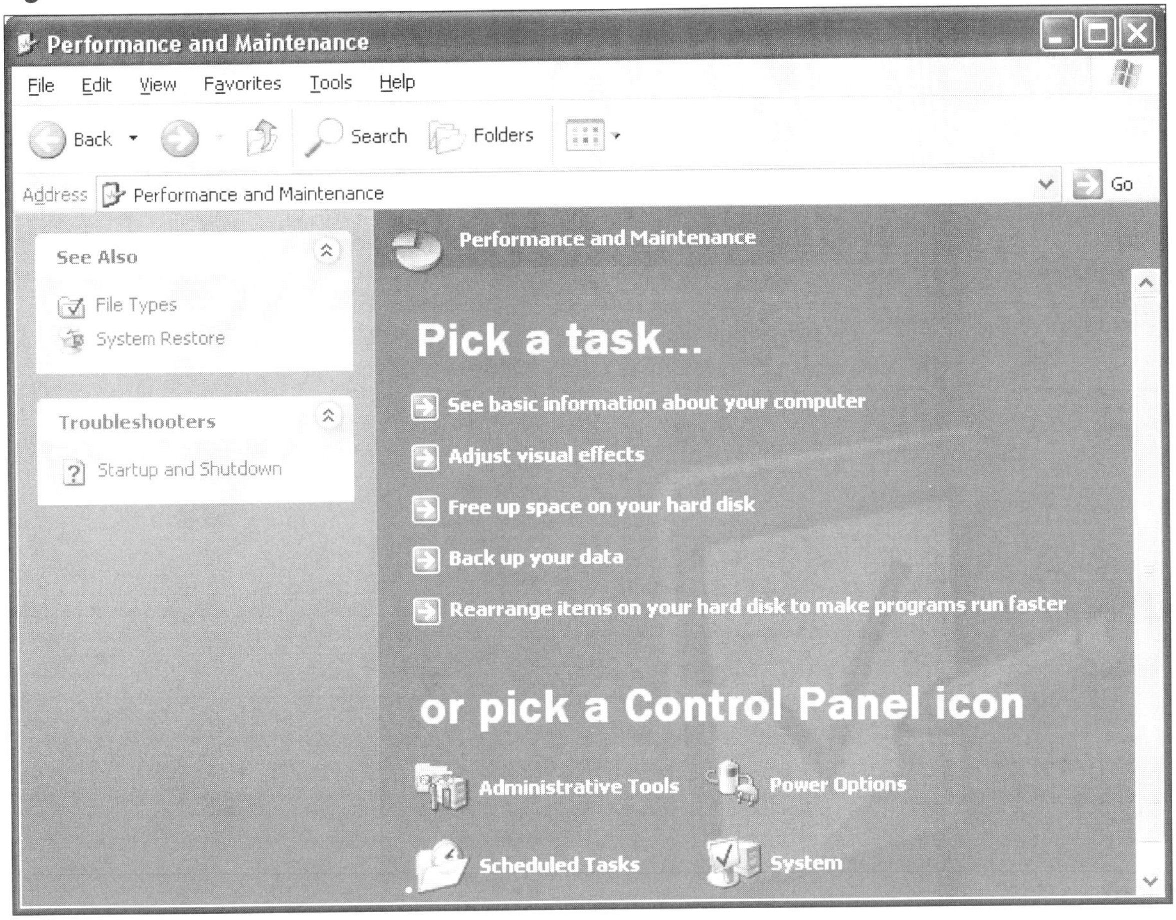

Figure 2-5 Selecting a power scheme

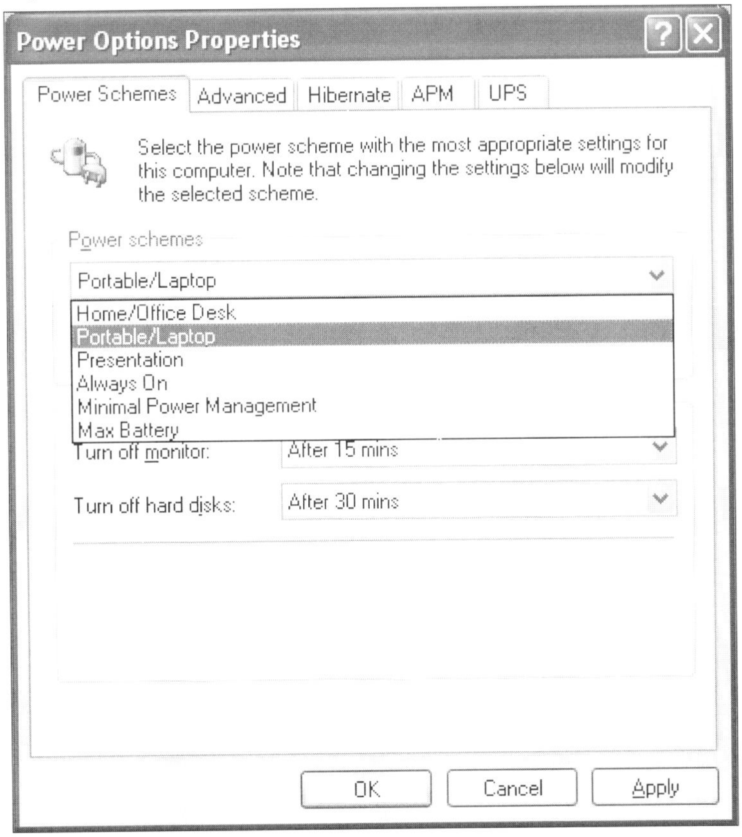

project 2.4

Introducing Windows XP Enhanced File Management Features

exam objective

Basic knowledge

overview

You have installed Windows XP Professional on a user's computer. The user is in the Accounting Department, and she often stores confidential files on her computer. You have explained to her that one of the key reasons for upgrading to Windows XP Professional is to better protect confidential files. You need to verify the current file system on her hard disk and answer her questions about file protection.

learning objective

After completing this project, you will be able to identify the current file system and select a file system based on security requirements.

specific requirements

See General Requirements.

estimated completion time

10 minutes

project steps

1. Click **Start** and then **My Computer** to open the **My Computer** window (**Figure 2-6**).
2. Right-click **Local Disk** (**C:**) and select **Properties** to open the **Local Disk** (**C:**) **Properties** dialog box on the **General** tab (**Figure 2-7**).
3. Which file system was used to format the drive?
4. Does this file system support file permissions?
5. Does this file system support Encrypting File System?
6. Click **Cancel** to close the Properties dialog box.
7. Close My Computer.

Figure 2-6 The My Computer window

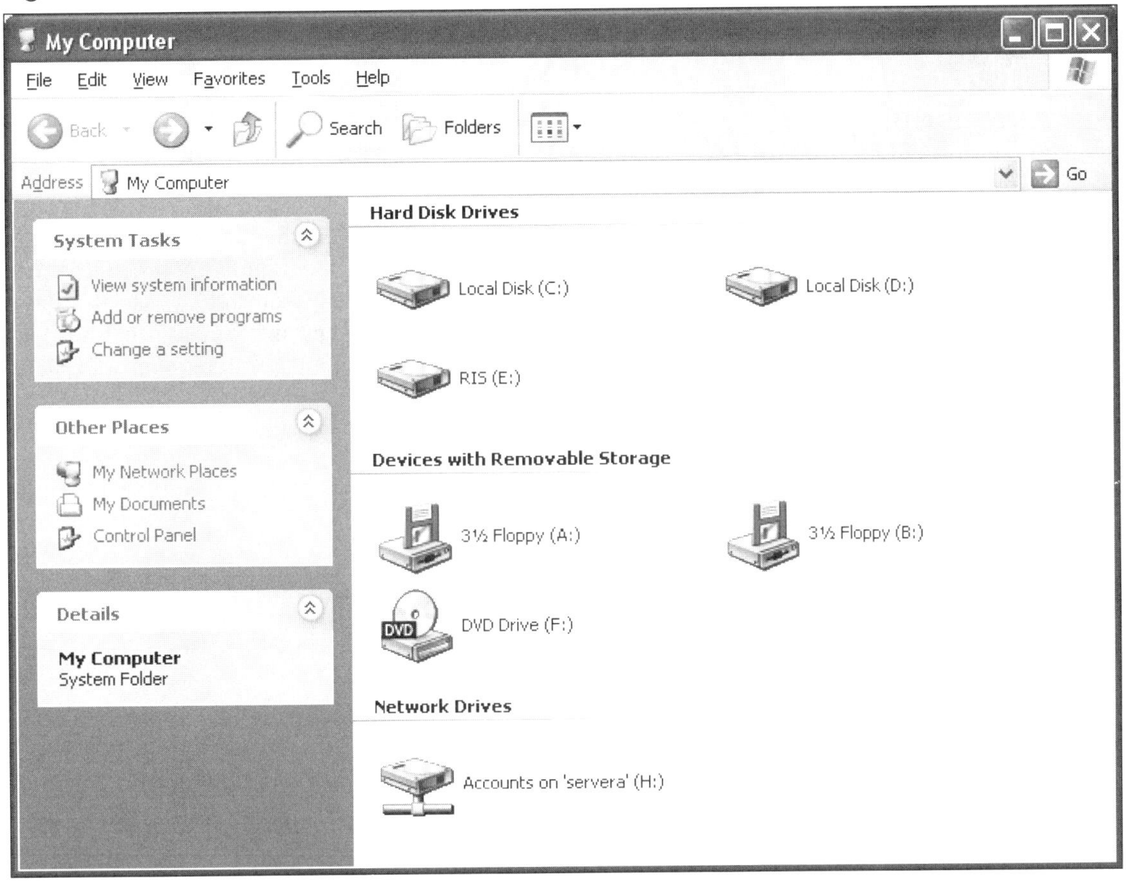

Figure 2-7 Verifying the file system

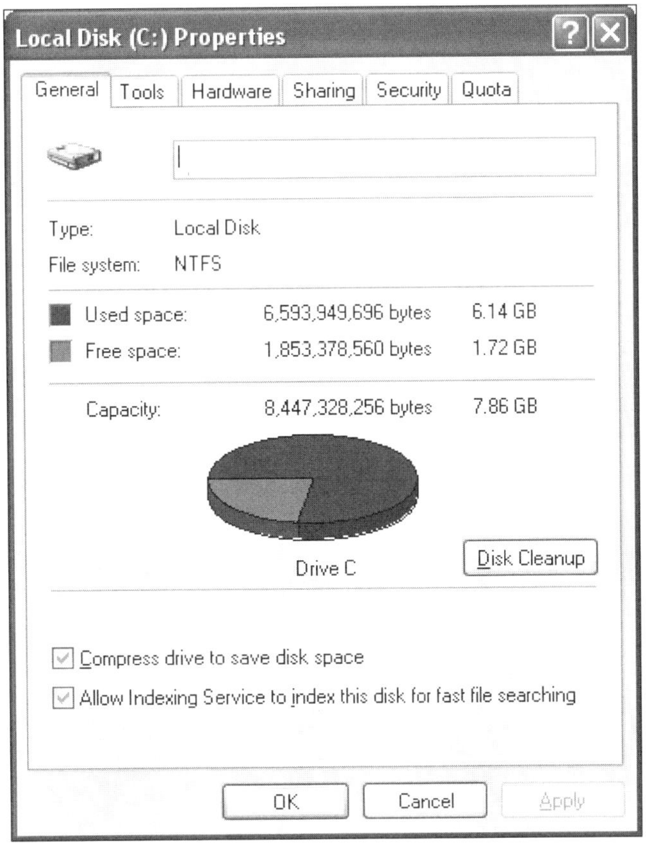

project 2.5

Introducing Windows XP Security Features

exam objective

Basic knowledge

overview

The owner of Ads R Us read a news report about another company that lost billions of dollars because some confidential company data was obtained by a competitor. You explain that upgrading to Windows XP Professional will help you to better secure the data on client computers. She has asked for a report describing the security features of Windows XP Professional. Answer the following questions about the features shown in **Figure 2-8**.

learning objective

After completing this project, you will be able to describe how Windows XP Professional can increase the security of a network.

specific requirements

None

estimated completion time

15 minutes

project steps

1. Which feature or features can help to ensure that only authorized users log on to a computer?
2. Which feature or features can be used to protect files while they are stored on the hard disk?
3. Which feature or features can be used to protect files while they are transmitted across the network?

Figure 2-8 Windows XP Professional security features

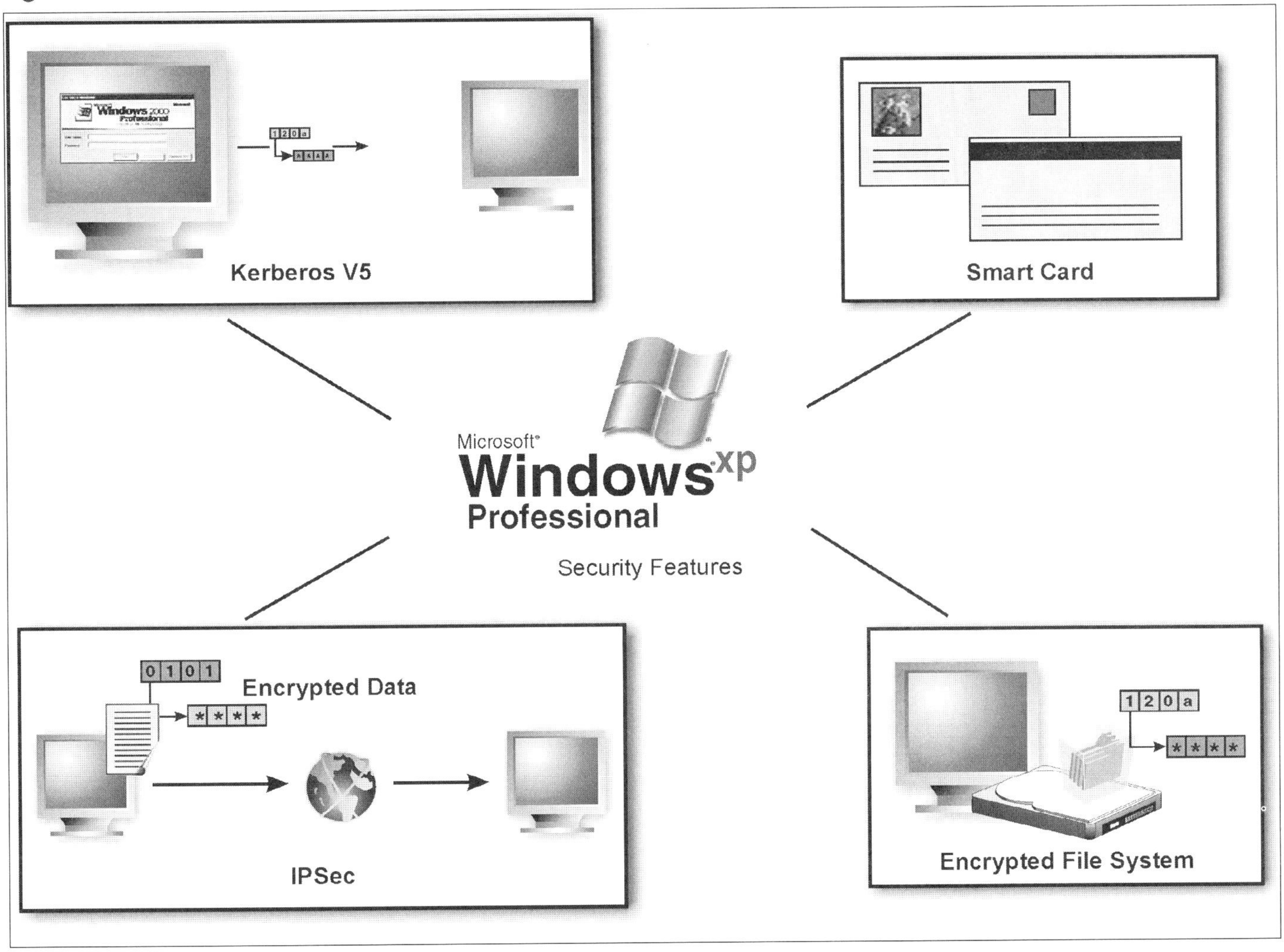

project 2.6

Introducing Windows XP Troubleshooting Features

exam objective

Basic knowledge

overview

You installed Windows XP Professional on a test computer. You are preparing a troubleshooting guide for other members of the IT Help Desk team. You must teach the other team members how they can use the Help and Support Center to obtain system information and troubleshoot a problem. Explore the Help and Support Center to locate various tools.

learning objective

After completing this project, you will be familiar how to use the Help and Support Center.

specific requirements

See General Requirements

estimated completion time

15 minutes

project steps

1. Click **Start** and then **Help and Support** to open the **Help and Support Center**.
2. Click the **Use Tools to view your computer information and diagnose problems** link to display a list of tools (**Figure 2-9**).
3. On the **Tools** list, select the **My Computer Information** link.
4. Click the **View general system information about this computer** link and record the following information:
   a. Processor speed
   b. Windows XP Professional version
   c. Amount of RAM
5. On the **Tools** list, select the **Advanced System Information** link.
6. Click **View detailed system information** (**Msinfo32.exe**) to open the **System Information** console.
7. Expand the **Hardware Resources** node.
8. Select **Conflicts/Sharing** (**Figure 2-10**). Are any devices configured to use the same IRQ?
9. Expand the **Software Environment** node, select **Signed Drivers**, and read the list of devices (**Figure 2-11**).
10. Close the System Information console.
11. In the **Advanced System Information** window, click the **View the error log** link (**Figure 2-12**). Have any errors occurred?
12. On the **Tools** list, select **System Configuration Utility**.
13. Click the **Open System Configuration Utility** link.
14. Review the options on the **General** tab. When would you use Diagnostic Startup?
15. Click the **Services** tab (**Figure 2-13**). How would you display only non-Microsoft services?
16. Click **Cancel** to close the System Configuration Utility.
17. Close the Help and Support Center.

Figure 2-9 The Help and Support Center Tools window

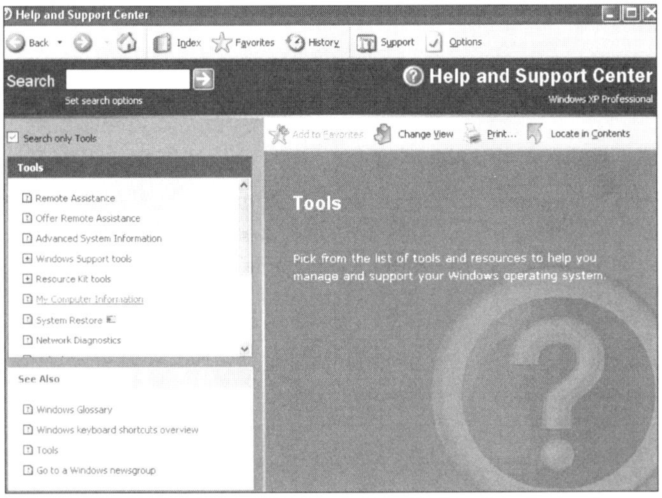

Figure 2-10 The System Information console-Conflicts/Sharing node

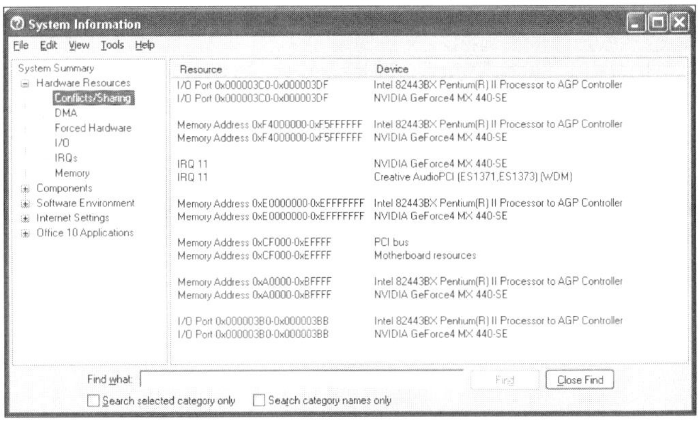

Figure 2-11 The System Information console-Signed Drivers node

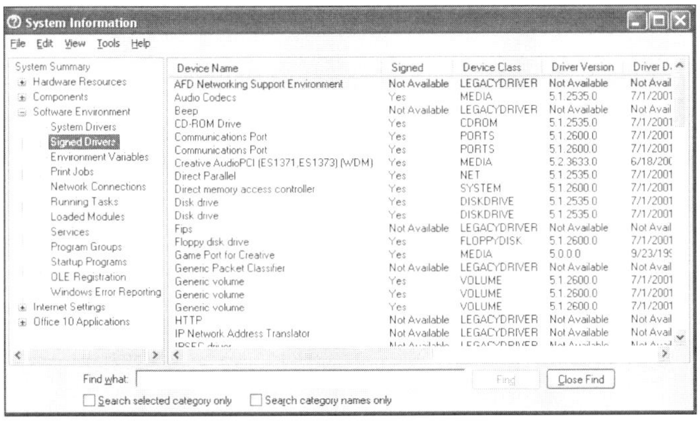

Figure 2-12 Advanced System Information-Error Log

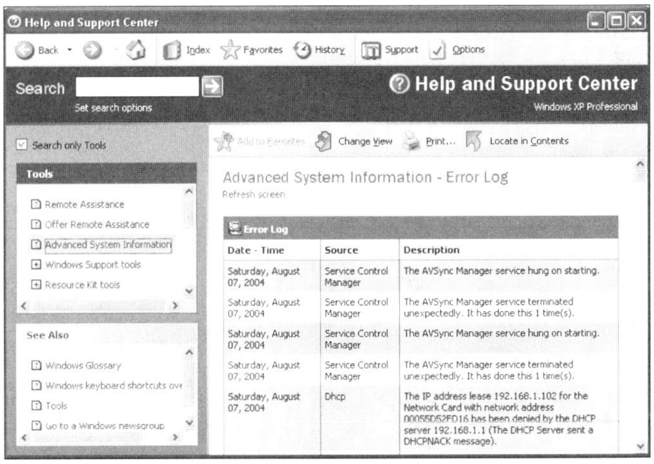

Figure 2-13 System Configuration Utility-Services tab

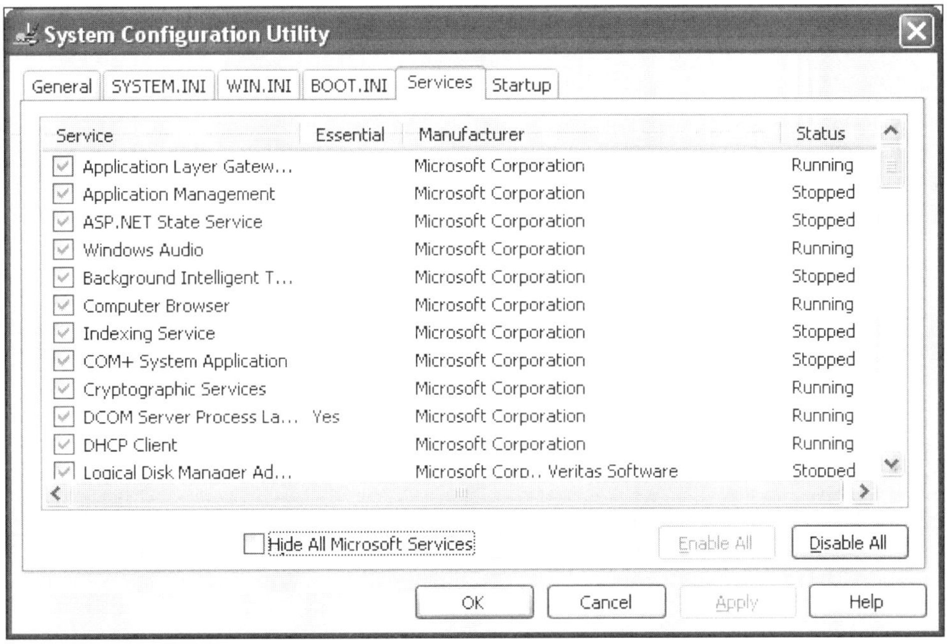

project 2.7

Introducing Workgroups and Domains

exam objective

Basic knowledge

overview

The Ads R Us network is currently configured as a workgroup **(Figure 2-14)**. Users share folders on the desktop computers and create accounts for other users as needed. As the company has grown, managing the network has become difficult and the manager of the IT department has suggested moving to a domain configuration using a Windows Server 2003 domain controller **(Figure 2-15)**. The manager has asked you to document the benefits of a domain configuration to help convince the decision-makers that the initial cost will be recouped in savings due to better manageability and security.

learning objective

After completing this project, you will be able to describe how moving from a workgroup to a domain can lower the total cost of ownership.

specific requirements

See General Requirements.

estimated completion time

30 minutes

project steps

Create a PowerPoint or other form of presentation that shows how implementing the network as a domain can help save management costs and increase security. Consider the following points:

- Where is user account information stored when the network is implemented as a workgroup?
- Where is user account information stored in a domain?
- Who will create domain user accounts?
- How does a domain improve security?

Figure 2-14 A Windows workgroup

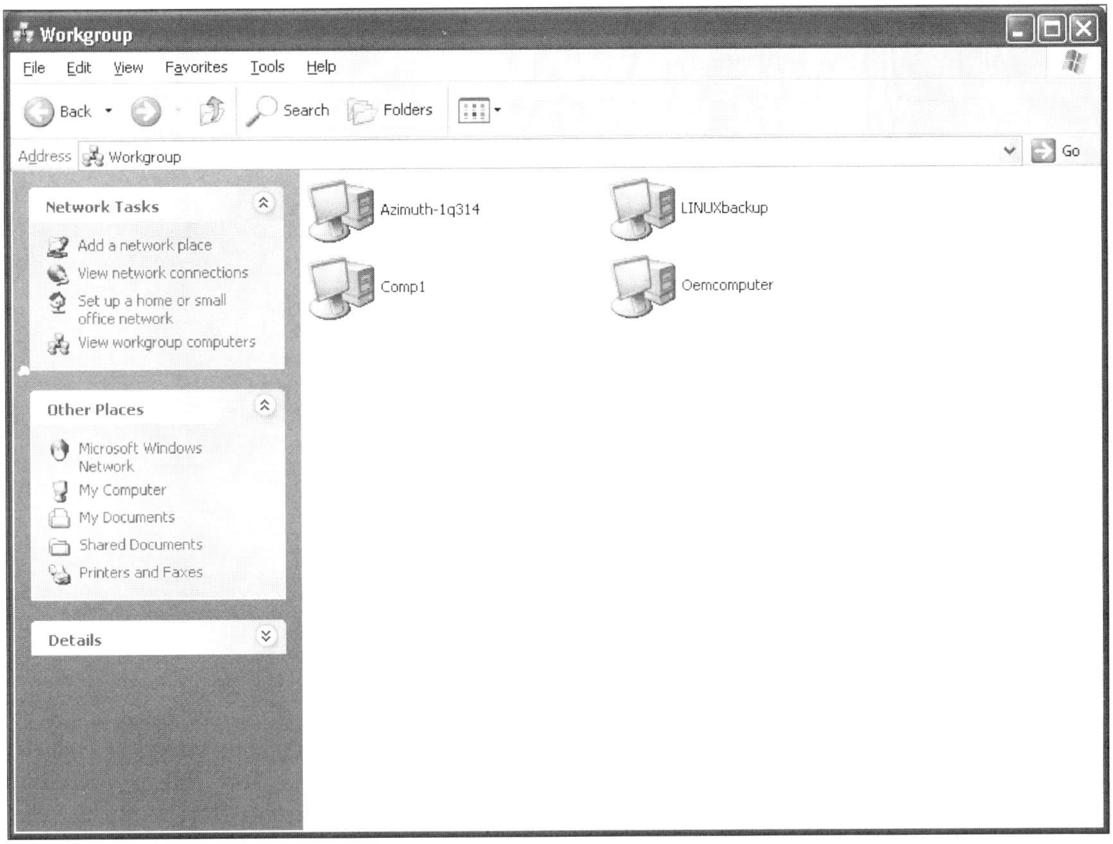

Figure 2-15 A Windows domain

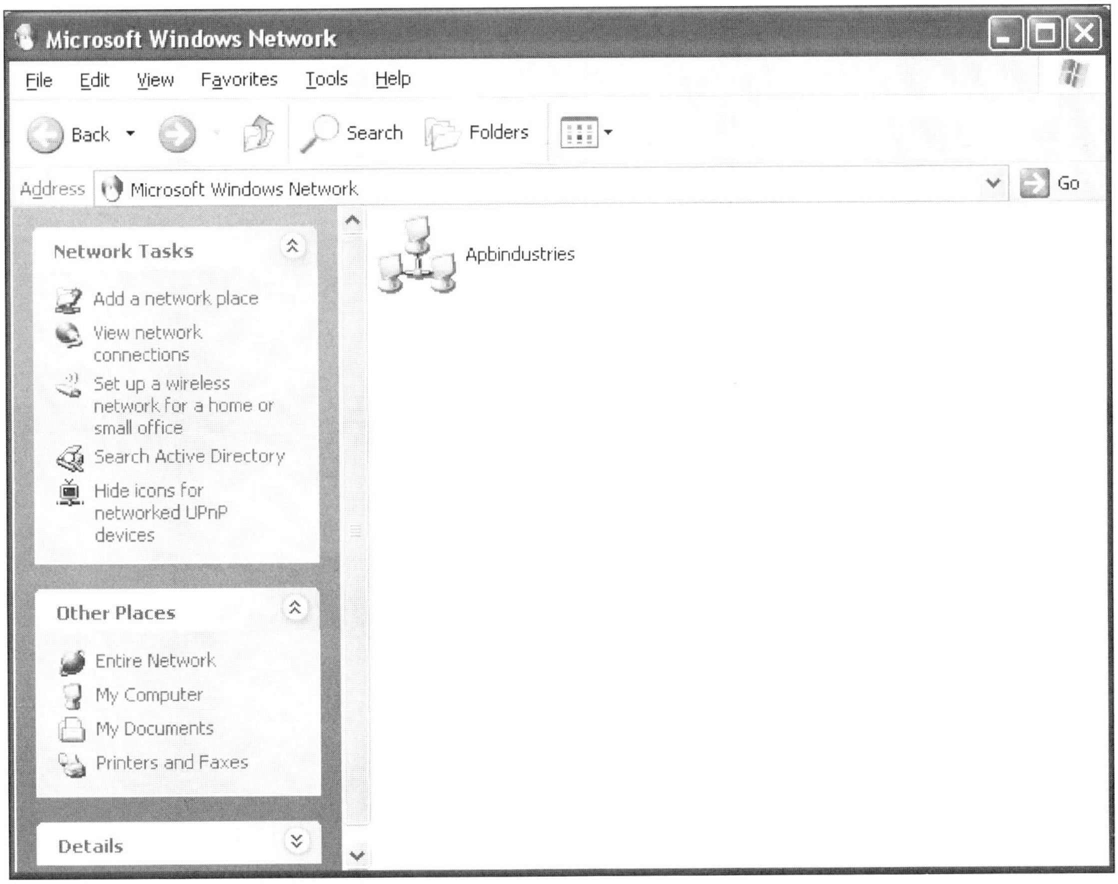

LESSON

3 Installing Windows XP

Understanding installation requirements and available options is critical to successfully deploying Windows XP. Before you can start an installation, you must complete preinstallation activities and choose your installation type and method.

You can perform a clean installation (also referred to as a new installation) of Windows XP as long as you understand that none of the previous settings or applications will be retained. If you want to maintain your current applications and settings, you can perform an upgrade installation. Finally, if you want to configure your computer to boot other operating systems in addition to Windows XP, you can perform a multiple-boot installation.

The installation type can be either attended or unattended. During an attended installation, the user is prompted for installation information. An unattended installation takes this information from an answer file, which is prepared in advance.

Certain preinstallation checks and tasks must always be performed. Some of these, such as partitioning the hard disk, are typically unnecessary when you perform an upgrade. Preparatory tasks include verifying that the minimum hardware requirements are met, checking for hardware and software compatibility, creating disk partitions and formatting them with either FAT or NTFS, and selecting the installation destination. If any potential hardware or software problems are detected, they must be corrected and you must identify any network configuration requirements.

For an upgrade installation, you must verify that installation requirements are met, that the current operating system can be upgraded to Windows XP, and that there are no system problems or incompatible applications running on the computer that might prevent the upgrade from running properly. You can check for problems by running Winnt32 /checkupgradeonly or by downloading and using the Microsoft Upgrade Advisor.

The installation procedures are determined by the installation type and method. You can install from a CD-ROM or a network source that contains the installation file set. You can also prepare a preconfigured disk image to ensure consistent installations when you deploy Windows XP to several computers.

When you install from a network source, there are two options: connecting to a distribution server that contains the installation file set and using Remote Installation Services (RIS). When you install from a CD-ROM, you can either boot from the CD-ROM or run the Setup program to initiate the installation. When you install from a network source, you must first boot the computer into the existing operating system or from a disk that includes a network client, which will enable the computer to connect to the server that contains the installation file set—unless you use RIS, which entails booting to a PXE-enabled network adapter (an RIS boot). You then connect to the shared folder containing the installation files and run Setup to initiate the installation.

The same information is required for attended or unattended installation, including the regional settings, name and organization, product key, computer name, administrator password, network settings, modem dialing information, and date and time settings. You can use the Setup Manager to prepare an answer file in advance that contains this information so that Setup is not required to prompt the user.

Scenario

You are responsible for designing an implementation plan for upgrading computers currently running Windows 98 to Windows XP Professional. You must evaluate the upgrade options, minimizing the interruptions to the user, the administrative time required, and the hardware and software costs. In addition to the 30 computers you are currently supporting, the company plans to receive five new computers in the next two weeks. You must present a written plan, including a proposed deployment budget, to a review committee. Your plan must include integration of the current upgrade into a planned network change. The company is planning to implement an Active Directory domain within six months.

Lesson 3 Installing Windows XP

Project	Exam 70-271 Objective
3.1 Choosing an Installation Method	**Perform and troubleshoot an attended installation of a Windows XP operating system**. Answer end-user questions related to performing an attended installation of a Windows XP operating system.
3.2 Identifying Preinstallation Tasks	**Perform and troubleshoot an attended installation of a Windows XP operating system**. Answer end-user questions related to performing an attended installation of a Windows XP operating system. **Perform and troubleshoot an unattended installation of a Windows desktop operating system**. Answer end-user questions related to performing an unattended installation of a Windows XP operating system. **Perform and troubleshoot an unattended installation of a Windows desktop operating system**. Answer end-user questions related to performing an unattended installation of a Windows XP operating System. Tasks include starting an installation, answering questions asked by an end user during an installation, and performing post-installation tasks. **Upgrade from a previous version of Windows**. Answer end-user questions related to upgrading from a previous version of Windows. Considerations include available upgrade paths and methods of transferring user state data.
3.3 Installing Windows XP Using a CD-ROM	**Perform and troubleshoot an attended installation of a Windows XP operating system**.
3.4 Performing a Network Installation	**Perform and troubleshoot an attended installation of a Windows XP operating system.**
3.5 Using Setup Manager	**Perform and troubleshoot an unattended installation of a Windows desktop operating system**. Perform an installation by using unattended installation files.
3.6 Using the System Preparation Tool	**Perform and troubleshoot an unattended installation of a Windows desktop operating system**.
3.7 Understanding Remote Installation Services (RIS)	**Perform and troubleshoot an unattended installation of a Windows desktop operating system**. Answer end-user questions related to performing an unattended installation of a Windows XP operating system. Tasks include starting an installation, answering questions asked by an end user during an installation, and performing post-installation tasks. Configure a PC to boot to a network device and start an installation of a Windows XP operating system. Tasks include configuring PXE-compliant network cards.
3.8 Upgrading from a Previous Version of Windows	**Upgrade from a previous version of Windows**. Answer end-user questions related to upgrading from a previous version of Windows. Considerations include available upgrade paths and methods of transferring user state data. Verify hardware compatibility for the upgrade. Considerations include minimum hardware and system resource requirements. Verify application compatibility for the upgrade. Tasks include ascertaining which applications can and cannot run and using application compatibility tools.

General Requirements

To complete the projects in this lesson, you will need administrative rights on a Windows XP Professional computer and a Windows XP Professional installation CD. You may also find it helpful to refer to Lesson 3 in your Prentice Hall Certification Series Exam 70-271 textbook for further information about the topics covered by the projects in this lesson.

project 3.1 Choosing an Installation Method

exam objective

Perform and troubleshoot an attended installation of a Windows XP operating system. Answer end-user questions related to performing an attended installation of a Windows XP operating system.

overview

You must determine the most appropriate Windows XP installation method. The same installation method may not be appropriate in all situations. Most of the current applications are Windows XP compatible. You have identified one custom application that is running on four of the desktop computers that is not Windows XP compatible. A compatible version of the application is not available. Refer to the scenario in the introduction for the computers on which Windows XP will be installed. Review the installation types in **Table 3-1** and the installation method requirements in **Table 3-2**. Make your installation type/method recommendations. Be prepared to justify your recommendations.

learning objective

After completing this project, you will know how to choose an installation type/method appropriate to your installation requirements.

specific requirements

None

estimated completion time

10 minutes

project steps

1. Most users, with the possible exception of those using incompatible applications, will continue to use the same applications after the upgrade. For users who will continue to use the same applications, which installation type would be most efficient for these users, and why?
2. How many computers will require a multiple-boot installation? Explain the need for the multiple-boot installation and how this might be avoided.
3. Identify the problems that could arise from each of the following and identify the factors that would prevent you from using the installation method described:
   - Run a clean installation on all computers.
   - Run an upgrade installation on all computers.
   - Use RIS to automate a Windows XP distribution.

Table 3-1 Clean installation versus upgrade installation

Perform a clean installation when:	Perform an upgrade when:
You have a new or newly formatted disk.	The current operating system supports upgrading.
The operating system on the computer is not on the upgrade list for the planned edition.	You intend to fully replace the previous Windows operating system with Windows XP.
The operating system on the computer and the settings associated with it can be replaced or are no longer needed.	You want to keep your existing files and preferences.
You want to create a multiple-boot configuration with Windows XP and another operating system or with the current operating system. (Note: Microsoft recommends using two partitions to avoid conflicts between overlapping program file directories and overlapping page files.)	You are willing to accept the risk that in some rare cases, applications or hardware will not immediately work as they do on the current operating system.

Table 3-2 Requirements for different installation methods

Installation method/type	Type of installation	Requirements	Windows XP edition
CD-ROM/attended	Upgrade or clean	CD-ROM drive	Both
CD-ROM/unattended	Upgrade or clean	CD-ROM drive and floppy disk drive	Both
Over-the-network/attended	Upgrade or clean	Distribution server	Both
Over-the-network/unattended	Upgrade or clean	Distribution server	Both
Sysprep	Clean only	All desktop computers must have similar hardware configurations	Windows XP Professional only
RIS	Clean only	PXE-enabled desktop computer; Windows Server 2003 or Windows 2000 Server with Active Directory, DNS, and DHCP.	Windows XP Professional only

project 3.2 Identifying Preinstallation Tasks

exam objective

Perform and troubleshoot an attended installation of a Windows XP operating system. Answer end-user questions related to performing an attended installation of a Windows XP operating system.

Perform and troubleshoot an unattended installation of a Windows desktop operating system. Answer end-user questions related to performing an unattended installation of a Windows XP operating system. Tasks include starting an installation, answering questions asked by an end user during an installation, and performing post-installation tasks.

Upgrade from a previous version of Windows. Answer end-user questions related to upgrading from a previous version of Windows. Considerations include available upgrade paths and methods of transferring user state data.

overview

You must identify action items that must be completed before the company can start deploying Windows XP. This includes verifying that all current computers meet the minimum hardware requirements **(Table 3-3)**.

You will be running upgrade installations on the majority of the current computers and multiple-boot installations when required to meet operational requirements. If the new computers do not come with an operating system installed, you will have to install Windows XP before delivering the computers to users. Your deployment solution must support planned network changes and upgrades. Key among these is the expectation to implement an Active Directory domain within six months.

learning objective

After completing this project, you will be more familiar with tasks that must be performed before installing Windows XP.

specific requirements

None

estimated completion time

15 minutes

project steps

1. Compare features of the FAT32 and NTFS file systems (**Figure 3-1**). Prepare guidelines for determining whether disk partitions on current computers should be converted to NTFS. Address issues of:
   - Interoperability
   - Security
   - Support for Windows XP Professional
2. Prepare a checklist that can be completed by users to identify whether a computer supports an upgrade to Windows XP. Include all hardware requirements.
3. Prepare a report for your superior that addresses how the plan to implement Active Directory impacts operating system selection.

Table 3-3 Hardware requirements for installing Windows XP

Component	Requirements
CPU	Intel Pentium/Celeron, AMD K6/Athlon/Duron or compatible processor; 233MHz supported, 300MHz recommended
Memory	64MB RAM supported, 128MB recommended
Hard disk space	1.5GB available
Networking	Appropriate network adapter card
Display	Super VGA (800 x 600) resolution or higher, Video Display Adapter (VDA), and monitor
Other devices	Recommended: CD-ROM or DVD drive 12x or faster, unless you are installing Windows XP Professional over a network
Accessories	Keyboard and mouse or other pointing devices, 14.4Kbps or higher modem for Internet access (33.6Kbps or higher for voice and videoconferencing)

Figure 3-1 Types of file systems supported by Windows XP

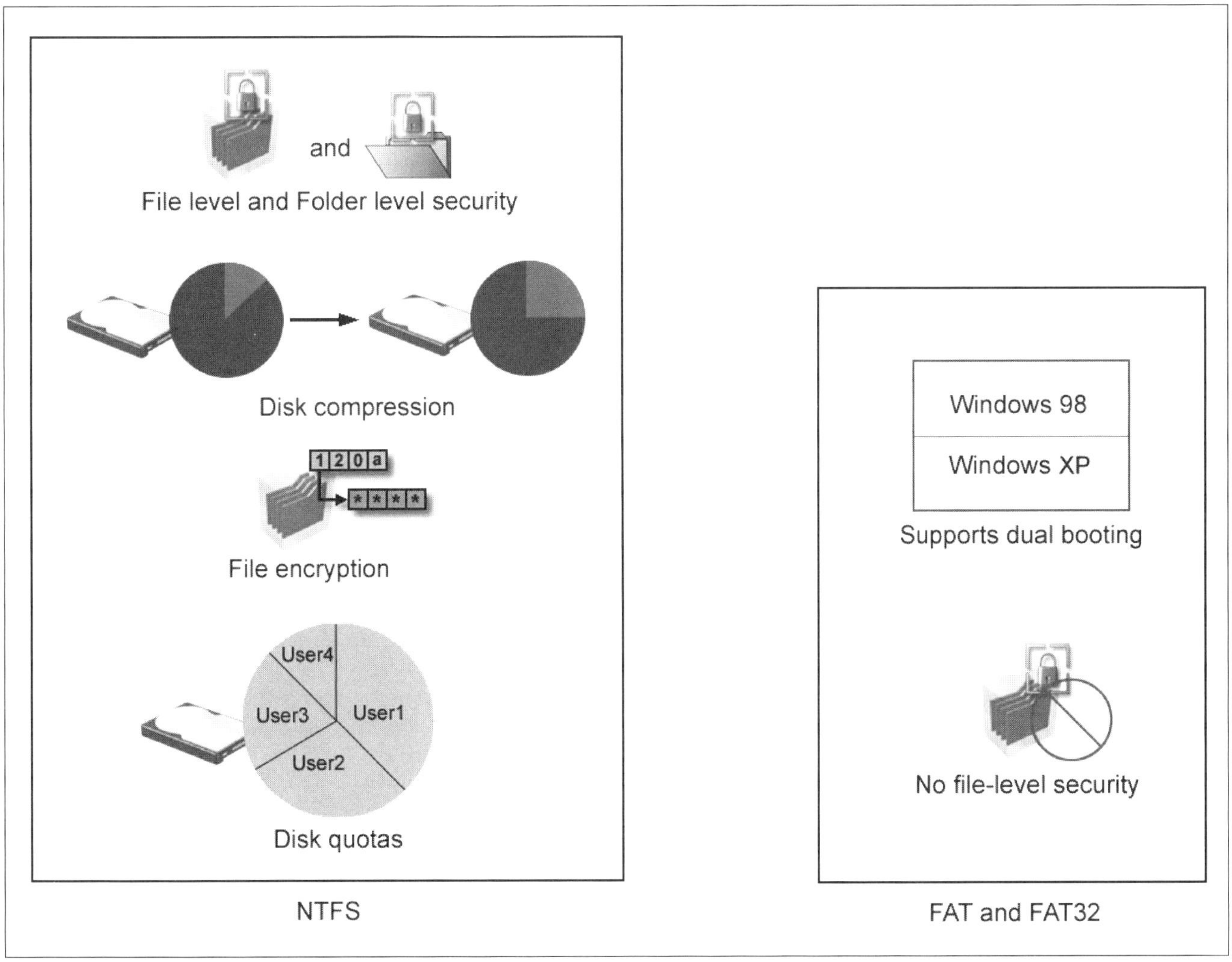

project 3.3

Installing Windows XP Using a CD-ROM

exam objective

Perform and troubleshoot an attended installation of a Windows XP operating system.

overview

You are preparing instructions for users who will be responsible for their own installations from a CD-ROM. You identify technically competent users who should be able to run an attended installation and later might be called upon to assist other users.

You must verify that the users understand the installation options listed in **Figure 3-2**. Prepare any support documentation needed to enable the users to complete the installation without further assistance.

learning objective

After completing this project, you will understand the basic procedures for installing Windows XP from a CD-ROM.

specific requirements

None

estimated completion time

10 minutes

project steps

1. Compare the procedures required when booting from a CD-ROM and when booting from the current operating system and running Setup. Which would you recommend for your users, and why?
2. Justify providing the following for users rather than allowing them to enter values they choose:
   - Computer name
   - Workgroup name
   - Administrator password
3. When must you have users select a custom network setup rather than accepting the default setup? The default network configuration settings are shown in **Figure 3-3**.

Figure 3-2 Attended installation prompts

- Regional settings
- Name and organization
- Product key
- Computer name
- Administrator password
- Modem dialing information
- Date and time
- Network components

Figure 3-3 Networking components installed by default

- Client for Microsoft Networks
- Enabled file and printer sharing
- Transmission Control Protocol/Internet Protocol (TCP/IP) as only protocol installed
- Automatic IP address assignment (DHCP client)

project 3.4 Performing a Network Installation

exam objective

Perform an attended installation of a Windows XP operating system.

overview

For users whose computers are currently running Windows 98, you must address installation issues. Your manager has requested that you review the requirements for using an over-the-network installation using a distribution server where the i386 folder from the Windows XP Professional CD-ROM has been stored, rather than a CD-ROM installation, to see whether this will be easier for the Windows 98 users **(Figure 3-4)**. You must recommend one of these installation methods for users who need to upgrade their computers and justify your recommendation.

learning objective

After completing this project, you will be able to identify the requirements for running a network installation.

specific requirements

None

estimated completion time

10 minutes

project steps

1. In addition to the preinstallation requirements for all installations, what are the preinstallation requirements for an over-the-network installation?
2. You must prepare step-by-step installation instructions for less experienced users. Which method requires less effort by users?
3. Explain why a network installation is not the best method for new computers that do not have an operating system installed.

Figure 3-4 Pre-Setup requirements to install Windows XP over a network

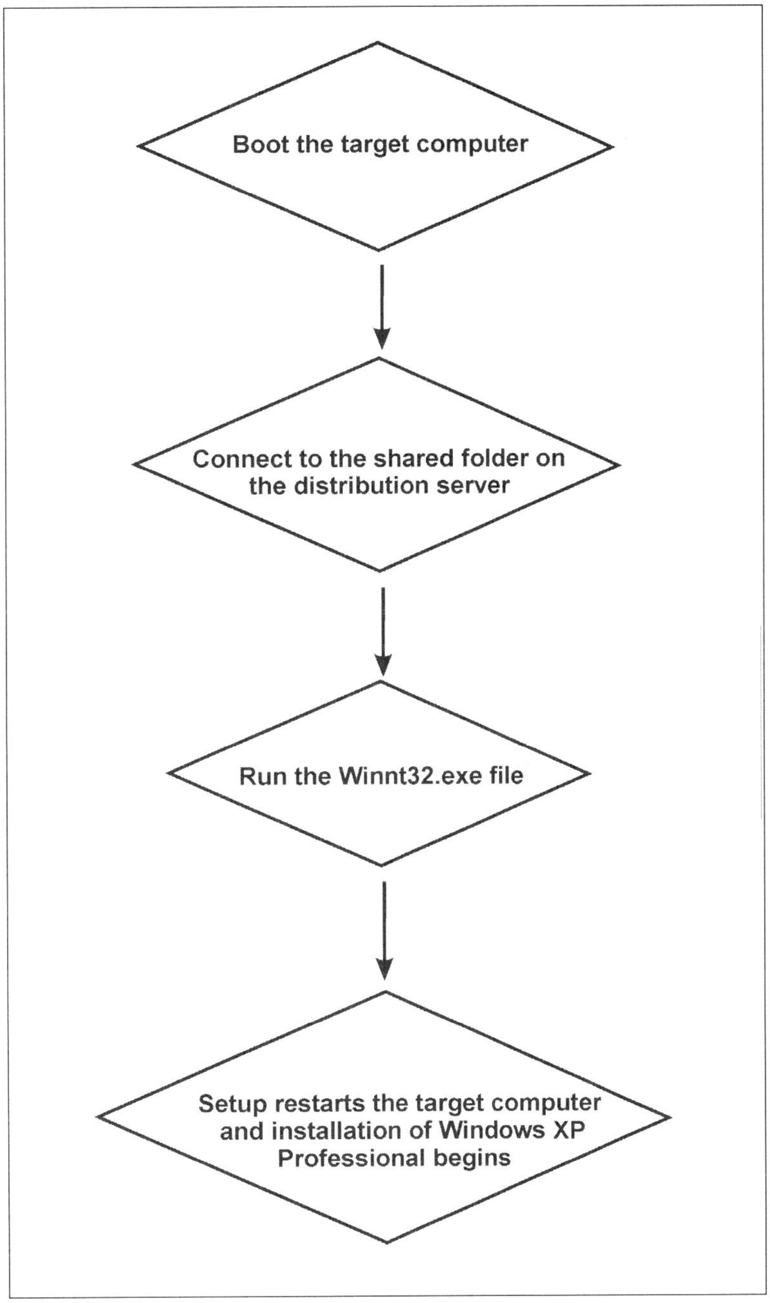

project 3.5

Using Setup Manager

exam objective

Perform and troubleshoot an unattended installation of a Windows desktop operating system. Perform an installation by using unattended installation files.

overview

You want to delegate the Windows XP installations on the newly purchased computers to an assistant. The computers all have the same hardware configuration. You must ensure consistent installations. You have extracted the Setup Manager. You need to justify the time required to prepare references for your assistant and explain the installation choices you have made.

learning objective

After completing this project, you will know how to use the Setup Manager to create custom installation scripts and answer files.

specific requirements

None

estimated completion time

10 minutes

project steps

1. Prepare a short memo to justify the time it requires to generate installation scripts using the Setup Manager.
2. Compare the User Interaction options (**Figure 3-5**). Explain why **Fully automated** is the most appropriate choice.
3. Include a brief explanation of what would be wrong with each of the other choices.

Figure 3-5 The User Interaction screen

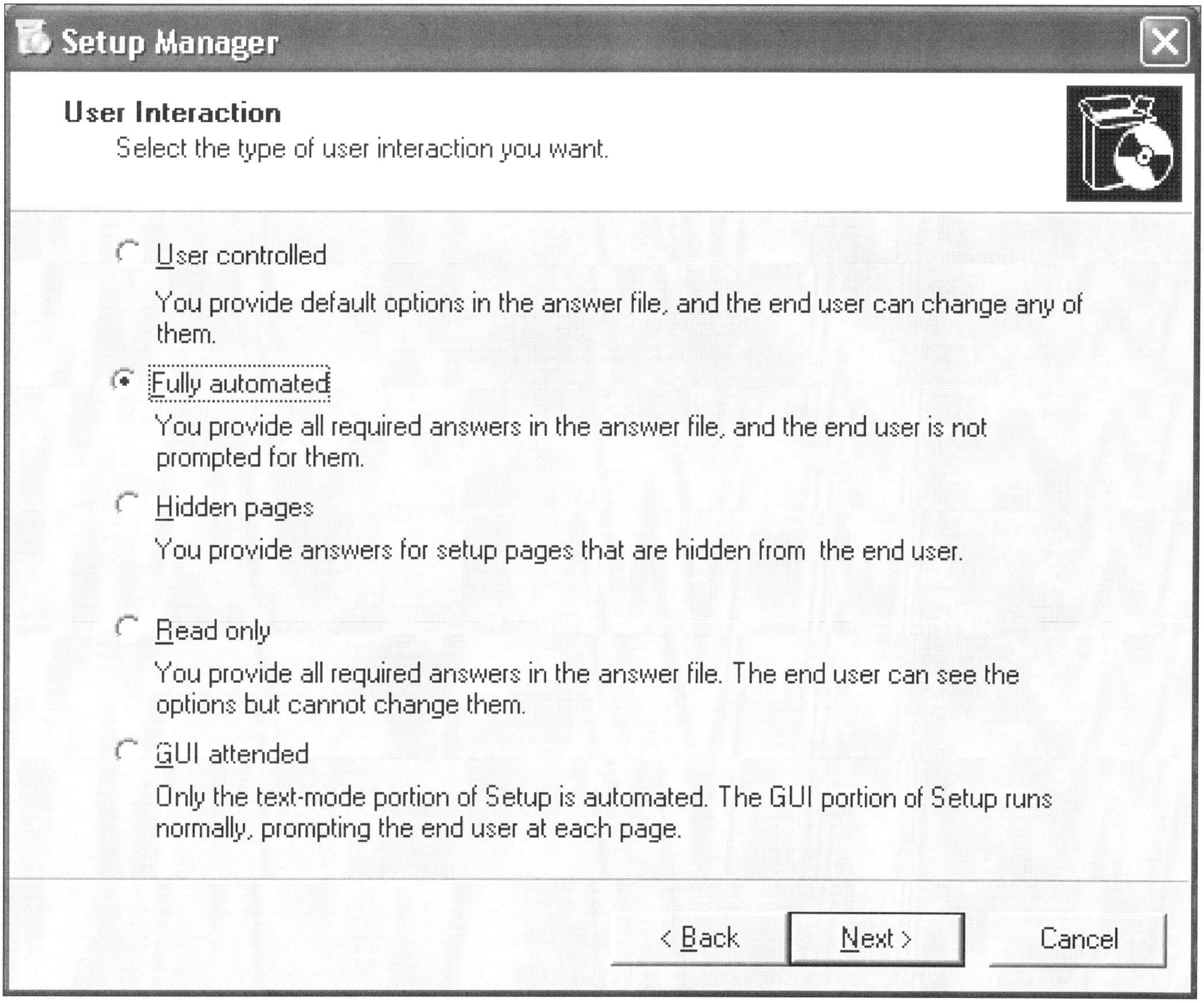

project 3.6

Using the System Preparation Tool

exam objective

Perform and troubleshoot an unattended installation of a Windows desktop operating system.

overview

You discover that a branch office is opening in 30 days. You are responsible for preparing the computers for use in the new office. You will receive one computer with the same hardware configuration as the computers being sent to the new office. The computers will be delivered with no operating system installed. You do not know the technical expertise of the users in the new office.

The branch office will have eight computers configured as a workgroup. All of the computers should have Windows XP Professional installed with identical configuration settings. Initially, users in the remote office will not have Internet access available. You must prepare the resources users in the remote office will need to set up the computers. You must also provide the users with written instructions.

learning objective

After completing this project, you will be more familiar with the procedures for using Sysprep to deploy Windows XP.

specific requirements

None

estimated completion time

15 minutes

project steps

1. Explain why you must review the hardware configurations of the computers being ordered for the new office to verify that they meet the requirements for using Sysprep (**Figure 3-6**).
2. You will be running Sysprep on the distribution model computer. Which switches will you use when you run Sysprep if you want to audit the distribution system (**Table 3-4**)?
3. You decide to have the installation run as a fully unattended installation. Which files must you produce for the Windows XP installation?
4. After preparing the files required for Windows XP installation, how should you distribute the files to the remote office? Explain why you would use this distribution method.

Figure 3-6 Components that must be identical in a Sysprep installation

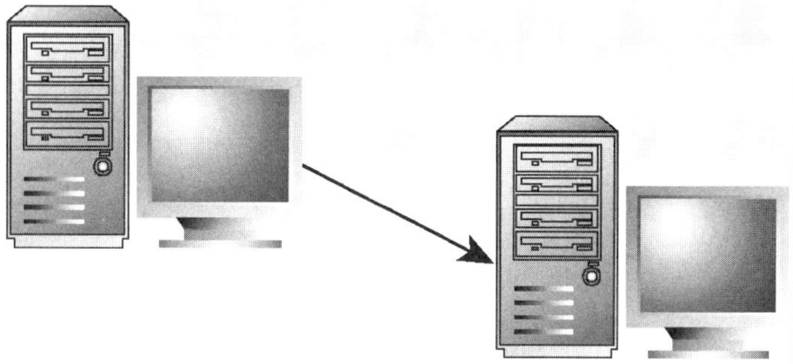

- Hardware Abstraction Layer (HAL)
- Hard disk controller
- Mass storage controllers
- Boot device
- Kernel

Table 3-4 Sysprep switches

Switch	Description
/quiet	Runs Sysprep in quiet mode. This switch stops the confirmation dialog boxes from displaying while Sysprep runs on the distribution model computer. It is used when you want to automate Sysprep by adding it to the GuiRunOnce key in the Unattend.txt file.
/pnp	Forces a full device detection on the target computer. This switch is optional. Use it when non-Plug and Play devices that cannot be dynamically detected exist on the target systems.
/reboot	Enables a reboot of the distribution model computer after the image has been created instead of shutting down and then starting the Mini-Setup Wizard. Use this switch for auditing the system and verifying that Mini-Setup is operating correctly.
/nosidgen	Runs Sysprep without generating any security ID. This switch is useful for the administrator who doesn't intend to clone the computer on which Sysprep is running.

project 3.7

Understanding Remote Installation Services (RIS)

exam objective

Perform and troubleshoot an unattended installation of a Windows desktop operating system. Tasks include starting the installation, answering questions asked by an end user during an installation, and performing post-installation tasks. Configure a PC to boot to a network device and start the installation of a Windows XP operating system. Tasks include configuring PXE-compliant network cards.

overview

Your supervisor hires a friend to act as a consultant to assist you in preparing for the Windows XP installation. The consultant convinces your supervisor that RIS is the most efficient way to install Windows XP on the 30 computers currently on the network.

learning objective

After completing this project, you will understand the requirements for, and limitations of, using RIS.

specific requirements

None

estimated completion time

15 minutes

project steps

1. Prepare a report explaining not only why RIS is an inappropriate solution, but also that RIS cannot be used in your current network configuration. The report should include
   - RIS components and their purposes **(Table 3-5)**
   - RIS network and computer hardware requirements **(Table 3-6)**
   - Impact on existing computers
2. As an example, describe a scenario in which it would be appropriate to use RIS.

Table 3-5 RIS components

Component	Description
Remote Installation Services Setup (Risetup.exe)	Used to set up the RIS server
Remote Installation Preparation tool (Riprep.exe)	Used to prepare and replicate an image of an installation for deployment via a RIS server on the network
Remote Boot Floppy Generator (Rbfg.exe)	Used to create the RIS bootable floppy disk required to simulate a PXE-enabled boot ROM for systems without them
Client Installation Wizard (CIW) (Oschooser.exe)	Used on a client computer to select the RIS image to be installed

Table 3-6 RIS network services and computer hardware requirements

Requirement	Description
Active Directory domain	RIS is supported in a Windows 2000 Server or Windows Server 2003 domain environment only. The Active Directory domain environment must include DHCP support with one or more DHCP servers. The network services required to support RIS are DNS and the DHCP service. DNS is a requirement of Active Directory. Client computers use Active Directory to locate the RIS server. Client computers performing a network boot receive an IP address from the DHCP server, and DNS must be functioning so that they can locate a server or domain controller running Active Directory.
Distribution server (RIS server)	The distribution server must be running Windows 2000 Server or Windows Server 2003. This is the role performed by the RIS server(s).
Installation images	One or more installation images must be created as the installation source files. The installation image will overwrite the destination disk partition. Installation images are maintained on the RIS server(s).
PXE-compliant network adapter	RIS clients must either have a PXE-compliant network adapter or you must prepare RIS boot disks for the client computers to simulate the PXE boot process.

project 3.8

Upgrading from a Previous Version of Windows

exam objective

Upgrade from a previous version of Windows. Answer end-user questions related to upgrading from a previous version of Windows. Considerations include available upgrade paths and methods of transferring user state data. Verify hardware compatibility for the upgrade. Considerations include minimum hardware and system resource requirements. Verify application compatibility for the upgrade. Tasks include ascertaining which applications can and cannot run and using application compatibility tools.

learning objective

You have final responsibility for identifying potential upgrade problems. You have verified that the current Windows version supports an upgrade to Windows XP **(Table 3-7)**. You want to use the most accurate and up-to-date tools available to assist you. As part of your preparation, you will compare using the Upgrade Advisor available on the Microsoft Web site and the compatibility check run from the Windows XP installation CD-ROM **(Figures 3-7** and **3-8)**. You have already run the Upgrade Advisor on several computers to provide baseline information.

overview

After completing this project, you will understand the procedures for verifying whether a computer can be upgraded to Windows XP.

specific requirements

See General Requirements. This project assumes that you have the Windows XP installation CD-ROM.

estimated completion time

15 minutes

project steps

1. Compare the available methods for compatibility checking.
2. Prepare a report with your recommendations answering the following:
   - Which method is easier to use and is most readily available?
   - Which method is most up-to-date?
   - Which types of problems might prevent you from upgrading to Windows XP?
   - What are optional solutions if an upgrade is not possible because of software incompatibility?

Table 3-7 Upgrade paths to Windows XP

Version of Windows	Upgrade Path
Windows 95	Must upgrade to Windows 98 first.
Windows 98/Windows 98 Second Edition	Can be directly upgraded to either Windows XP Home Edition or Windows XP Professional.
Windows Me	Can be directly upgraded to either Windows XP Home Edition or Windows XP Professional.
Windows NT Workstation 3.51	Must upgrade to Windows NT 4.0 SP5 first.
Windows NT Workstation 4.0 without SP5 or later	Upgrade to Windows NT 4.0 SP5 first.
Windows NT Workstation with SP5 or later	Can be directly upgraded to Windows XP Professional.
Windows 2000 Professional	Can be directly upgraded to Windows XP Professional.
Windows XP Home Edition	Can be directly upgraded to Windows XP Professional.
Windows Server operating systems	Cannot be "downgraded" to Windows XP.

Figure 3-7 Windows Upgrade Advisor

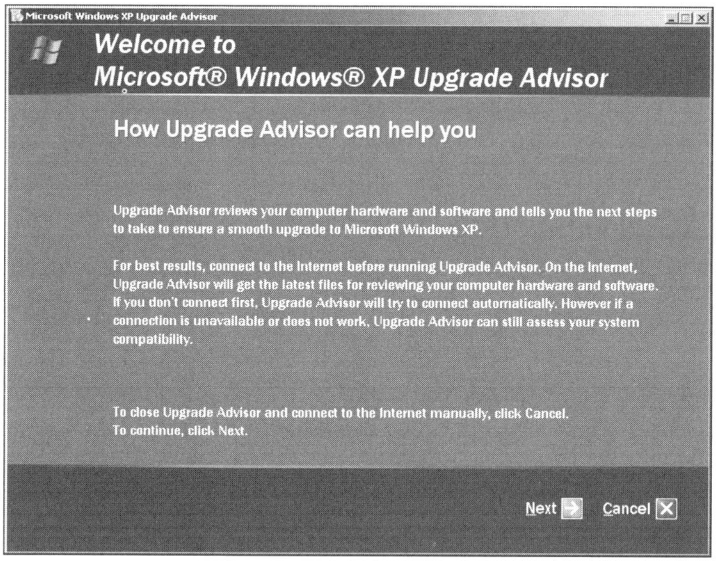

Figure 3-8 The Welcome to Microsoft XP screen

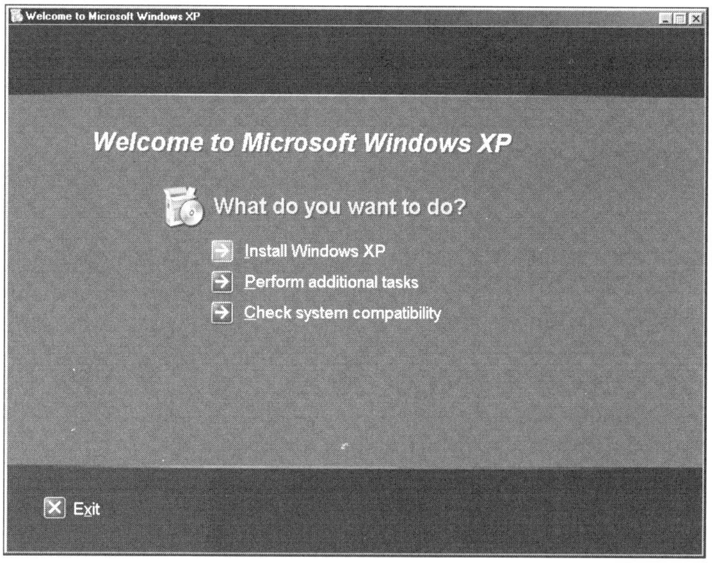

LESSON 4

Troubleshooting Windows XP Installations

Although with proper planning, most installations of Windows XP complete successfully, it is important that your deployment planning includes installation troubleshooting methods and recovery procedures for failed installations.

A failed installation is one that does not start, one that terminates before it completes, or one that appears to complete but fails when the operating system is started for the first time. Installation failures can be caused when the system does not meet the hardware requirements, the system includes hardware that is incompatible with Windows XP, or device drivers are not upgraded during installation and are incompatible with Windows XP. The operating system can also fail to install if the system has not been properly prepared for the installation media, if applications exist that are incompatible with Windows XP, or if the installation media is damaged or inaccessible.

Although the specifics of installation troubleshooting differ depending on the type of installation and the error reported, troubleshooting a failed installation is similar to other troubleshooting scenarios. You should isolate the cause systematically, starting with the system itself.

If an installation cannot be started, it is important to verify that the installation media is accessible. If you are booting from a CD-ROM, you should verify that the BIOS configuration lists the CD-ROM drive as the first device in the boot order and that the CD-ROM can be read. If you are installing from the network, you should verify that the installation files are shared on the network and that the computer can access the network share. If you are performing a RIS installation, you must verify that the network adapter in the computer is PXE enabled or that the computer can boot from the RIS disk and that the RIS server and a DHCP server are accessible.

If an installation fails after it has started, the problem might be due to installation media failure, incompatible hardware, or incompatible device drivers. The following log files can help you isolate the problem:

- Setupact.log
- Setupapi.log
- Setuperr.log
- Setuplog.txt

Some errors, such as insufficient disk space, are reported by the Setup program. Post-installation problems are more likely to occur after an upgrade installation. Depending on the nature of the problem, you might need to reinstall or replace an application, upgrade a device driver, or even uninstall Windows XP.

Scenario

You are planning to deploy Windows XP throughout the Ads R Us network. As part of the planning process, you must develop a recovery plan that you and those assisting you can use if an installation fails. Your plan should include methods to employ if new installations fail to start, for new installations that fail before they complete, for upgrade installations that fail before they complete, and for handling potential problems after an upgrade.

Lesson 4 Troubleshooting Windows XP Installations

Project	Exam 70-271 Objective
4.1 Troubleshooting an Installation that Fails to Start	**Perform and troubleshoot an attended installation of a Windows XP operating system**. Troubleshoot and complete installations in which an installation does not start. Tasks include configuring the device boot order and ascertaining probable cause of the failure to start.
4.2 Troubleshooting an Installation that Fails to Complete	**Perform and troubleshoot an attended installation of a Windows XP operating system**. Troubleshoot and complete installations in which an installation fails to complete. Tasks include reviewing the setup log file and providing needed files.
4.3 Troubleshooting an Upgrade Installation	**Upgrade from a previous version of Windows**. Answer end-user questions related to upgrading from a previous version of Windows. Considerations include available upgrade paths and methods for transferring user state data.

General Requirements

To complete the projects in this lesson, you will need administrative rights on a Windows XP Professional computer that can access the Internet. You may also find it helpful to refer to Lesson 4 in your Prentice Hall Certification Series Exam 70-271 textbook for further information about the topics covered by the projects in this lesson.

project 4.1

Troubleshooting an Installation that Fails to Start

exam objective

Perform and troubleshoot an attended installation of a Windows XP operating system. Troubleshoot and complete installations in which an installation does not start. Tasks include configuring the device boot order and ascertaining probable cause of the failure to start.

overview

You are documenting the installation procedures that will be used when Windows XP Professional is installed by booting from a CD-ROM. Some of the common problems are shown in **Table 4-1**. You must document the procedure for verifying the boot order in the BIOS. You must also document the procedure for creating Windows XP Setup boot disks if necessary.

learning objective

After completing this project, you will know how to resolve an installation that fails to start.

specific requirements

See General Requirements.

estimated completion time

20 minutes

project steps

1. Shut down your computer.
2. Start your computer. As it is restarting, press the key that enables you to enter the BIOS configuration. This key differs depending on the computer manufacturer. On most computers, the [**Delete**] or [**Escape**] key works. If not, try pressing either [**F2**] or [**F10**].
3. View the current boot order. This procedure differs depending on the manufacturer. Older systems are configured to boot from the floppy disk first and the hard drive second. Newer systems are typically configured to boot from the hard drive first because floppy drives are slowly being omitted from new computers.
4. If you are installing Windows XP by booting from a CD-ROM, which device should be listed first?
5. Exit from the BIOS configuration without saving the changes.
6. Allow your computer to start normally.
7. Launch **Internet Explorer**.
8. Navigate to the following URL: **http://support.microsoft.com**, type **KB article 310994** in the **Search the Knowledge Base** field and click **Go**.
9. Review the information about creating and using the Windows XP Setup boot disks.
10. How many disks are required to start a Windows XP installation by booting from a floppy disk?
11. What other requirements must be met?
12. Under what circumstances will using the Windows XP Setup boot disks resolve an installation failure?

Table 4-1 Common problems that prevent an installation from starting

Problem	Things to Check
Setup cannot find the CD-ROM drive	• Verify that your hardware is listed in the Windows Catalog. The Windows Catalog is available online at **http://www.microsoft.com/windows/catalog/**. • Use the startup disk that came with your CD-ROM to reload the drivers for the CD-ROM drive. Updated drivers might also be available from the manufacturer. • Try another installation method, such as a network installation. • If you are performing a new installation and you start the installation from Windows 95, Windows 98, or Windows NT, click Advanced Options during Setup and copy the files to your hard disk.
Setup cannot read the CD-ROM	• Verify that the CD-ROM or DVD drive is working. • Clean the CD. • Use a different CD or obtain a replacement.
Windows XP will not install or will not start	• Verify that the hardware is listed in the Windows Catalog. • Simplify the hardware configuration as much as possible by temporarily removing hardware not required by Setup (modems, sound cards, and network cards). • Make sure that the latest drivers, firmware, and BIOS for the computer and all hardware are installed.
Insufficient disk space	• Free up space on an existing partition by deleting files that are no longer necessary and emptying the Recycle Bin or, if there is more than one drive or partition, by moving files to another partition. • Remove existing partitions and create a new partition large enough for installation (1.5+ GB). If the hard disk already contains an operating system or data files, make sure you don't destroy them without saving what you need.
You are unable to connect to your network installation	Make sure that • The [Caps Lock] key is not on when you type the password to begin. Windows XP passwords are case sensitive. • The username and password are correct. • The correct domain name is selected. • The network cable is properly attached to the computer and the network connection. • The network settings on the computer have not been changed.
Media errors	Check/clean the CD-ROM drive and the installation CD.
The SCSI disk is not detected	Press [F6] during the text mode portion of Setup and install the drivers.
A "Setup was unable to build the list of files to be copied" error message displays	This occurs when you use the /copydir switch during a Windows XP installation. There is a slight difference between the syntax in Windows 2000 and Windows XP. The correct syntax for Windows XP is **/copydir:i386\tempfiles**, in which **tempfiles** is the folder designated for temporary files.
A "The file Asms on the Windows XP Professional CD-ROM is needed" error message displays during Windows XP installation	This can occur if Windows XP Setup cannot communicate with the CD-ROM drive. See Microsoft Knowledge Base Article 311755 for the best approach if you cannot use a network installation as an alternative.

project 4.2

Troubleshooting an Installation that Fails to Complete

exam objective

Perform and troubleshoot an attended installation of a Windows XP operating system. Troubleshoot and complete installations in which an installation fails to complete. Tasks include reviewing the setup log files and providing needed files.

overview

You are preparing documentation that will be used to troubleshoot installation errors that might occur when an installation starts but fails to complete. Your documentation should include information that will be used to diagnose problems that produce STOP errors, also known as Blue Screen of Death (BSOD) messages. Common STOP errors caused by software and device driver issues are described in **Table 4-2**. You will analyze some symptoms and make recommendations for troubleshooting the problem. You will also examine the log files created during installation.

learning objective

After completing this project, you will know how to diagnose and resolve problems that occur during Windows XP installation.

specific requirements

You must be logged on as Administrator, the default administrator account created during Windows XP installation. You may need to refer to **Table 4-2** and **Table 4-3** in your Prentice Hall Certification Series Exam 70-271 textbook for common hardware-related STOP errors.

estimated completion time

20 minutes

project steps

1. An installation fails with a STOP error number 0x00000050. What might you try to correct the problem?
2. You are installing Windows XP by booting from a CD-ROM. The installation fails with a STOP error number 0x0000007B. What might you try to correct the problem?
3. Open **My Computer** and navigate to the **C:\Windows** directory.
4. Locate and open the **setupact.log** file.
5. Scroll through the file and notice the types of entries. In particular, look for error messages regarding the hardware device/driver that may be causing the problem.
6. When would you use **setupact.log** to diagnose an installation problem?
7. Close setupact.log.
8. Locate and open **setuperr.log**, which is located in the **C:\Windows** directory.
9. Does it contain any entries?
10. Close setuperr.log.
11. Take a few moments to review **setupapi.log** and **setuplog.txt**, which are located in the **C:\Windows** directory.

Table 4-2 Common software- and device driver-related STOP errors

Error Number	Description
0x0000000A	IRQL_NOT_LESS_OR_EQUAL. The STOP 0xA message indicates that a kernel-mode process or driver attempted to access a memory location to which it did not have permission or at a kernel interrupt request level (IRQL) that was too high. A kernel-mode process can only access other processes that have an IRQL lower than, or equal to, its own. This STOP message is typically due to faulty or incompatible hardware or software.
0x0000001E	KMODE_EXCEPTION_NOT_HANDLED. The STOP 0x1E message indicates that the Windows XP Professional kernel detected an illegal or unknown processor instruction. The problems that cause STOP 0x1E messages share similarities with those that generate STOP 0xA errors in that they can be due to invalid memory and access violations. This default Windows XP error handler typically intercepts these problems if error-handling routines are not present in the code itself.
0x00000050	PAGE_FAULT_IN_NONPAGED_AREA. The STOP 0x50 message indicates that the requested data was not in memory. The system generates an exception error when using a reference to an invalid system memory address. Defective memory (including main memory, L2 RAM cache, and video RAM) or incompatible software (including remote control and antivirus software) can cause STOP 0x50 messages.
0x0000007B	INACCESSIBLE_BOOT_DEVICE. The STOP 0x7B message indicates that Windows XP Professional has lost access to the system partition or boot volume during the startup process. Installing incorrect device drivers when installing or upgrading storage adapter hardware typically causes STOP 0x7B errors. STOP 0x7B errors could also indicate possible virus infection.
0x0000009F	DRIVER_POWER_STATE_FAILURE. The STOP 0x9F message indicates that a driver is in an inconsistent or invalid power state.
0x000000D1	DRIVER_IRQL_NOT_LESS_OR_EQUAL. The STOP 0xD1 message indicates that the system attempted to access pageable memory using a kernel process IRQL that was too high. Drivers that have used improper addresses typically cause this error.
0x000000EA	THREAD_STUCK_IN_DEVICE_DRIVER. A device driver problem is causing the system to pause indefinitely. Typically, this problem is caused by a display driver waiting for the video hardware to enter an idle state. This might indicate a hardware problem with the video adapter or a faulty video driver.
0xC000021A	STATUS_SYSTEM_PROCESS_TERMINATED. The STOP 0xC000021 A message occurs when Windows XP Professional switches into kernel mode and a user-mode subsystem, such as Winlogon or the Client Server Runtime Subsystem (CSRSS), is compromised and security can no longer be guaranteed. Because Windows XP Professional cannot run without Winlogon or CSRSS, this is one of the few situations in which the failure of a user-mode service can cause the system to stop responding. You cannot use the kernel debugger in this situation because the error occurred in a user-mode process. A STOP 0xC000021A message can also occur when the computer is restarted after a system administrator has modified permissions in such a way that the SYSTEM account no longer has adequate permissions to access system files and folders.
0xC0000221	STATUS_IMAGE_CHECKSUM_MISMATCH. This STOP message indicates driver, system file, or disk corruption problems (such as a damaged paging file). Faulty memory hardware can also cause this STOP message to appear.

Note: STOP errors 0x0000001E, 0x0000000A, and 0x0000007B can also be caused by general hardware errors; see **Table 4-3** in your Prentice Hall Certification Series Exam 70-271 textbook.

project 4.3

Troubleshooting an Upgrade Installation

exam objective

Upgrade from a previous version of Windows. Answer end-user questions related to upgrading from a previous version of Windows. Considerations include available upgrade paths and methods for transferring user state data.

overview

You are preparing documentation that will help users troubleshoot any problems they might experience when they upgrade their computers from Windows 98 to Windows XP.

learning objective

After completing this project, you will know how to troubleshoot problems with an upgrade installation.

specific requirements

None

estimated completion time

25 minutes

project steps

1. Prepare a frequently asked questions document (FAQ) that can be distributed to users. Make sure to answer the following questions:
   - Why are some of my Control Panel icons missing?
   - Why can't I connect to the Internet using my dial-up connection?
   - My data entry application used to start automatically. Now it doesn't. How can I correct the problem?
2. Document the procedures for uninstalling Windows XP and reverting to Windows 98. Include the following considerations:
   - What factors will prevent the Uninstall program from running?
   - The user upgraded to Windows XP and then installed a new application. Which steps must the user take to revert to Windows 98 but still be able to run the new application?
3. The Help and Support Center can connect to the Windows Catalog **(Figure 4-1)**. Why might you need to access the Windows Catalog after you upgrade from Windows 98 to Windows XP?

Figure 4-1 The Windows Catalog

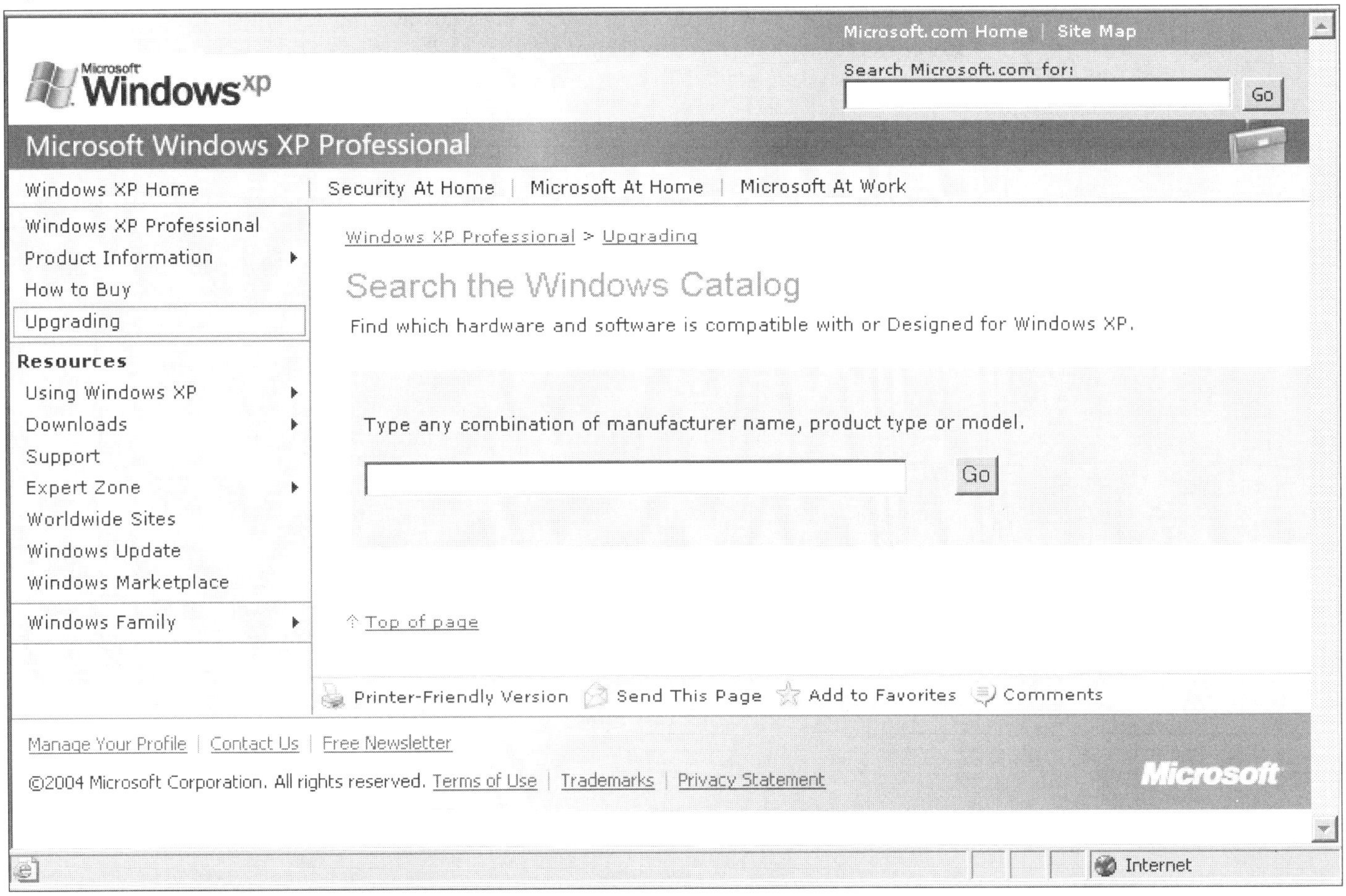

LESSON

5 Performing Post-Installation Tasks

Post-installation tasks include tasks that must be completed immediately after installation as well as ongoing activities. Required tasks will depend on the type of installation and the user support requirements.

After an upgrade installation, you must verify that there are no compatibility issues because, unfortunately, preinstallation checks do not always find all possible incompatibilities. Windows XP includes compatibility tools that enable you to run applications in an environment that emulates an earlier Windows version, such as Windows 95 or Windows Me.

Multiple-boot installations often mean that system configuration issues must be addressed. Primary among these are where, or if, you will be using the NTFS file system. You may also need to update the other operating systems on the computer to ensure compatibility with your preferred configuration.

Even a clean installation on a new computer can have additional configuration requirements. If the computer is replacing another computer, you might need to transfers files and settings from the user's original computer.

Ongoing tasks include installing updates, which are released as patches, hotfixes, security fixes, and service packs. Whichever form they are released in, you will need to install applicable updates as they become available. You can simplify the process somewhat for new installations by applying the most recent service pack to the installation file set through slipstreaming. You can also automate the Windows update process by configuring Windows XP to periodically check, download, and install updates.

Scenario

You have completed the Windows XP deployment plan and identified the installation requirements and recovery procedures. Before you can start the physical installations, you must identify the actions, by both computer and user, which must be taken after installation. You will also assign the responsibility for these tasks to either the end user or technical support personnel. As part of this process, you must address concerns about ongoing updates. Develop a plan for applying updates with minimal user interaction requirements.

Lesson 5 Performing Post-Installation Tasks

Project	*Exam 70-271 Objective*
5.1 Using Windows XP and Multiple Operating Systems	**Upgrade from a previous version of Windows**. Install a second instance of an operating system on a computer.
5.2 Transferring Files and Settings	**Upgrade from a previous version of Windows**. Migrate user state data from an existing PC to a new PC. Answer end-user questions relating to upgrading from a previous version of Windows. Considerations include available upgrade paths and methods of transferring user state data. **Perform and troubleshoot an attended installation of a Windows XP operating system**. Perform post-installation configuration. Tasks include customizing installations for individual users and applying service packs.
5.3 Using Application Compatibility Tools	**Upgrade from a previous version of Windows**. Verify application compatibility for upgrade. Tasks include ascertaining which applications can and cannot run and using the application compatibility tools.
5.4 Installing Service Packs and Hotfixes	**Perform and troubleshoot an attended installation of a Windows XP operating system**. Perform post-installation configuration. Tasks include customizing installations for individual users and applying service packs.
5.5 Updating Windows XP After Installation	**Perform and troubleshoot an attended installation of a Windows XP operating system**. Perform post-installation configuration. Tasks include customizing installations for individual users and applying service packs.

General Requirements

To complete the projects in this lesson, you will need administrative rights on a Windows XP computer with access to the Internet. You may also find it helpful to refer to Lesson 5 in your Prentice Hall Certification Series Exam 70-271 textbook for further information about the topics covered by the projects in this lesson.

project 5.1

Using Windows XP and Multiple Operating Systems

exam objective

Upgrade from a previous version of Windows. Install a second instance of an operating system on a computer.

overview

The deployment plan calls for you to install Windows XP Professional on four computers in a multiple-boot configuration with Windows 98 Second Edition. All four computers are configured with two hard disks. Each disk has a single FAT32 disk partition. Windows 98, Second Edition has already been installed on drive C:. You will install Windows XP Professional on drive D:. Users are currently using the D: drive to store files while working in applications on Windows 98. You must determine possible compatibility problems (Table 5-1) and prepare suggested post-installation configuration guidelines.

learning objective

After completing this project, you will be know how to review a computer's current configuration and configure a computer to support multiple operating system instances in a multiple-boot configuration.

specific requirements

None

estimated completion time

15 minutes

project steps

1. Drive D: is compressed with DriveSpace 3 and formatted as FAT32. What preinstallation actions, if any, are required?
2. Compare and contrast the possible consequences of each of the following actions during Windows XP installation:
   - Convert drive D: to NTFS.
   - Reformat drive D: as NTFS.
   - Convert all drives to NTFS.
   - Make no changes to any current file systems.
3. Which file system features would require you to convert at least one hard disk to NTFS?

Table 5-1 Installing Windows XP with another operating system: Requirements and cautions

Windows XP and:	Requirements/Cautions
Any of the other operating systems listed in this table	• Install each operating system on its own partition. • Install the applications used with each operating system on the same partition as the respective operating system. If you plan to run an application on both operating systems, you should install the application on both partitions.
MS-DOS	• Install MS-DOS first. • Format the system partition with FAT because it is the only file system that both operating systems can read.
Either Windows 95 or Windows 95 OSR2	• Install Windows 95 first. • If using Windows 95, format the system partition with FAT. • If using Windows 95 OSR2 (also called Windows 97), the primary partition should be formatted with FAT32 for efficiency reasons, although you can use FAT. • If you intend to access a compressed DriveSpace or DoubleSpace volume from Windows XP, you must uncompress it.
Windows 98, Windows 98 Second Edition, or Windows Me	• Format the system partition, as FAT or FAT32. FAT32 is more efficient. • If you intend to access a compressed DriveSpace or DoubleSpace volume from Windows XP, you must uncompress it.
Windows NT 4.0 (SP4 or above)	• Make sure that Windows NT 4.0 has been updated with at least SP4 or later. • Using NTFS as the only file system on a computer that contains both Windows XP Professional and Windows NT is not recommended unless SP6 has been installed on Windows NT first. • Windows XP Professional should be installed on a compressed volume only if the volume was compressed with NTFS compression. If the computer is going to be part of a domain, you must use a different computer name for each installation.
Windows 2000 or Windows XP Home Edition (single or multiple instances) or Windows XP Professional (single or multiple instances)	• If you want, you can install Windows XP Professional on one partition and Windows XP Home Edition on an other partition on the same volume, but you must use basic disks. • If the computer will be part of a domain, you must use a different computer name for each installation.

project 5.2

Transferring Files and Settings

exam objective

Upgrade from a previous version of Windows. Migrate user state data from an existing PC to a new PC. Answer end-user questions relating to upgrading from a previous version of Windows. Considerations include available upgrade paths and methods of transferring user state data.

Perform and troubleshoot an attended installation of a Windows XP operating system. Perform post-installation configuration. Tasks include customizing installations for individual users and applying service packs.

overview

The final deployment of the computers in the local office is as follows:

- Twenty-six computers will be upgraded from Windows 98 to Windows XP.
- Four computers will have Windows XP installed in a multiple-boot configuration.
- Five computers will have a new installation of Windows XP installed, sometimes referred to as a "clean install."

Five of the new computers will be assigned to current employees. Five of the upgraded computers will be assigned to newly hired employees after the original employees' files and application settings are transferred to the new computers.

learning objective

After completing this project, you will be more familiar with the procedures for transferring files and settings between computers.

specific requirements

None

estimated completion time

15 minutes

project steps

1. How many times will it be necessary to run the Files and Settings Transfer Wizard after the Windows XP installations are finished? Explain how you determined this value.
2. Consider the following alternative scenario: You want to transfer the users' files to the new computers before the computers are delivered. You want to make sure that none of the current applications or data files are left on the "old" computers before they are delivered to their new users. Prepare a set of instructions describing the steps necessary to meet this scenario's requirements. Refer to **Table 5-2** and **Table 5-3** for transfer requirements.
3. What will be the easiest way to connect the source and destination computers for file and settings transfer?

Table 5-2 File and Settings Transfer Wizard requirements

Windows XP installation CD-ROM
Source computer running supported operating system
Destination computer running Windows XP
Direct or local area network connection

Table 5-3 Support source operating systems

Windows 95
Windows 98
Windows 98, Second Edition
Windows NT 4.0
Windows 2000
Windows XP

project 5.3

Using Application Compatibility Tools

exam objective

Upgrade from a previous version of Windows. Verify application compatibility for upgrade. Tasks include ascertaining which applications can and cannot run and using the application compatibility tools.

overview

After installing Windows XP on a test computer, you discover an application that was not reported as incompatible during the preinstallation checks but which does not run correctly on Windows XP. You must compare available application compatibility configuration options and determine the best solution.

learning objective

After completing this project, you will know how to use application compatibility tools to correct software compatibility problems.

specific requirements

See General Requirements. Internet access is not required for this project.

estimated completion time

10 minutes

project steps

Test the procedures for setting application compatibility properties:

1. Prepare a list of actions to take to correct compatibility problems before editing file properties.
2. Click **Start**, point to **All Programs**, point to **Accessories**, and click **Command Prompt** to open a command prompt window.
3. Type **copy con c:\test.bat** and press [**Enter**].
4. Press [**Ctrl+Z**] and press [**Enter**] (**Figure 5-1**). This action creates an empty file named **test.bat** at the root of drive **C:**. The action also gives you a file that the operating system recognizes as executable, so that you can access the compatibility properties for the file, without affecting system and application executables.
5. Type **exit** and press [**Enter**] to close the command prompt window.
6. Click **Start** and select **My Computer** to open the **My Computer** window.
7. On the **My Computer** toolbar, click **Folders** to open the **Folders** pane on the left side of the **My Computer** window.
8. In the **Folders** pane, select **Local Disk** (**C:**).
9. In the C: drive detail window, locate the **test.bat** file you created in step 4.
10. Right-click **test.bat** and select **Properties** to open the **test.bat Properties** dialog box on the **General** tab (**Figure 5-2**).
11. Click the **Compatibility** tab.
12. Select the **Run this program in compatibility mode for** check box.
13. Click the list arrow. What are the available operating system compatibility settings (**Figure 5-3**)?
14. Which additional configuration settings are supported?
15. Click the **Cancel** button to close the Properties dialog box without making any changes.
16. Open the **File** menu and select **Close** to exit My Computer.
17. Prepare a report explaining potential problems that could result from having less-experienced end users run the **Program Compatibility Wizard** to attempt to correct compatibility problems.

Figure 5-1 Creating a test batch file

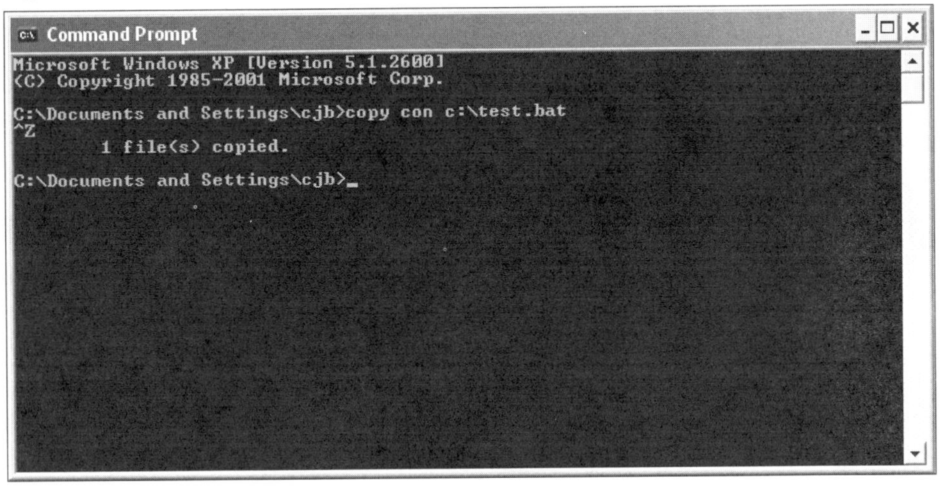

Figure 5-2 The test Properties dialog box – General tab

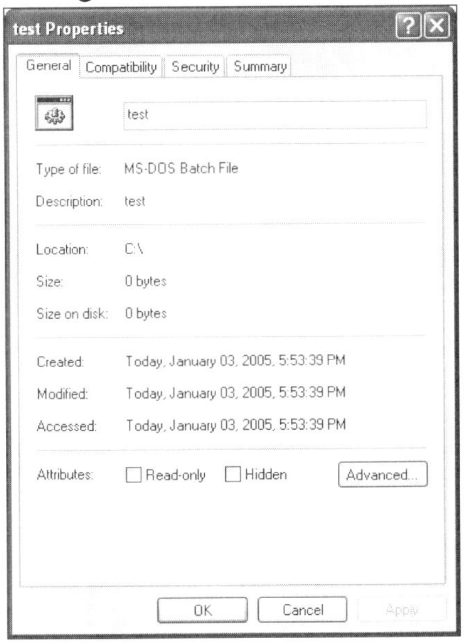

Figure 5-3 Operating system compatibility choices

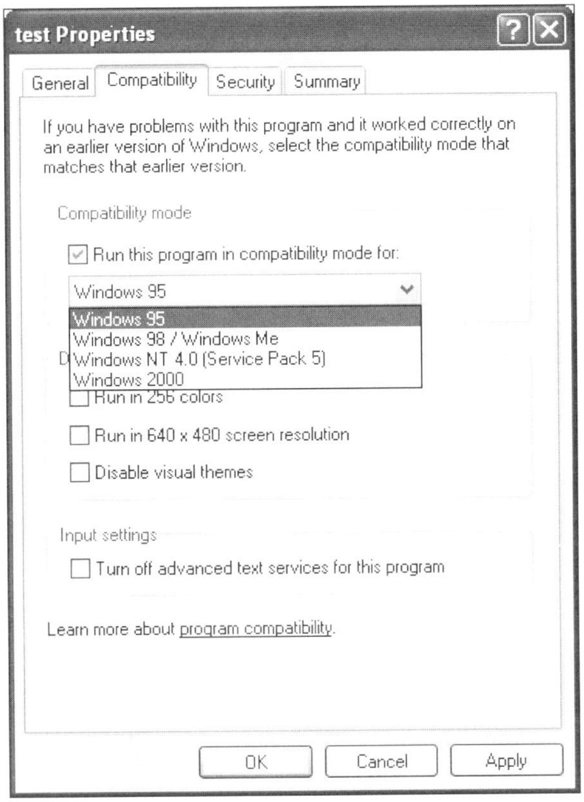

Figure 5-4 Other compatibility settings

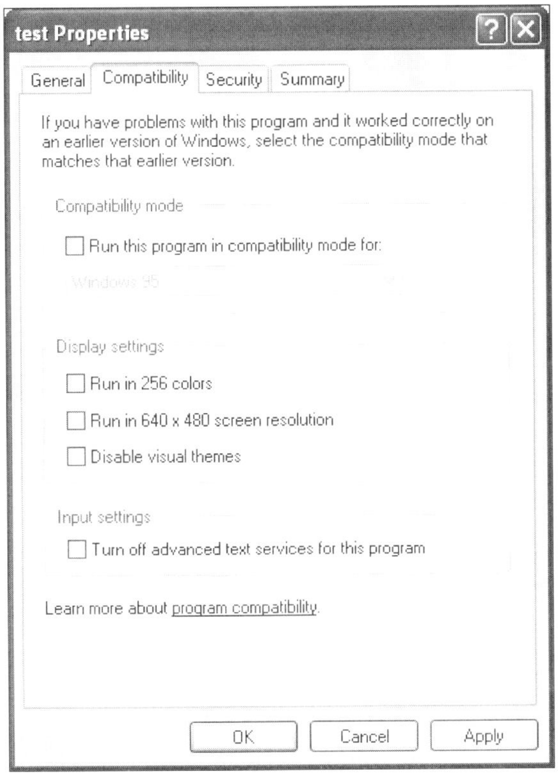

project 5.4

Installing Service Packs and Hotfixes

exam objective

Perform and troubleshoot an attended installation of a Windows XP operating system. Perform post-installation configuration. Tasks include customizing installations for individual users and applying service packs.

overview

The business management staff is concerned about articles they have read recently about security breaches and data loss. They want to verify that the computers will be protected after you have installed Windows XP. They specifically asked how you plan to ensure that the security enhancements in Service Pack 2 will be applied to the computers.

You are asked to draw up a plan for applying Service Pack 2 to newly installed computers and for applying any other applicable security fixes.

learning objective

After completing this project, you will know how to apply service packs and updates.

specific requirements

See General Requirements. Internet access is required for this project.

estimated completion time

Approximately 15 minutes, depending on Internet connection

project steps

1. Launch **Internet Explorer** and navigate to **http://windowsupdate.microsoft.com**.
2. If a **Security Warning** dialog box opens, click **Yes** (**Figure 5-5**).
3. Click the **Custom Install: High Priority and Optional Updates for Your Computer** link to view the available updates (**Figure 5-6**).
4. If prompted to install a new version of Windows Update software, click **Install Now** and following the installation prompts.
5. Review the available updates. Do not install any updates at this time.
6. Close Internet Explorer.
7. What are the advantages of integrating a service pack with the Windows XP Professional installation files (referred to as slipstreaming) before you start your Windows XP installations?
8. Describe the requirements for using an integrated installation set as your installation source. Include any special requirements for client computers. Refer to Project 5.2 for installation requirements.

Figure 5-5 Security Warning dialog box

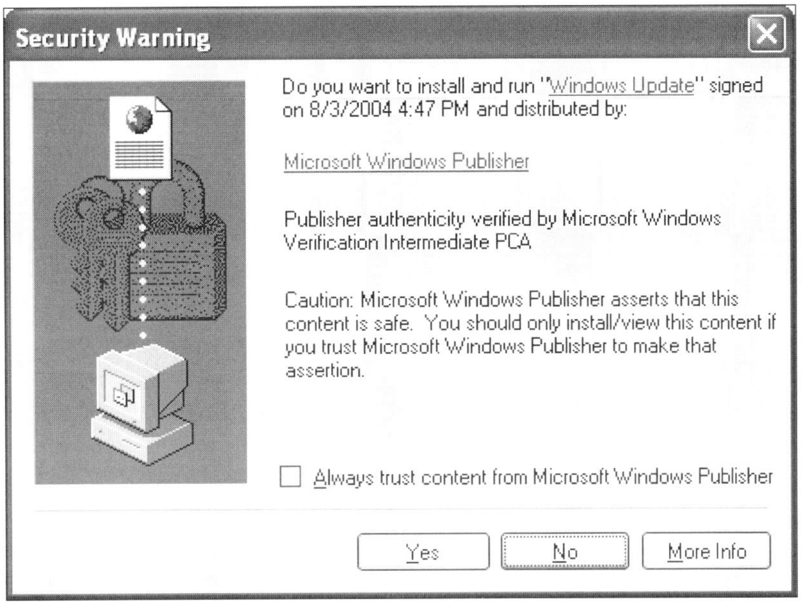

Figure 5-6 Windows Update installation options

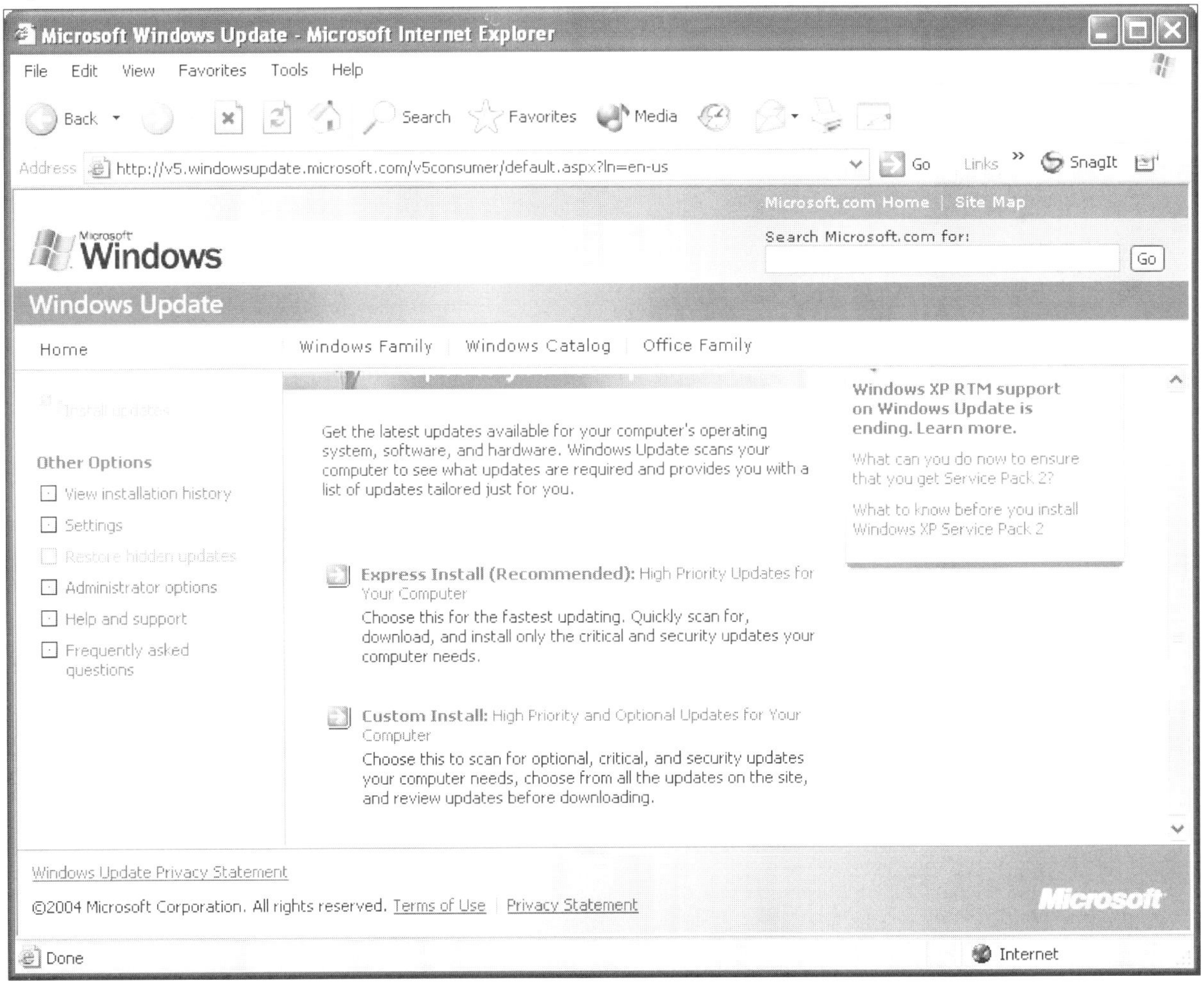

project 5.5

Updating Windows XP After Installation

exam objective

Perform and troubleshoot an attended installation of a Windows XP operating system. Perform post-installation configuration. Tasks include customizing installations for individual users and applying service packs.

overview

Based on recent requests, you must determine the best way to keep users' computers up-to-date. All computers will have Internet access available. The solution you choose should be applicable in both workgroup and Active Directory domain environments. You must submit your plan for review and approval before you can start installing Windows XP.

learning objective

After completing this project, you will be more familiar with configuring Windows Updates to meet update preferences.

specific requirements

None

estimated completion time

10 minutes

project steps

1. Updates should be a completely transparent process. How should Automatic Updates be configured (**Figure 5-7**)?
2. Prepare a set of step-by-step instructions that walks users through configuring Automatic Updates.
3. How can users bring their systems up-to-date as a baseline before configuring Automatic Updates?

Figure 5-7 The Automatic Updates tab on the System Properties dialog box

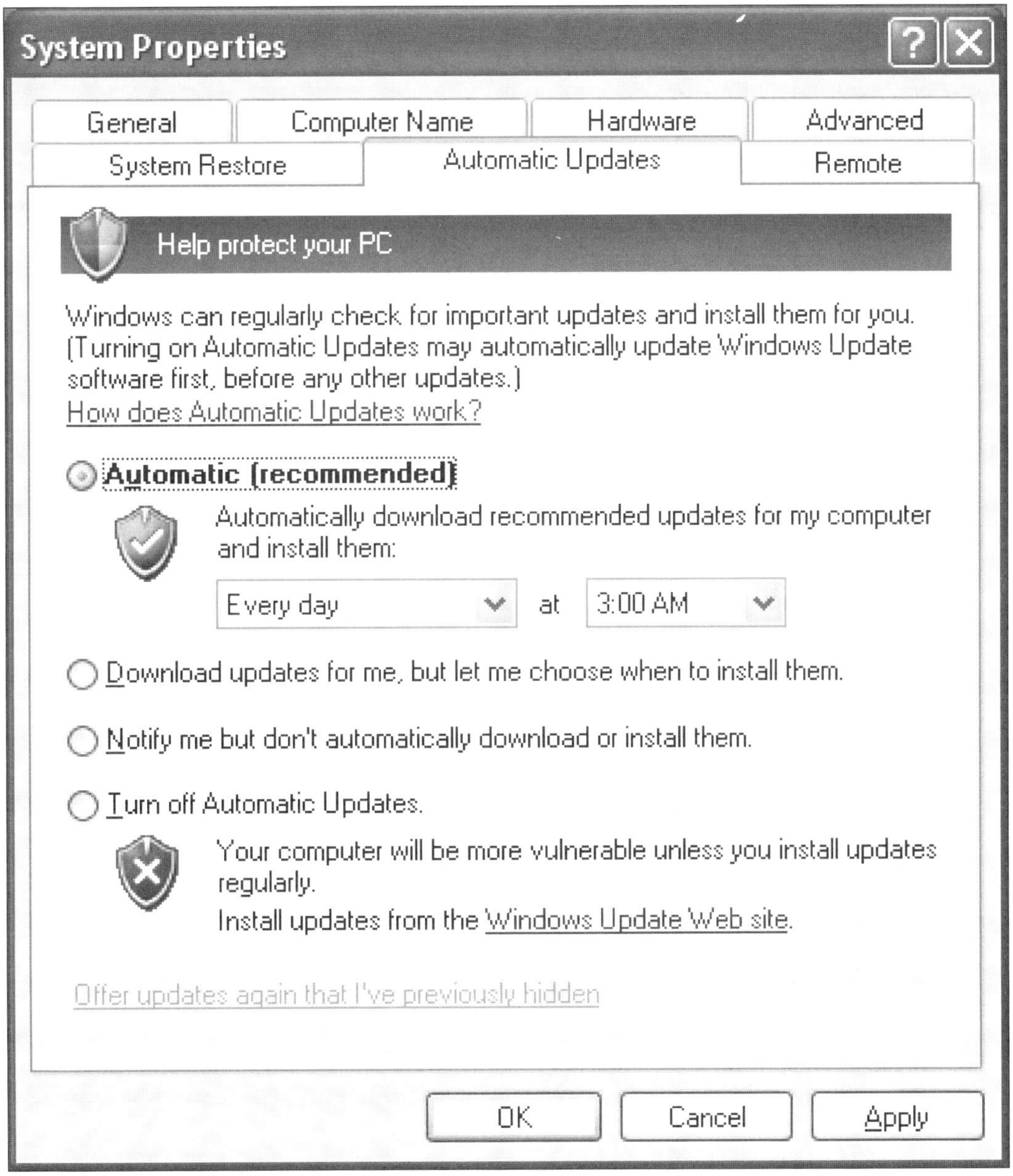

LESSON

6 Monitoring, Managing, and Troubleshooting File and Folder Access

Using Windows XP, you can share files between multiple users whether they are logged on locally or over the network. However, understanding how shared files can be protected from unauthorized access is critical to ensuring the security of network resources. Users should be educated about file protection and instructed on the best practices for file sharing.

Simple File Sharing, which is enabled by default on Windows XP Home Edition, allows you to share files, but with very limited protection. In fact, Simple File Sharing is the only choice for file sharing on Windows XP Home. Simple File Sharing allows users to share files with other users on their computer by dragging the folder and its contents to the Shared Documents folder. You can also share folders with other users on the network. However, all shared folders are accessed over the network using the built-in Guest account. This means that when you use Simple File Sharing, you cannot select which users can and cannot access a folder. Protection can be provided for folders stored in the user's personal profile (C:\Documents and Settings*username*).

Windows XP Professional also supports Simple File Sharing. In fact, it is enabled by default when a computer running Windows XP Professional is a member of a workgroup. Simple File Sharing is not supported on domain members. If you require user-specific file security, you should disable Simple File Sharing and use NTFS file permissions instead. NTFS file permissions protect files both when they are accessed locally and when they are accessed over the network. NTFS permissions are supported only on volumes formatted with the NTFS file system. Shared folders on any file system can be protected using share permissions. When both share permissions and NTFS permissions are defined and a file is accessed over the network, the most restrictive permissions are used to determine a user's access level.

Encrypting File System (EFS), available on NTFS volumes only, is another key file protection feature of Windows XP Professional. EFS uses keys that are obtained from the certificate of the user to encrypt files. Only users who have a certificate used to encrypt the file can decrypt it. EFS protects files not only when Windows XP Professional is running, but even if an intruder starts the computer using another operating system or removes the hard drive and places the drive in another system. An encrypted file can be copied only by a user with a certificate used to encrypt the file. One limitation to EFS is that a compressed file must be uncompressed before it can be encrypted.

Scenario

A number of users at Ads R Us store confidential files on their computers. Some of these files must be accessed by other users in the company; others are sensitive and must be carefully protected against unauthorized access. You have been asked to develop a training program to help users understand the importance of file security and the procedures that can be used to protect the files on their computers. You will consider situations in which Simple File Sharing is appropriate and situations in which NTFS permissions should be used. You will also make recommendations for using EFS.

Lesson 6 Monitoring, Managing, and Troubleshooting File and Folder Access

Project	Exam 70-271 Objective
6.1 Monitoring, Managing, and Troubleshooting Simple File Sharing	**Monitor, manage, and troubleshoot access to files and folders.** Manage and troubleshoot simple file sharing. Answer end-user questions related to managing and troubleshooting access to files and folders.
6.2 Monitoring, Managing, and Troubleshooting NTFS File Permissions	**Monitor, manage, and troubleshoot access to files and folders.** Monitor, manage, and troubleshoot NTFS file permissions. Answer end-user questions related to managing and troubleshooting access to files and folders.
6.3 Monitoring, Managing, and Troubleshooting File Encryption	**Monitor, manage, and troubleshoot access to files and folders.** Manage and troubleshoot file encryption. Answer end-user questions related to managing and troubleshooting access to files and folders.

General Requirements

To complete the projects in this lesson, you will need administrative rights on either a standalone Windows XP Professional computer or a Windows XP Professional computer that is a member of a workgroup. You may also find it helpful to refer to Lesson 6 in your Prentice Hall Certification Series Exam 70-271 textbook for further information about topics covered by the projects in this lesson.

project 6.1

Monitoring, Managing, and Troubleshooting Simple File Sharing

exam objective

Monitor, manage, and troubleshoot access to files and folders. Manage and troubleshoot simple file sharing. Answer end-user questions related to managing and troubleshooting access to files and folders.

overview

One of the members of the Marketing Department uses her home computer to work on ads outside of office hours. Her home computer is running Windows XP Professional. Other members of her family use the computer, and she wants to ensure that they cannot access her work files.

learning objective

After completing this project, you will know how to use Simple File Sharing to protect files from unauthorized access.

specific requirements

In addition to the General Requirements, to follow the project steps, you must create a user account and make the password on the account blank. If you use an account that you have already created, first log on using the Administrator account and change the password for the user account to blank.

estimated completion time

5 minutes

project steps

1. Click **Start**, and then **Control Panel** to open the **Control Panel**.
2. In **Category view**, click the **User Accounts** link to open the **User Accounts** window.
3. Click the **Create a new account** link to open the **User Accounts** window on the **Name the new account** screen.
4. Type a username in the **Type a name for the new account** text box and click **Next**.
5. On the **Pick an account type** screen, make sure that the **Computer administrator** option button is selected and click the **Create Account** button.
6. Log off and log back on using the user account you just created.
7. Click **Start** and then **My Documents** to open the **My Documents** window.
8. Right-click an empty area of the window and click **Properties** to open the **My Documents Properties** dialog box.
9. Click the **Sharing** tab.
10. Select the **Make this folder private** check box (**Figure 6-1**).
11. Click **OK** to close the My Documents Properties dialog box.
12. The **Sharing** warning dialog box opens. Click **Yes** to create a password for the user account (**Figure 6-2**).
13. The **User Accounts** window opens on the **Create a password for your account** screen.
14. Type the same password in the **Type a new password** and **Type the new password again to confirm** fields.
15. Type a password hint in the **Type a word or phrase to use as a password hint** field.
16. Click the **Create Password** button (**Figure 6-3**).
17. Close the User Accounts window.
18. Close the My Documents window.

Figure 6-1 The Make this folder private check box

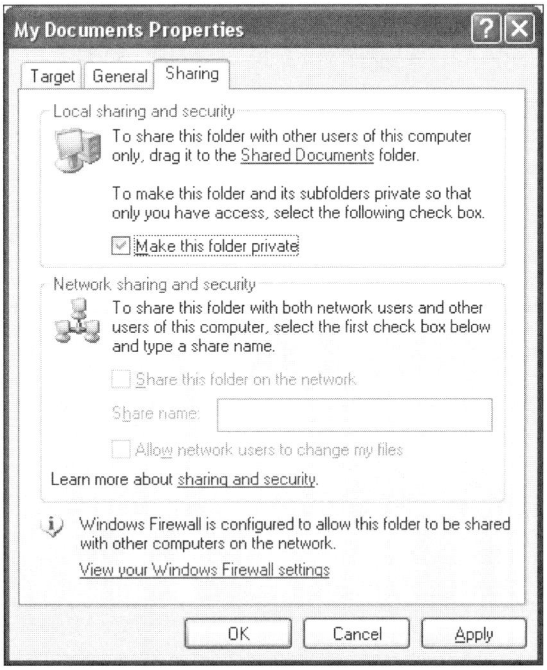

Figure 6-2 The Sharing warning dialog box

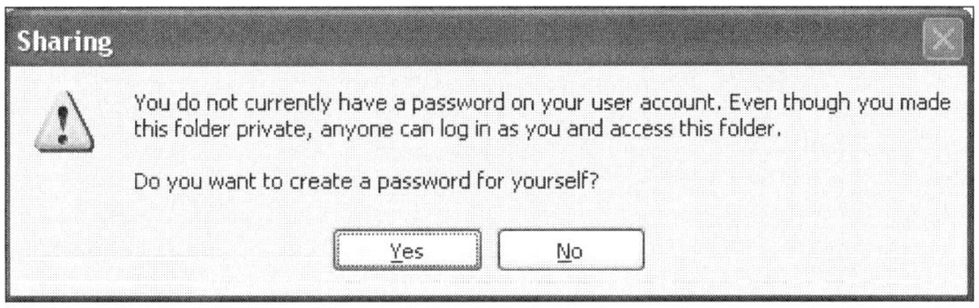

Figure 6-3 Creating a password for your user account

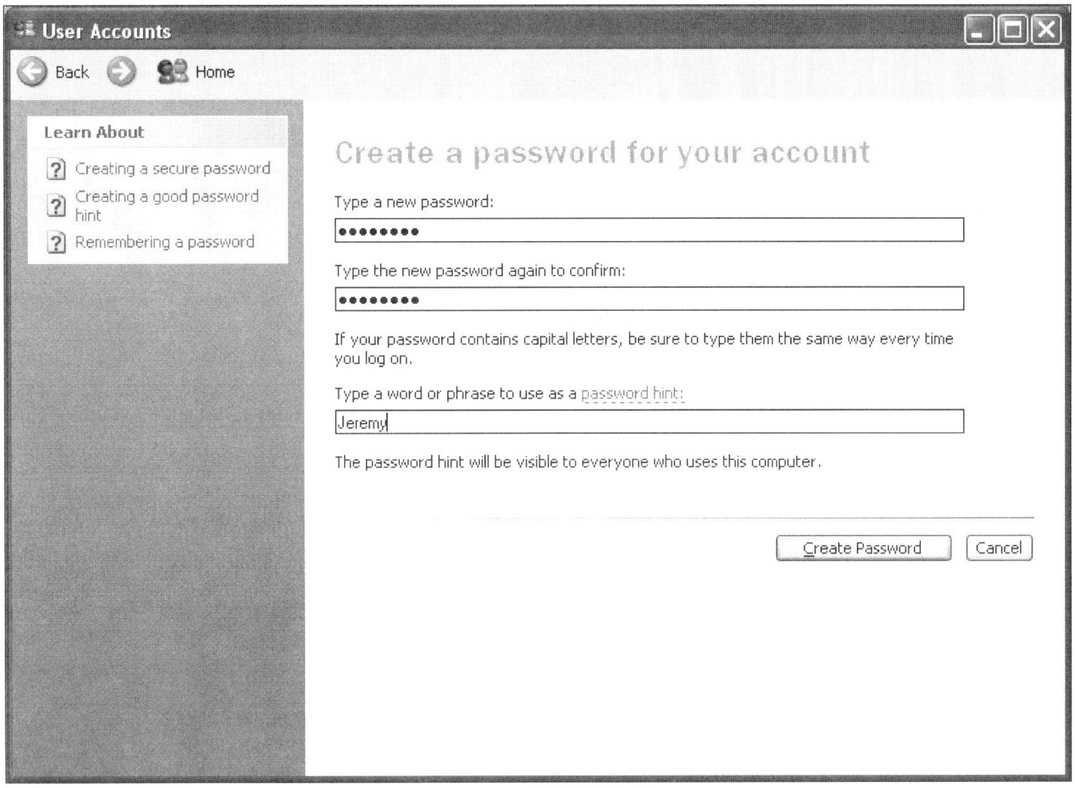

project 6.2

Monitoring, Managing, and Troubleshooting NTFS File Permissions

exam objective

Monitor, manage, and troubleshoot access to files and folders. Manage and troubleshoot NTFS file permissions. Answer end-user questions related to managing and troubleshooting access to files and folders.

overview

Two employees at Ads R Us are responsible for billing customers. These employees store customer billing information, including credit card numbers, on their computers. You must ensure that only members in the Accounting Department can access the files that contain credit card numbers. The computers are currently members of a workgroup with Simple File Sharing enabled. You are not sure which file system is used to format the volume. You will check the file system, convert it to NTFS if necessary, and disable Simple File Sharing. Then you will create a group and a folder that only members of that group can access.

learning objective

After completing this project, you will know how to protect files and folders using NTFS permissions.

specific requirements

See General Requirements. You should be logged on as Administrator, the default administrator account created during the Windows XP installation.

estimated completion time

30 minutes

project steps

1. Log off and log back on using the **Administrator** account.
2. Click **Start** and then **Control Panel** to open the **Control Panel**.
3. In **Category view**, click the **Performance and Maintenance** link to open the **Performance and Maintenance** window.
4. Click **Administrative Tools** to open the **Administrative Tools** window.
5. Double-click the **Computer Management** icon to open the **Computer Management** console.
6. Select the **Disk Management** node.
7. Note the file system of drive C. If it is not NTFS, you will need to convert it. To do so
   a. Click **Start**, point to **All Programs**, point to **Accessories**, and click **Command Prompt** to open the command prompt.
   b. Type the following command: **convert c: /FS:NTFS**, and press **Enter**.
   c. Type the volume label for volume C and press **Enter**. The label is shown in the **Volume** column in the **Computer Management** console.
8. The Convert utility warns you that it cannot gain exclusive access to the drive and asks if you want to schedule the conversion for the next time the system starts. Click **Yes** to close the dialog box.
9. Restart the computer to convert the volume to NTFS.
10. When the computer restarts, follow steps 1-4 to reopen the **Computer Management** console.
11. Expand the **Local Users and Groups** node.
12. Select the **Groups** folder (**Figure 6-4**).
13. Right-click **Groups** and select **New Group** to open the **New Group** dialog box.
14. Enter the values in the **Group name** and **Description** text boxes shown in **Figure 6-5**.
15. Click the **Add** button to open the **Select Users** dialog box and add a user to the group.
16. Type **Administrator** in the **Enter the object names to select** box and click the **Check Names** button (**Figure 6-6**).

Figure 6-4 Groups

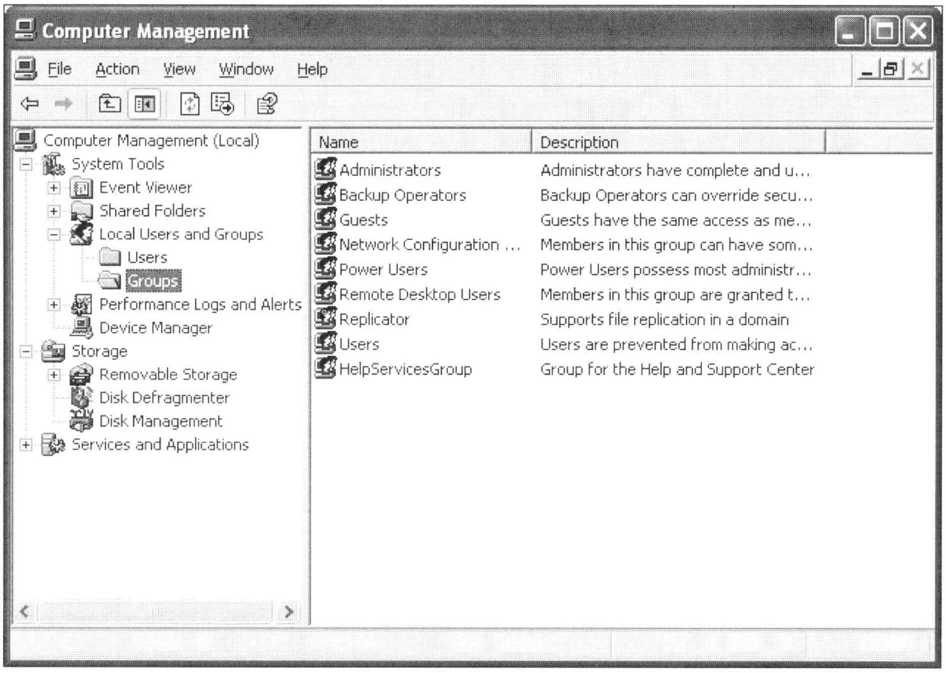

Figure 6-5 Creating a new group

Figure 6-6 Adding the Administrator account to the group

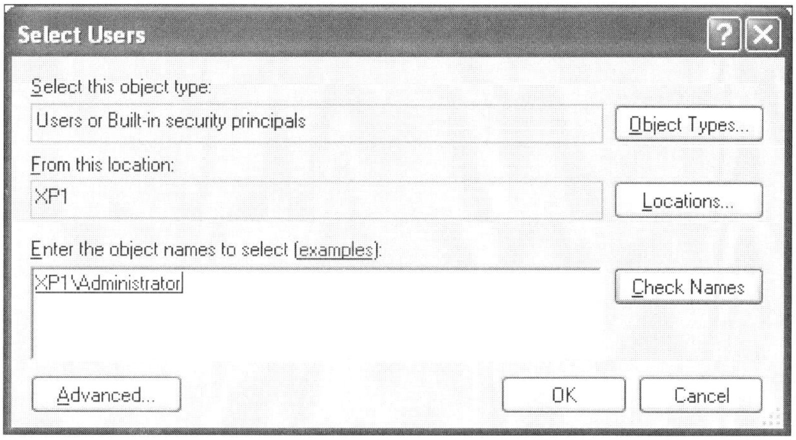

project 6.2 Monitoring, Managing, and Troubleshooting NTFS File Permissions (cont'd)

exam objective

Monitor, manage, and troubleshoot access to files and folders. Manage and troubleshoot NTFS file permissions. Answer end-user questions related to managing and troubleshooting access to files and folders.

project steps

17. Click **OK** to add the Administrator account to the group and close the Select Users dialog box.
18. Click the **Create** button to create the group.
19. Click the **Close** button to close the New Group dialog box.
20. Close the Computer Management console and the Administrative Tools window.
21. Click **Start** and then **My Computer** to open the **My Computer** window.
22. Double-click **Local Disk (C:)**.
23. If you are prompted that the files are hidden, click **Show the contents of this folder**.
24. Open the **File** menu, point to **New**, and click **Folder** to create a new folder. Name it **CustomerInfo** and press **[Enter]**.
25. Right-click the **CustomerInfo** folder and click **Sharing and Security** to open the **CustomerInfo Properties** dialog box on the **Sharing** tab. Why doesn't the Security tab appear?
26. Open the **Tools** menu and select **Folder Options** to open the **Folder Options** dialog box.
27. Click the **View** tab.
28. Scroll down and clear the **Use simple file sharing** (**Recommended**) check box (**Figure 6-7**).
29. Click **OK** to close the Folder Options dialog box.
30. Right-click the **CustomerInfo** folder and click **Sharing and Security** to open the **CustomerInfo Properties** dialog box on the **Sharing** tab.
31. Click the **Share this folder** option button.
32. Click the **Apply** button.
33. Click the **Security** tab. In the **Group or user names** box, select the **Administrators** group. Notice that the permissions for Administrators are grayed out and unavailable (**Figure 6-8**). What does this mean?
34. Click the **Advanced** button to open the **Advanced Security Settings for CustomerInfo** dialog box (**Figure 6-9**).
35. Clear the **Inherit from parent the permission entries that apply to child objects** check box.
36. When the **Security** dialog box opens, click the **Remove** button.
37. Click **OK** to close the Advanced Security Settings for CustomerInfo dialog box.
38. Another **Security** warning dialog box cautions you that you have denied everyone access to the CustomerInfo folder. No one will be able to access the folder and only the owner will be able to change permissions. Click **Yes** (**Figure 6-10**).
39. Click the **Add** button to open the **Select Users or Groups** dialog box.
40. Type **Accounting** in the **Enter the object names to select** box and click the **Check Names** button.
41. Click **OK** to add the **Accounting** group to the list and close the Select Users or Groups dialog box.
42. Grant the **Accounting** group **Full Control** access to the CustomerInfo folder (**Figure 6-11**).
43. Click **OK** to close the CustomerInfo Properties dialog box.
44. How will granting permission to a group instead of a user make the transition from a workgroup to a domain easier to manage?

Figure 6-7 Disabling Simple File Sharing

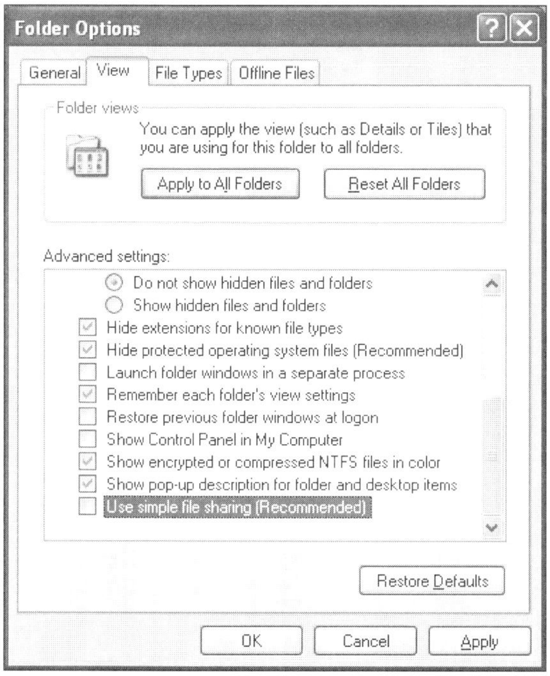

Figure 6-8 Inherited permissions

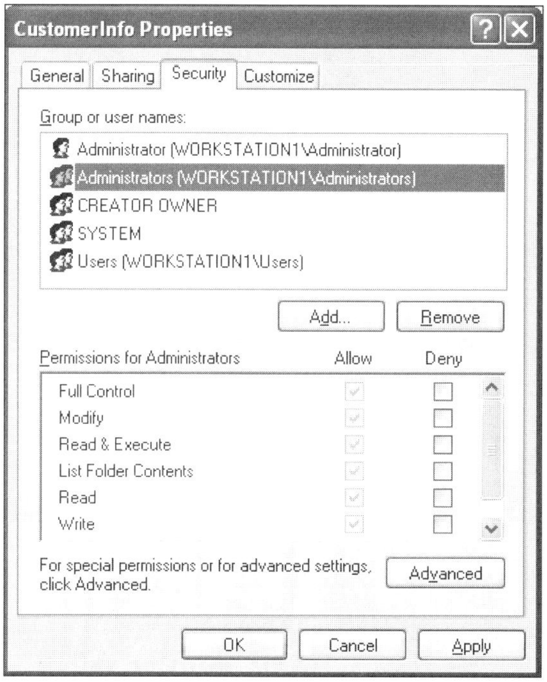

Figure 6-9 Preventing inheritance

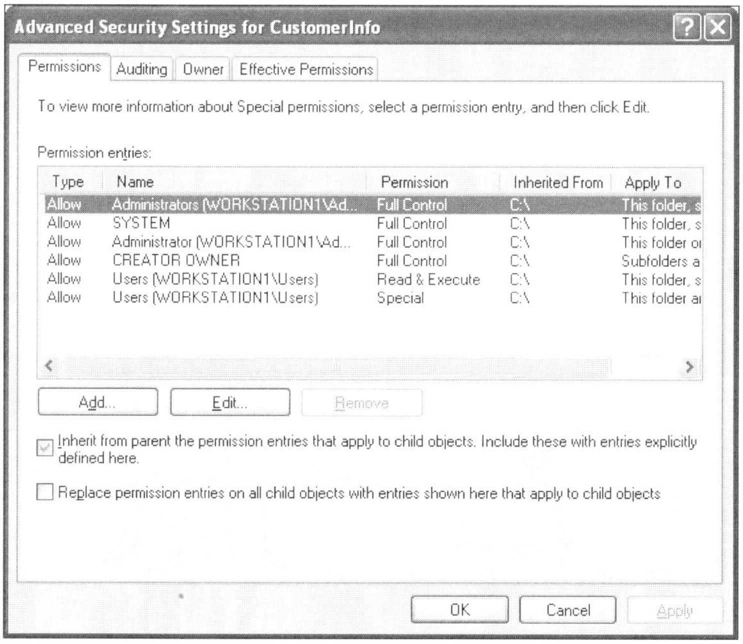

Figure 6-10 A Security warning dialog box

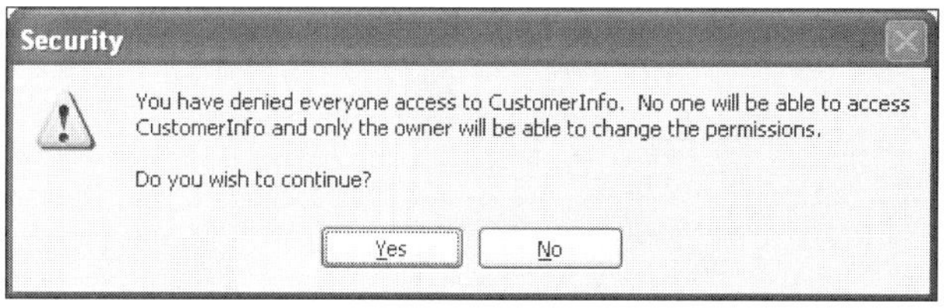

Figure 6-11 Explicit permissions

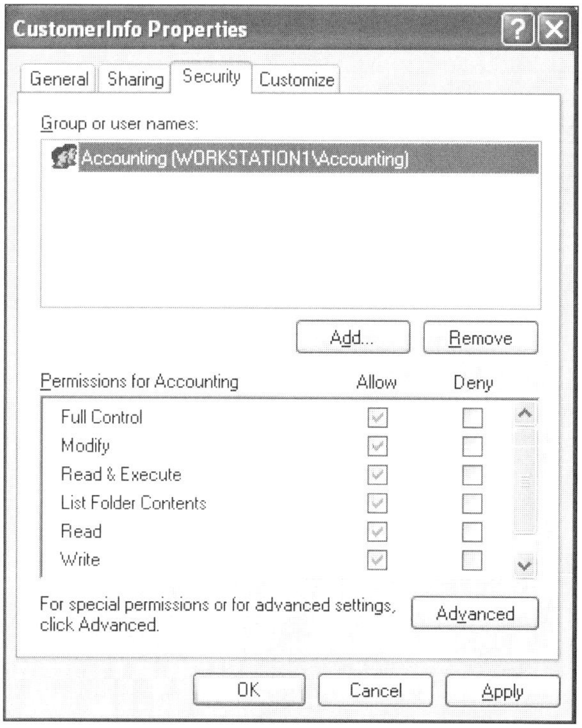

project 6.3

Monitoring, Managing, and Troubleshooting File Encryption

exam objective

Monitor, manage, and troubleshoot access to files and folders. Manage and troubleshoot file encryption. Answer end-user questions related to managing and troubleshooting access to files and folders.

overview

You are configuring a laptop computer that will be used by the president of Ads R Us when he is traveling. He is concerned that the laptop might be stolen and his confidential financial records might be accessed. His financial files are stored in the Money directory on the C drive. He is currently located in a different time zone and would like you to send him a batch file that he can run to protect his files. You will create and test a batch file that uses the cipher command.

learning objective

After completing this project, you will know how to use the Cipher command to encrypt files.

specific requirements

See General Requirements. You should be logged on as Administrator, the default administrator account created during the Windows XP installation.

estimated completion time

15 minutes

project steps

1. Create a folder named **Money** at the root of drive **C**.
2. Open **C:\Money**.
3. Open the **File** menu, point to **New**, and click **Text Document**. Name the document **January.txt**.
4. Repeat step 3 twice, naming the files **February.txt** and **March.txt**.
5. Navigate to the root of drive **C**.
6. Open the **Tools** menu and click **Folder Options** to open the **Folder Options** dialog box.
7. Click the **View** tab.
8. Clear the **Hide extensions for known file types** check box (**Figure 6-12**).
9. Click **OK** to close the Folder Options dialog box.
10. Open the **File** menu, point to **New**, and click **Text Document**. Name the document **MakeSecret.bat**. This is created in the root of drive C.
11. The **Rename** dialog box warns you that the file may become unusable if you change its extension. Click **Yes** (**Figure 6-13**).
12. Right-click the **MakeSecret.bat** file and click **Edit** to open the file in **Notepad**.
13. Type the following command **(Figure 6-14)**: **cipher /e /s:c:\money /acd moneycipher**
14. In the **Notepad** window, open the **File** menu and select **Save** to save the file.
15. Close Notepad.
16. Click **Start**, point to **All Programs**, point to **Accessories**, and click **Command Prompt** to open the command prompt.
17. Type **cd c:** and press **[Enter]** to change the directory to the root of the C: drive.
18. Type **makesecret** and press **[Enter]**.
19. Review the results (**Figure 6-15**).
20. Close the command prompt and view the **C** drive window. How can you tell that the Money directory is encrypted?
21. Double-click the **Money** folder to open it.
22. Create a new text document named **April.txt**. Is it encrypted?
23. Close the Money folder.

Figure 6-12 Displaying well-known file extensions

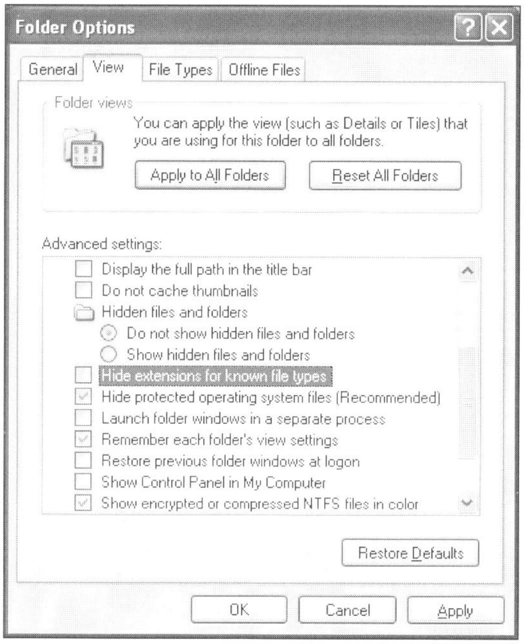

Figure 6-13 The Rename warning dialog box

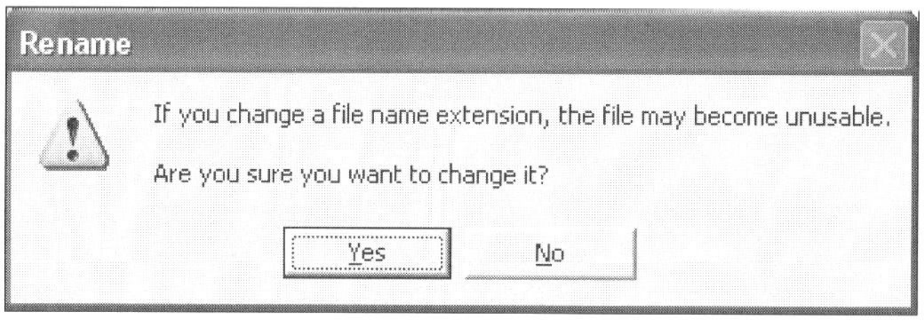

Figure 6-14 Creating a batch file to encrypt a folder

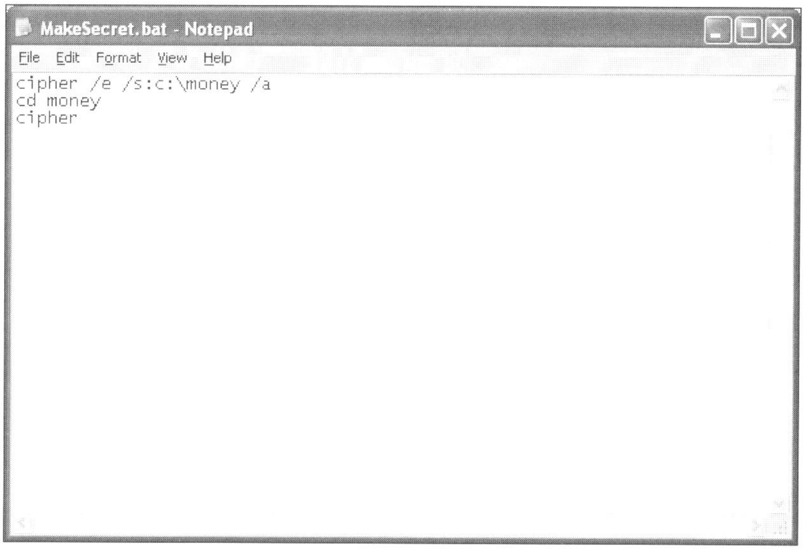

Figure 6-15 Running a batch file

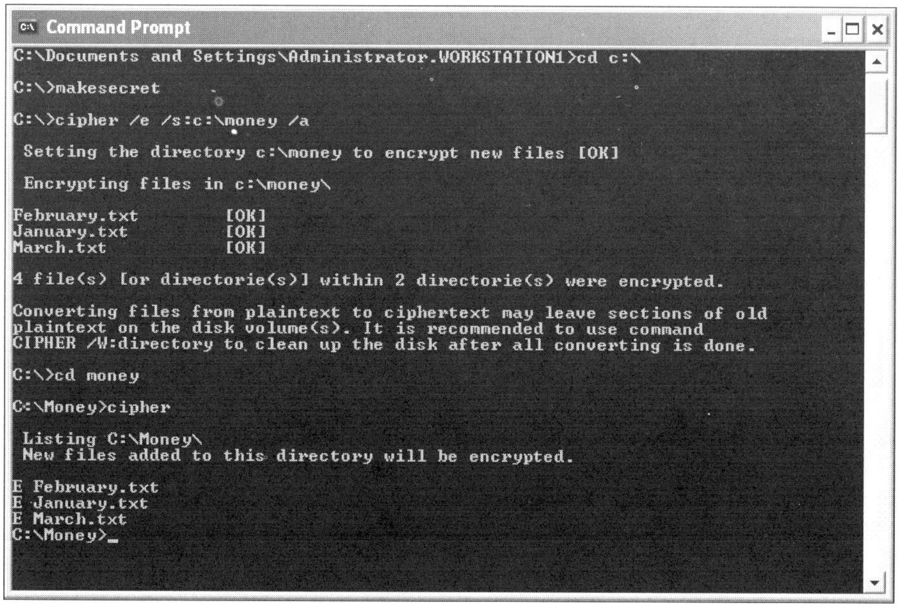

LESSON

7 Managing and Troubleshooting Access to Shared Folders

Resource sharing, specifically folder and file sharing, is typically a prime justification for networking computers. Thus, it is critical that you understand the procedures for sharing files, potential security issues, how to configure and manage access security, how to synchronize offline files, and how to troubleshoot connectivity and access errors.

In an Active Directory domain environment, most resource sharing is at least somewhat centralized. In a workgroup environment, sharing and security typically are left up to individual users.

File sharing is supported by Windows XP by default, but it must be enabled manually. Depending on how the computer is configured, the share properties you can manage include whether the folder is shared, the share name, a descriptive comment, the maximum concurrent user limit, access permissions, and file caching.

There are three methods you can use to share a folder: the Share a Folder Wizard, the Properties dialog box for a folder, and the NET SHARE command-line command.

Access to resources is controlled through the use of share and NTFS permissions. When a user is assigned both share and NTFS permissions for a folder, the more restrictive of the two becomes their effective permission. NTFS permissions, which apply locally as well as over the network, are supported only when the NTFS file system is used to format the partition or volume. Folders on a FAT partition can only have share permissions applied. The share permissions are Read, Change, and Full Control.

In addition to folders you designate as shared, Windows XP Professional creates and shares folders that are used for remote administrative purposes (C$, D$, ADMIN$, PRINT$). These are known as administrative shares, which are hidden by adding a dollar sign ($) to the end of the share name. These folders are automatically created and shared during the installation of the operating system and cannot be deleted. Other folders that you designate as shared can also be hidden from browsing by including the dollar sign ($). These shares, created by users, can be deleted.

Access is denied when a user has insufficient rights. This can be due to shared or NTFS permissions. The permissions that apply include those that are explicitly assigned to a user, those that are explicitly assigned to a group to which the user belongs, and inherited permissions.

A common problem occurs when an access permission is configured as Denied at some point in the permission hierarchy, which takes precedence over allowed permissions. When you test permission changes, the user must log off and log back on. On an Active Directory domain, you must allow time for permission changes to propagate through the domain controllers.

Files and folders can be made available for offline access. This allows a user to view and modify files when he or she is not connected to the network or when the files are not available on the network. Offline files are cached locally. Cached files can be synchronized every time the user logs on or logs off, at specified intervals (when the system is idle), or at scheduled times. Common causes of synchronization errors include improper property settings, insufficient permissions, insufficient disk space on the user's computer, insufficient disk space allocated to cached files, and network communication errors. Some Windows XP features, such as Terminal Services and Fast User Switching, are incompatible with offline file access and file synchronization.

Scenario

You have finished the initial deployment of Windows XP. After answering questions and concerns related to the initial learning curve, the users are comfortable with Windows XP. Support requests have significantly dropped. After reading your report on how well the transition has gone, the management staff has decided to move up the schedule for converting the network to an Active Directory domain environment. As part of the preparation, you have been assigned two additional tasks: to have all users stop using simple file sharing to prepare for file sharing in Active Directory and to implement offline file access for users who telecommute. You have already added one computer running Windows Server 2003 that will be used as the corporate file server. The server has been configured to make files available offline and will host all confidential files and all files to which offline access is needed. Users will continue to share less sensitive files on their own computers.

Lesson 7 Managing and Troubleshooting Access to Shared Folders

Project	Exam 70-271 Objective
7.1 Creating Shared Folders	**Manage and troubleshoot access to shared folders**. Create shared folders. Answer end-user questions related to managing and troubleshooting access to files and folders.
7.2 Configuring Access Permissions for Shared Folders on NTFS Partitions	**Manage and troubleshoot access to shared folders**. Configure access permissions for shared folders on NTFS partitions. Answer end-user questions related to managing and troubleshooting access to files and folders.
7.3 Troubleshooting and Interpreting Troubleshoot Access Denied Messages	**Manage and troubleshoot access to shared folders**. and interpret Access Denied messages. Answer end-user questions related to managing and troubleshooting access to files and folders.
7.4 Configuring and Troubleshooting Offline Files	**Manage and troubleshoot access to and synchronization of offline files**. Configure and troubleshoot offline files. Answer end-user questions related to configuring and synchronizing offline files.
7.5 Configuring and Troubleshooting Offline File Synchronization	**Manage and troubleshoot access to and synchronization of offline files**. Configure and troubleshoot offline file synchronization. Answer end-user questions related to configuring and synchronizing offline files.

General Requirements

To complete the projects in this lesson, you will need administrative rights on either a standalone Windows XP computer or a Windows XP computer that is a member of a workgroup. You may also find it helpful to refer to Lesson 7 in your Prentice Hall Certification Series Exam 70-271 textbook for further information about the topics covered by the projects in this lesson.

project 7.1 Creating Shared Folders

exam objective

Manage and troubleshoot access to shared folders. Create shared folders. Answer end-user questions related to managing and troubleshooting access to files and folders.

overview

You must prepare a document that reinforces the file sharing concepts users have learned and explains the procedures for sharing files when Simple File Sharing is disabled. It has been decided that hidden shares will be used to provide an added layer of protection for some folders containing confidential information. Hidden shares are created manually by the user to hide non-administrative shares from users who browse the network. They are not used for remote administration purposes and they can be deleted.

learning objective

After completing this project, you will know how to manage folder and file sharing.

specific requirements

See General Requirements.

estimated completion time

10 minutes

project steps

1. Prepare a document reviewing basic file sharing and file access concepts, including the use of hidden shares (**Figure 7-1**).
2. Prepare a document describing the prompts and available properties on the **Sharing** tab in the **Properties** dialog box for a folder when Simple File Sharing is disabled (**Figure 7-2**).

Figure 7-1 The Windows Properties dialog box

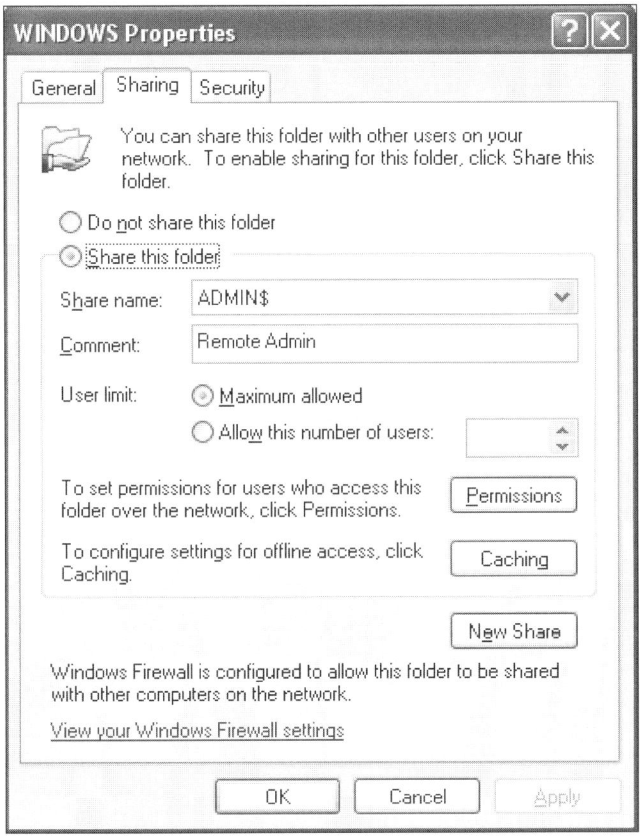

Figure 7-2 The Sharing tab in the General Properties dialog box

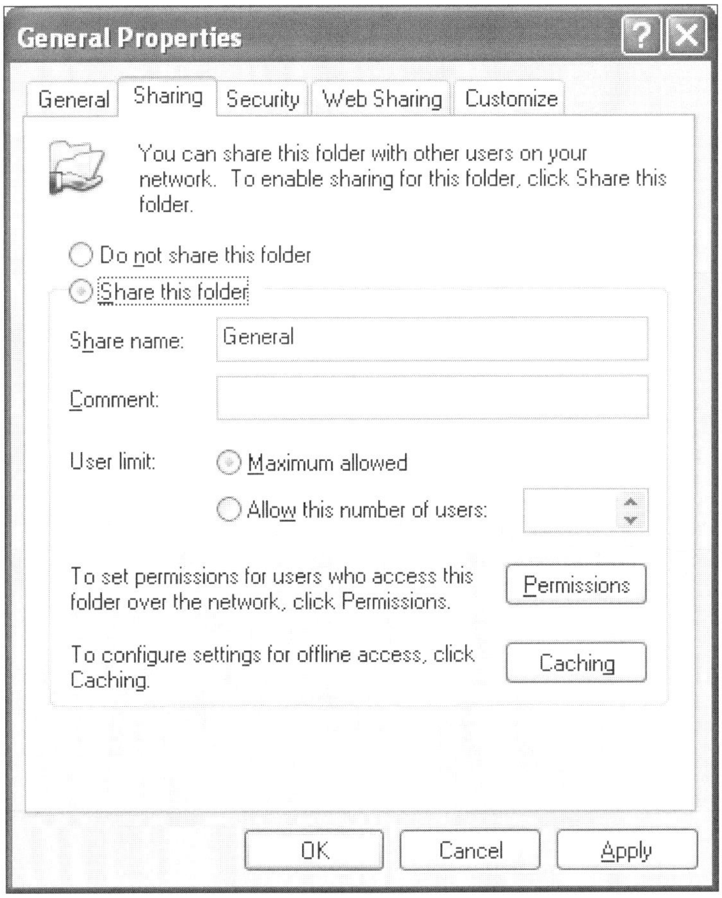

project 7.2

Configuring Access Permissions for Shared Folders on NTFS Partitions

exam objective

Manage and troubleshoot access to shared folders. Configure access permissions for shared folders on NTFS partitions. Answer end-user questions related to managing and troubleshooting access to files and folders.

overview

It is already obvious that share permissions are going to be a problem for some users. You decide to write up a short guide that helps users understand how to configure share permissions.

learning objective

After completing this project, you will know how to manage shared folder access permissions.

specific requirements

See General Requirements.

estimated completion time

15 minutes

project steps

1. Click **Start** and then **Control Panel** to open the **Control Panel**.
2. If the **Control Panel** is in Classic view, click **Switch to Category View**.
3. Click the **Performance and Maintenance** link to open the **Performance and Maintenance** window.
4. Click **Administrative Tools** to open the **Administrative Tools** window.
5. Double-click the **Computer Management** icon to open the **Computer Management** console.
6. Expand the **Local User and Groups** node and select the **Groups** folder.
7. Right-click the **Groups** folder and select **New Group** to open the **New Group** dialog box.
8. Type **SecTest** in the **Group name** text box and click the **Add** button to open the **Select Users** dialog box.
9. Type the username for the account you created in Project 6.1 in the **Enter the object names to select** box and click **OK**. The user account is added to the **Members** box (**Figure 7-3**).
10. Click the **Create** button to create the group.
11. Click the **Close** button to close the **New Group** dialog box.
12. Close the Computer Management console and the Administrative Tools window.
13. Click **Start** and then **My Computer** to open the **My Computer** window.
14. Open the **Tools** menu and select **Folder Options** to open the **Folder Options** dialog box.
15. Click the **View** tab and scroll down to verify that **Simple File Sharing** is disabled, as shown in **Figure 7-4**.
16. Click **OK** to close the Folder Options dialog box.
17. Click **Folders** on the **My Computer** toolbar to display the folder tree view in the left window pane.
18. In the folder tree, select **Local Disk (C:)**.
19. Open the **File** menu, point to **New**, and click **Folder**.
20. Type **Security** and press [**Enter**] to name the folder.
21. In the folder tree, select **C:\Security**.
22. Follow the procedures in steps 19 and 20 to create a folder named **All** in **C:\Security.**
23. Follow the procedures in steps 19 and 20 to create a folder named **None** in **C:\Security**.

Figure 7-3 The New Group dialog box with a user added as a member

Figure 7-4 Simple File Sharing disabled

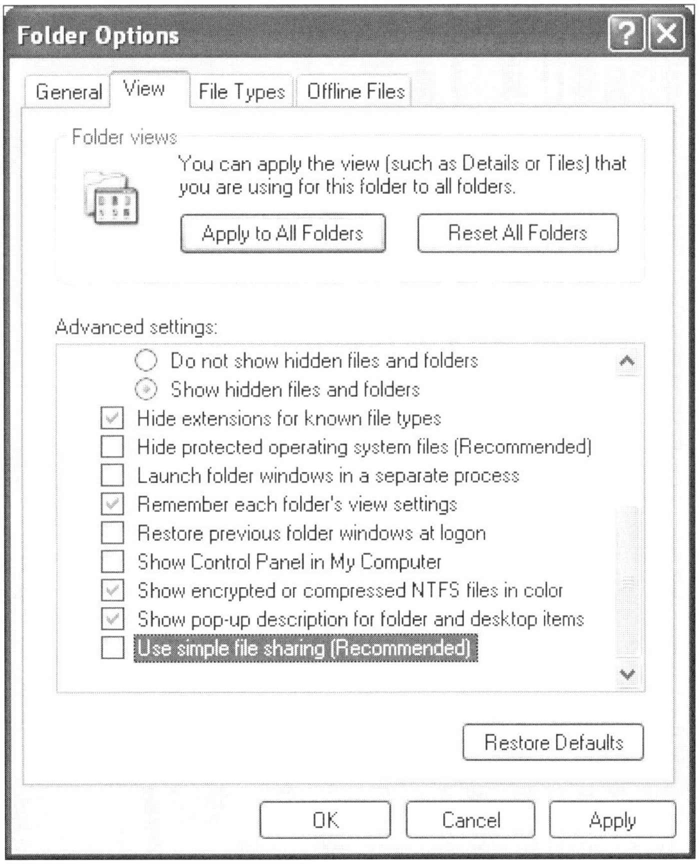

project 7.2

Configuring Access Permissions for Shared Folders on NTFS Partitions *(cont'd)*

exam objective

Manage and troubleshoot access to shared folders. Configure access permissions for shared folders on NTFS partitions. Answer end-user questions related to managing and troubleshooting access to files and folders.

project steps

24. In the folder tree, click the plus sign (+) to the left of the **Security** folder to expand its contents. Select the **All** folder.
25. Open the **File** menu, point to **New**, and click **Text Document** to create a text document. You can name the text document whatever you want, such as **test1.txt**.
26. Select the **None** folder and follow the same procedure to create a text document in the **None** folder.
27. Right-click the **All** folder in the folder tree, and select **Properties** to open the **All Properties** dialog box.
28. Click the **Sharing** tab and share the folder using the default share name **(Figure 7-5)**.
29. Click the **Permissions** button to open the **Permissions for All** dialog box.
30. Click the **Add** button to open the **Select Users or Groups** dialog box.
31. Type **SecTest** in the **Enter the object names to select** box and click **OK** to add the group to the **Group or user names** box in the **Permissions for All** dialog box.
32. Grant **Full Control** access to the **All** folder for the **SecTest** group **(Figure 7-6)**.
33. Click **OK** to save the permissions and close the Permissions for All dialog box.
34. Click **OK** to close the All Properties dialog box.
35. Right-click the **None** folder in the folder tree, and select **Properties** to open the **None Properties** dialog box.
36. Click the **Sharing** tab and share the folder using the default share name.
37. Click the **Permissions** button to open the **Permissions for None** dialog box.
38. Click the **Add** button to open the **Select Users or Groups** dialog box.
39. Type **SecTest** in the **Enter the object names to select** box and click **OK** to add the group to the **Group or user names** box in the **Permissions for None** dialog box.
40. Deny **Full Control** access to the **None** folder for the **SecTest** group **(Figure 7-7)**.
41. Click **OK** to save the permissions and close the Permissions for None dialog box.
42. A **Security** warning dialog box cautions you that deny permission entries take precedence over allow entries; click **Yes (Figure 7-8)**.
43. Click **OK** to close the None Properties dialog box.
44. Close the My Computer window.
45. From a management standpoint, what is the potential impact of denying access to the **None** folder for the SecTest group?

Figure 7-5 Sharing the All folder

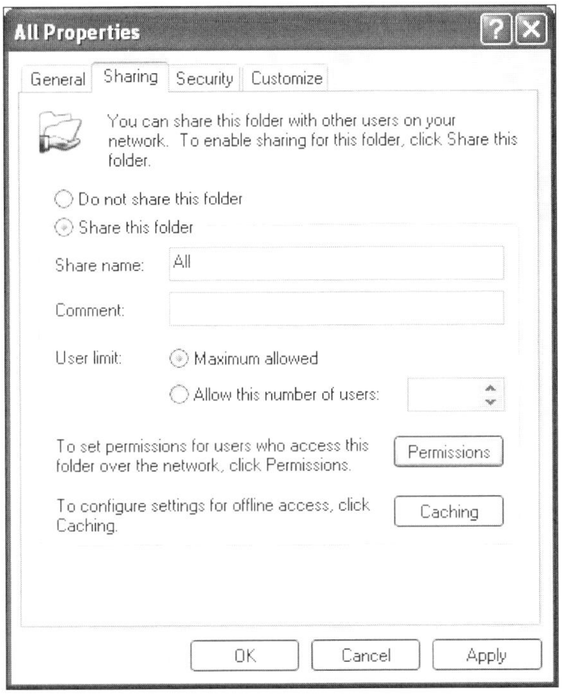

Figure 7-6 Allowing Full Control to the SecTest group for the All folder

Figure 7-7 Denying Full Control to the SecTest group for the None folder

Figure 7-8 Security warning for deny permission entries

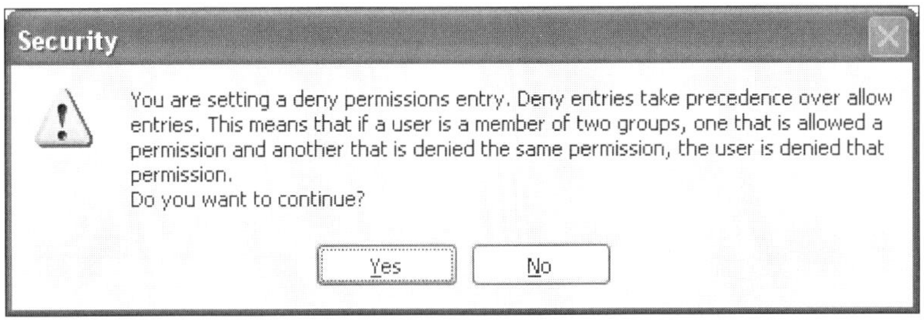

project 7.3

Troubleshooting and Interpreting Access Denied Messages

exam objective

Manage and troubleshoot access to shared folders. Troubleshoot and interpret Access Denied messages. Answer end-user questions related to managing and troubleshooting access to files and folders.

overview

Users continue to have questions about share permissions and their impact. You decide to prepare a short guide that will enable them to recognize when they encounter denied permissions. Users will need a checklist of items to check when Access is denied errors occur (**Table 7-1**).

learning objective

After completing this project, you will be more familiar with interpreting Access Denied errors and troubleshooting shared file and folder access problems.

specific requirements

See General Requirements. You also must complete Project 7.2 before starting this project.

estimated completion time

15 minutes

project steps

1. Click **Start** and then **Control Panel** to open the **Control Panel**.
2. If the **Control Panel** is in Classic View, click **Switch to Category View**.
3. Click the **Performance and Maintenance** link to open the **Performance and Maintenance** window.
4. Click **Administrative Tools** to open the **Administrative Tools** window.
5. Double-click **Computer Management** to launch the **Computer Management** console.
6. Expand the **Local User and Groups** node and select the **Users** folder.
7. Open the **Action** menu and select **New User** to open the **New User** dialog box.
8. Type **Test User** in the **User name** text box.
9. Clear the **User must change password at next logon** check box **(Figure 7-9)**.
10. Type a password in the **Password** and **Confirm password** text boxes.
11. Click the **Create** button to create the user.
12. Click the **Close** button to close the New User dialog box.
13. In the **Users** details pane, right-click **Test User** and select **Properties** to open the **Test User Properties** dialog box.
14. Click the **Member Of** tab to view and manage group membership.
15. Click the **Add** button to open the **Select Groups** dialog box.
16. Type **SecTest** in the **Enter the object names to select** box and click **OK** to add **Test User** to the **SecTest** group **(Figure 7-10)**.
17. Click **OK** to save the membership changes and close the Test User Properties dialog box.
18. Click **Start** and then **Log Off**.
19. In the **Log Off Windows** dialog box, click the **Log Off** button.
20. Log on as **Test User**.
21. Click **Start** and then **My Computer** to open the **My Computer** window.
22. Click **Folders** on the **My Computer** toolbar to display the folder tree view.
23. In the folder tree, right-click **My Computer** and select **Properties** to open the **System Properties** dialog box.
24. Click the **Computer Name** tab. Record your computer name, which is listed after the **Full computer name** label, for use in the following steps and click **OK** to close the System Properties dialog box.

Table 7-1 Steps to follow when you receive an "Access is denied" message

- Make sure that there is a valid network connection.
- Check the permissions on the share:
  - √ Is the user granted permissions directly or through group memberships?
  - √ Through group memberships, does the group have the proper level of permissions for what the user is trying to do?
  - √ Are there NTFS permissions that are further restricting the share permissions for the group?
  - √ Is the user actually a member of the group?
  - √ Does the Everyone group have the proper permissions (especially if SP1 has been applied)?
  - √ Has the user logged off and on since relevant changes to permissions were made (such as a change in group membership)?
  - √ If permissions were recently changed, has adequate time passed to ensure replication across all domain controllers?

Figure 7-9 Creating a new user

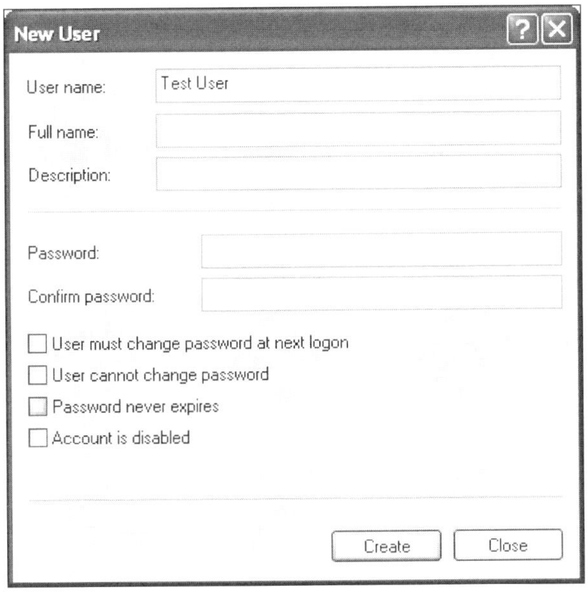

Figure 7-10 Adding a user to a group

project 7.3

Troubleshooting and Interpreting Access Denied Messages (cont'd)

exam objective

Manage and troubleshoot access to shared folders. Troubleshoot and interpret Access Denied messages. Answer end-user questions related to managing and troubleshooting access to files and folders.

project steps

25. In the folder tree, right-click **My Computer** and click **Map Network Drive** to open the **Map Network Drive** dialog box.
26. Accept the default drive letter that is automatically assigned and type ***computername*\All** in the **Folder** text box **(Figure 7-11)**. Replace ***computername*** with your computer name from step 24.
27. Record the drive letter assigned and click the **Finish** button to map the drive and close the **Map Network Drive** dialog box.
28. When the new window opens, verify that the text document (test1.txt) you created in Project 7.2 is listed.
29. Open the **File** menu and select **Close** to close the mapped drive window.
30. In the folder tree in **My Computer**, right-click **My Computer** and select **Map Network Drive** to open the **Map Network Drive** dialog box.
31. Accept the default drive letter that is automatically assigned and type ***computername*\None** in the **Folder** text box. Replace ***computername*** with your computer name from step 24.
32. Record the drive letter assigned and click the **Finish** button to map the drive and close the **Map Network Drive** dialog box.
33. When the **Windows Explorer** "Access is denied" message box opens, click **OK** **(Figure 7-12).**
34. Right-click the mapped drive for the **None** folder and select **Properties**. The properties should resemble those in **Figure 7-13**.
35. Click the **Cancel** button to close the mapped drive Properties dialog box.
36. Open the **File** menu and select **Close** to close the My Computer window.
37. Log off and log back on with a user account that has administrative permissions.
38. Click **Start** and then **Control Panel** to open the **Control Panel**.
39. In **Category View**, click the **Performance and Maintenance** link to open the **Performance and Maintenance** window.
40. Click **Administrative Tools** to open the **Administrative Tools** window.
41. Double-click **Computer Management** to launch the **Computer Management** console.
42. Expand the **Local User and Groups** node and select the **Users** folder.
43. Right-click **Test User** and select **Properties** to open the **Test User Properties** dialog box.
44. Click the **Member Of** tab.
45. Select **SecTest** and click the **Remove** button to remove **Test User** from the **SecTest** group.
46. Click **OK** to save the change and close the Test User Properties dialog box.
47. Close the Computer Management console and the Administrative Tools window.
48. Log off and log back on as **Test User**.
49. Launch **My Computer** and click **Folders** on the **My Computer** toolbar to display the folder tree view.
50. Locate and select the drive mapped in step 31 (***computername*\none**). You should now be able to view the drive contents.
51. Right-click the mapped drive for the **None** folder and click **Properties**. The properties should resemble those in **Figure 7-14.**
52. Click the **Cancel** button to close the mapped drive's Properties dialog box.
53. Close My Computer.
54. Log off and log back on with a user account that has administrative permissions.

Figure 7-11 Mapping a shared folder to a network drive

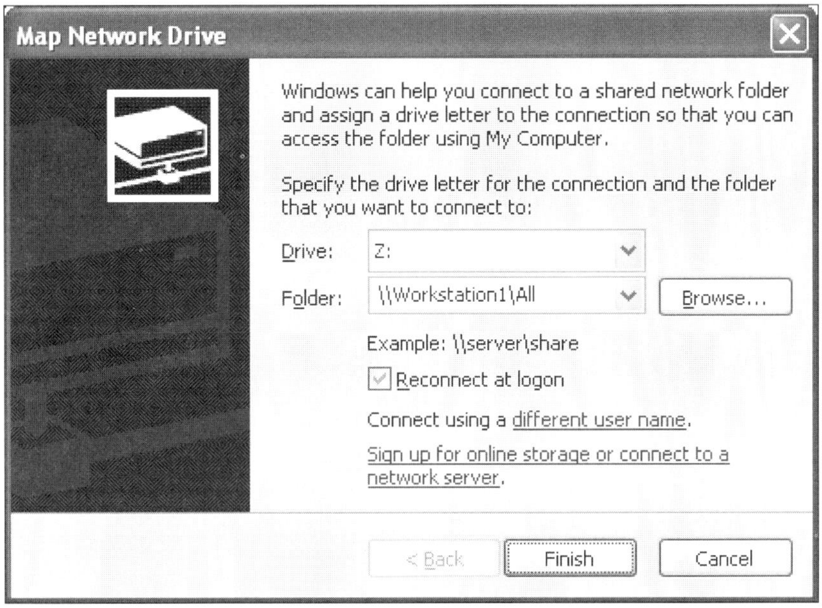

Figure 7-12 Access is denied message

Figure 7-13 Drive properties displayed when access is denied

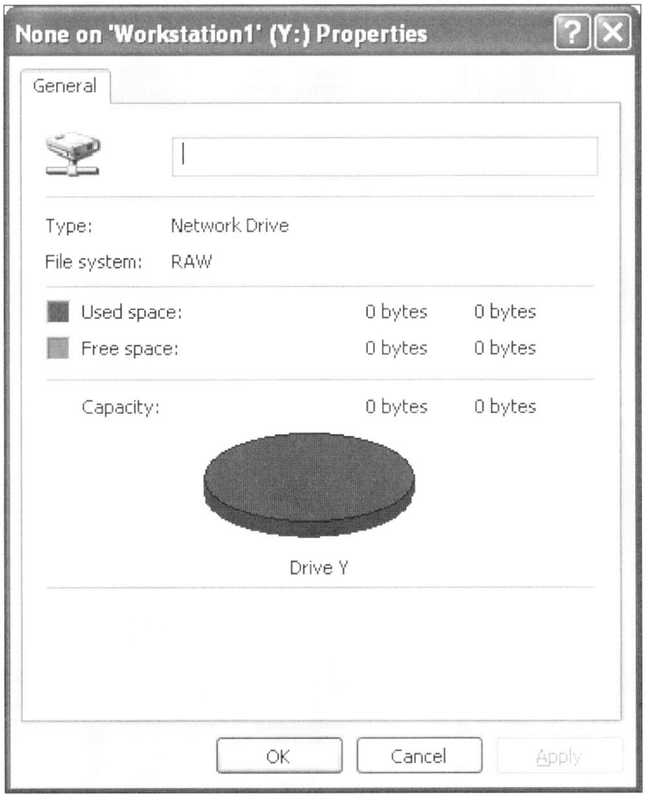

Figure 7-14 Drive properties displayed when Read access is allowed

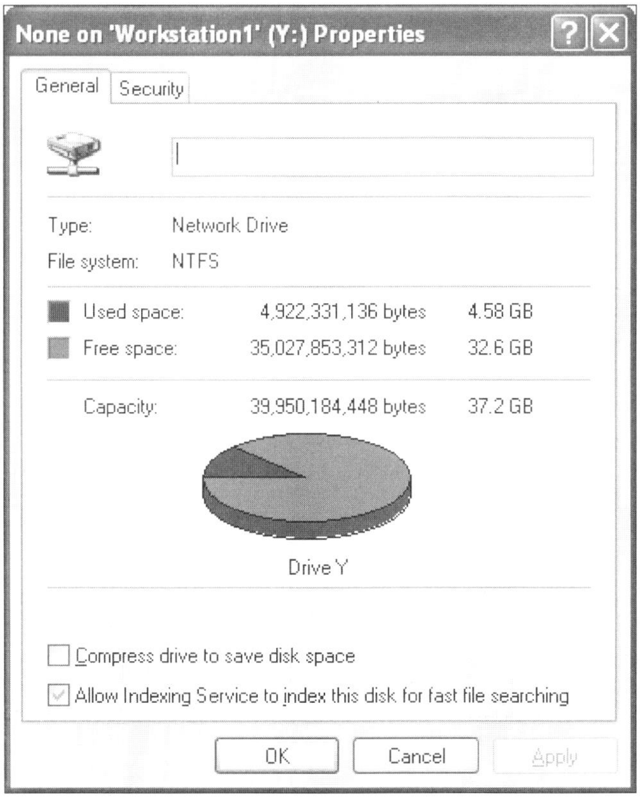

project 7.4

Configuring and Troubleshooting Offline Files

exam objective

Manage and troubleshoot access to synchronization of offline files. Configure and troubleshoot offline files. Answer end-user questions related to configuring and synchronizing offline files.

overview

The network does not currently support offline file access and you need to configure it. You are responsible for training end users and support personnel in using offline file access.

learning objective

After completing this project, you will understand the procedures to enable and configure Offline Files on Windows XP Professional.

specific requirements

See General Requirements. Before you can perform offline files configuration, you must make sure that Fast User Switching is disabled on the client.

estimated completion time

10 minutes

project steps

1. Click **Start** and then **Control Panel** to open the **Control Panel** window.
2. In **Category view**, click the **User Accounts** link to open the **User Accounts** window.
3. Click the **Change the way users log on or off** link **(Figure 7-15)**.
4. If **Offline Files** is enabled, a **User Accounts** message box opens. Fast User Switching cannot be used when **Offline Files** is enabled **(Figure 7-16)**.
5. Click **OK** to close the User Accounts message box and open the **Offline Files Settings** dialog box.
6. Clear the **Enable Offline Files** check box.
7. Click **OK** to disable **Offline Files** and close the Offline Files Settings dialog box.
8. Click the **Change the way users log on and off** link again.
9. If necessary, select the **Use the Welcome screen** check box and clear the **Use Fast User Switching** check box **(Figure 7-17)**.
10. Click the Apply Options button.
11. Close the User Accounts window.
12. Close the Control Panel.
13. Click **Start** and then click **My Computer** to open the **My Computer** window.
14. Open the **Tools** menu and select **Folder Options** to open the **Folder Options** dialog box.
15. Click the **Offline Files** tab.
16. Configure the **Offline Files** properties shown in **Figure 7-18**. Leave the disk space allocated for temporary files at the default value.
17. Click **OK** to close the Folder Options dialog box.
18. Exit My Computer.

Figure 7-15 The User Accounts window

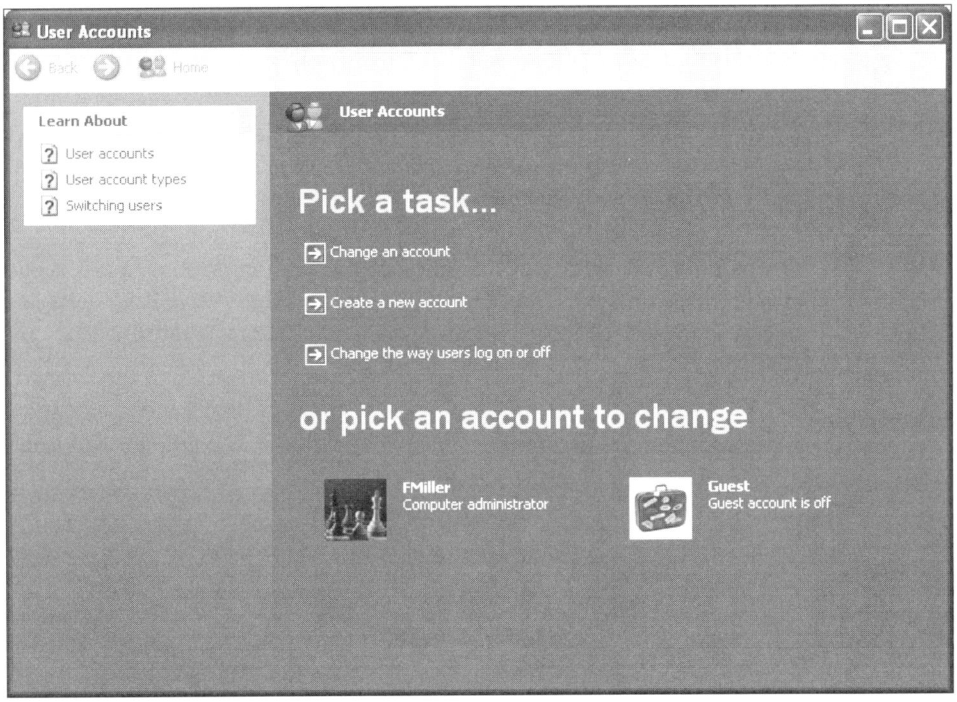

Figure 7-16 A Users Accounts message box

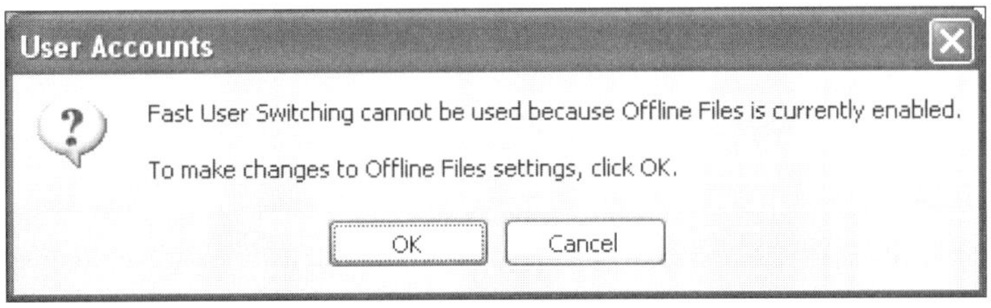

Figure 7-17 Disabling Fast User Switching

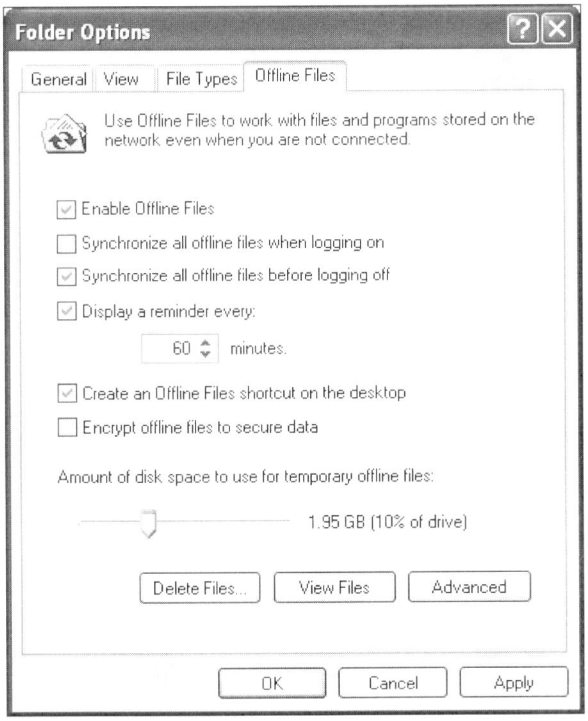

Figure 7-18 Offline Files tab in the Folder Options dialog box

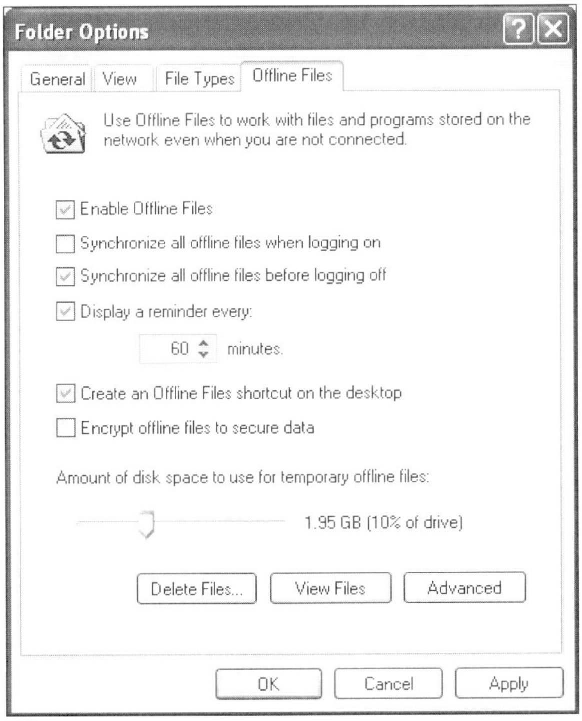

project 7.5

Configuring and Troubleshooting Offline File Synchronization

exam objective

Manage and troubleshoot access to and synchronization of offline files. Configure and troubleshoot offline file synchronization. Answer end-user questions related to configuring and synchronizing offline files.

overview

One possible concern is offline file synchronization. Problems can occur with keeping files synchronized and with server-based files being overwritten. Both users and support personnel must understand the available synchronization options **(Figure 7-19)**.

learning objective

After completing this project, you will know how to configure and troubleshoot offline file synchronization.

specific requirements

None

estimated completion time

10 minutes

project steps

1. Prepare guidelines for when synchronization should occur for users who are accessing the network through a LAN connection. You want to ensure that users are working with current file versions and that any changes are written to the server **(Figure 7-20)**.
2. Explain how you would change the settings to ensure that the server-based files are up-to-date, but the user's cached version is used as the source file when connecting through a dial-up connection. How does this change bandwidth use compared to step 1?
3. Prepare a checklist of possible concerns when multiple remote users are accessing the same files **(Figure 7-21)**. Include suggestions for minimizing version problems.

Figure 7-19 Synchronization options

Synchronization Options

--Full synchronization - All files: All files are kept up to date. A full synchronization takes longer, but it ensures that every file made available offline is the most current version.

--Quick synchronization - All files: There is no guarantee that files are up to date. A quick synchronization is much faster, but it may not provide the most current version of the file.

Figure 7-20 The Logon/Logoff tab in the Synchronization Settings dialog box

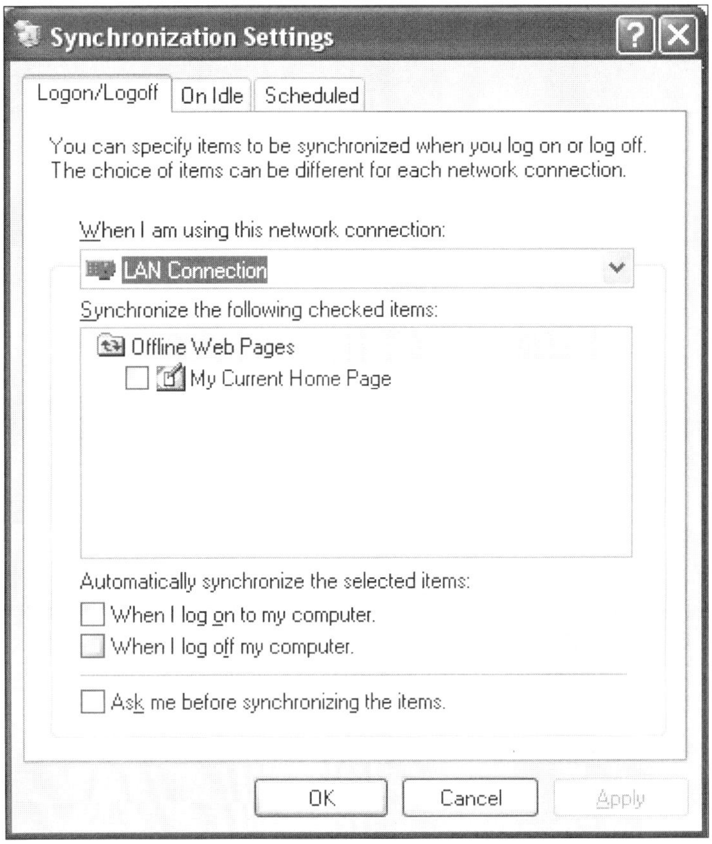

Figure 7-21 Multiple remote offline file user concerns

User Concerns

--User cannot synchronize until the files are closed.

--Deleting a file that is changed by another user deletes only the cached copy.

--User can save a version of a file or delete the local copy if a different user deletes the file.

--Files added while a user is offline are added locally at connection and synchronization.

LESSON

8 Connecting to Local and Network Print Devices

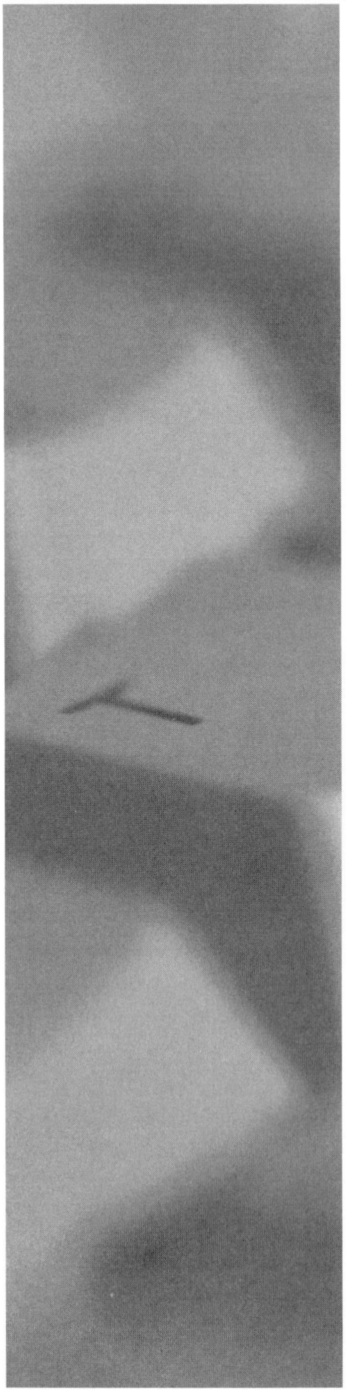

Printing is a key function on most networks. Many users are accustomed to working with a printed page instead of working with an onscreen document. Printing is also required for disseminating information, such as invoices, marketing materials, and reports, and for archiving important data.

Unfortunately, printing a document successfully requires that several components function in tandem. The document must be spooled to a print server or on the local hard disk and then sent to a physical print device. A problem on the print server, the local hard disk, or the print device can cause an error in the printing process.

Understanding how to correctly configure and manage both local and network print devices is essential. You will often be called upon to configure printers and resolve printing issues. As a review:

- A local print device is attached to the computer through a parallel, serial, USB, or infrared port.
- A network print device is shared on the network. It might be attached to the print server or directly to the network.
- A print queue contains a list of print jobs that have been sent to the printer. When jobs are in the queue, they can be canceled, paused, and restarted.
- A print device can be used only if a device driver for that print device is installed on the computer.
- A printer (the logical object) has a number of properties that can be configured. These include:
    - Separator page
    - Priority
    - Share name
    - Permissions
    - Paper size
    - Paper tray settings
    - Port
- Multiple print devices with the same device driver can be pooled. When a printer is pooled, a job is sent to the first available print device.
- The owner of a print job can manage that job. Only users with the Manage Documents permission can manage print jobs belonging to other users.
- Only members of the Administrators and Power Users (Windows XP Professional only) groups can install a printer.
- Shared network printers can be accessed by UNC, by browsing, or if IIS is installed on the print server, by typing the printer's URL.

Scenario

Ads R Us has an expensive, high-quality color printer that is used to print ad copy for customers. A second identical color printer will be purchased for the branch office. The company also has four inexpensive laser printers for general use, including printing invoices and reports.The color printer at the branch office should be used only by the Ad Development and Customer Representative departments. The other printers should be accessible by all users in the company. You have installed Windows XP Professional on the computer that will be used as the print server for the new color printer. Now you must configure the printer. You must also provide documented guidelines for troubleshooting printing problems. These guidelines will be used by the help desk person at the new branch office.

Lesson 8 Connecting to Local and Network Print Devices

Project	Exam 70-271 Objective
8.1 Adding a Local Printer	**Connect to local and network print devices**. Answer end-user questions related to printing locally. Configure and manage local printing.
8.2 Configuring and Managing a Local Printer	**Connect to local and network print devices**. Answer end-user questions related to printing locally. Configure and manage local printing.
8.3 Connecting to a Network Printer	**Connect to local and network print devices**. Answer end-user questions related to network-based printing. Connect to and manage printing to a network-based printer.
8.4 Configuring a Network Printer	**Connect to local and network print devices**. Answer end-user questions related to network-based printing. Connect to and manage printing to a network-based printer.
8.5 Troubleshooting Printers	**Connect to local and network print devices**. Answer end-user questions related to printing locally. Configure and manage local printing. Answer end-user questions related to network-based printing. Connect to and manage printing to a network-based printer.

General Requirements

To complete the projects in this lesson, you will need administrative rights on a Windows XP Professional computer and access to Windows XP installation files. You do not need a print device. You must create groups named CustomerReps and AdDevelopers before you begin the projects in this lesson. You may also find it helpful to refer to Lesson 8 in your Prentice Hall Certification Series Exam 70-271 textbook for further information about the topics covered by the projects in this lesson.

project 8.1 Adding a Local Printer

exam objective

Connect to local and network print devices. Answer end-user questions related to printing locally. Configure and manage local printing.

overview

You are configuring a Windows XP Professional computer that will perform the role of a print server for the color printer at the branch office. The printer has been ordered and will be shipped directly to the branch office. Therefore, you cannot install the printer using Plug and Play and you use the Add Printer Wizard to create a printer for the print device.

learning objective

After completing this project, you will know how to create a print device using the Add Printer Wizard.

specific requirements

See General Requirements. You also must be logged on using the Administrator account created during installation. This project is a prerequisite for Projects 8.2, 8.3, and 8.4. You must create groups named CustomerReps and AdDevelopers before you begin this project.

estimated completion time

15 minutes

project steps

1. Click **Start** and then **Printers and Faxes** to open the **Printers and Faxes** window.
2. On the **Printer Tasks** list, click the **Add a printer** link to start the **Add Printer Wizard**.
3. Click **Next** to view the **Local or Network Printer** screen.
4. Clear the **Automatically detect and install my Plug and Play printer** check box (**Figure 8-1**).
5. Click **Next** to view the **Select a Printer Port** screen.
6. Keep the default selection **(LPT1: (Recommended Printer Port))** and click **Next** to view the **Install Printer Software** screen.
7. On the **Manufacturer** list, select **HP**.
8. On the **Printers** list, select **HP Color LaserJet 8550 PCL (Figure 8-2)**.
9. Click **Next** to view the **Name Your Printer** screen.
10. Type **AdPrinter** in the **Printer name** text box. If another printer is installed on the computer, select the **Yes** option button to use this printer as the default printer, and click **Next** to view the **Printer Sharing** screen.
11. Select the **Share name** option button and keep the default share name (**Figure 8-3**).
12. Click **Next** to view the **Location and Comment** screen.
13. Type **Branch Office** in the **Location** text box and click **Next** to open the **Print Test Page** screen.
14. Select the **No** option button.
15. Click **Next** to open the **Completing the Add Printer Wizard** screen.
16. Click **Finish** to create the printer.
17. Right-click the **AdPrinter** icon and select **Properties** to open the **AdPrinter Properties** dialog box.
18. Click the **Security** tab.
19. Select the **Everyone** group and click the **Remove** button.
20. Select the **Power Users** group and click the **Remove** button.
21. Click the **Add** button to open the **Select Users or Groups** dialog box.
22. Type **CustomerReps** in the **Enter the object name to select** box and click the **Check Names** button.

Figure 8-1 The Local or Network Printer screen

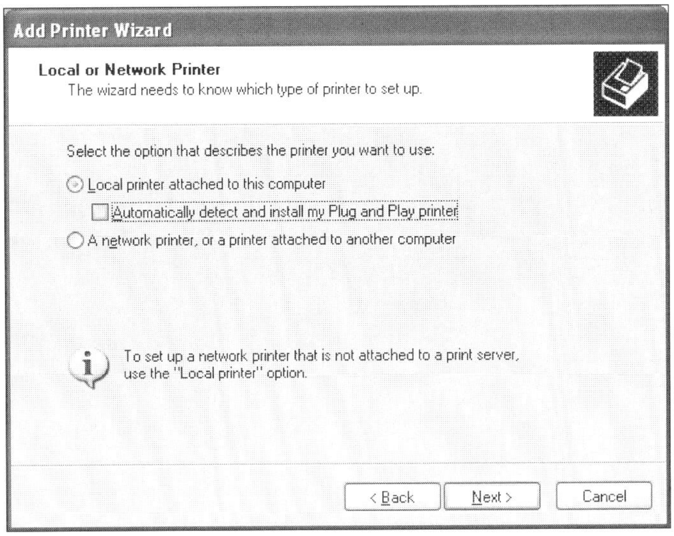

Figure 8-2 The Install Printer Software screen

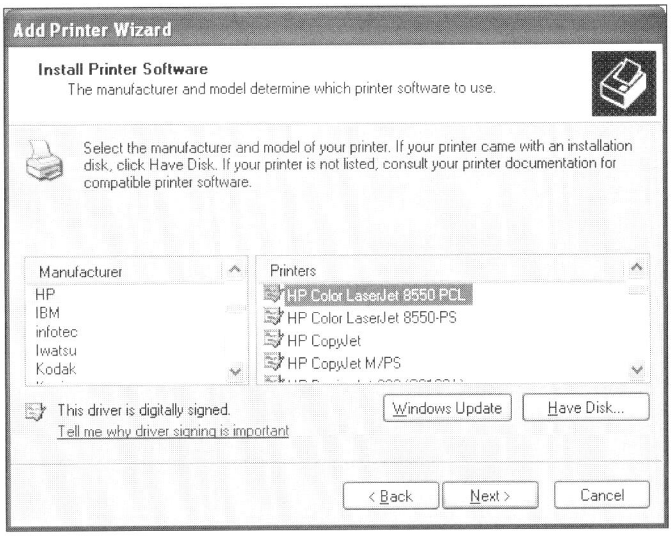

Figure 8-3 The Printer Sharing screen

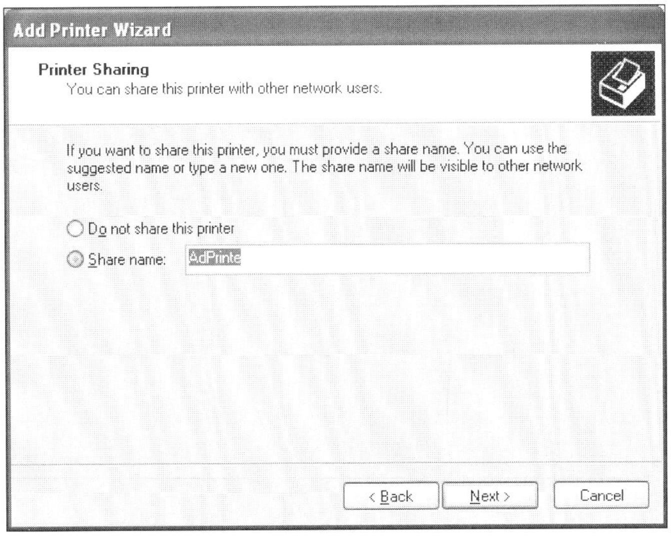

project 8.1

Adding a Local Printer *(cont'd)*

exam objective

Connect to local and network print devices. Answer end-user questions related to printing locally. Configure and manage local printing.

project steps

23. Type a colon, press the space bar, and type **AdDevelopers** in the **Enter the object name to select** box. Click the **Check Names** button.
24. Click **OK** to close the Select Users or Groups dialog box and add the two groups to the **Group or user names** box. Only Administrators, the CREATOR OWNER, and the CustomerReps and AdDevelopers groups will be able to print on this print device **(Figure 8-4)**.
25. Click **OK** to close the AdPrinter Properties dialog box.
26. Close the **Printers and Faxes** window.

Figure 8-4 Setting printer permissions

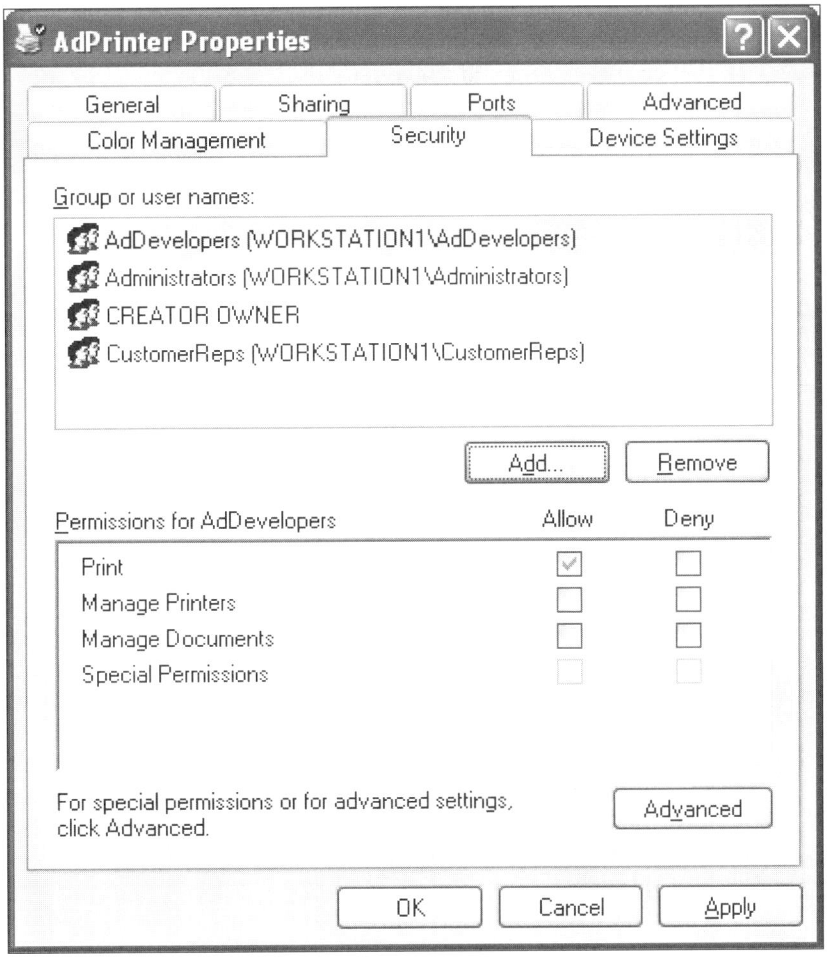

project 8.2

Configuring and Managing a Local Printer

exam objective

Connect to local and network print devices. Answer end-user questions related to printing locally. Configure and manage local printing.

overview

Multiple users will be sending documents to the color printer (AdPrinter) in the branch office. You want to configure a separator page, also called a banner page, to allow these users to easily locate their documents after they have been printed. Separator pages are printed between each print job and usually include the name of the user who requested it along with the date and time.

learning objective

After completing this project, you will know how to set a separator page.

specific requirements

See General Requirements. You should be logged on as Administrator, the default administrator account created during the Windows XP installation. Project 8.1 is a prerequisite.

estimated completion time

10 minutes

project steps

1. Click **Start** and then **Printers and Faxes** to open the **Printers and Faxes** window.
2. Right-click **AdPrinter** and select **Properties** to open the **Properties** dialog box for the printer.
3. Click the **Advanced** tab **(Figure 8-5)**.
4. Review the current settings. What advantage is gained by spooling the print documents? Which hardware resource must you monitor to ensure documents can be spooled?
5. Click the **Separator Page** button to open the **Separator Page** dialog box **(Figure 8-6)**.
6. Click the **Browse** button to open the **Separator Page** search dialog box in the **System 32** folder.
7. Select **sysprint.sep (Figure 8-7)**.
8. Click the **Open** button to set the separator page **(Figure 8-8)**.
9. Click **OK** to close the Separator Page dialog box.
10. Click **OK** to close the AdPrinter Properties dialog box.
11. Close the Printer and Faxes window.

Figure 8-5 Advanced printer properties

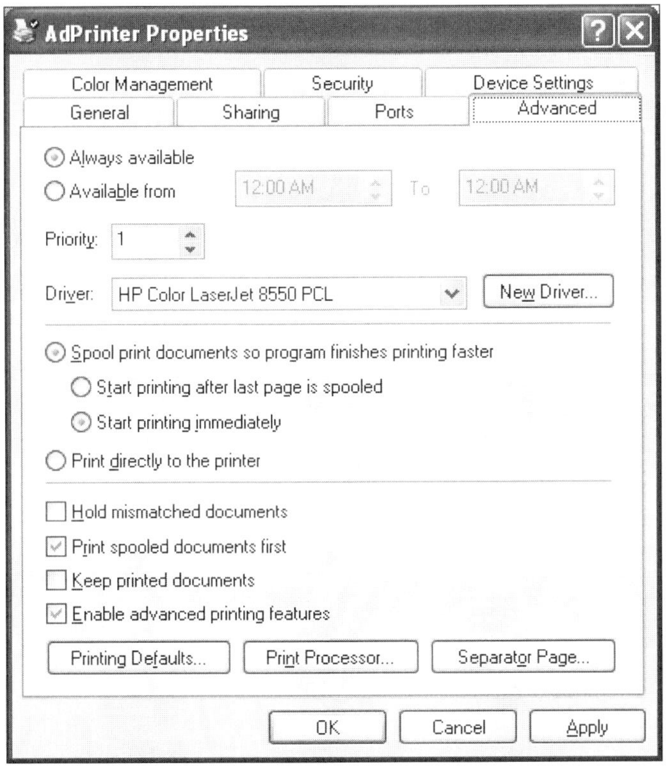

Figure 8-6 The Separator Page dialog box

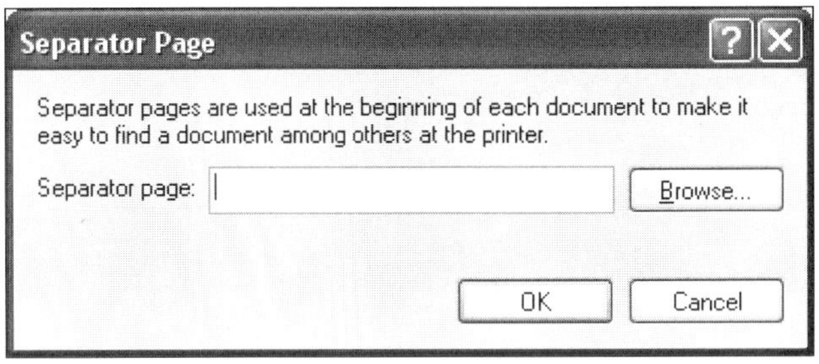

Figure 8-7 Selecting a separator page

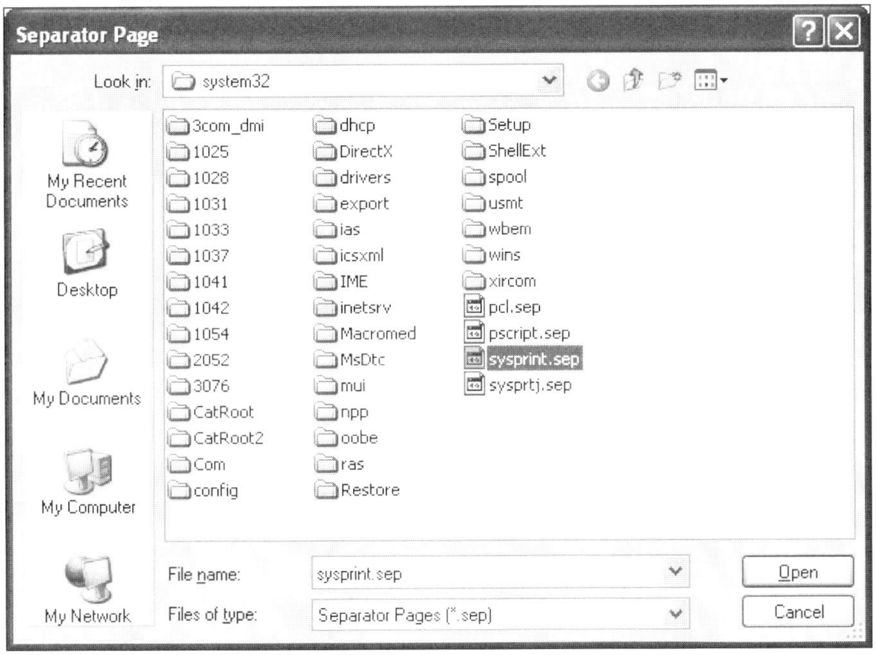

Figure 8-8 The path to the separator page

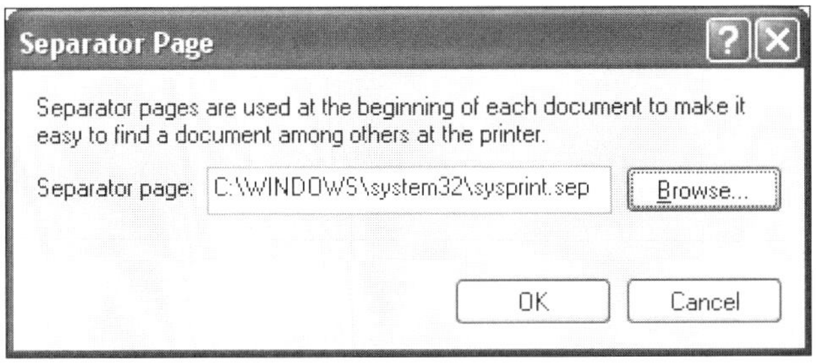

project 8.3 Connecting to a Network Printer

exam objective

Connect to local and network print devices. Answer end-user questions related to network-based printing. Connect to and manage printing to a network-based printer.

overview

Because ad designers work at the main office and sometimes telecommute, they must be able to send documents to the color printer (AdPrinter) from across the Internet. You must configure the Windows XP Professional computer that is performing the print server role to support this capability.

learning objective

After completing this project, you will know how to install IIS and connect to a printer using its Uniform Resource Locator (URL) address.

specific requirements

See General Requirements. You should be logged on as Administrator, the default administrator account created during Windows XP installation. Project 8.1 is a prerequisite. You will need access to the Windows XP Professional installation files to complete the project.

estimated completion time

15 minutes

project steps

1. Click **Start** and then **Control Panel** to open the **Control Panel**.
2. In **Category view**, click the **Add or Remove Programs** link to open the **Add or Remove Programs** window.
3. Click **Add/Remove Windows Components** to start the **Add/Remove Windows Components Wizard**.
4. Select the **Internet Information Services** (**IIS**) check box **(Figure 8-9)**.
5. Click **Next** to open the **Configuring Components** screen while the files are copied to your computer.
6. If prompted, insert the Windows XP Professional CD-ROM and click **OK** to close the Insert Disk dialog box.
7. Click **Finish**.
8. Close the Add or Remove Programs window.
9. Close the Control Panel.
10. Restart the computer and log on as Administrator.
11. Click **Start** and then **Internet Explorer**.
12. Type **http://localhost/printers/** in the **Address** bar and click **Go**.
13. The servername ***localhost*** is a special keyword used to identify the local computer. The printers attached to the local computer are displayed **(Figure 8-10)**.
14. Click **AdPrinter** to view the **AdPrinter** queue **(Figure 8-11)**.
15. Take a few moments to explore what you can do from this window.
16. Close the browser window.

Figure 8-9 Adding IIS

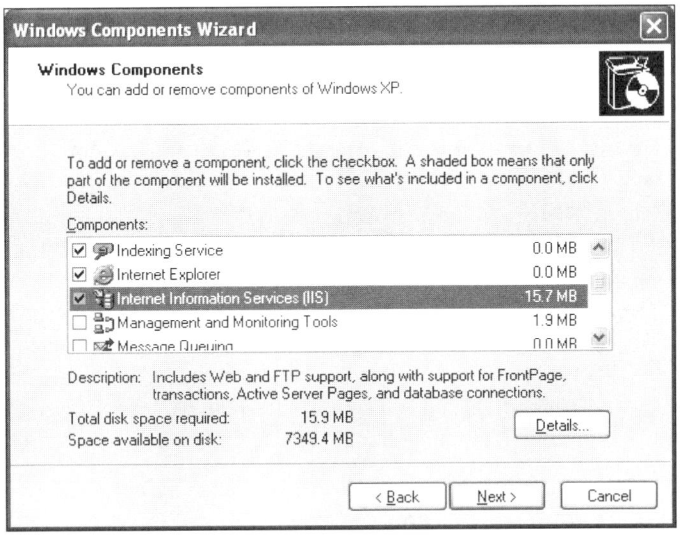

Figure 8-10 Displaying a list of printers

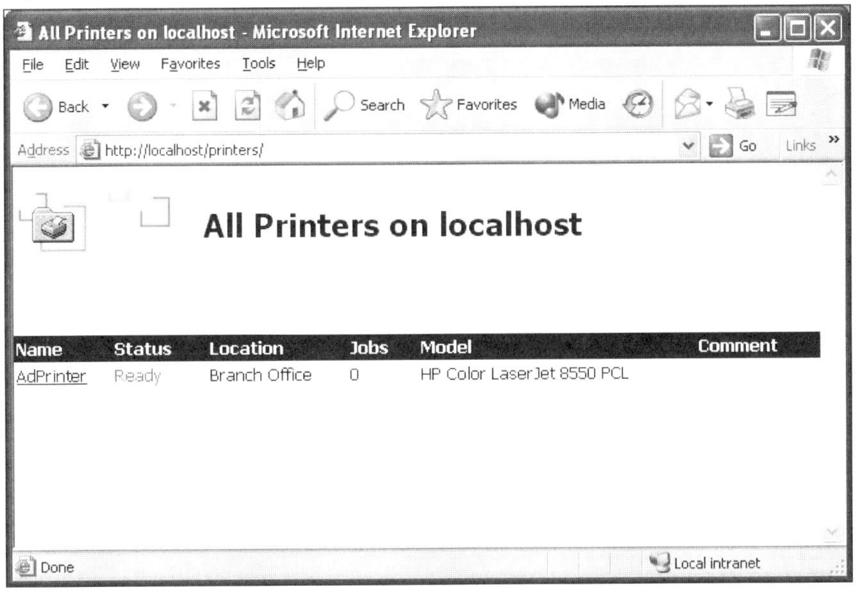

Figure 8-11 AdPrinter queue

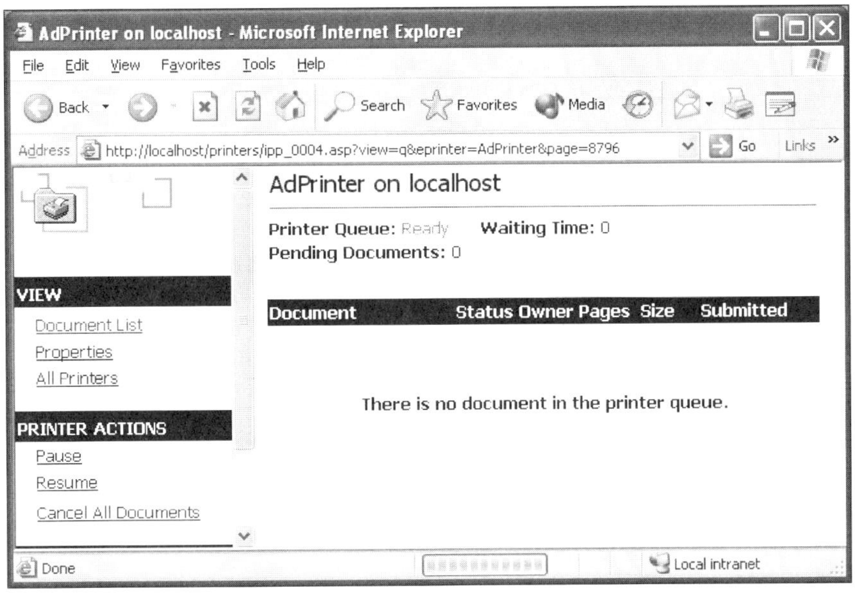

project 8.4

Configuring a Network Printer

exam objective

Connect to local and network print devices. Answer end-user questions related to network-based printing. Connect to and manage printing to a network-based printer.

overview

Ad designers and customer representatives often send documents to AdPrinter at the same time. Customer representatives complain that customers have had to wait while a document prints. They would like their print jobs to have a higher priority than those sent by the Ad designers. You decide to create a new logical printer (RepPrinter) for the existing print device connected on LPT1. Permissions must then be set on the new logical printer to grant the Print permission to the CustomerReps group. To ensure that documents sent from the customer representatives are printed first, the new logical printer will be assigned a higher printer priority.

learning objective

After completing this project, you will know how to manage printer priority and permissions.

specific requirements

See General Requirements. You should be logged on as Administrator, the default administrator account created during Windows XP installation. You also must have already created the CustomerReps group.

estimated completion time

20 minutes

project steps

1. Click **Start** and then **Printers and Faxes** to open the **Printers and Faxes** window.
2. On the **Printer Tasks** list, click the **Add a printer** link to start the **Add Printer Wizard**.
3. Click **Next** to view the **Local or Network Printer** screen.
4. If necessary, clear the **Automatically detect and install my Plug and Play printer** check box.
5. Click **Next** to view the **Select a Printer Port** screen.
6. Keep the default selection, **LPT1: (Recommended Printer Port)**, and click **Next** to view the **Install Printer Software** screen.
7. On the **Manufacturer** list, select **HP**.
8. On the **Printers** list, select **HP Color LaserJet 8550 PCL**.
9. Click **Next** to open the **Use Existing Driver** screen.
10. Make sure that the **Keep existing driver** (**recommended**) option button is selected **(Figure 8-12)**.
11. Click **Next** to view the **Name Your Printer** screen.
12. Type **RepPrinter** in the **Printer name** text box and select the **No** option button to keep AdPrinter as the default printer.
13. Click **Next** to view the **Printer Sharing** screen. Keep the default share name.
14. Click **Next** to view the **Location and Comment** screen.
15. Type **Branch Office** in the **Location** text box and click **Next** to open the **Print Test Page** screen.
16. Select the **No** option button.
17. Click **Next** to open the **Completing the Add Printer Wizard** screen.
18. Click **Finish** to create the printer.
19. Right-click **RepPrinter** and select **Properties** to open the **Properties** dialog box for the printer.
20. Click the **Advanced** tab.

Figure 8-12 Select to keep the existing driver

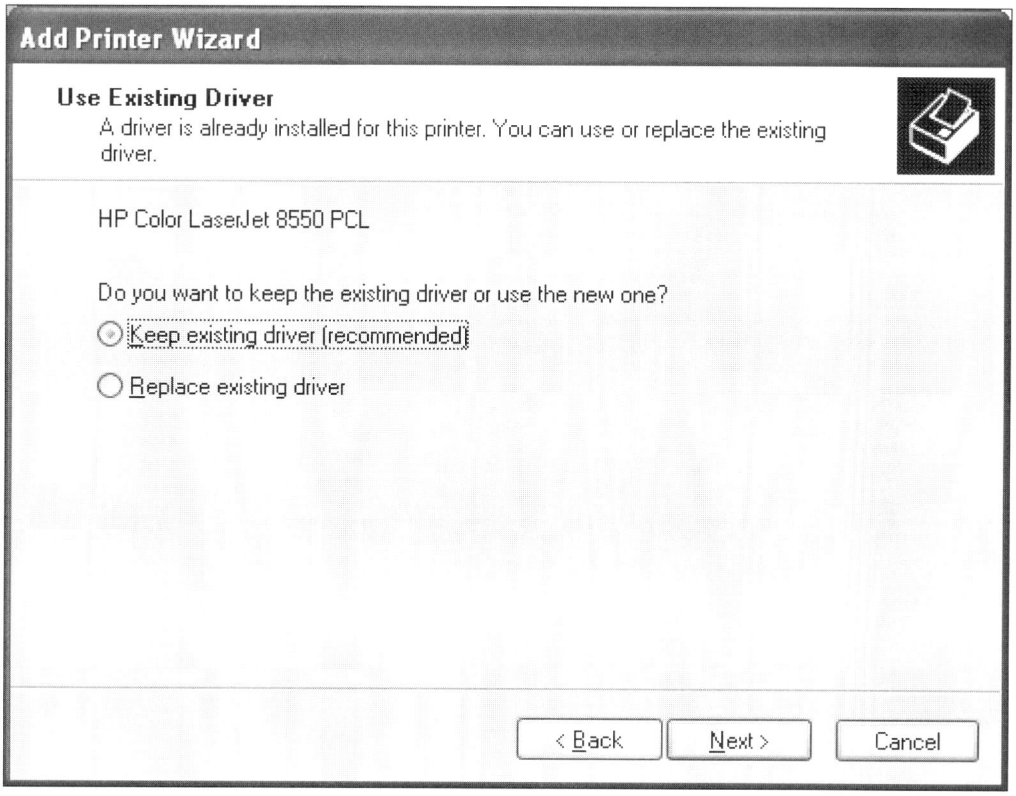

project 8.4

Configuring a Network Printer (cont'd)

exam objective

Connect to local and network print devices. Answer end-user questions related to network-based printing. Connect to and manage printing to a network-based printer.

project steps

21. Type **50** in the **Priority** spin box to change the printer priority to 50 **(Figure 8-13)**. Note: The default priority setting of 1 was used for the other logical printer on LPT1 (AdPrinter). Therefore, documents sent to RepPrinter will have priority over documents sent to AdPrinter.
22. Click the **Security** tab to display the permissions for the printer.
23. Select **Everyone** and click the **Remove** button.
24. Select **Power Users** and click the **Remove** button. At this point only **Administrators** and **CREATOR OWNER** should be listed **(Figure 8-14)**.
25. Click the **Add** button to open the **Select Users or Groups** dialog box.
26. Type **CustomerReps** in the **Enter the object names to select** box and click the **Check Names** button.
27. Click **OK** to close the Select Users or Groups dialog box.
28. Verify that the **CustomerReps** group is assigned only the **Print** permission **(Figure 8-15)**.
29. Click **OK** to close the RepPrinter Properties dialog box.
30. Close the Printer and Faxes window.

Figure 8-13 Modified priority setting

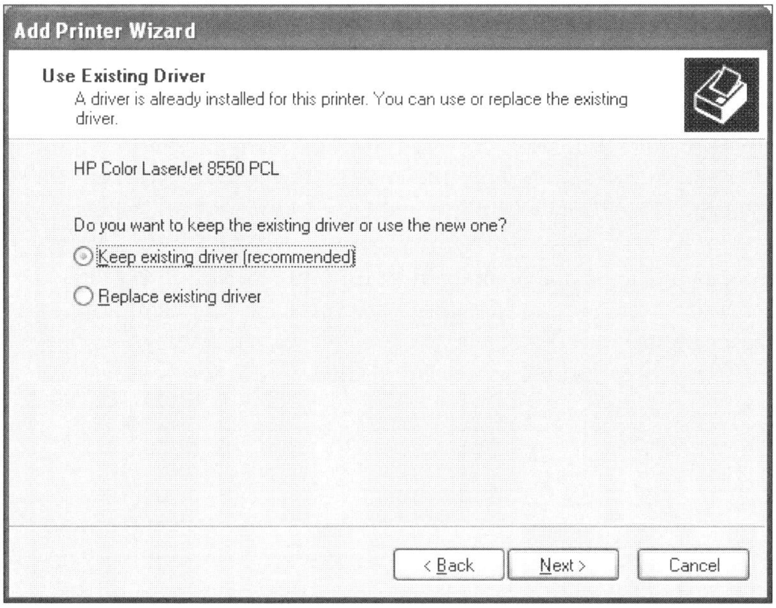

Figure 8-14 Security settings after removing users

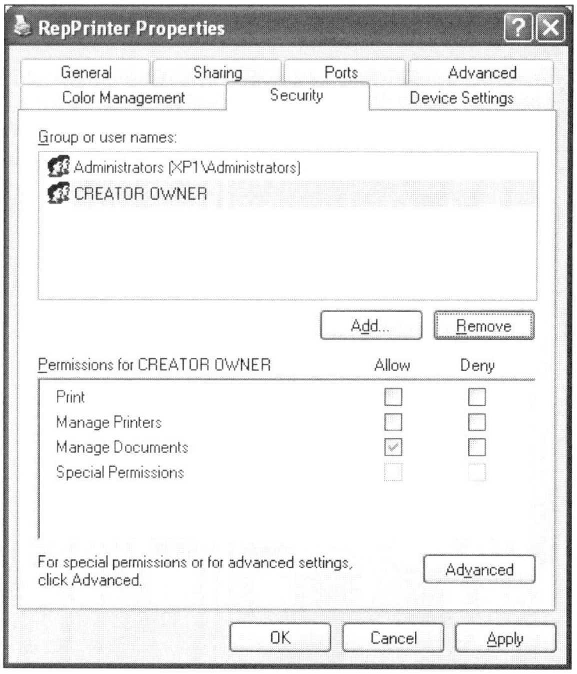

Figure 8-15 The default permission is Print

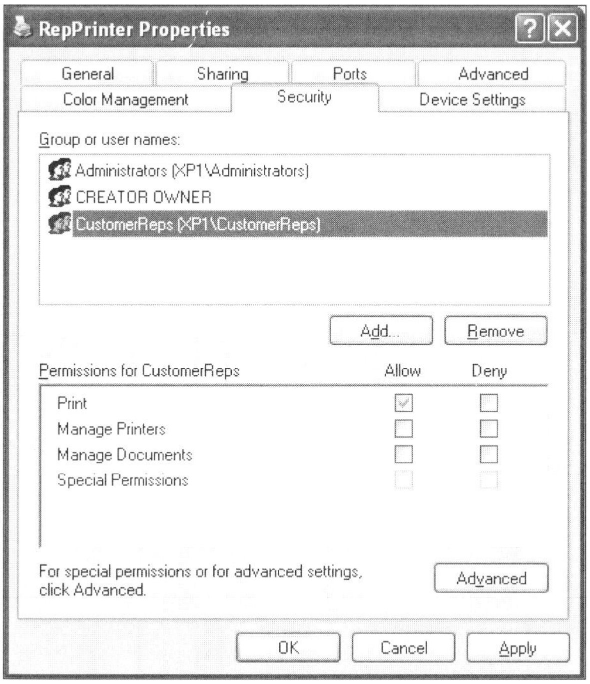

project 8.5

Troubleshooting Printers

exam objective

Connect to local and network print devices. Answer end-user questions related to printing locally. Connect to and manage printing to a local printer. Answer end-user questions related to network-based printing. Connect to and manage printing to a network-based printer.

overview

You are ready to send the computer to the branch office. However, you need to provide the help desk person there with printer troubleshooting guidelines. Some potential printing problems are illustrated in **Figure 8-16**. You must create a document outlining the types of problems that can occur and some guidelines for resolving them.

learning objective

After completing this project, you will know how to troubleshoot printing problems.

specific requirements

None

estimated completion time

25 minutes

project steps

Create a document describing typical printer problems and how to resolve them. Make sure your document includes:

- Problems related to the print device
- Problems related to resource shortages on the print server
- Insufficient access permissions
- Queue management procedures
- Steps for isolating the cause of the problem

Figure 8-16 Printer problems

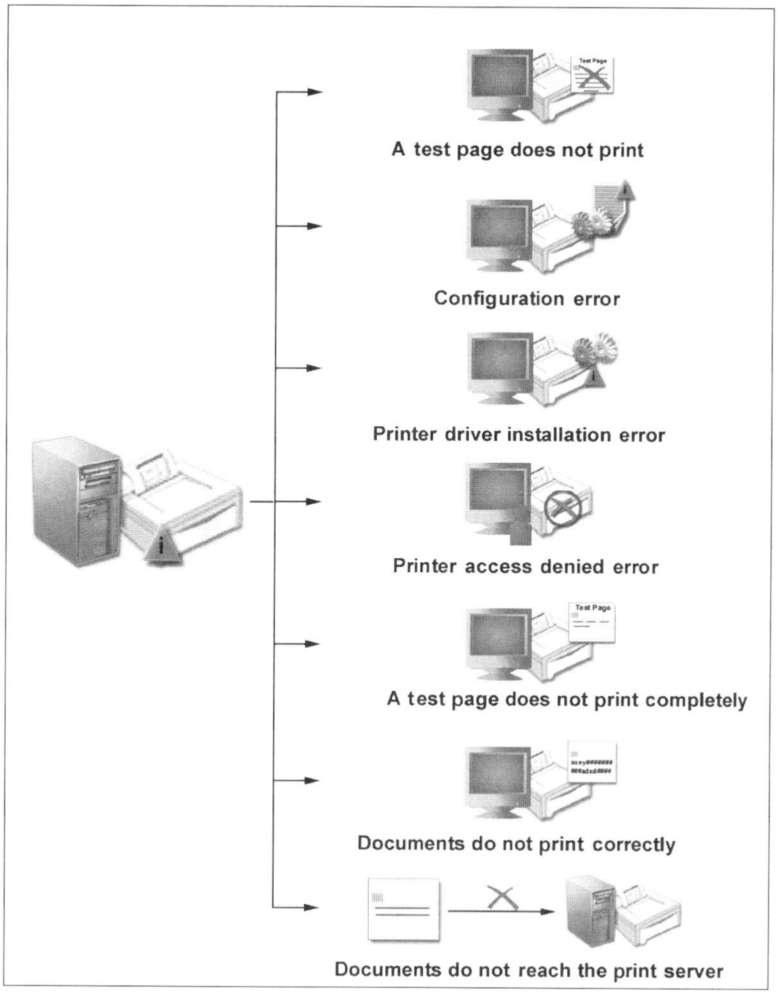

LESSON

9 Configuring and Troubleshooting Storage Devices

Ensuring that data is reliable and that it can be retrieved without errors is a primary responsibility of every IT department. Fortunately, Windows XP provides numerous features that aid technicians can use to ensure disk reliability and efficient hard disk management.

Windows XP provides two primary storage types: basic and dynamic. The default disk type is basic, which allows you to create partitions using unallocated disk space. Unlike basic disks, dynamic disks are divided into volumes that can be composed of a single disk or a portion of several disks. Dynamic disks are divided into five categories: simple, spanned, striped, mirrored, and RAID 5. However, only simple, spanned, and striped volumes are supported by Windows XP Professional.

The easiest way to access Windows XP disk management options is to use the Disk Management snap-in. Using the Disk Management snap-in you can:

- View disk status.
- Create new partitions.
- Create a new volume.
- Set an active partition.
- Assign and change drive letters.
- Change a basic disk to a dynamic disk.
- Increase the size of an existing volume.

Right-clicking a disk in the Disk Management console allows you to access other utilities that you can use to defragment, check, and repair a disk and to set data saving limits.

This lesson contains projects that will familiarize you with the various storage options provided by Windows XP. You will practice creating an additional partition, extending the size of an existing volume, and configuring disk quota limits.

Scenario

You have been asked to set up Windows XP Professional computers at a new City Hospital branch office. You are responsible for choosing the best storage options for the branch office, and you will need to set up storage devices and perform periodic maintenance on them.

Lesson 9 Configuring and Troubleshooting Storage Devices

Project	Exam 70-271 Objective
9.1 Understanding Disk Storage in Windows XP	**Configure and troubleshoot storage devices.** Answer end-user questions related to configuring hard disks and partitions or volumes.
9.2 Creating an Extended Partition and a Logical Drive	**Configure and troubleshoot storage devices.** Answer end-user questions related to configuring hard disks and partitions or volumes.
9.3 Updating a Disk from Basic to Dynamic	**Configure and troubleshoot storage devices.** Answer end-user questions related to configuring hard disks and partitions or volumes.
9.4 Extending an Existing Volume	**Configure and troubleshoot storage devices.** Answer end-user questions related to configuring hard disks and partitions or volumes.
9.5 Using Disk Management on Remote Disks	**Configure and troubleshoot storage devices.** Answer end-user questions related to configuring hard disks and partitions or volumes.
9.6 Configuring Disk Quotas	**Configure and troubleshoot storage devices.** Answer end-user questions related to configuring hard disks and partitions or volumes.
9.7 Troubleshooting Disks and Volumes	**Configure and troubleshoot storage devices.** Answer end-user questions related to configuring hard disks and partitions or volumes. Manage and troubleshoot disk partitioning.

General Requirements

To complete the projects in this lesson, you will need administrative rights on a Windows XP Professional computer with at least two disks installed, as well as free disk space to create volumes and partitions. You may also find it helpful to refer to Lesson 9 in your Prentice Hall Certification Series Exam 70-271 textbook for further information about the topics covered by the projects in this lesson.

project 9.1

Understanding Disk Storage in Windows XP

exam objective

Configure and troubleshoot storage devices. Answer end-user questions related to configuring hard disks and partitions or volumes.

overview

You are preparing for a meeting with the IT staff of a City Hospital branch office. You will be discussing the best storage configuration for branch office computers. In order to prepare for the meeting, you review the types of storage configurations provided by Windows XP and create handouts for the IT staff.

learning objective

After completing this project, you will be more familiar with the storage options provided by Windows XP.

specific requirements

None

estimated completion time

30 minutes

project steps

1. Prepare a PowerPoint or Word handout describing the advantages and disadvantages of basic versus dynamic storage.
2. Describe the difference between a basic disk partition and extended partitions (**Figure 9-1**).
3. Describe each of the following types of dynamic volumes and their uses:
   - Simple volume
   - Spanned volume
   - Striped volume (**Figure 9-2**)

Figure 9-1 Types of partitions on a basic disk

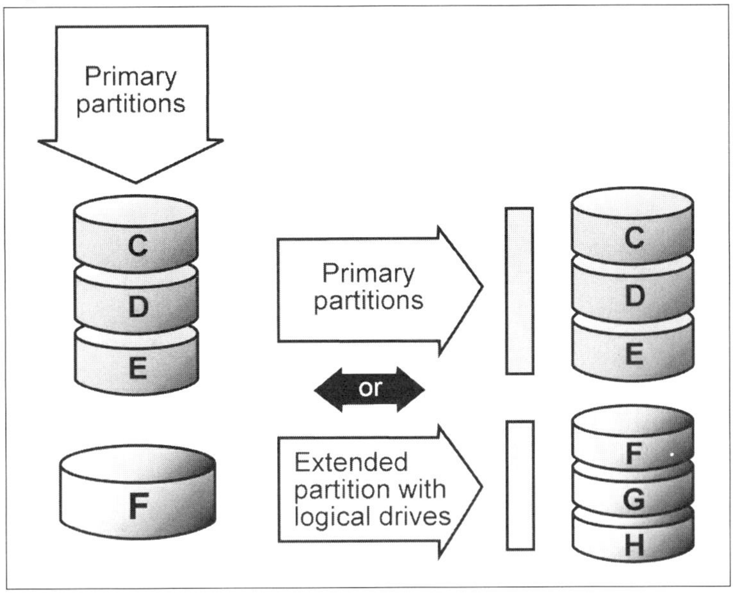

Figure 9-2 Types of volumes available on Windows XP dynamic disks

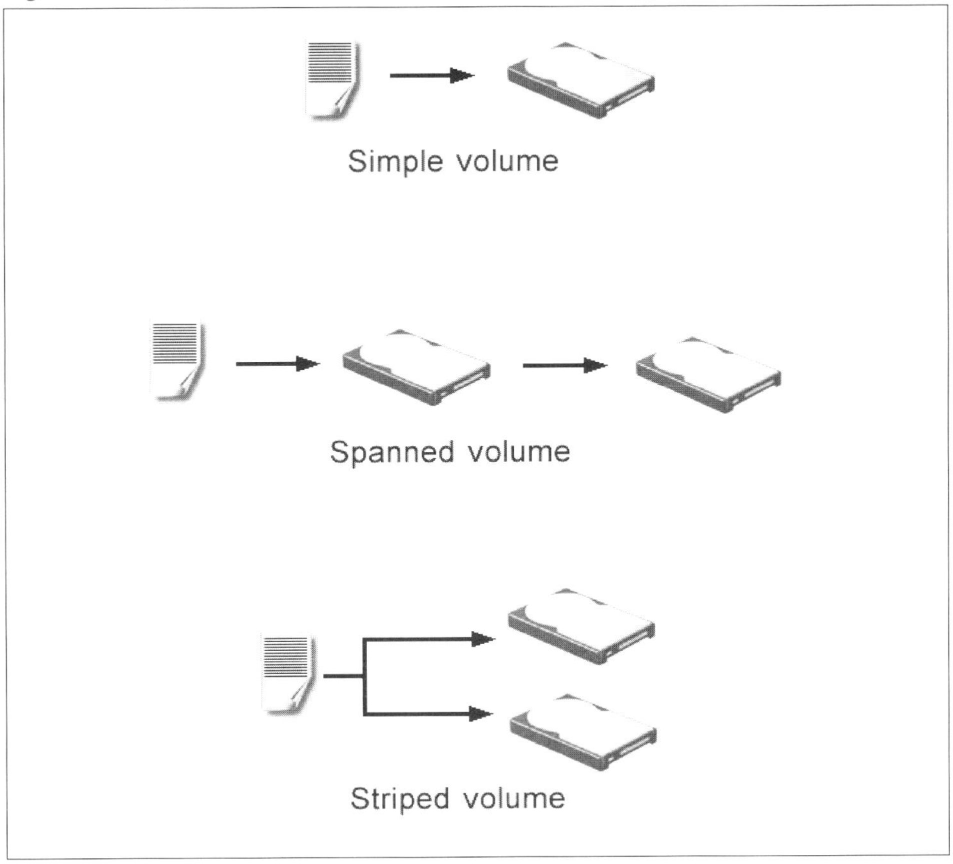

project 9.2

Creating an Extended Partition and a Logical Drive

exam objective

Configure and troubleshoot storage devices. Answer end-user questions related to configuring hard disks and partitions or volumes.

overview

One of the computers at the City Hospital field office is used to store patient information. To provide additional storage space for the patient files, you decide to install a new hard drive and create a logical drive for the patient files. You will create a logical drive on an extended partition to store the patient files.

learning objective

After completing this project, you will know how to create partitions from unpartitioned disk space.

specific requirements

See General Requirements.

estimated completion time

25 minutes

project steps

1. Click **Start**, right-click **My Computer**, and select **Manage** to open the **Computer Management** console.
2. In the scope pane, double-click the **Storage** node to expand it, if necessary.
3. Click the **Disk Management** snap-in to display the disk configuration in the details pane.
4. Right-click the **Unallocated** disk space and click **New Partition** to start the **New Partition Wizard** (**Figure 9-3**).
5. Click **Next** to open the **Select Partition Type** screen.
6. Select the **Extended partition** option button to create an extended partition.
7. Click **Next** to open the **Specify Partition Size** screen.
8. Type **1024** in the **Partition size in MB** spin box to set the size for the extended partition.
9. Click **Next** to open the **Completing the New Partition Wizard** screen.
10. Click **Finish** to create the extended partition **(Figure 9-4)**.
11. To create a logical drive on this extended partition, right-click the **Free space** in the extended partition and click **New Logical Drive** to open the **New Partition Wizard** (**Figure 9-5**).
12. Click **Next** to open the **Select Partition Type** screen. Note that the **Logical drive** option button is selected by default and the other options are inactive.
13. Click **Next** to open the **Specify Partition Size** screen.
14. Type **1024** in the **Partition size in MB** spin box to set the size for the logical drive.
15. Click **Next** to open the **Assign Drive Letter or Path** screen. The **Assign the following drive letter** option button is selected by default.
16. Select **D** in the list box or another unused drive letter as appropriate.
17. Click **Next** to open the **Format Partition** screen.
18. By default, the file system selected to format your logical drive is **NTFS**. Accept the default file system and allocation unit size, and type **PATIENTS** in the **Volume label** text box as the label for the logical drive.
19. Click **Next** to open **Completing the New Partition Wizard** screen.
20. Click **Finish** to create the logical drive on the extended partition (**Figure 9-6**).
21. Close the Computer Management console.

Figure 9-3 Creating a new partition

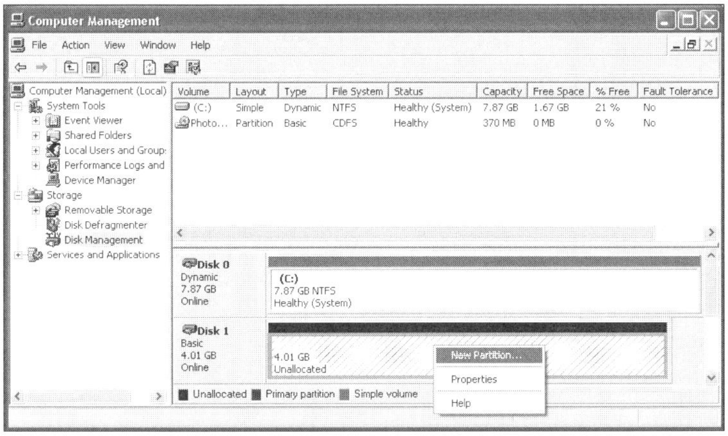

Figure 9-4 The extended partition

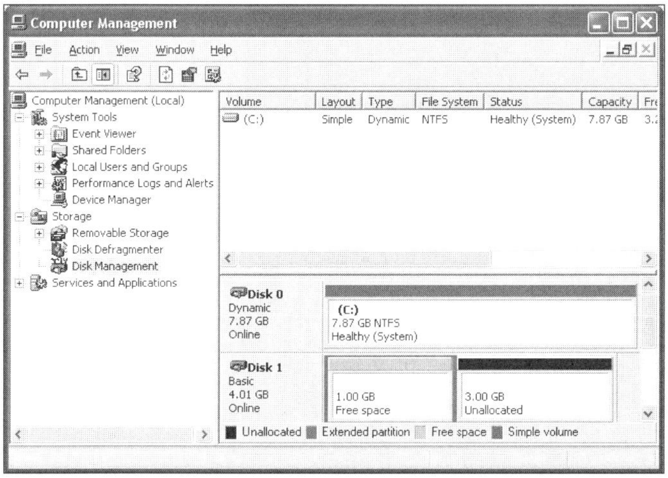

Figure 9-5 Creating a logical drive

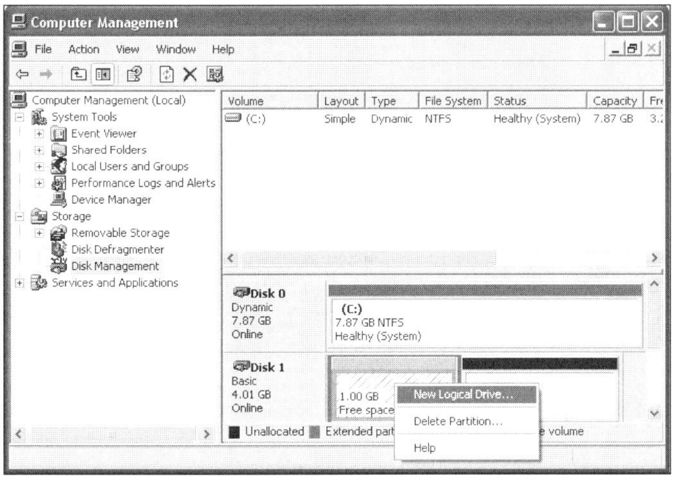

Figure 9-6 The PATIENTS logical drive

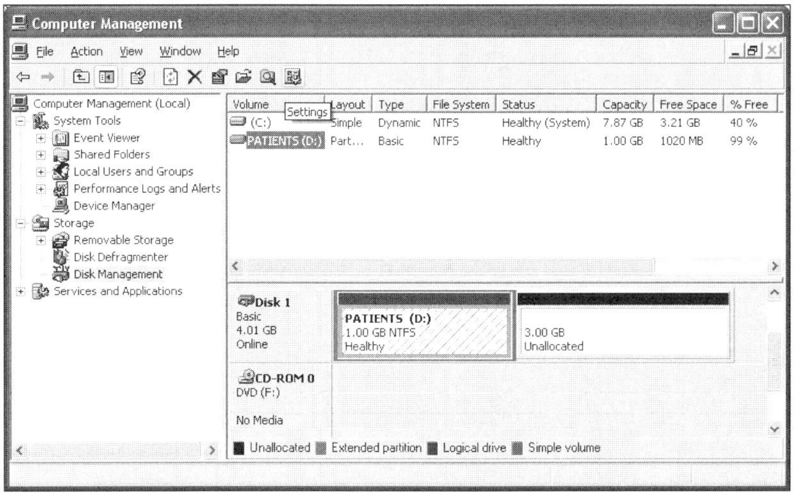

project 9.3

Updating a Disk from Basic to Dynamic

exam objective

Configure and troubleshoot storage devices. Answer end-user questions related to configuring hard disks and partitions or volumes.

overview

The field office manager informs you that in the next few months all patient files from all six of the satellite medical offices will be stored at this facility. You decide that you want to create a separate storage unit for the patient records from each office. Since basic disks are limited to four partitions, you decide to upgrade the disk to dynamic.

learning objective

After completing this project, you will know how to convert a basic disk to a dynamic disk.

specific requirements

See General Requirements.

estimated completion time

15 minutes

project steps

1. Click **Start**, right-click **My Computer**, and select **Manage** to open the **Computer Management** console.
2. In the scope pane, double-click the **Storage** node to expand it, if necessary.
3. Click the **Disk Management** snap-in to display the disk configuration in the details pane.
4. Right-click the disk, for example, **Disk 1,** and select **Convert to Dynamic Disk** (**Figure 9-7**).
5. The **Convert to Dynamic Disk** dialog box opens. The disk you selected should be listed as a check box in the Disks box and be selected. Click **OK** to convert the disk (**Figure 9-8**).
6. The **Disks to Convert** dialog box opens. The disk that you are going to convert to dynamic is listed in the **Disks** box. Click the **Convert** button.
7. A **Disk Management** information message box opens to caution you that if you convert the disk to dynamic, you will not be able to start other installed operating systems from any volume on the disk. Click **Yes** to confirm that you want to continue.
8. The **Convert Disk to Dynamic** warning message box opens to caution you that file systems on any of the disks to be converted will be dismounted. Click **Yes** to confirm that you want to continue.
9. If you are converting a disk that includes the system volume, the boot volume, or a volume that contains the paging file, the **Confirm alert** dialog box opens to inform you that your computer will be rebooted. Click **OK** to allow the computer to restart. After it does, the disk is upgraded from basic to dynamic.
10. If the Confirm alert dialog box does not open, the disk is automatically converted to the dynamic storage type. The extended partition is converted to a simple volume (**Figure 9-9**).
11. Close the Computer Management console.

Figure 9-7 Converting a basic disk to dynamic

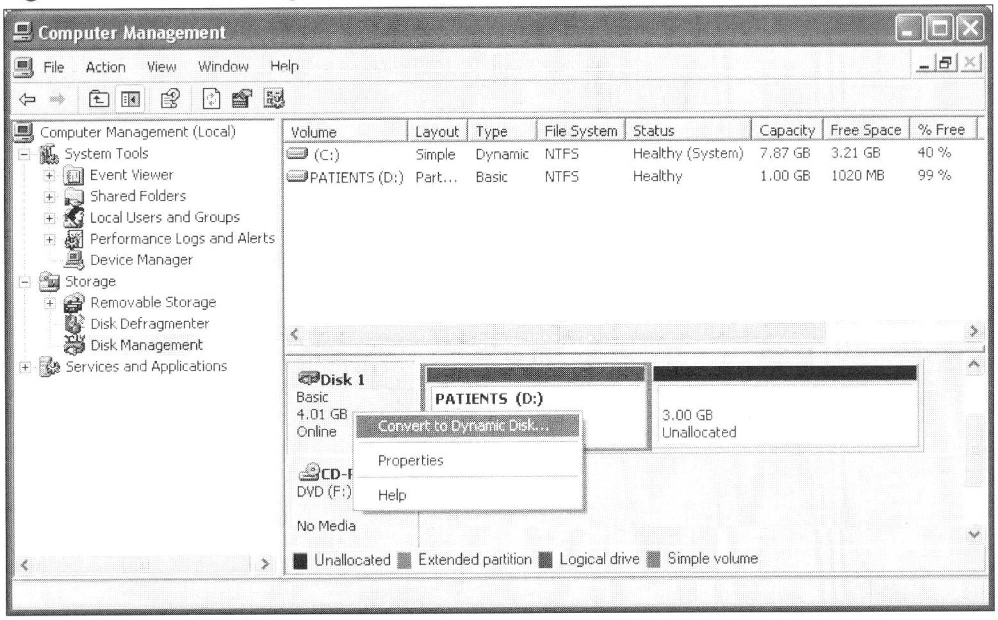

Figure 9-8 The Convert to Dynamic Disk dialog box

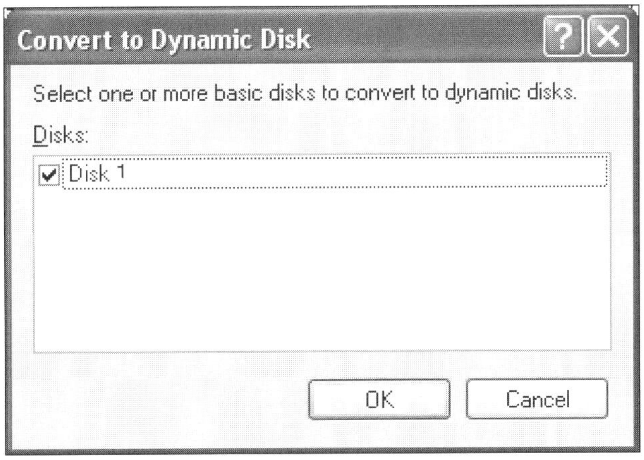

Figure 9-9 The extended partition converted to a simple volume

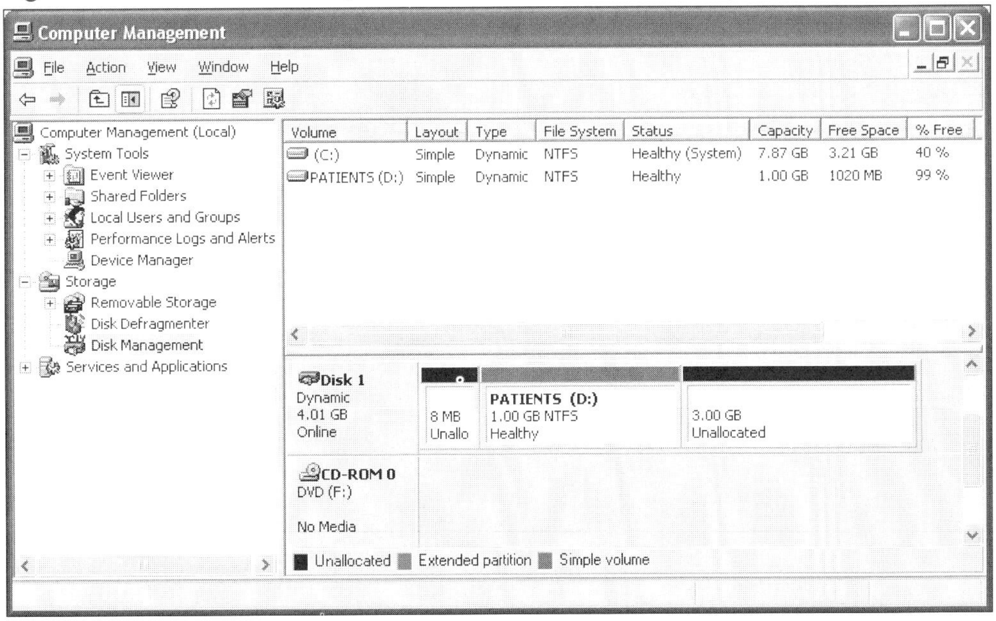

project 9.4

Extending an Existing Volume

exam objective

Configure and troubleshoot storage devices. Answer end-user questions related to configuring hard disks and partitions or volumes.

overview

After speaking to the field office manager again, you realize that 1 GB is not going to be a large enough storage space for the several large databases used to store the patient records at her office. You decide to use unallocated space on the same hard drive to extend the storage capacity of the PATIENTS volume.

learning objective

After completing this project, you will know how to increase the size of an existing volume.

specific requirements

See General Requirements.

estimated completion time

15 minutes

project steps

1. Click **Start**, right-click **My Computer**, and select **Manage** to open the **Computer Management** console.
2. In the scope pane, double-click the **Storage** node to expand it, if necessary.
3. Click the **Disk Management** snap-in to display the disk configuration in the details pane.
4. Right-click the **PATIENTS** volume and click **Extend Volume** (**Figure 9-10**) to start the **Extend Volume Wizard**.
5. Click **Next** to open the **Select Disks** screen.
6. The disk you are using to extend the volume should be selected in the **Selected** box with the amount of free space available.
7. Type **1024** in the **Select the amount of space in MB** spin box to extend the volume by 1GB. If you do not have sufficient disk space, you can extend the volume by a smaller amount (**Figure 9-11**).
8. Click **Next** to open the **Completing the Extend Volume Wizard** screen.
9. Click **Finish** to extend the volume.
10. In the **Disk Management** snap-in, there are now two **Patients (D:)** volumes with a total of 2 GB of disk space (**Figure 9-12**).
11. Close the Computer Management console.

Figure 9-10 Extending a volume

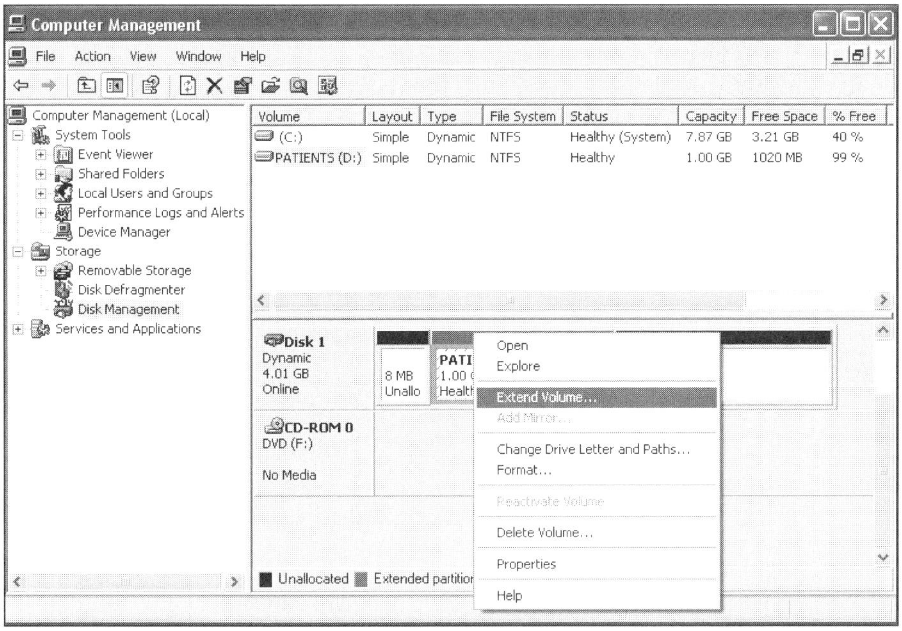

Figure 9-11 Selecting the disk and setting the size

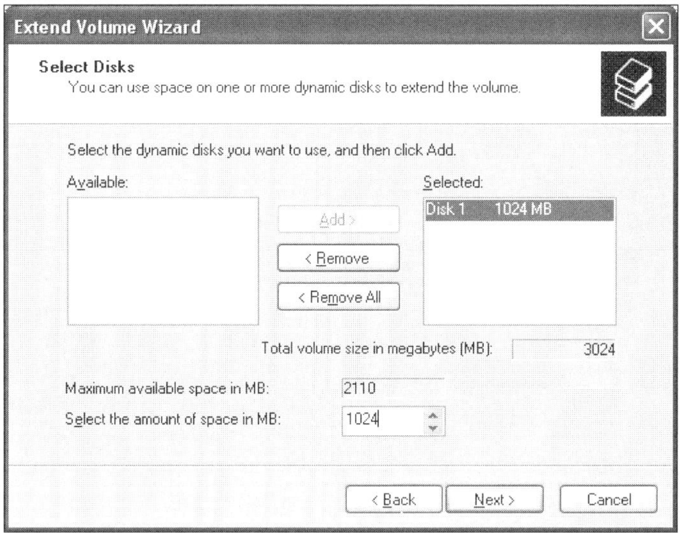

Figure 9-12 The extended PATIENTS volume

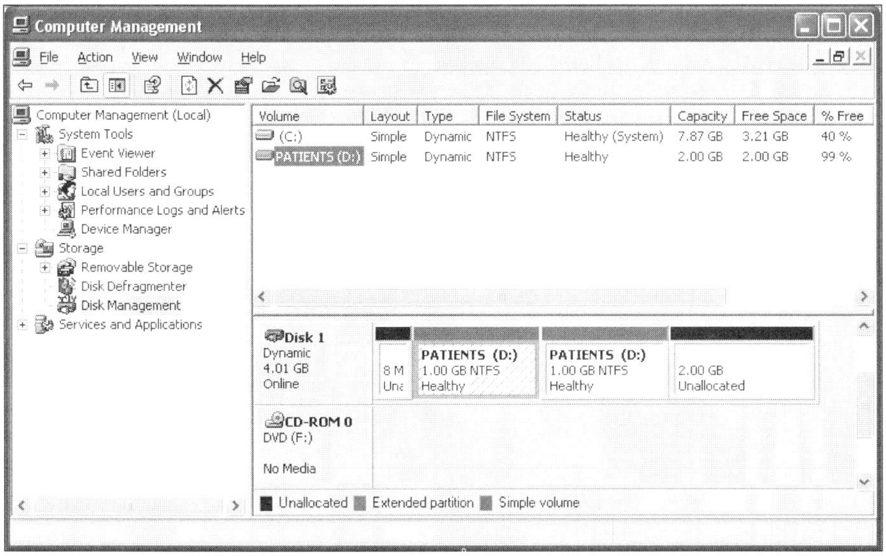

project 9.5

Using Disk Management on Remote Disks

exam objective

Configure and troubleshoot storage devices. Answer end-user questions related to configuring hard disks and partitions or volumes.

overview

You want to run the Disk Management snap-in on several computers, but you do not want to walk from desktop to desktop. To save time, you create a console to access other computers remotely. In order to do this, you must log on using an account with administrative rights on a domain network or with administrative rights on each remote computer on a workgroup network.

learning objective

After completing this project, you will know how to create a Microsoft Management Console to run disk management functions remotely.

specific requirements

See General Requirements. To complete this project, you must be on a workgroup or domain network and be logged on with an account that has administrative rights on the domain or on one of the remote computers on a workgroup network..

estimated completion time

15 minutes

project steps

1. Click **Start** and then **Run** to open the **Run** dialog box.
2. In the **Open** text box, type **mmc** and press [**Enter**] to open an empty Microsoft management console.
3. Open the **File** menu and select **Add Remove Snap-in** to open the **Add Remove Snap-in** dialog box. Make sure the **Standalone** tab is selected.
4. Click the **Add** button to open the **Add Standalone Snap-in** dialog box.
5. In the **Available Standalone Snap-ins** box, select **Disk Management** (**Figure 9-13**).
6. Click the **Add** button to add the Disk Management snap-in to the **Add/Remove Snap-in** dialog box.
7. The **Disk Management Wizard** opens so that you can select the computer you want to use the console to manage. Select the **The following computer** option button and enter the name of the computer you want to access, or click the **Browse** button to search for computers on the network (**Figure 9-14**).
8. Click **Finish** to close the wizard.
9. Repeat Steps 6 and 7 to add the Disk Management snap-in for the other computers you want to remotely manage to the console.
10. Click the **Close** button to close the Add Standalone Snap-in dialog box.
11. Click **OK** to close the Add/Remove Snap-in dialog box.
12. Click **Disk Management** (***computername***) to open the **Disk Management** console on the remote computer (**Figure 9-15**).
13. Open the **File** menu and select **Save As** to open the **Save As** dialog box.
14. Save the console as **Remote Disk Management** in the **Administrative Tools** folder.
15. Close the Remote Disk Management console.

caution

If you have Service Pack 2 installed, after Step 12, a Disk Management warning dialog box opens to inform you that the console could not connect because the Disk Management remoting service is not in the Windows Firewall exception list. Click OK to close the dialog box and then follow the steps on page 9.14.

Figure 9-13 Selecting the Disk Management snap-in

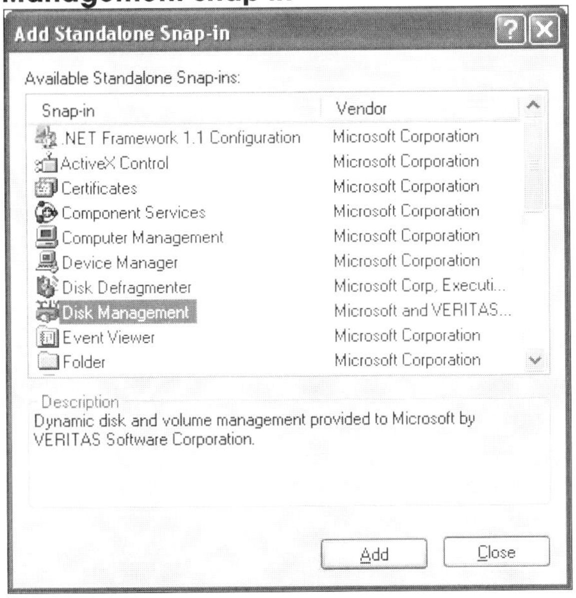

Figure 9-14 The Disk Management Wizard

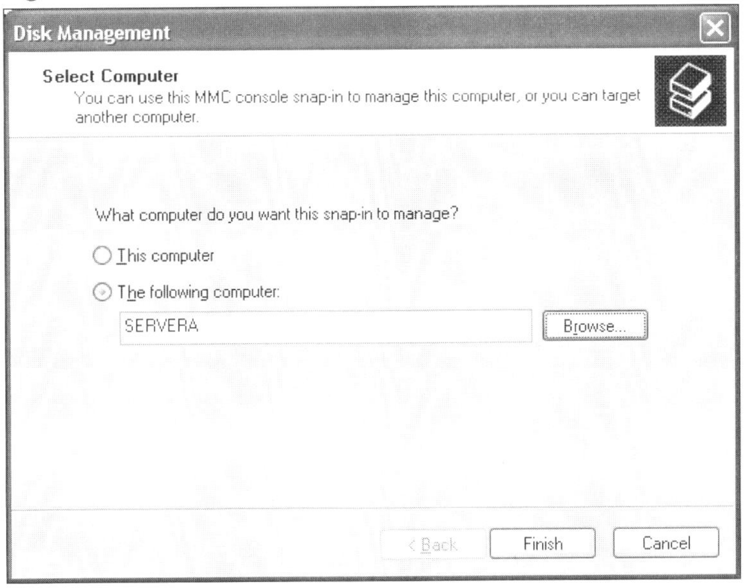

Figure 9-15 Running the Disk Management snap-in on remote computers

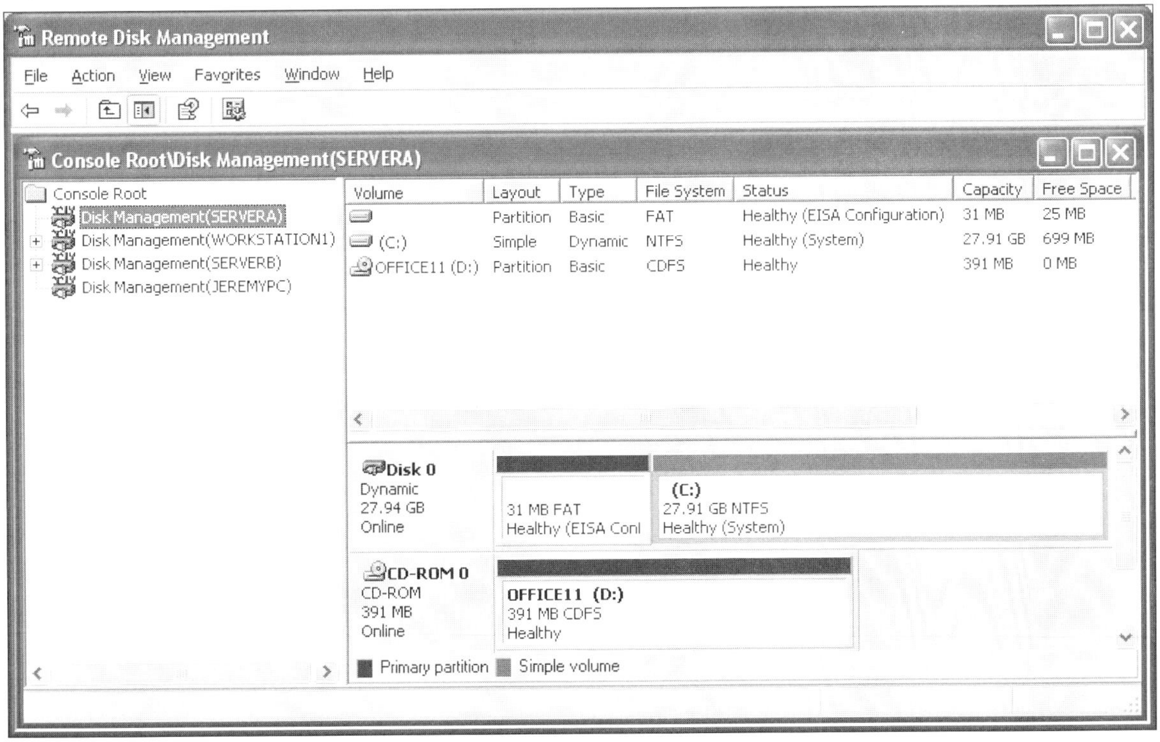

project 9.5

Using Disk Management on Remote Disks *(cont'd)*

exam objective

Configure and troubleshoot storage devices. Answer end-user questions related to configuring hard disks and partitions or volumes.

project steps

If you have Service Pack 2 installed, follow the steps below to add the remoting service to the firewall exception list and open the necessary ports.

1. Click **Start** and then **Control Panel** to open the **Control Panel**.
2. In **Category view**, click **Security Center** to open the **Windows Security Center**.
3. Under **Manage security settings for**, click **Windows Firewall** to open the **Windows Firewall** dialog box.
4. Click the **Exceptions** tab.
5. Click the **Add Program** button to open the **Add a Program** dialog box.
6. Click the **Browse** button to open the **Browse** dialog box.
7. In the **Look in** list box, navigate to %Systemroot%\Windows\System32 and locate and select **dmremote.exe** (**Figure 9-16**).
8. Click the **Open** button to add **dmremote.exe** to the **Programs** box and the path to the program to the **Path** label (**Figure 9-17**).
9. Click the **Change scope** button to open the **Change Scope** dialog box.
10. Select the **My network** (**subnet**) **only** option button (**Figure 9-18**).
11. Click **OK** to close the Add a Program dialog box.
12. Click the **Add Port** button to open the **Add a Port** dialog box.
13. Type **TCP Port 135** in the **Name** text box and **135** in the **Port number** text box (**Figure 9-19**).
14. Click the **Change scope** button to open the **Change Scope** dialog box.
15. Select the **My network** (**subnet**) **only** option button.
16. Click **OK** to close the Change Scope dialog box.
17. Click **OK** to close the Add a Port dialog box.
18. Click **OK** to close the Windows Firewall dialog box.
19. Close the Windows Security Center.

Figure 9-16 Locating the Disk Management remoting service

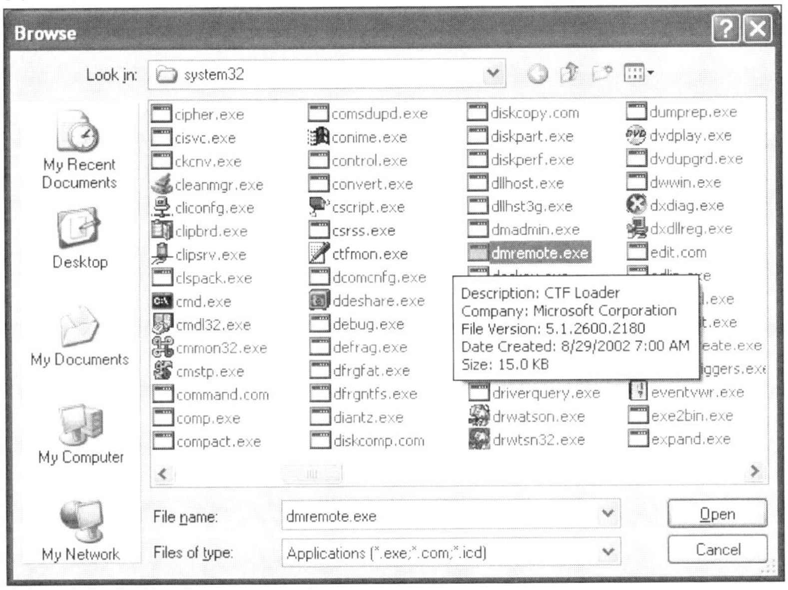

Figure 9-17 Adding dmremote.exe to firewall exceptions

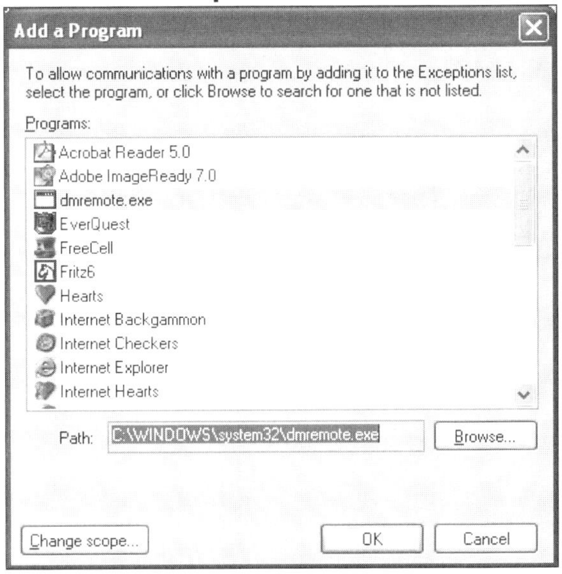

Figure 9-18 Changing the scope for a program

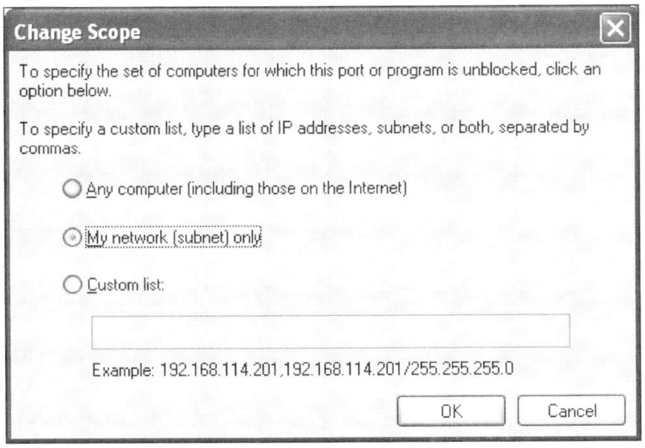

Figure 9-19 Adding TCP port 135

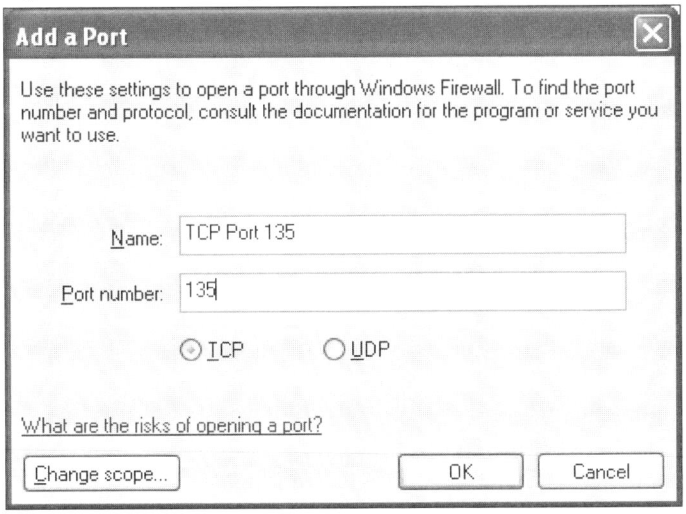

project 9.6 Configuring Disk Quotas

exam objective

Configure and troubleshoot storage devices. Answer end-user questions related to configuring hard disks and partitions or volumes.

overview

One of the City Hospital field offices will be used exclusively for training hospital and medical office personnel. Employees will use the computers to learn everything from database design to digital imaging. To ensure that all applications run efficiently and that no users "hog" disk space with their files, you decide to set disk quotas.

learning objective

After completing this project, you will know how to set disk quotas to set limits on the amount of disk space users can consume on a volume or partition.

specific requirements

See General Requirements.

estimated completion time

15 minutes

project steps

tip

The local administrator will be the only entry in the Quota Entries for the PATIENTS volume. The Administrator account has no quota limit by default. When a new user who has never placed any data on the volume before adds a folder to the volume his or her account will be automatically added to the quota entries with the amount used and the warning/limits. You must create quota entries for users who have data on the volume before the quota is set.

1. Click **Start**, right-click **My Computer**, and select **Manage** to open the **Computer Management** console.
2. In the scope pane, double-click the **Storage** node to expand it, if necessary.
3. Click the **Disk Management** snap-in to display the disk configuration in the details pane.
4. Right-click the volume you want to access. For example, right-click **PATIENTS D:** and click Properties to open the **PATIENTS (D:) Properties** dialog box (**Figure 9-20**).
5. Click the **Quota** tab.
6. Select the **Enable quota management** check box.
7. Select the **Deny disk space to users exceeding quota limit** check box.
8. Select the **Limit disk space to** option button. Type **500** in the text box and select **MB** in the list box to limit users to 500MB of storage space.
9. In the **Set warning level to** text box, type **450** and then select **MB** in the corresponding list box to configure a warning to display when the user reaches 450MB of disk space (**Figure 9-21**).
10. If you want to record log entries when the user exceeds his quota, select either or both quota logging option check boxes.
11. Click **OK** to close the Patients (D:) Properties dialog box.

Figure 9-20 Disk Properties dialog box – General tab

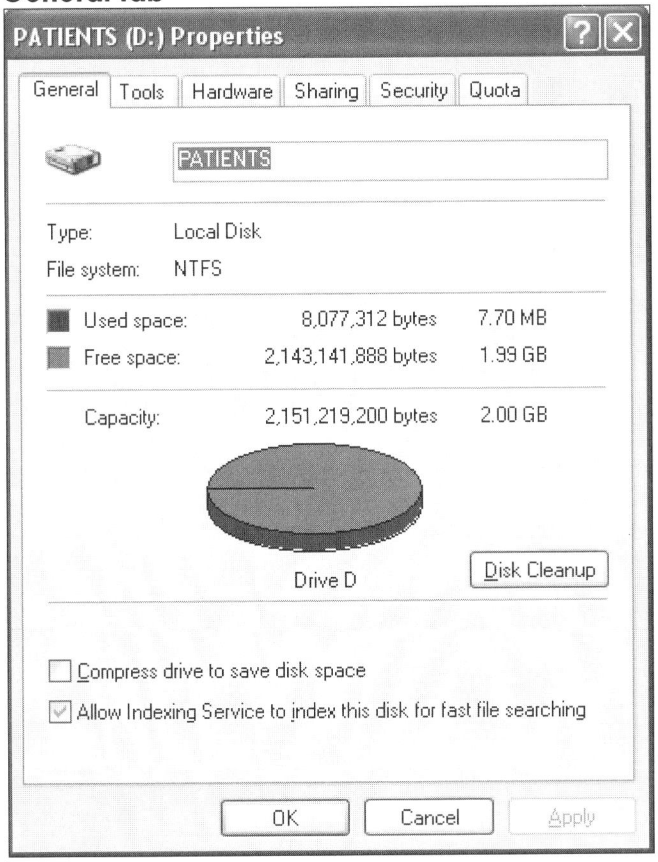

Figure 9-21 Disk Properties dialog box – Quota tab

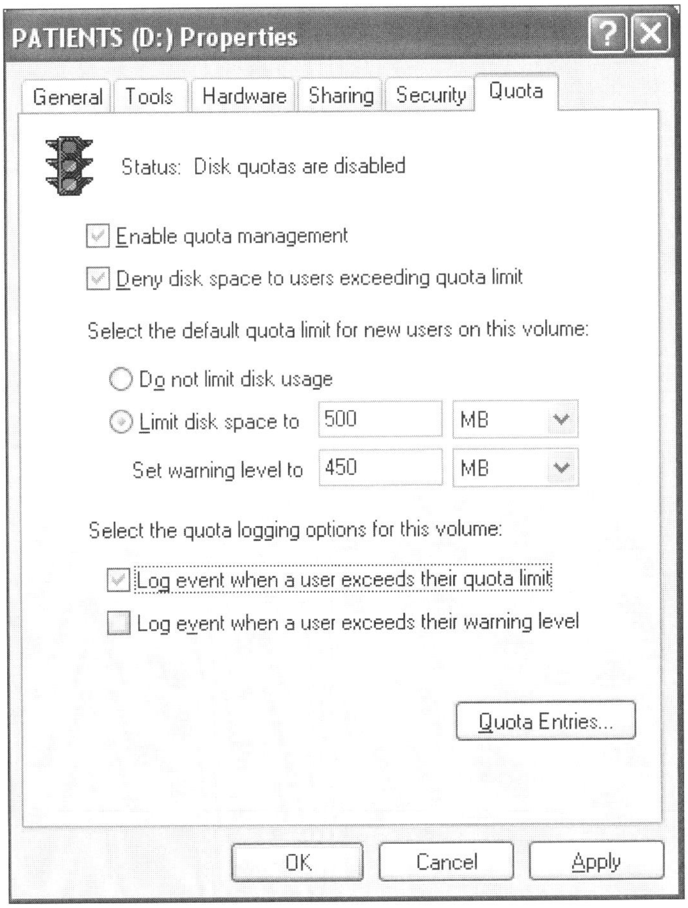

project 9.7 Troubleshooting Disks and Volumes

exam objective

Configure and troubleshoot storage devices. Answer end-user questions related to configuring hard disks and partitions or volumes. Manage and troubleshoot disk partitioning.

overview

One of the users at the City Hospital branch office informs you that one of the disks on his computer no longer appears in My Computer. You open the Disk Management console, rescan the disk, and run the Check Disk utility to try to fix disk errors.

learning objective

After completing this project, you will know how to rescan a disk and run the Check Disk utility.

specific requirements

See General Requirements.

estimated completion time

30 minutes

project steps

1. Click **Start**, right-click **My Computer**, and select **Manage** to open the **Computer Management** console.
2. In the scope pane, double-click the **Storage** node to expand it, if necessary.
3. Click the **Disk Management** snap-in to display the disk configuration in the details pane.
4. To simulate troubleshooting a disk that is offline or missing, select the volume, open the **Action** menu, and select **Rescan Disks** (**Figure 9-22**).
5. Right-click the volume you are troubleshooting and select **Properties** to open the **Properties** dialog box for the disk volume.
6. Click the **Tools** tab.
7. In the **Error-checking** section, click the **Check Now** button to open the **Check Disk** <***volumename (driveletter:***)> dialog box.
8. Select the **Automatically fix file** system **errors** and **Scan for and attempt recovery of bad sectors** check boxes (**Figure 9-23).**
9. Click the **Start** button to initiate the scan. If you are currently on the volume that you want to check or if there are any programs running, a **Checking Disk** <***volumename (driveletter:***)> information dialog box opens to inform you that the scan cannot run because the Check Disk utility needs exclusive access to some Windows files on the disk. Click **Yes** to schedule the disk check to occur at the next reboot (**Figure 9-24**).
10. When the scan is complete, the **Checking Disk** <***volumename (driveletter***:)> dialog box opens (**Figure 9-25**).
11. Click **OK** to close the Checking Disk dialog box.
12. Click **OK** to close the Properties dialog box for the volume.
13. Close the Computer Management console.

Figure 9-22 Rescanning a disk volume

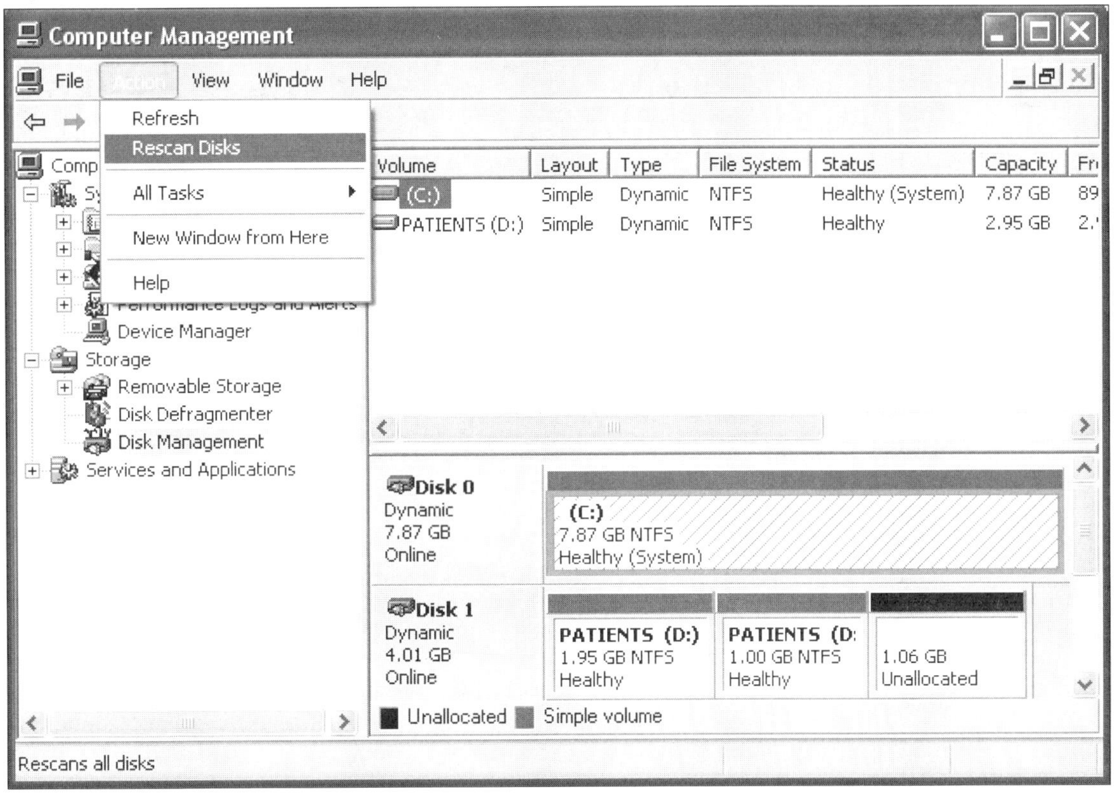

Figure 9-23 The Check Disk PATIENTS (D:) dialog box

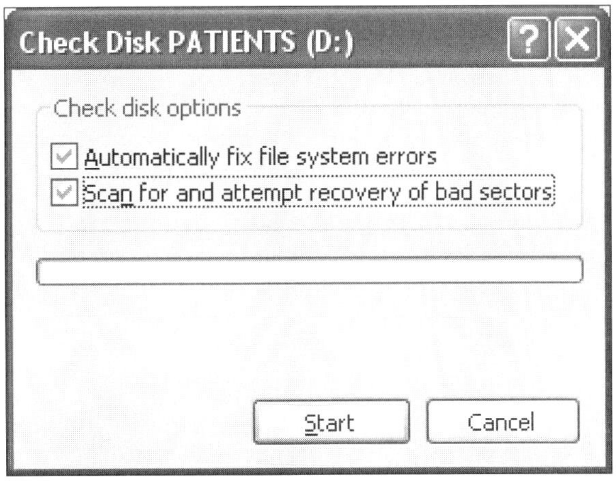

Figure 9-24 Checking Disk Local Disk (C:) information dialog box

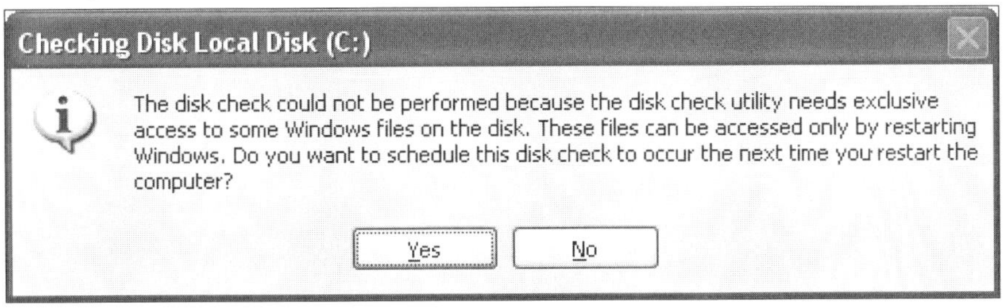

Figure 9-25 Checking Disk PATIENTS (D:) dialog box - Disk Check Complete

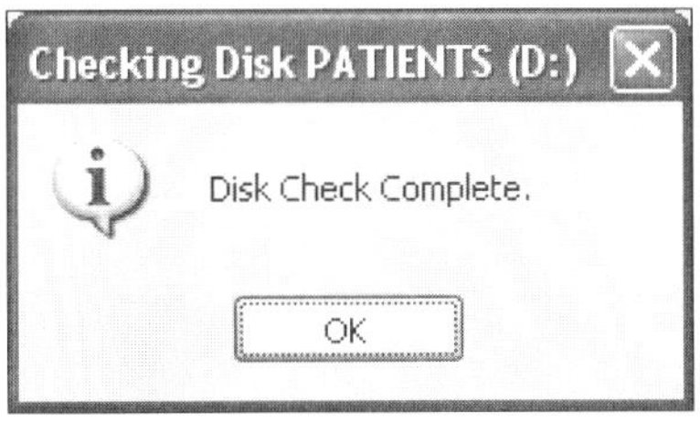

LESSON 10

Configuring and Troubleshooting Display, Power, and I/O Devices

Windows XP is a truly versatile system. Keyboards, modems, pointing devices, network cards, and video displays from different manufacturers can all be connected to an XP workstation. However, successfully configuring all these different devices and peripherals is not always an easy chore.

Windows XP provides numerous utilities that can help you configure and troubleshoot display and input/output devices. Many peripherals can be configured through the Control Panel, including pointing devices, keyboards, monitors, and modems. The Power Options utility is used to conserve energy when the computer is not in use. On laptop computers, you can set alarms to warn you when battery power is getting low or approaching a critically low level.

From the System Properties dialog box, you can access the Device Manager, which can be used to configure and troubleshoot device drivers--programs that help manage the interaction between the operating system and hardware devices. Although Windows XP automatically installs many device drivers, hardware and software modifications can require that the drivers be updated.

To help safeguard XP workstation reliability, you can configure the Driver Signing utility to prevent installing drivers that are not Windows Logo approved. You can also create different hardware profiles for mobile computers. For example, you can create a hardware profile for an office configuration that is different from the profile a laptop uses at a remote location.

This lesson provides practice configuring and troubleshooting display settings, power options, and I/O devices. You will also learn how to configure and troubleshoot hardware profiles.

Scenario

You have been asked to set up computers at a new City Hospital branch office. You will need to install monitors from a variety of vendors as well as set up laptops for different field workers.

Lesson 10 Configuring and Troubleshooting Display, Power, and I/O Devices

Project	*Exam 70-271 Objective*
10.1 Setting Display Properties	**Configure and troubleshoot display devices**. Answer end-user questions related to configuring desktop display settings. Configure display devices and display settings.
10.2 Troubleshooting Display Settings	**Configure and troubleshoot display devices**. Troubleshoot display device settings.
10.3 Configuring and Troubleshooting Power ACPI Settings	**Configure and troubleshoot Advanced Configuration and Interface (ACPI)**. Answer end-user questions related to configuring ACPI settings. Configure and troubleshoot operating system power settings. Configure and troubleshoot system standby and hibernate settings.
10.4 Configuring and Troubleshooting I/O Devices	**Configure and troubleshoot I/O devices**. Answer end-user questions related to configuring I/O devices. Configure and troubleshoot device settings.
10.5 Configuring and Troubleshooting Universal Serial Bus (USB) Devices	**Configure and troubleshoot I/O devices**. Answer end-user questions related to configuring I/O devices. Configure and troubleshoot devices settings.
10.6 Troubleshooting Driver Signing	**Configure and troubleshoot I/O devices**. Configure and troubleshoot device drivers for I/O devices.
10.7 Configuring and Troubleshooting Hardware Profiles	**Configure and troubleshoot I/O devices**. Configure and troubleshoot hardware profiles.

General Requirements

To complete the projects in this lesson, you will need administrative rights on a Windows XP Professional computer, a modem, and a USB device. For Project 10.3, you will need a laptop computer running Windows XP Professional. You may also find it helpful to refer to Lesson 10 in your Prentice Hall Certification Series Exam 70-271 textbook for further information about the topics covered by the projects in this lesson.

project 10.1 Setting Display Properties

exam objective

Configure and troubleshoot display devices. Answer end-user questions related to configuring desktop display settings. Configure display devices and display settings.

overview

A graphic artist at the City Hospital field office is creating a black-and-white user handbook. He will be shooting screen shots, and he needs the screen resolution set to 800 by 600 pixels. He would like you to change the Windows Display Properties color scheme and font size attributes so the printouts of the screen shots are easier to read.

learning objective

After completing this project, you will know how to change video display settings.

specific requirements

None

estimated completion time

10 minutes

project steps

1. Click **Start** and select **Control Panel** to open the **Control Panel**.
2. In **Category View**, click the **Appearance and Themes** link to open the **Appearance and Themes** window.
3. Click the **Change the screen resolution** link to open the **Display Properties** dialog box on the **Settings** tab.
4. Drag the **Screen resolution** slider to change the resolution to **800 by 600** (**Figure 10-1**).
5. Click the **Appearance** tab.
6. In the **Color scheme** list box, select **Silver**.
7. In the **Font size** list box, select **Large Fonts** (**Figure 10-2**).
8. Click **OK** to apply the new settings and close the Display Properties dialog box.
9. Close the Appearance and Themes window.

Figure 10-1 Display Properties dialog box–Settings tab

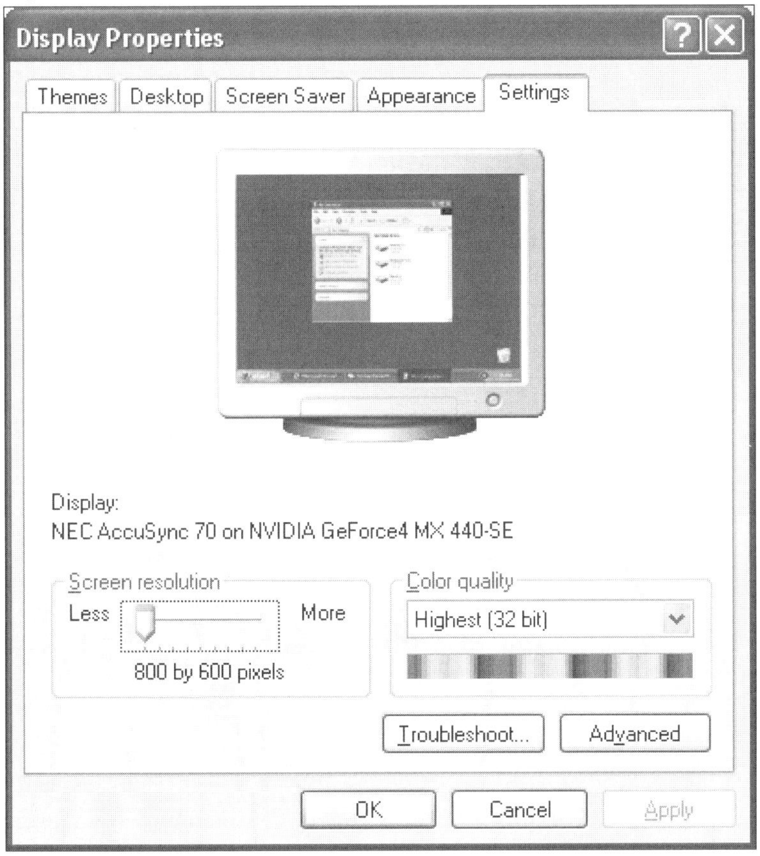

Figure 10-2 Display Properties dialog box–Appearance tab

project 10.2 Troubleshooting Display Settings

exam objective

Configure and troubleshoot display devices. Troubleshoot display device settings.

overview

The art director at the City Hospital field office has just installed a 21-inch monitor on a graphics workstation. When the art director boots up the computer, the screen is blank. To get the monitor up and running, you start the computer in VGA mode and use the Microsoft Help and Support to troubleshoot.

learning objective

After completing this project, you will know how to troubleshoot monitor settings and how to use the Help and Support Center.

specific requirements

See General Requirements.

estimated completion time

15 minutes

project steps

1. Click **Start** and select **Turn off computer** or **Shut Down**, depending on the network configuration, to shut down the computer.
2. In the **Shut Down Windows** dialog box, select **Restart** in the **What do you want the computer to do**? list box and click **OK**.
3. As the computer is starting up, press [**F8**] to access the **Windows Advanced Options Menu**.
4. Use the arrow keys to select **Enable VGA Mode** and press [**Enter**].
5. After the computer reboots and you log back on, click **Start** and then **Control Panel** to open the **Control Panel**.
6. In **Category View**, click the **Performance and Maintenance** link to open the **Performance and Maintenance** window.
7. Click the **See basic information about your computer** link to open the **System Properties** dialog box.
8. Click the **Hardware** tab.
9. Click the **Device Manager** button to open the **Device Manager**.
10. Double click **Display adapters** to expand the node (**Figure 10-3**).
11. Double-click the display adapter icon to open the **Properties** dialog box for the video card (**Figure 10-4**).
12. Click the **Troubleshoot** button to open the **Help and Support Center** to the **Video Display Troubleshooter**.
13. Select the **I cannot install my monitor** option button (**Figure 10-5**).
14. Follow the help and support path to learn about reinstalling the display driver.
15. When you are finished, close all open dialog boxes and windows.
16. Restart the computer.

tip

If you were using a computer with an incorrectly configured monitor, you would have to restart the computer by pressing the restart button.

Figure 10-3 Display adapters node in Device Manager

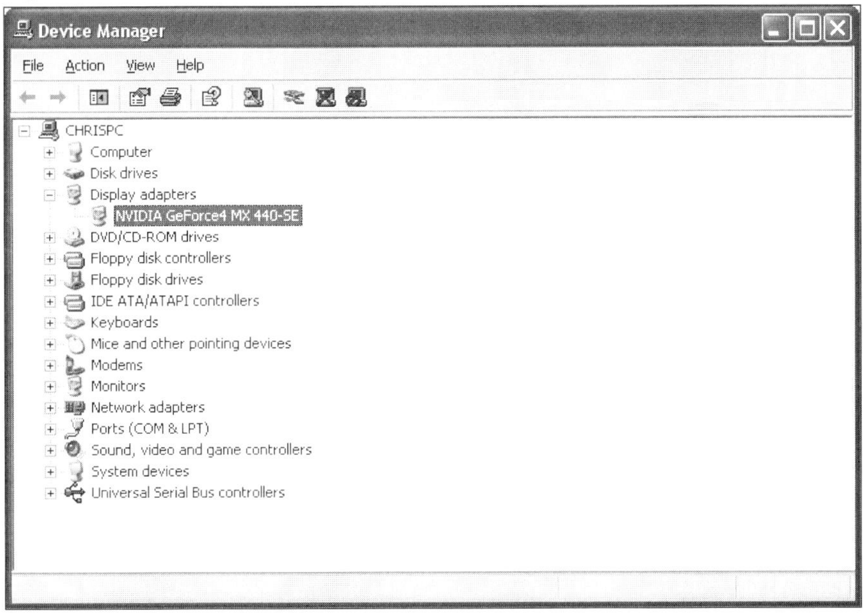

Figure 10-4 Properties dialog box for a video card

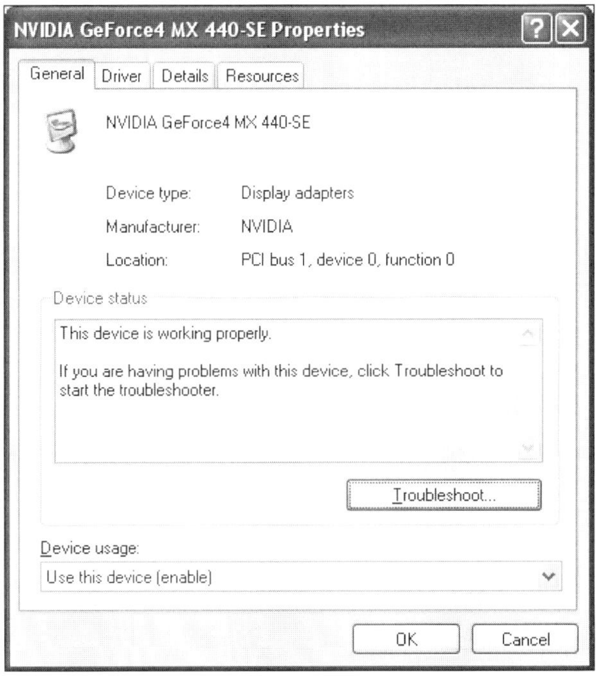

Figure 10-5 Video Display Troubleshooter page in the Help and Support Center

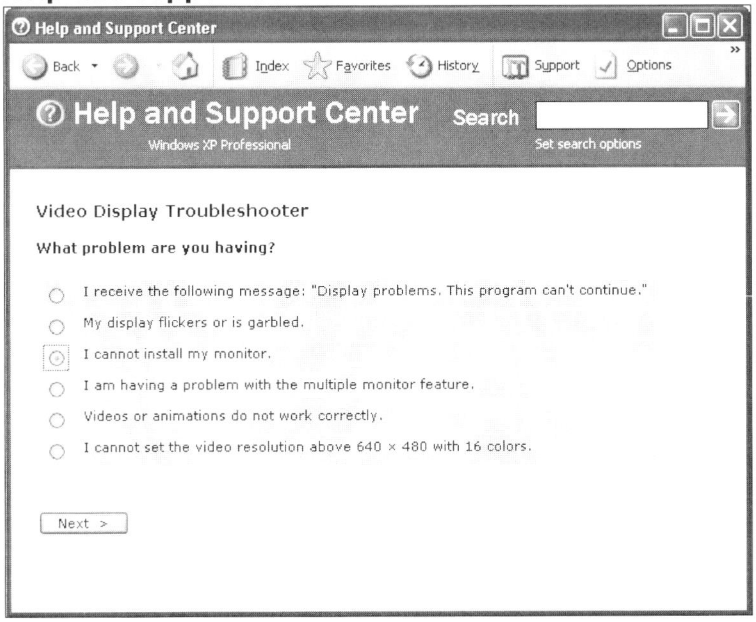

project 10.3

Configuring and Troubleshooting ACPI Settings

exam objective

Configure and troubleshoot Advanced Configuration and Power Interface (ACPI). Answer end-user questions related to configuring ACPI settings. Configure and troubleshoot operating system power settings. Configure and troubleshoot system standby and hibernate settings.

overview

One of the users at the City Hospital branch office complains that she needs a new laptop battery. She says that she can barely work more than half an hour before her battery runs out. When the battery does lose power, she says she loses her work. You decide to help her to change the Low battery and Critical battery alarm timing settings and to configure an alarm sound and make the laptop hibernate when the battery hits a critical stage. In hibernate mode, the computer writes an image of the files that are currently open to a file on the hard drive. When the user restarts the computer, the computer screen will look exactly as it did before the shut down. You also have her view the manufacturing details for the battery so that she can gather the appropriate information needed to replace it if necessary.

learning objective

After completing this project, you will know how to set system power settings and how to set an alarm for when battery power is running low on a laptop computer.

specific requirements

Laptop computer with Windows XP Professional installed

estimated completion time

15 minutes

project steps

1. Click **Start** and select **Control Panel** to open the **Control Panel** window.
2. In **Category view**, click the **Performance and Maintenance** link to open the **Performance and Maintenance** window.
3. Under **or pick a Control Panel icon**, click **Power Options** to open the **Power Options Properties** dialog box.
4. Click the **Alarms** tab to view the settings for low and critical battery (**Figure 10-6**).
5. In the **Low battery alarm** section, select the **Activate low battery alarm when power level reaches** check box, if necessary.
6. Drag the **Low battery alarm** slider to **25** percent.
7. In the **Critical battery alarm** section, select the **Activate critical battery alarm when power level reaches** check box, if necessary.
8. Drag the **Critical battery alarm** slider to **10** percent.
9. Click the **Alarm Action** button to open the **Critical Battery Alarm Actions** dialog box.
10. In the **Notifications** section, select the **Sound Alarm** check box.
11. In the **Alarm action** section, select the **When the alarm goes off the computer will** check box, if necessary, and select **Hibernate** in the list box (**Figure 10-7**).
12. Click **OK** to close the Critical Battery Alarm Actions dialog box.
13. Click the **Power Meter** tab.
14. Select the **Show details for each battery** check box.
15. Click the battery icon to open the **Detailed Information for Battery #** dialog box (**Figure 10-8**).
16. Click **OK** to close the Detailed Information for Battery # dialog box.
17. Click **OK** to close the Power Options Properties dialog box.
18. Close the Performance and Maintenance window.

Figure 10-6 Alarm settings for low and critical battery

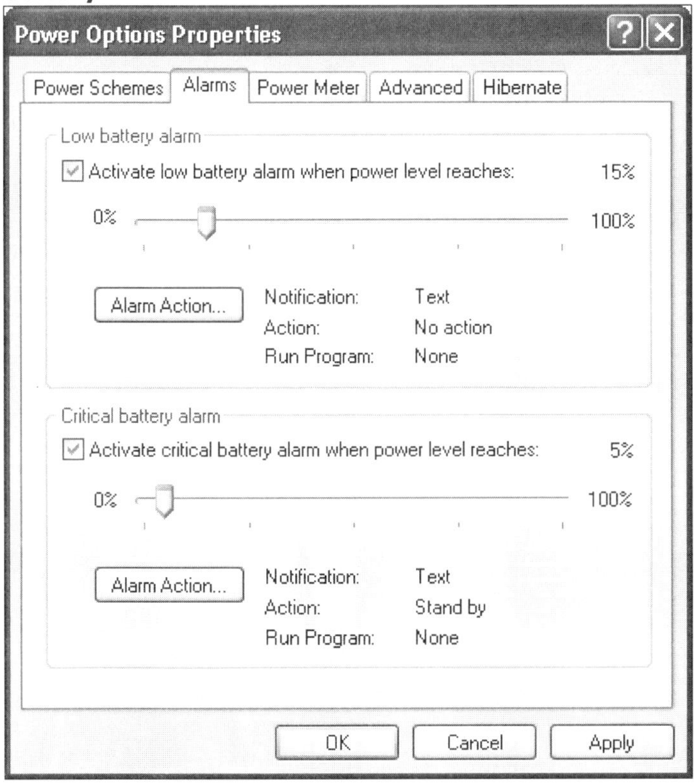

Figure 10-7 Changing critical battery alarm actions

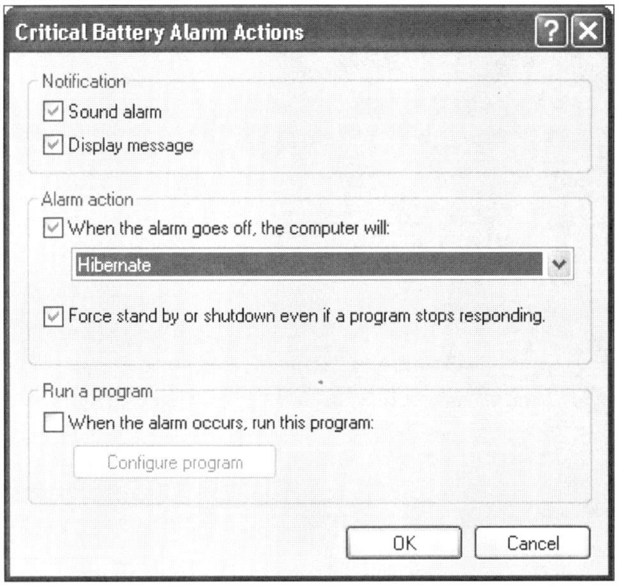

Figure 10-8 Power meter battery details

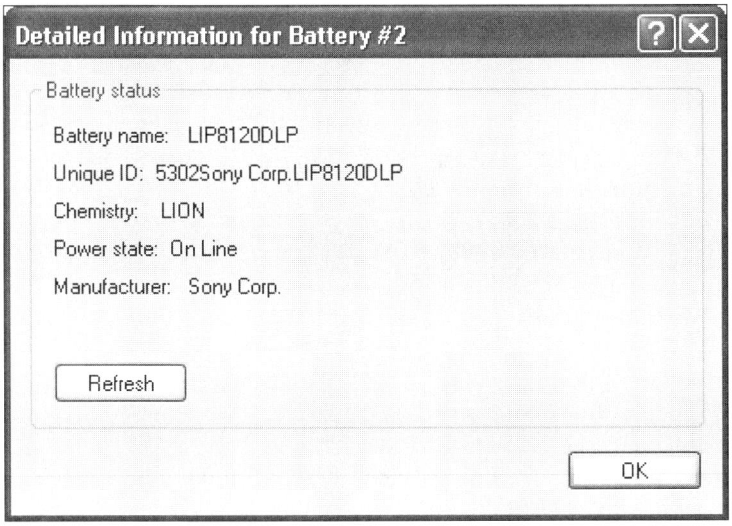

project 10.4

Configuring and Troubleshooting I/O Devices

exam objective

Configure and troubleshoot I/O devices. Answer end-user questions related to configuring I/O devices. Configure and troubleshoot device settings.

overview

A left-handed employee at the City Hospital branch office is having problems using the mouse. You decide to reconfigure the mouse to make it easier for her to use. You are going to have her reverse the left and right mouse button settings and enable large mouse icons. Because she is successfully using a modem and you will need to purchase modem cards for different computers, you want to check whether the modem is completely XP compatible. You find the modem name in the Device Manager and then search for the modem on the Web at the Microsoft Catalog. If the modem is XP compatible, you will purchase the same model for other XP machines.

learning objective

After completing this project, you will be more familiar with reconfiguring mouse settings and using the Windows Catalog.

specific requirements

See General Requirements.

estimated completion time

15 minutes

project steps

1. Click **Start** and select **Control Panel** to open the **Control Panel**.
2. In **Category view**, click the **Printers and Other Hardware** link to open the **Printers and Other Hardware** window.
3. Under **or pick a Control Panel icon**, click **Mouse** to open the **Mouse Properties** dialog box.
4. Click the **Buttons** tab, if necessary.
5. To reverse the left and right mouse button settings:
   a. **USB mouse**: Select the **Swap left and right button functions of USB mouse** check box (**Figure 10-9**).
   b. **Serial mouse (laptop):** Select **Shortcut menu** in the **Left Button** list box and select **Click** in the **Right Button** list box.
   c. **Serial mouse (PC):** Select the **Switch primary and secondary buttons** check box in the **Button configuration** section (**Figure 10-10**).
6. If you want to keep these changes, click **OK**; otherwise, click the **Cancel** button.
7. Click the **Phone and Modem Options** link. If no area code has yet been recorded for the computer, the **Location Information** dialog box opens. If the **Phone and Modem Options** dialog box opens, skip to Step 11.
8. Enter your area code in the **What area code (or city code) are you in now**? text box.
9. Click **OK** to close the **Location Information** dialog box.
10. Click the **Phone and Modem Options** link to open the **Phone and Modem Options** dialog box.
11. Click the **Modems** tab and write down the name of the listed modem (**Figure 10-11**).
12. Click **OK** to close the Phone and Modem Options dialog box.
13. Close the Printers and Other Hardware window.
14. Open Internet Explorer and go to the Windows Catalog Web site at the following URL: **http://www.microsoft.com/windows/catalog/**.

Figure 10-9 Mouse Properties (Laptop) - Buttons tab (USB mouse)

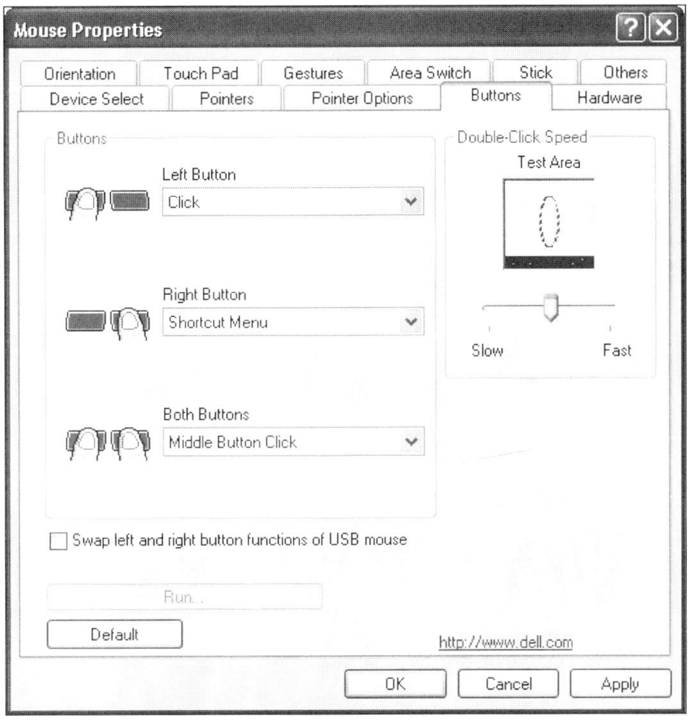

Figure 10-11 Phone and Modem Options dialog box - Modem tab

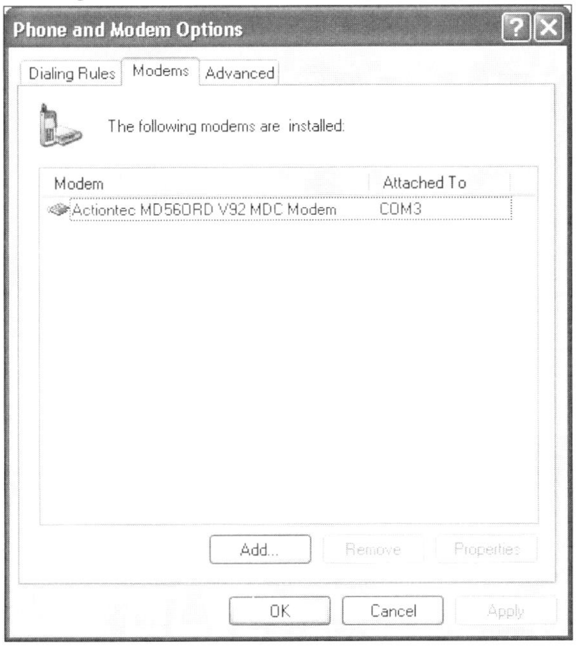

Figure 10-10 Mouse Properties - Buttons tab

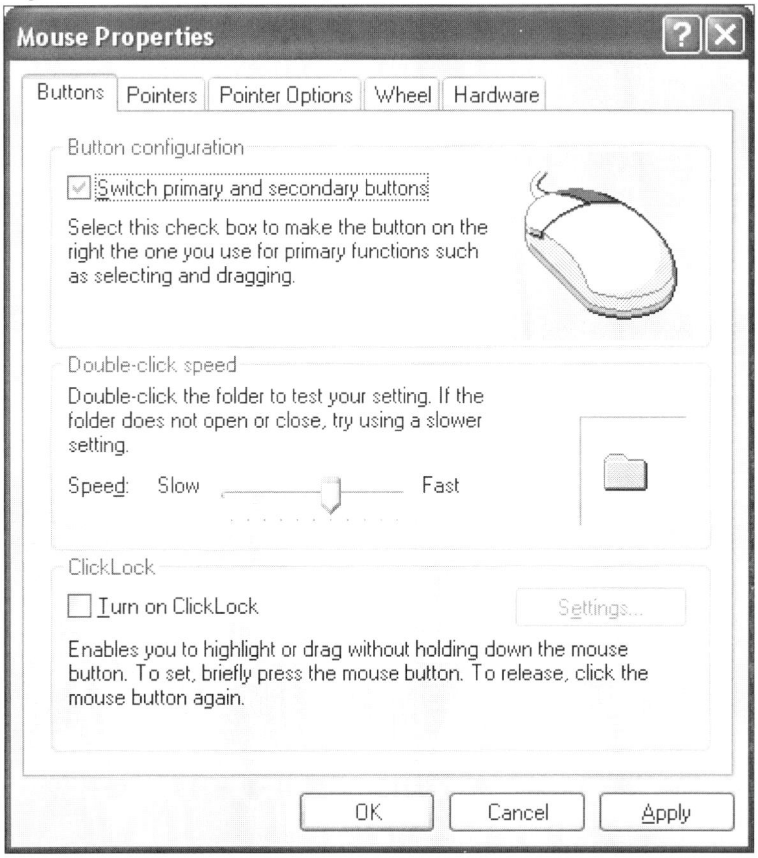

project 10.4

Configuring and Troubleshooting I/O Devices *(cont'd)*

exam objective

Configure and troubleshoot I/O devices. Answer end-user questions related to configuring I/O devices. Configure and troubleshoot device settings.

project steps

15. Enter the name of the modem in the **Search for** field and click **Go** to conduct a product search.

16. View the search results to see whether the modem is listed as **Designed for Windows XP (Figure 10-12)**.

17. Close Internet Explorer.

Figure 10-12 Search results for modem displayed on the Windows Catalog page

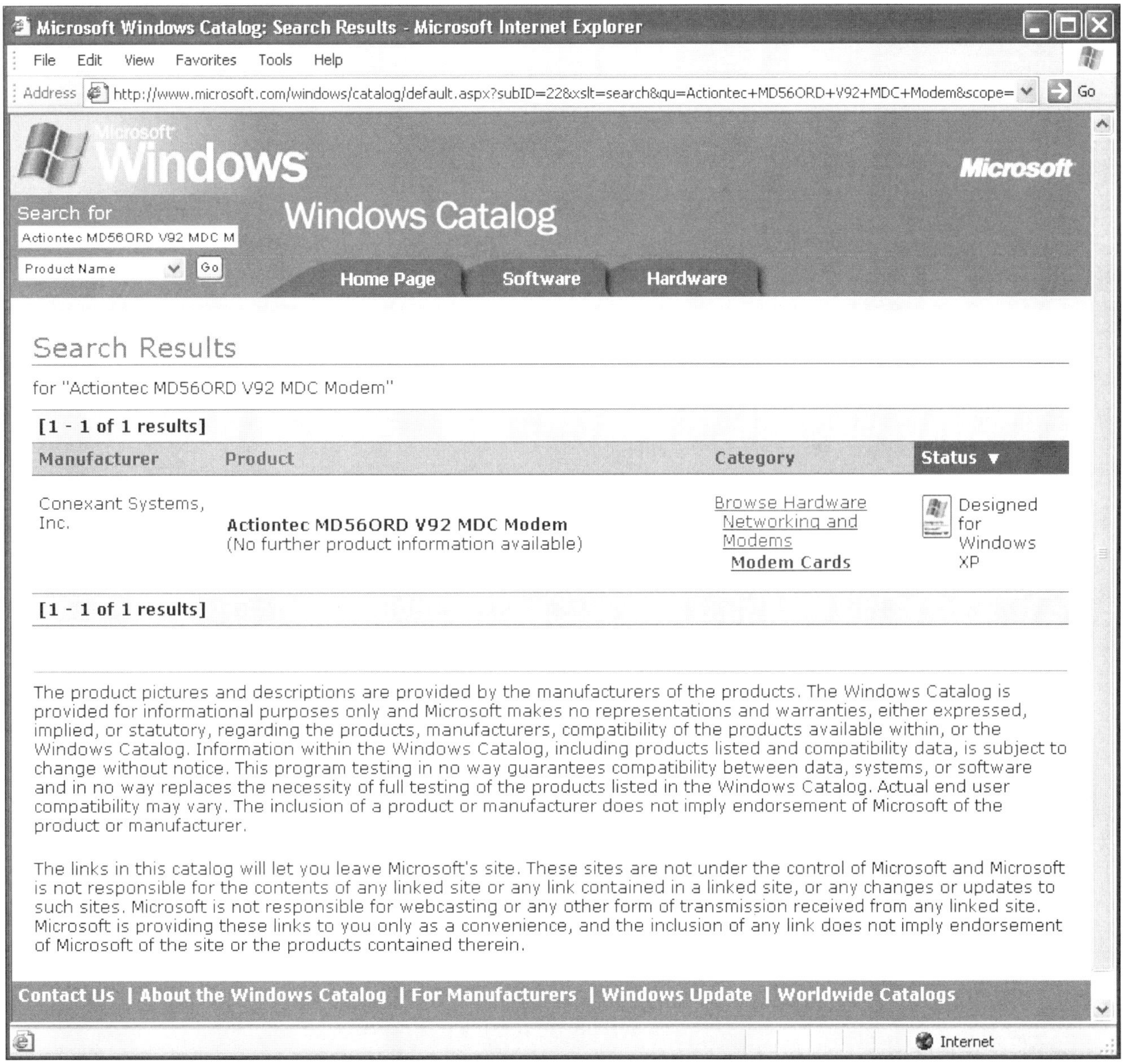

project 10.5

Configuring and Troubleshooting Universal Serial Bus (USB) Devices

exam objective

Configure and troubleshoot I/O devices. Answer end-user questions related to configuring I/O devices. Configure and troubleshoot devices settings.

overview

A project director at the City Hospital branch office needs a USB color inkjet printer installed. You turn on the printer and follow the instructions for installing the printer.

learning objective

After completing this project, you will be more familiar with installing a USB device.

specific requirements

See General Requirements.

estimated completion time

15 minutes

project steps

1. Plug the printer into the USB port and turn on the printer. A **Found New Hardware** message balloon opens from the system tray (**Figure 10-13**).
2. After a few moments, the **Found New Hardware Wizard** opens. Leave the **Install the software automatically (Recommended)** option button selected. If you have a disk containing the device drivers, insert the disk (**Figure 10-14**).
3. Click **Next**. The wizard searches for the proper device driver. When the driver is located, the wizard installs the necessary software.
4. The **Completing the Found New Hardware Wizard** screen opens (**Figure 10-15**).
5. Click **Finish** to complete the installation of the printer.
6. Your USB printer may run its own installation setup program. When all of the files have been installed and the installation is complete, click **Finish**.
7. Click **Start**, right-click **My Computer**, and select **Properties** to open the **System Properties** dialog box.
8. Click the **Hardware** tab.
9. Click the **Device Manager** button to open the **Device Manager** console.
10. Double-click the **Universal Serial Bus controllers** node. **USB Printing Support** is now listed (**Figure 10-16**).
11. Close the Device Manager.
12. Close the System Properties dialog box.

Figure 10-13 The Found New Hardware balloon

Figure 10-14 The Found New Hardware Wizard

Figure 10-15 The Completing the Found New Hardware Wizard screen

Figure 10-16 Device Manager– USB Printing Support

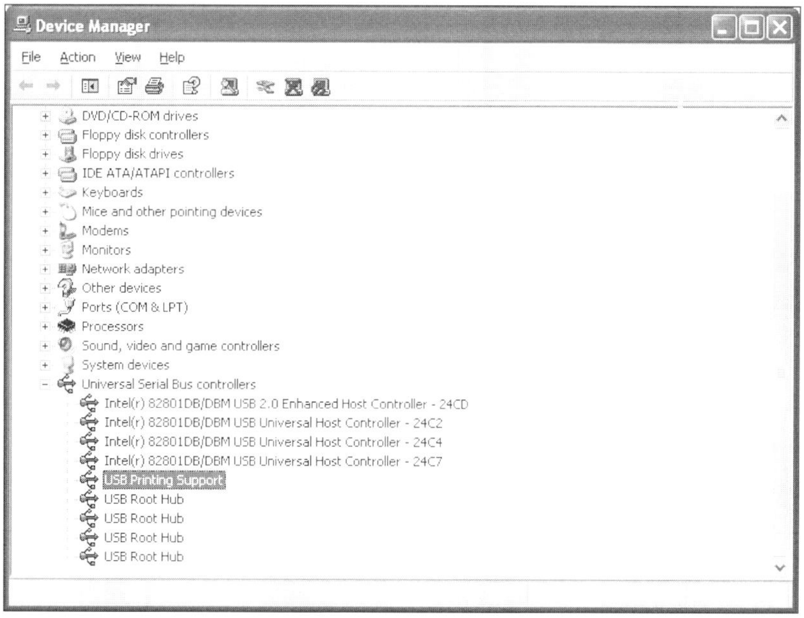

project 10.6

Troubleshooting Driver Signing

exam objective

Configure and troubleshoot I/O devices. Configure and troubleshoot device drivers for I/O devices.

overview

To help ensure a stable operating environment for all of the computers used by City Hospital employees, you implement a policy requiring that all device driver files have passed the Microsoft Certification process. You decide to run the File Signature Verification utility (sigverif) to view the unsigned driver files installed on various workstations. You also decide to save the sigverif.txt log file to disk so that you can evaluate all of the files at a later time.

learning objective

After completing this project, you will be more familiar with driver signing and using sigverif.exe.

specific requirements

See General Requirements. You should be logged on as Administrator, the default administrator account created during Windows XP installation.

estimated completion time

15 minutes

project steps

1. Click **Start** and then **Run** to open the **Run** dialog box.
2. Type **Sigverif** in the **Open** text box and click **OK** to open the **File Signature Verification** dialog box (**Figure 10-17).**
3. Click the **Start** button to search for unsigned driver files on the system.
4. If the computer has the default installation of Windows XP Professional, a message box opens indicating that all files are digitally signed. Skip to Step 6. If the **Signature Verification Results** dialog box opens, scroll through the list of unsigned drivers (**Figure 10-18**).
5. Click the **Close** button to exit the Signature Verification Results dialog box.
6. Click the **Advanced** button to open the **Advanced File Signature Verification Settings** dialog box.
7. Click the **Logging** tab (**Figure10-19**).
8. Click the **View Log** button to open the log in **Notepad (Figure 10-20)**.
9. In Notepad, open the **File** menu and select **Save As** to open the **Save As** dialog box. Save the **Sigverif.txt** file to a convenient location for further analysis and close the file.
10. Click **OK** to close the Advanced File Signature Verification Settings dialog box.
11. Click the **Close** button to close the File Signature Verification dialog box.

tip

Users can change driver signing installation behavior to make it more restrictive, but they cannot make it less restrictive. Only the Administrator can make the driver signing installation options less restrictive.

Figure 10-17 File Signature Verification dialog box

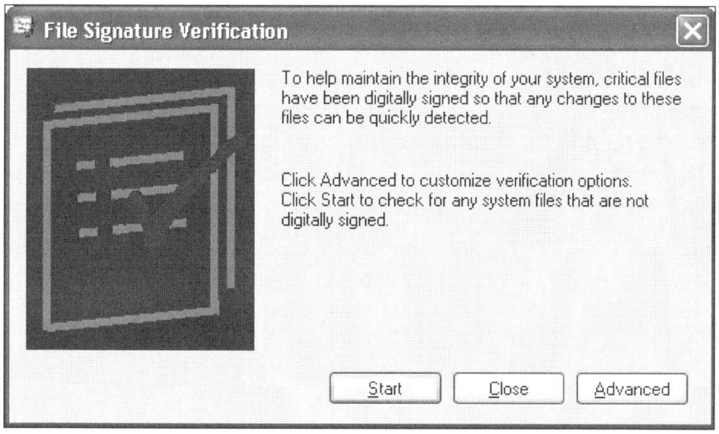

Figure 10-18 Signature Verification Results dialog box

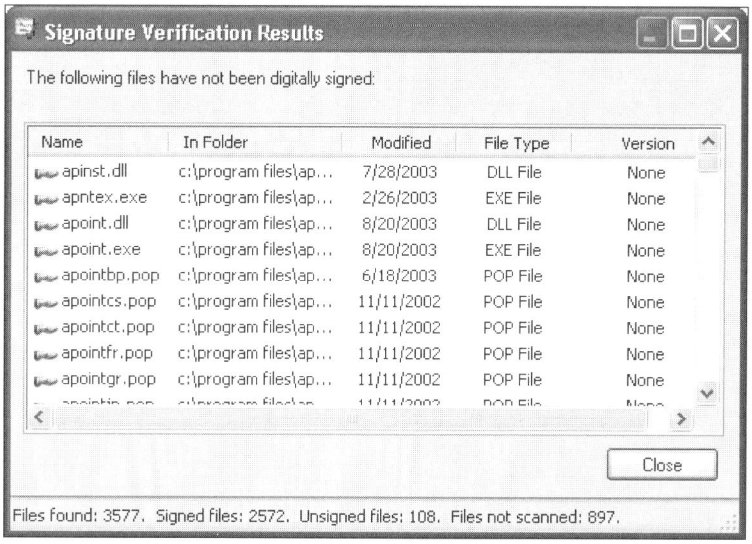

Figure 10-19 Advanced File Signature Verification Settings–Logging tab

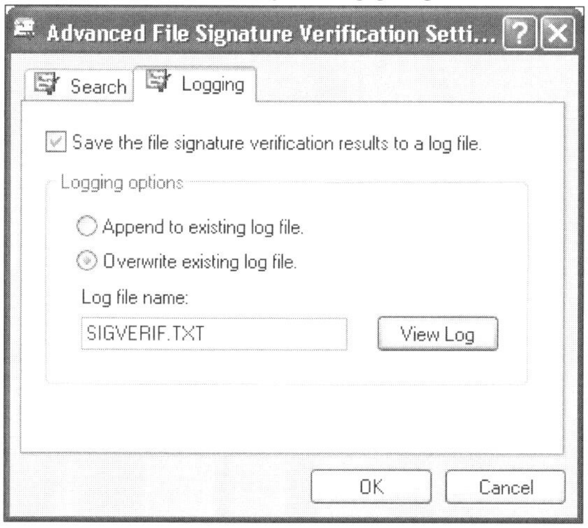

Figure 10-20 Sigverif file in Notepad

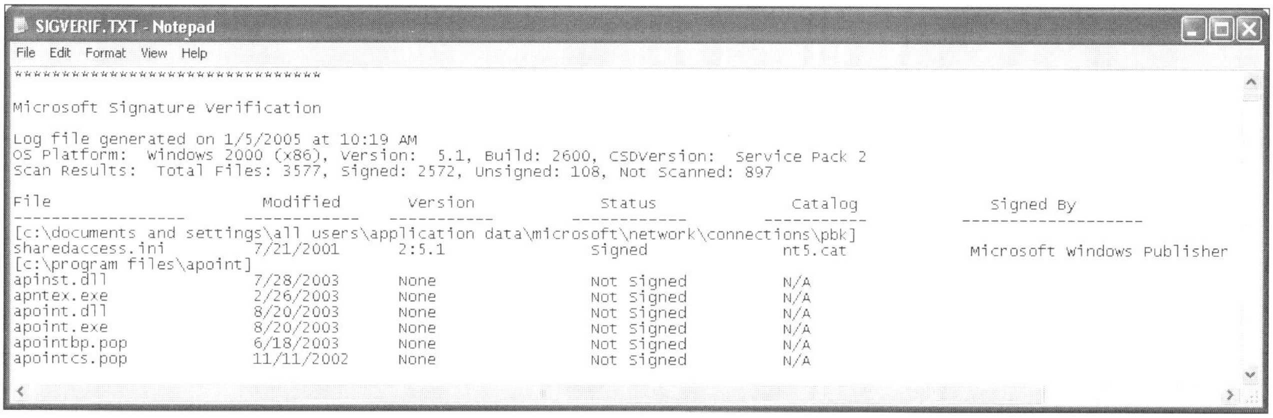

project 10.7

Configuring and Troubleshooting Hardware Profiles

exam objective

Configure and troubleshoot I/O devices. Configure and troubleshoot hardware profiles.

overview

One of the sales representatives at the City Hospital branch frequently uses his laptop at his home office. You decide to create a home office hardware profile so he can switch between the hardware profile for his office and the hardware profile he uses at home.

learning objective

After completing this project, you will be more familiar with configuring hardware profiles.

specific requirements

See General Requirements.

estimated completion time

30 minutes

project steps

1. Click **Start**, right-click **My Computer**, and click **Properties** to open the **System Properties** dialog box.
2. Click the **Hardware** tab.
3. Click the **Hardware Profiles** button to open the **Hardware Profiles** dialog box (**Figure 10-21**).
4. If **Profile 1** is not selected, select it and click the **Rename** button to open the **Rename Profile** dialog box.
5. Type **City Hospital** in the **To** text box and click **OK** to close the **Rename Profile** dialog box.
6. Click the **Copy** button to open the **Copy Profile** dialog box.
7. Type a name for the profile, **Home Office**, in the **To** text box (**Figure 10-22**).
8. Click **OK** to close the Copy Profile dialog box.
9. In the **Hardware Profiles** dialog box, select the **Wait until I select a hardware profile** option button.
10. Click **OK** to close the Hardware Profiles dialog box.
11. Click **OK** to close the System Properties dialog box.
12. Restart the computer. When the computer restarts, it waits until you select a hardware profile before booting up. Use the arrow keys to select **Home Office** and press [**Enter**].
13. You can now disable drivers that are not used at the user's home office. To disable a printer port, click **Start**, right-click **My Computer**, and click **Properties** to open the **System Properties** dialog box.
14. Click the **Hardware** tab.
15. Click the **Device Manager** button to open the **Device Manager**.
16. Double-click the **Ports** (**COM & LPT**) node to expand it.
17. Double-click **ECP Printer Port** (**LPT1**) to open the **ECP Printer Port** (**LPT1**) **Properties** dialog box.
18. In the **Device Usage** list box, select **Do not use this device in the current hardware profile (disable)** (**Figure 10-23**).
19. Click **OK** to close the ECP Printer Port (LPT1) dialog box. A red **X** appears over the disabled printer port.
20. Close the Device Manager.
21. Close the System Properties dialog box.

Figure 10-21 Hardware Profiles dialog box

Figure 10-22 Creating a new profile name

Figure 10-23 Disabling a device for the current hardware profile

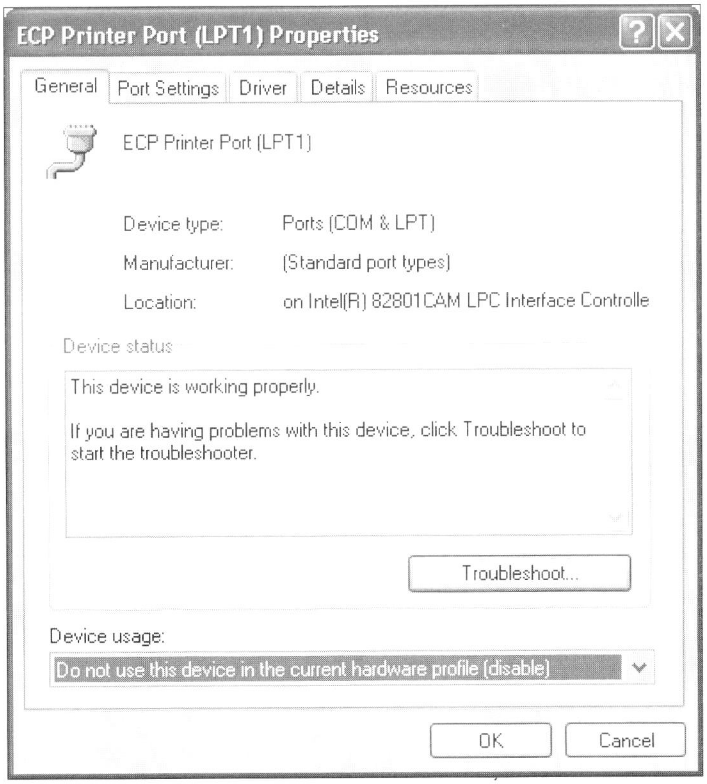

LESSON

11 Configuring and Troubleshooting the Desktop and User Environment

Computer workstations configured to meet the personal needs of individual users can improve productivity and enhance job performance. Windows XP provides numerous options that allow administrators and users to customize interface settings, thereby enhancing the digital working environment. If you take full advantage of these features, you can configure Windows XP to allow users to quickly log on to their systems and access their most important files in just one or two clicks of the mouse.

On Windows XP, you can enhance users' working environment by customizing setup options for the Start menu and Taskbar. The Start menu allows you to quickly access frequently used applications. Taskbar settings allow you to control the Taskbar appearance and provide Quick Launch buttons to instantly launch applications.

Using Windows XP Control Panel utilities, you can change accessibility options for users with special needs, such as altering settings for controlling the mouse and keyboard. You can also customize regional and language settings. This enables users to view date, time, or currencies in different formats or to view text in different language settings.

This lesson provides practice configuring the Windows XP user interface and desktop environment. You will practice configuring the Start menu and taskbar and changing the user interface options available in the Control Panel.

Scenario

You have been asked to customize Windows XP desktops at City Hospital's volunteer fundraising division. Because several of the workers in this department are elderly, you must take special care that the user interface settings meet their special needs.

Lesson 11 Configuring and Troubleshooting the Desktop and User Environment	
Project	***Exam 70-271 Objective***
11.1 Configuring and Troubleshooting Task and Toolbar Settings	**Configure the user environment**. Answer end-user questions related to configuring the desktop and user environment. Configure and troubleshoot task and toolbar settings.
11.2 Configuring and Troubleshooting Accessibility Options	**Configure the user environment**. Answer end-user questions related to configuring the desktop and user environment. Configure and troubleshoot accessibility options.
11.3 Configuring and Troubleshooting Keyboard and Pointing Device Settings	**Configure the user environment**. Answer end-user questions related to configuring the desktop and user environment. Configure and troubleshoot pointing device settings.
11.4 Configuring Welcome Screen Settings	**Configure the user environment**. Answer end-user questions related to configuring the desktop and user environment.
11.5 Configuring Regional and Language Options	**Configure support for multiple languages or multiple locations**. Answer end-user questions related to regional settings. Configure and troubleshoot regional settings. Answer end-user questions related to language settings. Configure and troubleshoot language settings.

General Requirements

To complete the projects in this lesson, you will need administrative rights on a Windows XP Professional computer. For Project 10.4, the computer must be a standalone computer or a member of a workgroup. You may also find it helpful to refer to Lesson 11 in your Prentice Hall Certification Series Exam 70-271 textbook for further information about the topics covered by the projects in this lesson.

project 11.1

Configuring and Troubleshooting Task and Toolbar Settings

exam objective

Configure the user environment. Answer end-user questions related to configuring the desktop and user environment. Configure and troubleshoot task and toolbar settings.

overview

You need to set up workstations for several users who have limited computer knowledge. You do not want them to access the Control Panel or the Help and Support Center from the Start menu. Nevertheless, you want them to be able to quickly access specific programs and their own documents. You decide to remove the Control Panel and the Windows Help and Support Center from the Start menu. You will also add Quick Launch programs and add a toolbar to the taskbar to enable users to quickly open their My Documents folders.

learning objective

After completing this project, you will know how to change Start menu and taskbar settings.

specific requirements

See General Requirements.

estimated completion time

15 minutes

project steps

1. Right-click **Start** and click **Properties** to open the **Taskbar and Start Menu Properties** dialog box on the **Start Menu** tab **(Figure 11-1)**.
2. Click the **Customize** button to open the **Customize Start Menu** dialog box.
3. Click the **Advanced** tab.
4. In the **Start menu items** list box, under **Control Panel**, select the **Don't display this item** option button **(Figure 11-2)**.
5. Scroll down the **Start menu items** list and clear the **Help and Support** link.
6. Click **OK** to close the Customize Start Menu dialog box.
7. In the **Taskbar and Start Menu Properties** dialog box, click the **Taskbar** tab.
8. Click the **Show Quick Launch** check box to select it, if necessary.
9. Click the **Hide inactive icons** check box **(Figure 11-3)**.
10. Click **OK** to close the Taskbar and Start Menu Properties dialog box. If desired, you can drag shortcut icons to the Quick Launch area of the taskbar.
11. Right-click the **Taskbar**, point to **Toolbars**, and select **New Toolbar** to open the **New Toolbar** dialog box.
12. Select **My Documents** and click **OK** to close the **New Toolbar** dialog box **(Figure 11-4)**.
13. The My Documents toolbar is added to the taskbar. Click the double-arrow to view the folders and documents in the My Documents folder.
14. Reopen the **Customize Start Menu** dialog box on the **Advanced** tab and reverse the changes to perform Project 11.2 on the same computer.
15. Close the Customize Start Menu and the Taskbar and Start Menu Properties dialog boxes.

Figure 11-1 Taskbar and Start Menu Properties dialog box

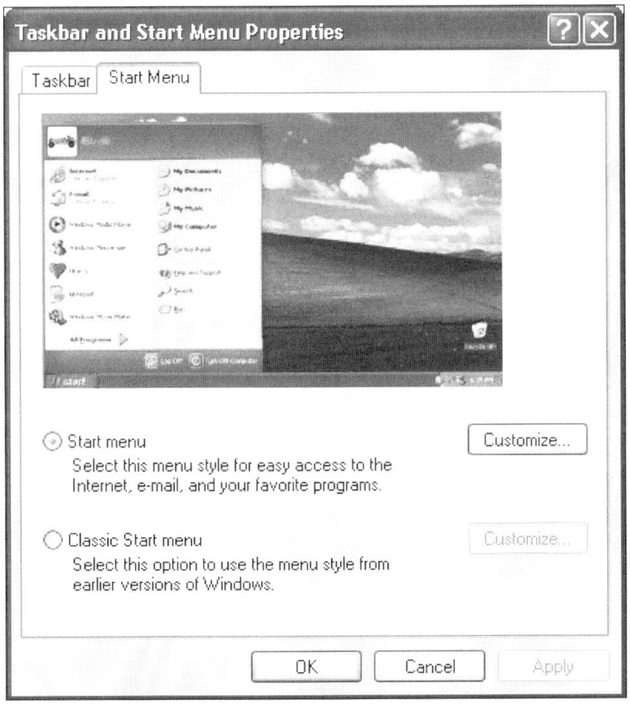

Figure 11-2 Advanced tab in the Customize Start Menu dialog box

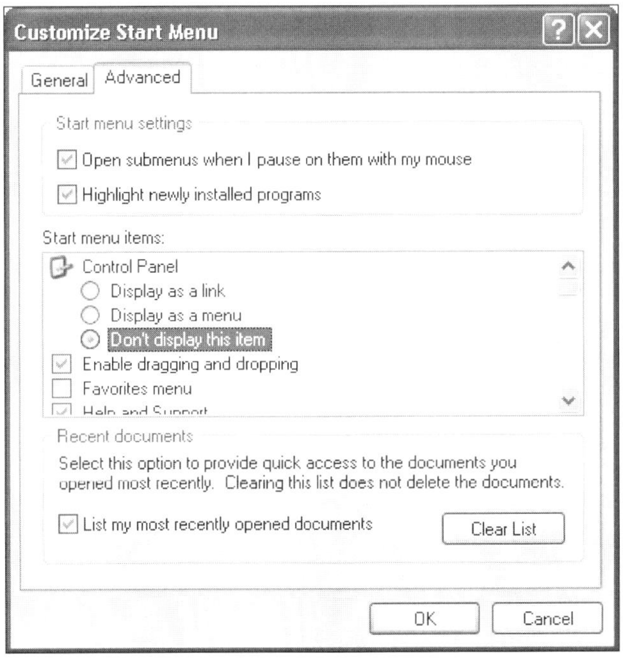

Figure 11-3 Taskbar tab

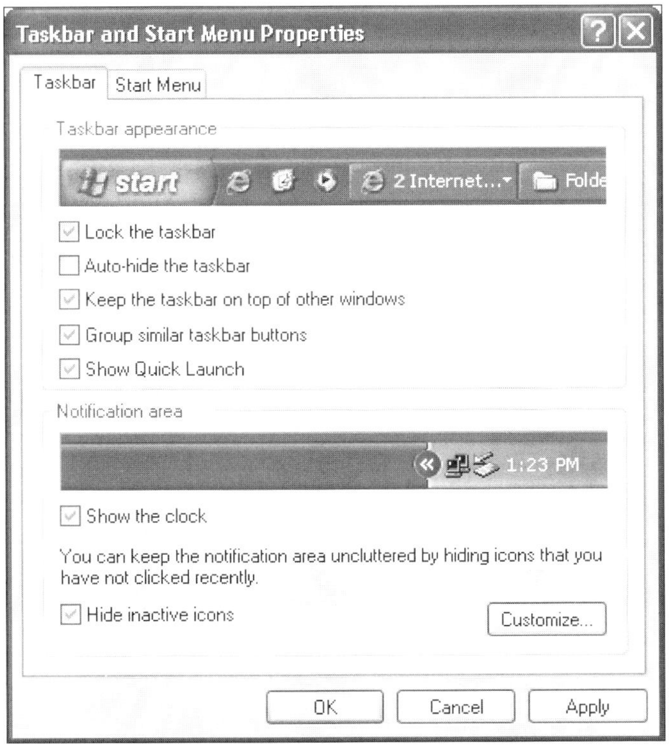

Figure 11-4 Creating a toolbar for My Documents

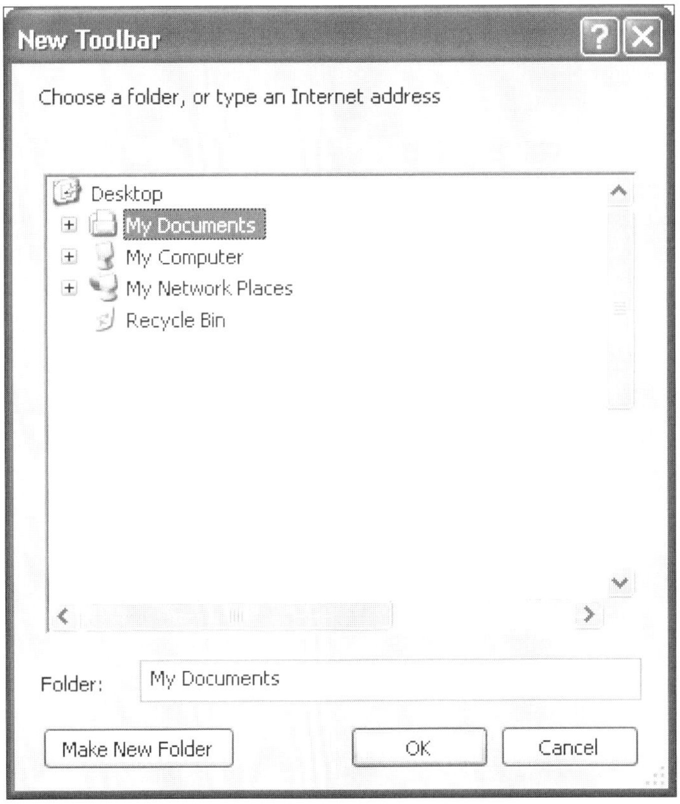

project 11.2

Configuring and Troubleshooting Accessibility Options

exam objective

Configure the user environment. Answer end-user questions related to configuring the desktop and user environment. Configure and troubleshoot accessibility options.

overview

Several users in the fundraising department have minor hearing, sight, and motor disabilities. You decide to set up a workstation for these users so that, if they do not lift their fingers from the keyboard keys quickly enough, keystrokes will not be repeated. You will also set up a visual warning for hearing-impaired users so that a visual alert appears when the computer emits a sound.

learning objective

After completing this project, you will know how to change keyboard and sound accessibility options.

specific requirements

See General Requirements.

estimated completion time

15 minutes

project steps

1. Click **Start** and select **Control Panel** to open the **Control Panel** window.
2. In **Category view**, click the **Accessibility Options** link to open the **Accessibility Options** window.
3. Under **or pick a Control Panel icon**, click the **Accessibility Options** link to open the **Accessibility Options** dialog box.
4. On the **Keyboard** tab in the **FilterKeys** section, select the **Use FilterKeys** check box **(Figure 11-5)**.
5. Click the **Settings** button to open the **Settings for FilterKeys** dialog box.
6. To test the change, click in the **Click and type here to test FilterKey settings** text box and press and hold down a key **(Figure 11-6)**.
7. Click **OK** to close the Settings for FilterKeys dialog box.
8. Click the **Sound** tab.
9. Select the **Use SoundSentry** check box.
10. In the **Choose the visual warning** list box, select **Flash active window (Figure 11-7)**.
11. Click the **General** tab.
12. In the **Administrative options** section, select the **Apply all settings to logon desktop** check box.
13. Click the **Cancel** button to close the Accessibility Options dialog box without saving the changes.
14. Close the Accessibility Options window.

Figure 11-5 Accessibility Options dialog box - Keyboard tab

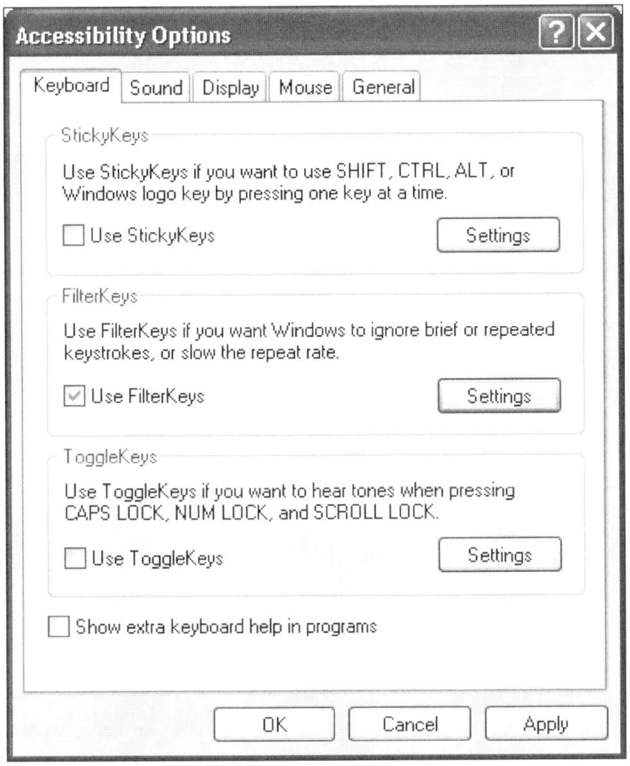

Figure 11-6 The Settings for FilterKeys dialog box

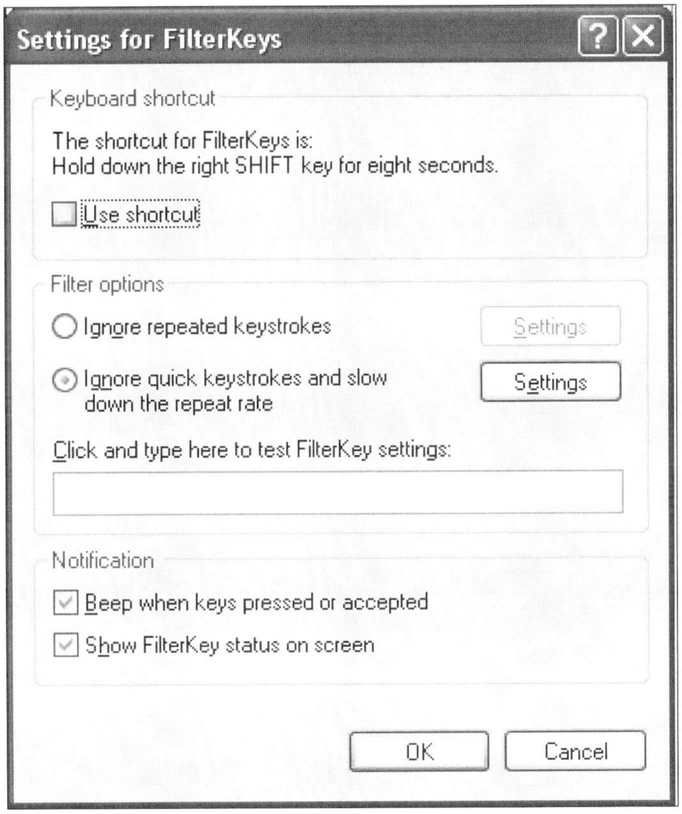

Figure 11-7 Accessibility Options dialog box - Sound tab

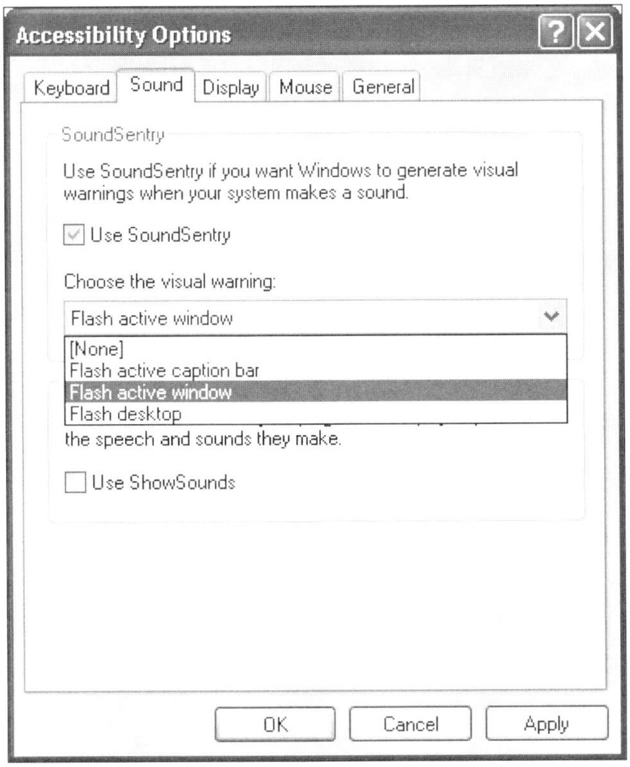

project 11.3

Configuring and Troubleshooting Keyboard and Pointing Device Settings

exam objective

Configure the user environment. Answer end-user questions related to configuring the desktop and user environment. Configure and troubleshoot pointing device settings.

overview

One of the users in the City Hospital fundraising department types very slowly and often loses track of the mouse pointer as he works. You decide to change the keyboard and mouse settings to make it easier for this user to type and work.

learning objective

After completing this project, you will be more familiar with using the Keyboard Properties and Mouse Properties dialog boxes.

specific requirements

See General Requirements.

estimated completion time

15 minutes

project steps

1. Click **Start** and select **Control Panel** to open the **Control Panel** window.
2. In **Category view**, click the **Printers and Other Hardware** link.
3. Under **or pick a Control Panel icon**, click the **Keyboard** link to open the **Keyboard Properties** dialog box on the **Speed** tab **(Figure 11-8)**.
4. Drag the **Repeat delay** slider one tick back toward **Long** on the slider bar to increase the amount of time that elapses before a character repeats when a user holds down a key.
5. Drag the **Repeat rate** slider back toward **Slow** to decrease the speed at which a character repeats when a user holds down a key.
6. Click **OK** to apply the changes and close the Keyboard Properties dialog box.
7. Under **or pick a Control Panel icon**, click the **Mouse** link to open the **Mouse Properties** dialog box.
8. Click the **Pointer Options** tab (**Figure 11-9**).
9. In the **Visibility** section, select the **Display pointer trails** check box.
10. Drag the slider midway between **Short** and **Long**.
11. Click **OK** to apply the changes and close the Mouse Properties dialog box.
12. Close the Printers and Other Hardware window.

Figure 11-8 The Keyboard Properties dialog box - Speed tab

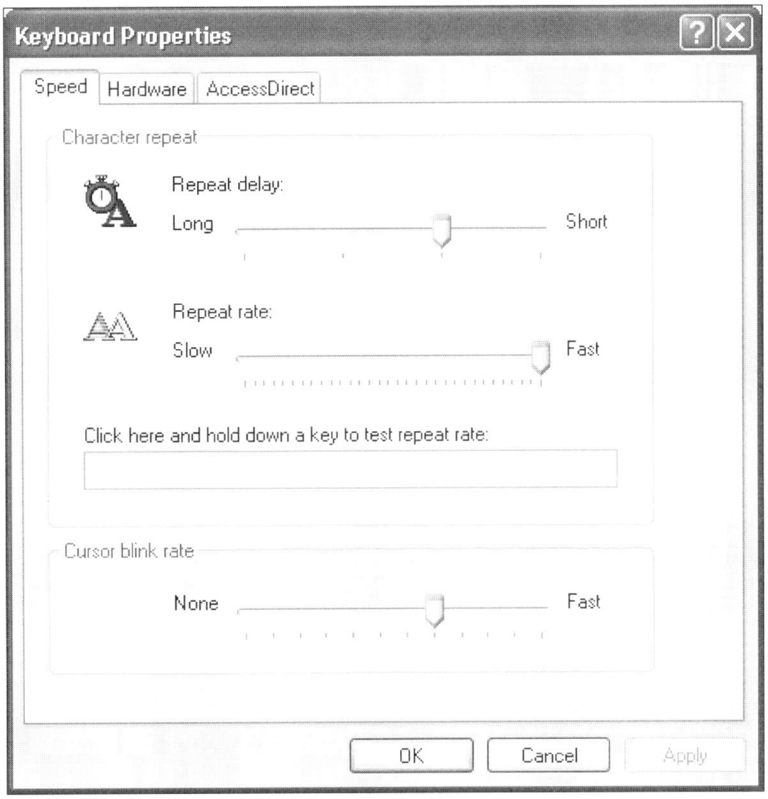

Figure 11-9 The Mouse Properties dialog box - Pointer Options tab

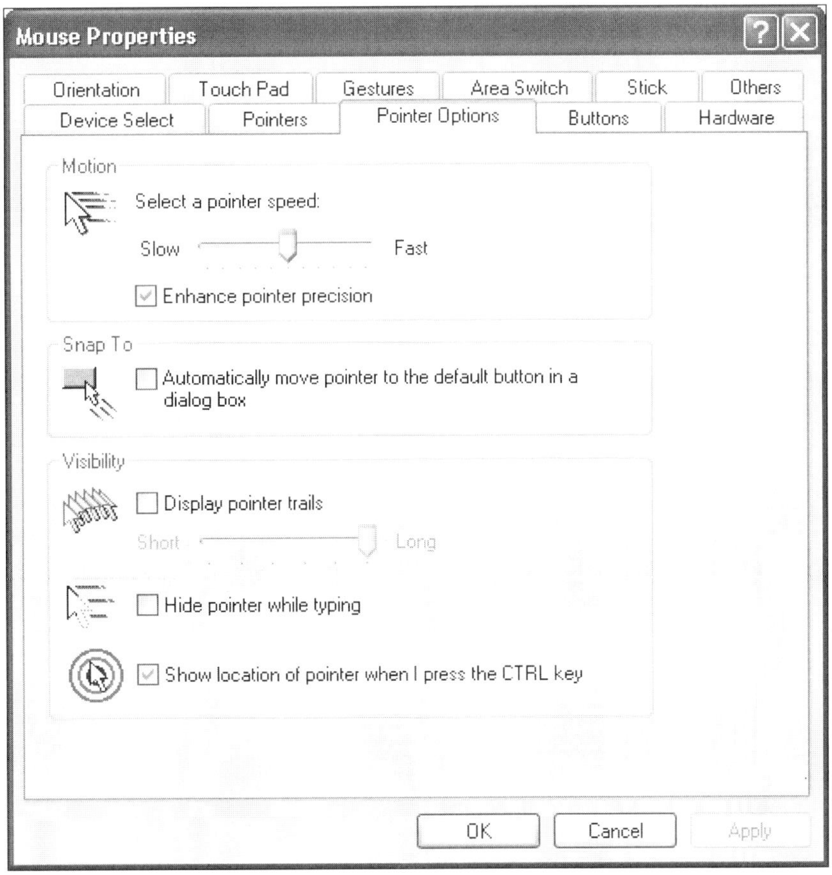

project 11.4 Configuring Welcome Screen Settings

exam objective

Configure the user environment. Answer end-user questions related to configuring the desktop and user environment.

overview

Several users at a doctor's office, which has a workgroup setting, ask you to change their user logon names on the Windows XP Welcome screen. They also want you to change the logon picture associated with their names. Some users like sports themes, and other users like nature themes. You want everybody to be happy with his or her work environment, so you decide to reconfigure their user accounts to satisfy their wishes.

learning objective

After completing this project, you will know how to modify the user Welcome screen.

specific requirements

A Windows XP Professional computer that is a standalone computer or a member of a workgroup

estimated completion time

15 minutes

project steps

To change user account options on a standalone computer running Windows XP Professional or a computer running Windows XP Professional that is a member of a workgroup, perform the following steps:

1. Click **Start** and select **Control Panel** to open the **Control Panel** window.
2. In **Category view**, click the **User Accounts** link to open the **User Accounts** window.
3. Click the **Change an account** link to view the **Pick an Account to change** window.
4. Click the account you want to edit to open the **What do you want to change about <*username*> account?** screen (**Figure 11-10**).
5. Click the **Change the name** link to view the **Provide a new name for <*username*> account** screen.
6. Type a new name for the user in the **Type a new name for <*username*>** text box (**Figure 11-11**).
7. Click the **Change Name** button to change the name and return to the previous screen.
8. Click the **Change the picture** link to view the **Pick a new picture for <*username*> account** screen.
9. Select the picture you want to associate with the account (**Figure 11-12**).
10. Click the **Change Picture** button to change the picture and return to the **What do you want to change about <*username*> account** screen.
11. Close the User Accounts window and the Control Panel.

Figure 11-10 Changing user account options

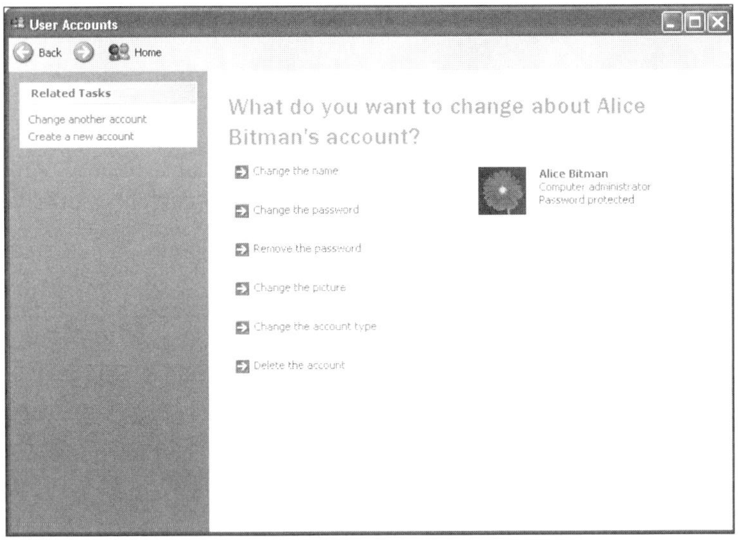

Figure 11-11 Changing the user account name

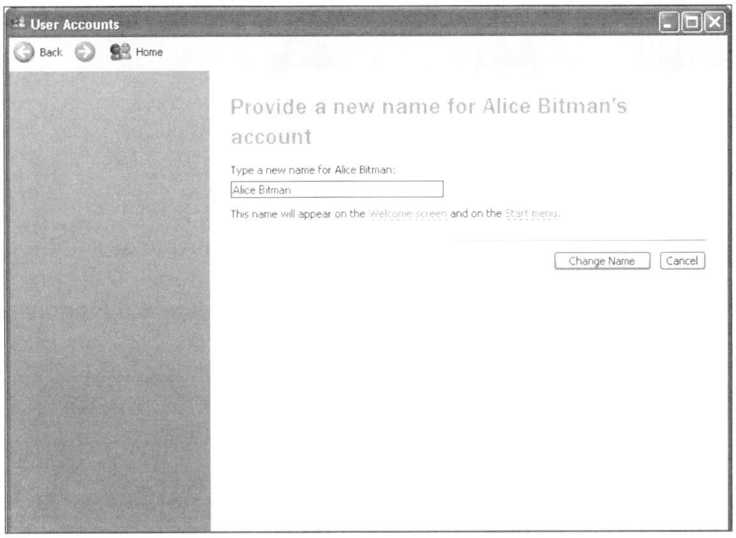

Figure 11-12 Picking a new picture for a user account

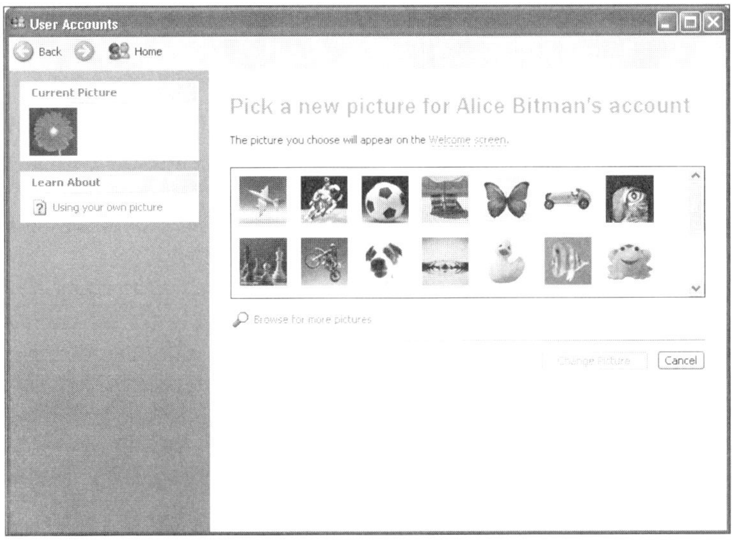

project 11.5

Configuring Regional and Language Options

exam objective

Configure support for multiple languages or multiple locations. Answer end-user questions related to regional settings. Configure and troubleshoot regional settings. Answer end-user questions related to language settings. Configure and troubleshoot language settings.

overview

One of the users in the City Hospital fundraising department is working on a project with a Canadian hospital. To make it easier for her to correspond with her colleagues in Canada, you decide to change the regional settings to French (Canada) and configure the Windows XP workstation so she can quickly switch between English and French keyboard assignments.

learning objective

After completing this project, you will be more familiar with the settings in the Regional and Language Options dialog box.

specific requirements

See General Requirements.

estimated completion time

15 minutes

project steps

1. Click **Start** and select **Control Panel** to open the **Control Panel** window.
2. In **Category view**, click the **Date, Time, Language, and Regional** Options link to open the **Date, Time, Language, and Regional Options** window.
3. Under or **pick a Control Panel icon**, click the **Regional and Language Options** link to open the **Regional and Language Options** dialog box.
4. On the **Regional Options** tab, in the **Standards and Formats** section select **French (Canada)** in the list box **(Figure 11-13)**.
5. Click the **Languages** tab.
6. Click the **Details** button to open the **Text Services and Input Languages** dialog box **(Figure 11-14)**.
7. In the **Installed services** section, click the **Add** button to open the **Add Input language** dialog box.
8. In the **Input** language list box, select **French (Canada) (Figure 11-15)**.
9. Click **OK** to close the **Add Input language** dialog box.
10. In the **Text Services and Input Languages** dialog box, click the **Apply** button to add **French (Canada)** to the installed input language services.
11. Click the **Language Bar** button to open the **Language Bar Settings** dialog box. These are the default settings for the **Language** bar.
12. Click **OK** to close the Language Bar Settings dialog box.
13. Click the **Key Settings** button to open the **Advanced Key Settings** dialog box. Here, you can change the keyboard shortcuts that are used to switch between input languages **(Figure 11-16)**.
14. Click **OK** to close the Advanced Key Settings dialog box.
15. Click **OK** to close the Text Services and Input Languages dialog box.
16. Click **OK** to close the Regional and Language Options dialog box.
17. Close the Date, Time, Language, and Regional Options window.
18. To see the different keyboard settings in action, open Microsoft Word and click the **EN** icon on the Taskbar.
19. Click **French (Canada)** to access the French-Canadian keyboard settings **(Figure 11-17)**.
20. Close Word.

Figure 11-13 French (Canada) chosen on the Regional Options tab

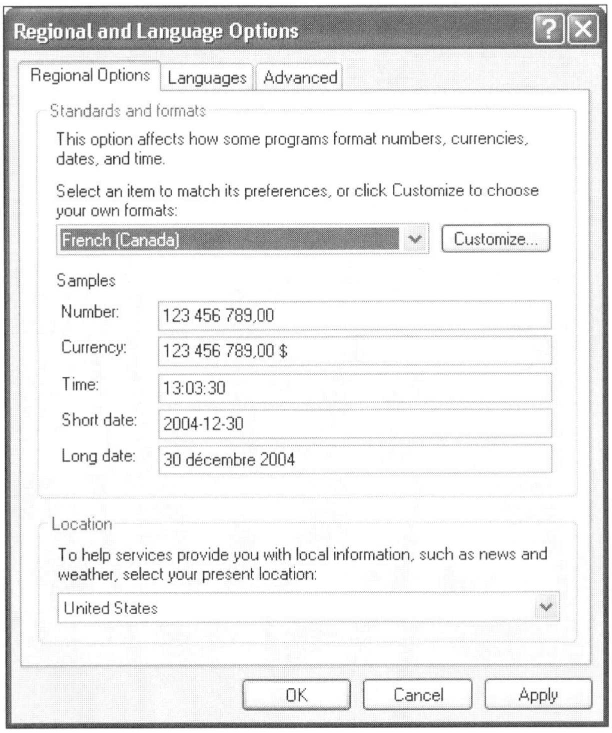

Figure 11-14 Text Services and Input Languages dialog box

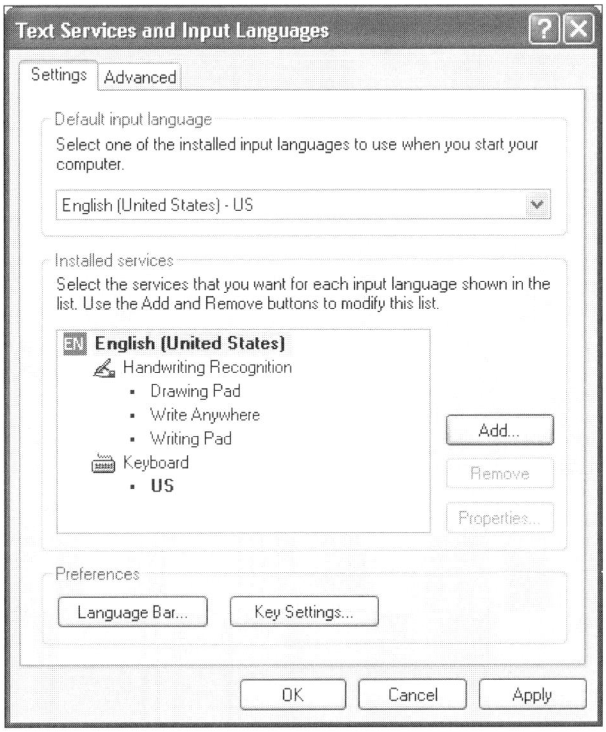

Figure 11-15 Choosing an input language

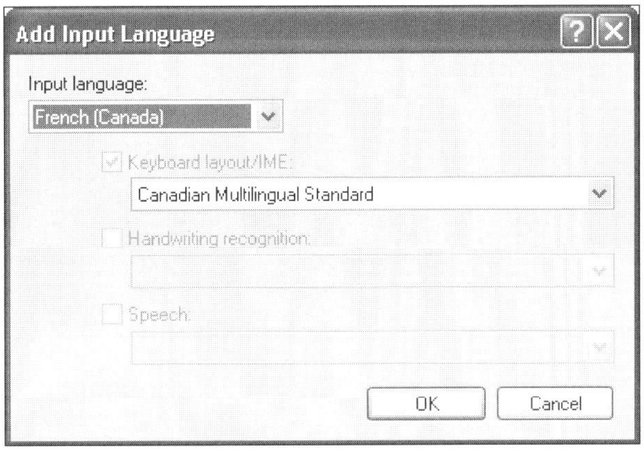

Figure 11-16 The Advanced Key Settings dialog box

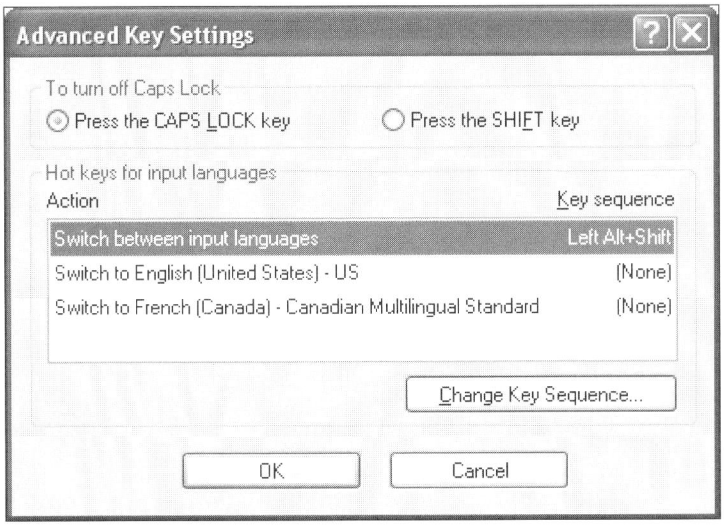

Figure 11-17 The Language bar

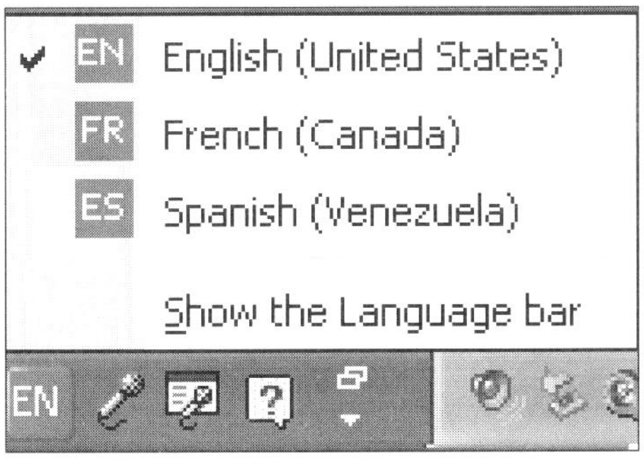

LESSON

12 Configuring and Troubleshooting Security

With megabytes of financial data and intellectual property stored on computers today, maintaining tight security policies has become essential for most modern companies, both large and small. However, security must be configured carefully. Too little security can lead to corrupted data and the loss of confidential information. Too much security can result in loss of productivity.

When you configure client security, you should always attempt to follow the principle of least privilege. The principle of least privilege stipulates that you grant users the absolute minimum levels of access needed to perform their duties. This is one of the best techniques for ensuring data security and confidentiality.

In Windows XP, Group Policies are used to configure and control the work environment for users. Many of the Group policy settings are implemented in the Registry, whereas others can be used to control the application of scripts as well as provide additional security options. Group policies are configured in the Group Policy snap-in. There are two nodes in the Group Policy snap-in: the User Configuration node and the Computer Configuration node. Group policy settings that affect the computer environment implement changes in the operating system settings, hardware, services, and much more. There are three main Computer Configuration setting nodes.

- **Software Settings:** Used to specify which applications will be distributed to users via Group Policy Objects (GPOs).
- **Windows Settings:** Divided into Scripts and Security Settings. The Security Setting node controls account lockout policy, password policy, user rights, audit policy, public\ key access, Registry and event log access, and system service operation. Scripts are used to assign scripts and batch files that are configured to run at specific times, such as during system startup or shutdown. In the User Configuration node, scripts run when users logon or logoff.
- **Administrative Templates:** Used to regulate Registry settings that control the behavior and appearance of the desktop and other Windows components and applications.

Group policy settings that affect the user environment include shortcuts, color schemes, access to Control Panel utilities, and other desktop settings. As with the Computer Configuration node, there are three main User Configuration setting nodes: Software Settings, Windows Settings and Administrative Templates.

Many of the features of Group policy are available only in domain-based group policies within Active Directory. However, you can still control many aspects of a Windows 2000 or greater system by editing the local policy on the system.

Perhaps the best way to become familiar with the vast array of policy settings is to open the Microsoft Management Console and the Group Policy snap-in. Here you can view the policy settings and review specific policy information in the Details pane. After you determine the level of security required for a computer, you can use a security template to set specify security policy for the computer.

This lesson provides practice configuring security settings in Windows XP. You will practice customizing account policies and using security tools and templates. You will also practice troubleshooting logon and startup problems.

Scenario

You have been asked to review computer security for City Hospital. Users at the hospital often review confidential patient records. Several departments receive confidential information from pharmaceutical companies. It is essential that the hospital's patient business data remain secure. You have been called on to change the security settings at branch offices and change the logon policy settings to ensure corporate security.

Lesson 12 Configuring and Troubleshooting Security

Project	Exam 70-271 Objective
12.1 Configuring Local Security Policy	**Troubleshoot security settings and local security policy**. Answer end-user questions related to security settings.
12.2 Analyzing and Setting Local Security Policy	**Troubleshoot security settings and local security policy**. Answer end-user questions related to security settings.
12.3 Identifying End User Issues Caused by Local Security Policies	**Troubleshoot security settings and local security policy**. Identify end-user issues caused by local security policies such as Local Security Settings and Security Configuration and Analysis.
12.4 Configuring and Managing Local User Accounts	**Configure and troubleshoot local user and group accounts**. Answer end-user questions related to user accounts. Configure and troubleshoot local user accounts.
12.5 Configuring and Troubleshooting Local Group Accounts	**Configure and troubleshoot local user and group accounts**. Answer end-user questions related to user accounts. Configure and troubleshoot local user accounts.
12.6 Troubleshooting System Startup Problems	**Troubleshoot system startup and user logon problems**. Answer end-user questions related to system startup issues. Troubleshoot system startup problems.
12.7 Troubleshooting Local User Logon Issues	**Troubleshoot system startup and user logon problems**. Answer end-user questions related to user logon issues. Troubleshoot local user logon issues.
12.8 Troubleshooting Startup Issues	**Troubleshoot system startup and user logon problems**. Answer end-user questions related to system startup issues. Troubleshoot system startup problems.

General Requirements

To complete the projects in this lesson, you will need administrative rights on a Windows XP Professional computer that is a standalone computer or a member of a workgroup network. To complete Project 12.6, you will also need a network card, and to complete Project 12.8, you will need a floppy disk and a backup storage medium sufficient to store the backup files. You also may find it helpful to refer to Lesson 12 in your Prentice Hall Certification Series Exam 271 textbook for additional information about the topics covered by the projects in this lesson.

project 12.1 Configuring Local Security Policy

exam objective

Troubleshoot security settings and local security policy. Answer end-user questions related to security settings.

overview

You are at a hospital branch and want to make simple specific changes to the local security policy of the workstation. You want make passwords more secure and keep a log of users who log on to the computer. To strengthen password security, you implement a policy that requires user passwords to be at least nine characters long and consist of three of the following four character types: uppercase letters, lowercase letters, numbers, and symbols. You use the Group Policy console to change security settings.

learning objective

After completing this project, you will know how to change security settings in the Group Policy console.

specific requirements

See General Requirements.

estimated completion time

30 minutes

project steps

1. Click **Start** and then **Run** to open the **Run** dialog box.
2. Type **gpedit.msc** in the **Open** text box and press **[Enter]** to open the **Group Policy** console (**Figure 12-1**).
3. In the scope pane, double-click **Computer Configuration** to expand the node, if necessary.
4. Double-click **Windows Settings** to expand the node.
5. Double-click **Security Settings** to expand the node.
6. Expand the **Account Policies** node and then the **Password Policy** node.
7. In the details pane, double-click **Minimum password length** to open the **Minimum password length Properties policy** dialog box.
8. Enter **9** in the **Password must be at least** spin box and click **OK** to close the dialog box.
9. Double-click **Password must meet complexity requirements** to open the **Password must meet complexity requirements Properties** dialog box.
10. Click the **Enabled** option button (**Figure 12-2**).
11. Click **OK** to close the dialog box.
12. In the scope pane, double-click **Local Policies** and then **Audit Policies** to expand the nodes.
13. Double-click **Audit logon events** to open the **Audit logon events Properties** dialog box.
14. Make sure that the **Success** and **Failure** check boxes are selected and click **OK** to close the dialog box (**Figure 12-3**).
15. Close the Group Policy console.
16. Click **Start** and then **Control Panel** to open the **Control Panel**.
17. In **Category view**, click the **User Accounts** link to open the **User Accounts** window.
18. Click the **Change an account** link to open the **Pick an account to change** screen.
19. Select the **Test User** account you created in Project 7.3.
20. Click the **Change the password** link to open the **Change Test User's password** screen.
21. Type the password you set for Test User in Project 7.3 in the **Type your current password** text box.

Figure 12-1 Group Policy console

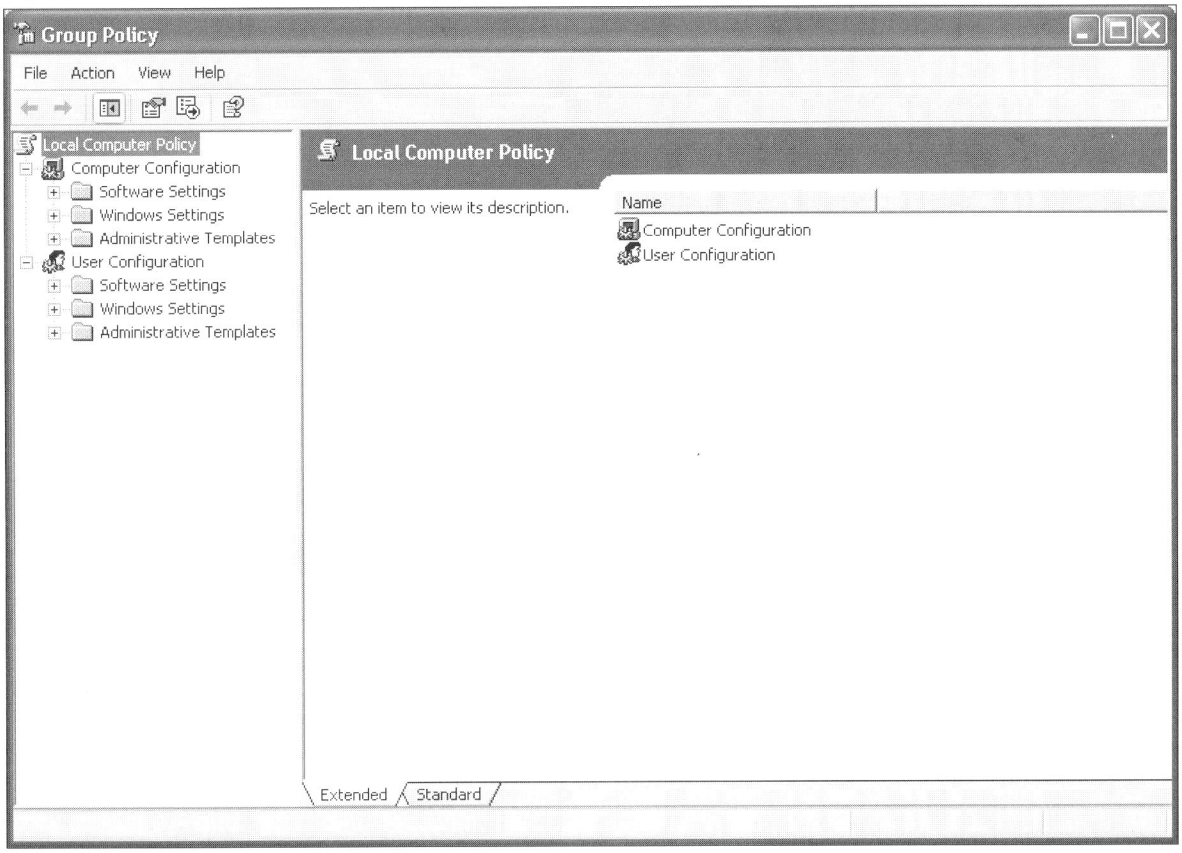

Figure 12-2 Enabling password complexity requirements

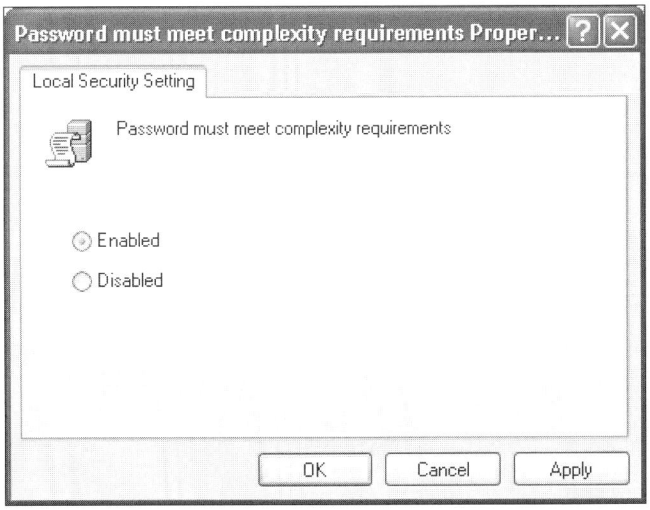

Figure 12-3 Auditing logon events

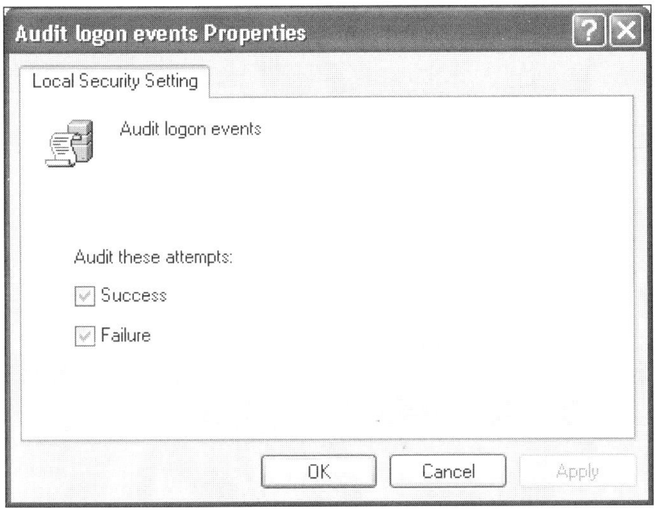

project 12.1

Configuring Local Security Policy

(cont'd)

exam objective

Troubleshoot security settings and local security policy. Answer end-user questions related to security settings.

project steps

22. Type a new password that is only eight letters long in the **Type a new password** and **Type the new password again to confirm** text boxes.
23. Click the **Change Password** button.
24. A **User Accounts** warning dialog box opens to inform you that the password does not meet the password policy requirements (**Figure 12-4).**
25. Click **OK** to close the User Accounts warning dialog box.
26. Type a new password that is at least nine characters long and that includes three of the four character types (upper case letters, lower case letters, digits, and non-alphanumeric characters) in the **Type a new password** and **Type the new password again to confirm** text boxes (**Figure 12-5**).
27. Click the **Change Password** button. The password should change successfully now.
28. Close the User Accounts window and the Control Panel.

Figure 12-4 User Accounts warning dialog box

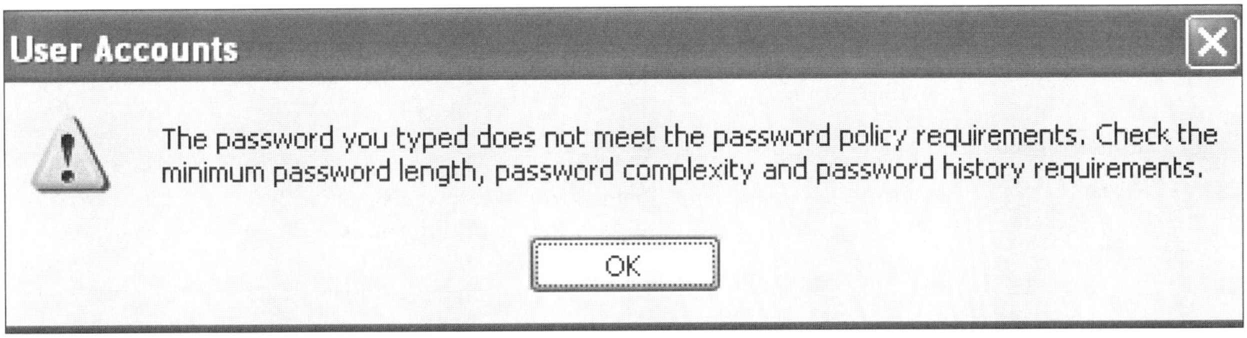

Figure 12-5 Changing a password

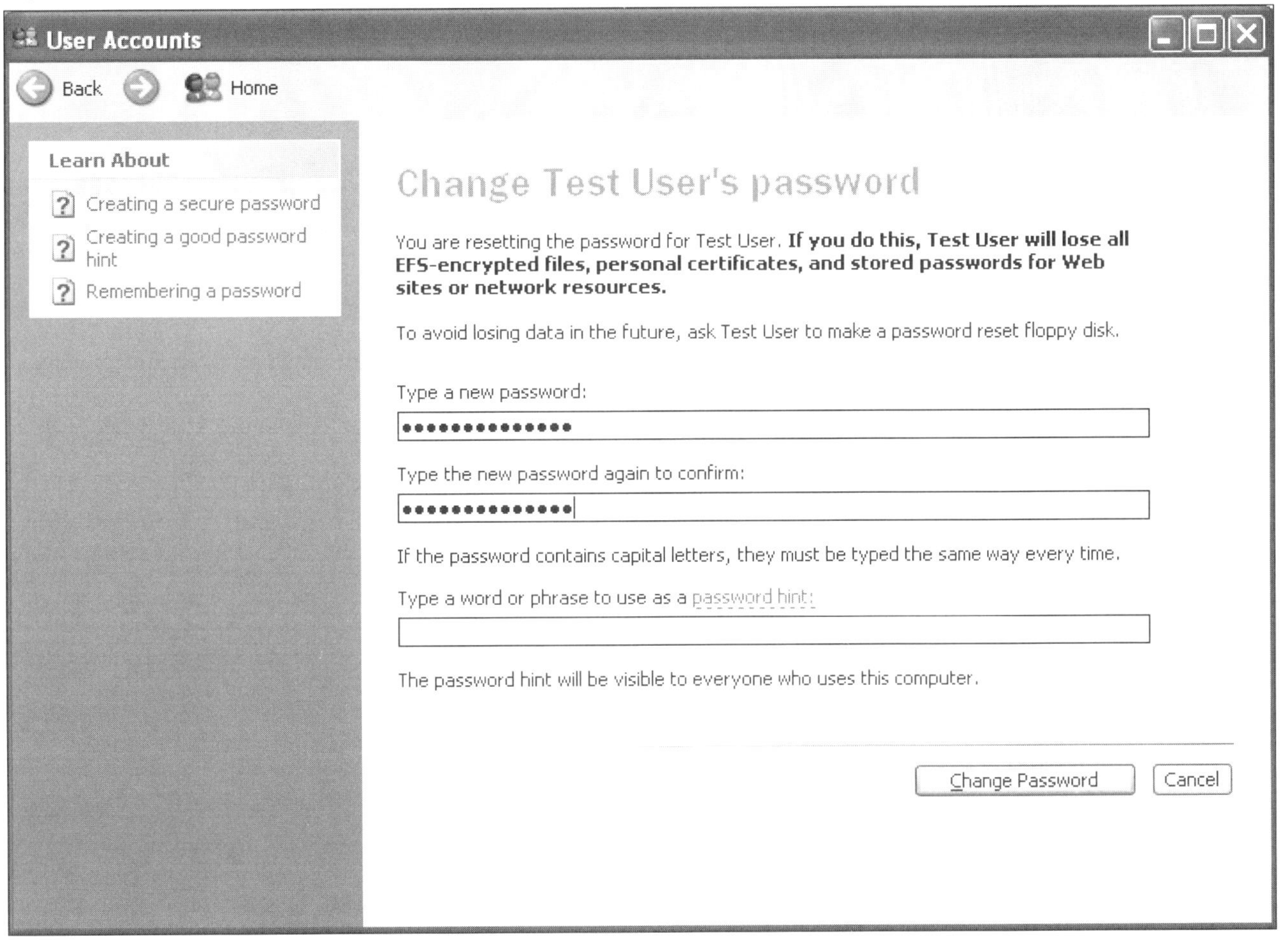

project 12.2

Analyzing and Setting Local Security Policy

exam objective

Troubleshoot security settings and local security policy. Answer end-user questions related to security settings.

overview

You are working with the Medical Analysis group at City Hospital. You want to tighten security on the workstation that is used for correspondence with drug companies and storing a physicians' database. You decide to run the Security and Configuration Analysis tool, import a predefined security template (securews.inf) into a database, and compare the current security settings on the computer with those in the template. After the analysis is complete, you modify the predefined template and apply it to the computer.

learning objective

After completing this project, you will know how to use the Security and Analysis Configuration tool and how to customize security options.

specific requirements

See General Requirements.

estimated completion time

30 minutes

project steps

1. Click **Start** and then **Run** to open the **Run** dialog box.
2. Type **mmc** in the **Open** text box and click **OK** to open an empty Microsoft Management console.
3. Open the **File** menu and select **Add/Remove Snap-in** to open the **Add/Remove Snap-in** dialog box.
4. Click the **Add** button to open the **Add Standalone Snap-in** dialog box.
5. On the **Available Standalone Snap-ins** list, select the **Security Configuration and Analysis** snap-in and click the **Add** button to add it to the **Add/Remove Snap-in** dialog box.
6. Click the **Close** button to close the Add Standalone Snap-in dialog box. The Security Configuration and Analysis snap-in has been added to the Add/Remove Snap-in dialog box (**Figure 12-6**).
7. Click **OK** to close the Add/Remove Snap-in dialog box.
8. Right-click the **Security Configuration and Analysis** node and select **Open Database to view the Open database** dialog box.
9. Type **Branch Office Security** in the **File name** text box and click the **Open** button to open the **Import Template** dialog box.
10. Select the **securews.inf** file (**Figure 12-7**).
11. Click the **Open** button to load the security template into the database.
12. Right-click the **Security Configuration and Analysis** node and select **Analyze Computer Now**.
13. The **Perform Analysis** dialog box opens.
14. Click **OK** to accept the default path in the **Error log file path** text box and close the dialog box.
15. Double-click **Security Configuration and Analysis** to expand the node.
16. Double-click the **Account Policies** node and then double-click the **Password Policy** node.
17. Red **X**s indicate current policies already configured on the computer that do not match the template's secure workstation settings (**Figure 12-8**).

Figure 12-6 Adding the Security Configuration and Analysis snap-in

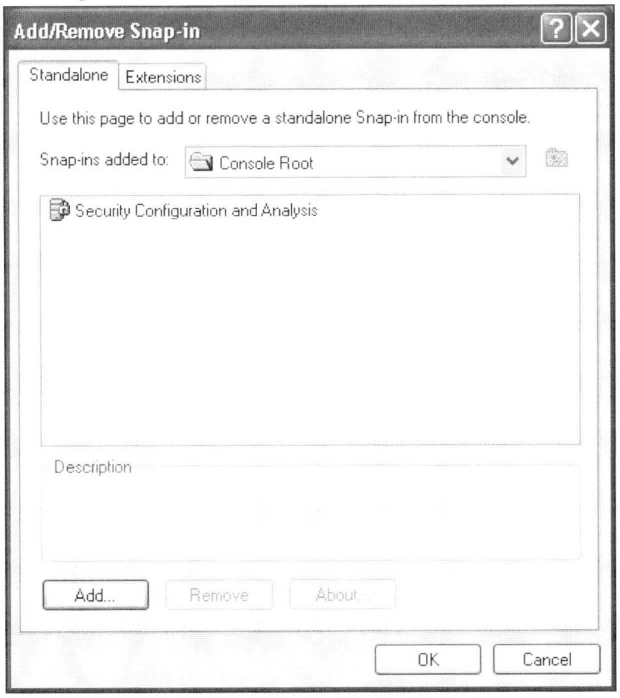

Figure 12-7 Importing the secure workstation template

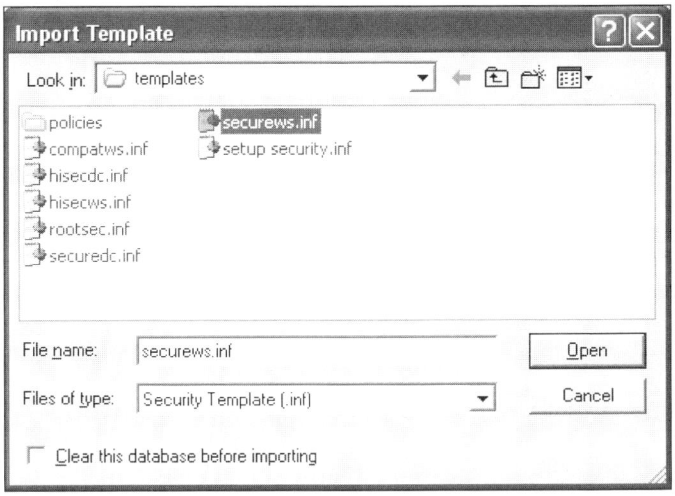

Figure 12-8 Analyzed password policy

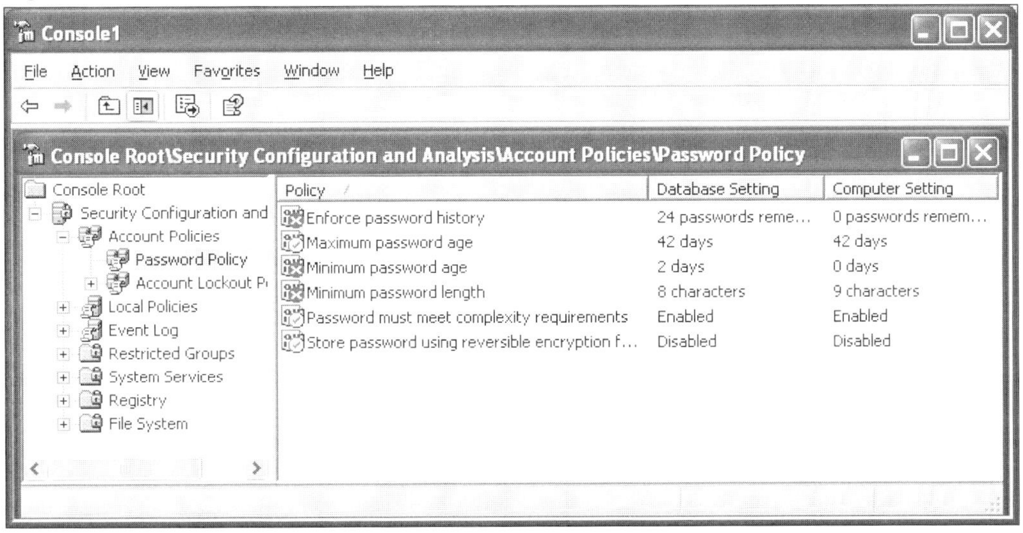

project 12.2

Analyzing and Setting Local Security Policy *(cont'd)*

exam objective

Troubleshoot security settings and local security policy. Answer end-user questions related to security settings.

project steps

18. In the details pane, double-click **Enforce password history** to open the **Enforce password history Properties** dialog box.
19. Select the **Define this policy in the database** check box, if necessary.
20. Enter **12** in the **Keep password history for** spin box and click **OK** to close the dialog box.
21. Double-click **Minimum password length** to open the **Minimum password length Properties** dialog box.
22. Select the **Define this policy in the database** check box, if necessary.
23. Enter **9** in the **Password must be at least–characters** spin box to set the password length in the database to nine characters (**Figure 12-9**).
24. Click **OK** to close the dialog box.
25. In the scope pane, double-click the **Account Lockout Policy** node to view the policies in the details pane.
26. Double-click **Account lockout threshold** to open the **Account lockout threshold Properties** dialog box.
27. Select the **Define this policy in the database** check box, if necessary.
28. Enter **3** in the **Account will lock out after–invalid logon attempts** spin box and click **OK** to close the dialog box (**Figure 12-10**).
29. To configure the computer with the custom template security settings, right-click the **Security Configuration and Analysis** node and click **Configure Computer Now**.
30. The **Configure System** dialog box opens (**Figure 12-11**).
31. Click **OK** to accept the default path in the Error log file path text box and close the dialog box.
32. After the computer is configured with the new settings, close the MMC console.
33. Do not save the console settings when prompted.

Figure 12-9 Setting the minimum password length

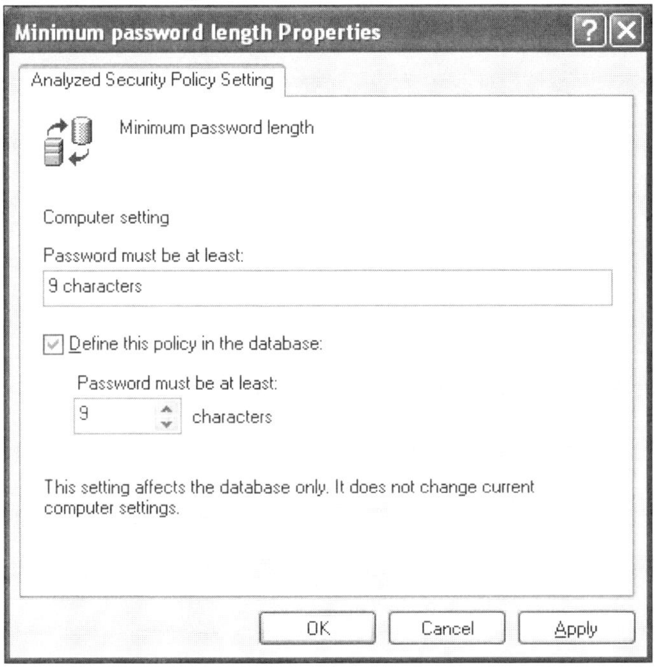

Figure 12-10 Setting the account lockout threshold

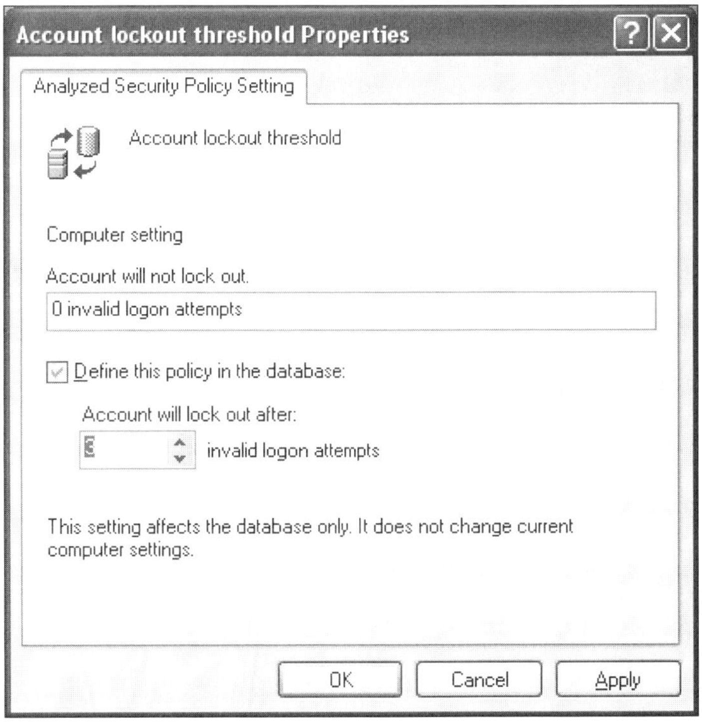

Figure 12-11 The Configure System dialog box

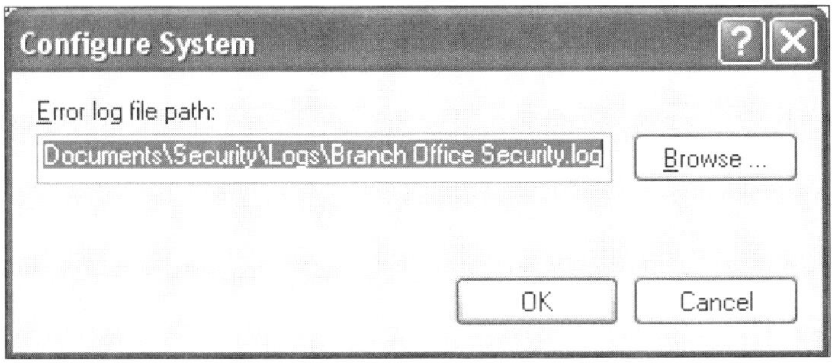

project 12.3

Identifying End User Issues Caused by Local Security Policies

exam objective

Troubleshoot security settings and local security policy. Identify end-user issues caused by local security policies such as Local Security Settings and Security Configuration and Analysis.

overview

You are at a new branch office at the hospital and want to quickly see the security settings for a specific computer. You want to create an easy to read report showing the Resultant Set of Policy (RSoP) for the computer. To create the report, you select the Group Policy option in the Windows XP Help and Support utility.

learning objective

After completing this project, you will be more familiar with using RSoP.

specific requirements

See General Requirements.

estimated completion time

30 minutes

project steps

1. Click **Start** and select **Help and Support** to open the **Help and Support** Center.
2. Under the heading, **Pick a Task**, click the **Use Tools to view your computer information and diagnose problems** link (**Figure 12-12**).
3. On the **Tools** list in the left pane of the window, click **Advanced System Information** to view the **Advanced System Information** choices in the right pane.
4. Click the **View Group Policy settings applied** link (**Figure 12-13**).
5. When the **Group Policy Results for <*computername*>** report opens, scroll through the report to review it (**Figure 12-14**).
6. Close the Help and Support Center.

Figure 12-12 Help and Support Center

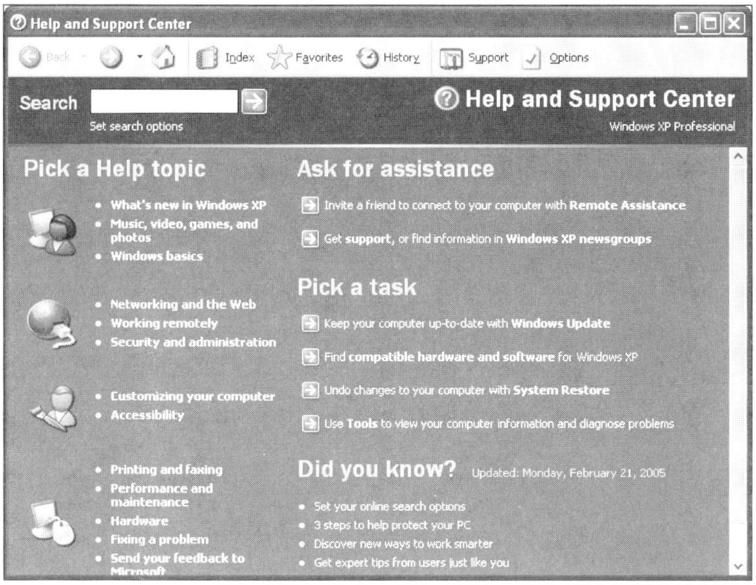

Figure 12-13 Advanced System Information page

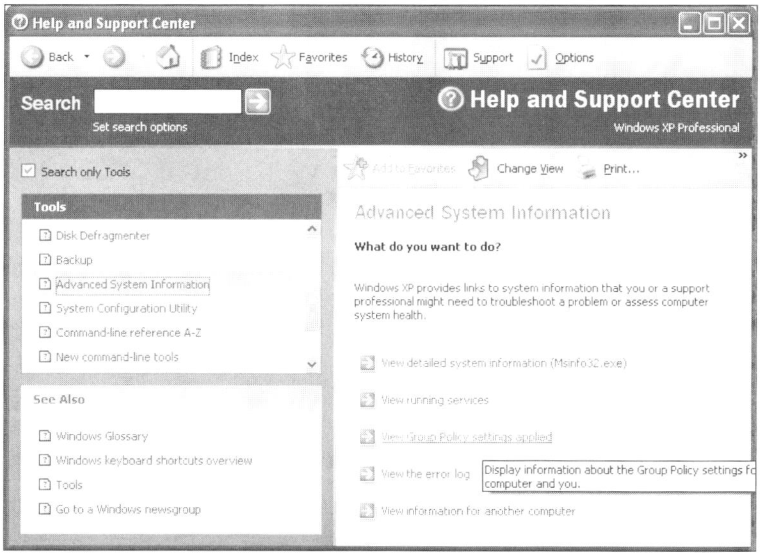

Figure 12-14 Group Policy Results

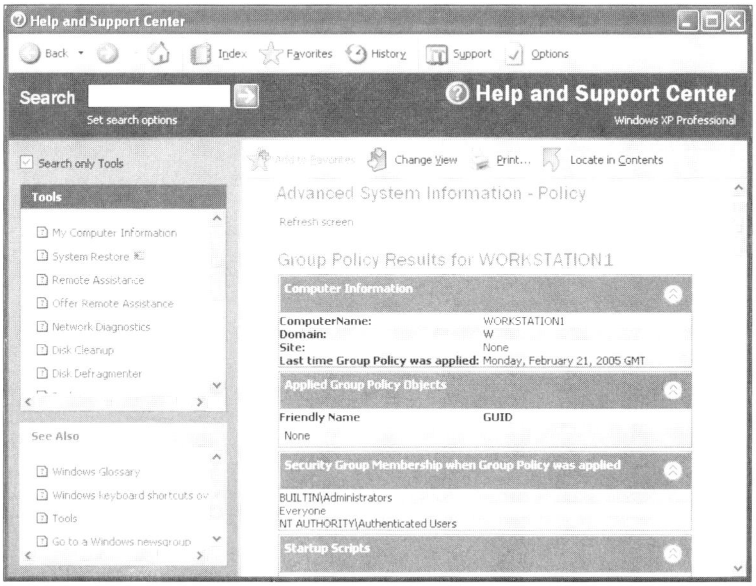

project 12.4

Configuring and Managing Local User Accounts

exam objective

Configure and troubleshoot local user and group accounts. Answer end-user questions related to user accounts. Configure and troubleshoot local user accounts.

overview

You visit a branch office that monitors drug trials for pharmaceutical companies. You want to disable the user account for an employee who is on pregnancy leave. You don't want to delete the account because she will be returning to work in a few months. In addition, you need to delete the user account for another employee who has left the company.

learning objective

After completing this project, you will be more familiar with configuring user accounts.

specific requirements

See General Requirements.

estimated completion time

15 minutes

project steps

1. Click **Start**, right-click **My Computer**, and select **Manage** to open the **Computer Management** console.
2. In the scope pane, double-click **Local Users and Groups** to expand it.
3. Select the **Users** folder (**Figure 12-15**).
4. Right-click the **Test User** account and select **Properties** to open the **Test User Properties** dialog box.
5. Select the **Account is disabled** check box (**Figure 12-16**).
6. Click **OK** to close the Test User Properties dialog box. A red X displays on the Test User account to indicate that it is disabled.
7. Reopen the **Test User Properties** dialog box and clear the **Account is disabled** check box to reactivate the account.
8. Click **OK** to close the Test User Properties dialog box.
9. Right-click the user account you created in Project 6.1 and click **Delete** to remove it from the user list (**Figure 12-17**).
10. Close the Computer Management console.

Figure 12-15 Users in the Computer Management console

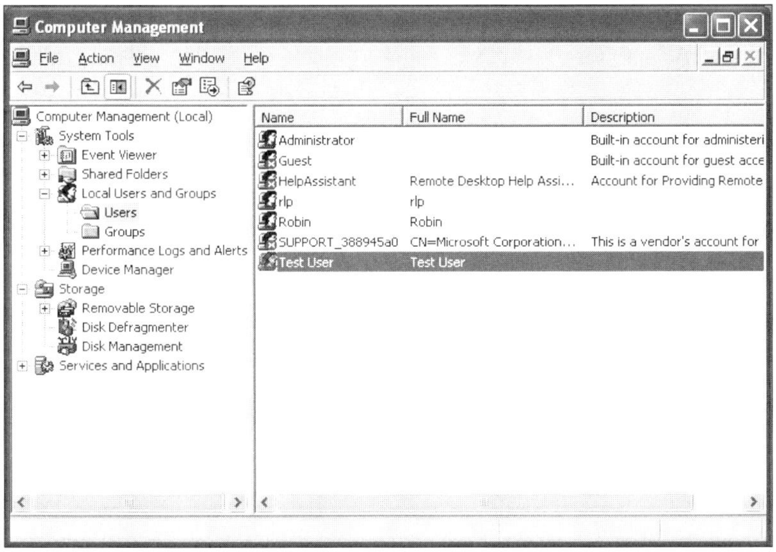

Figure 12-16 Disabling a user account

Figure 12-17 Deleting a user account

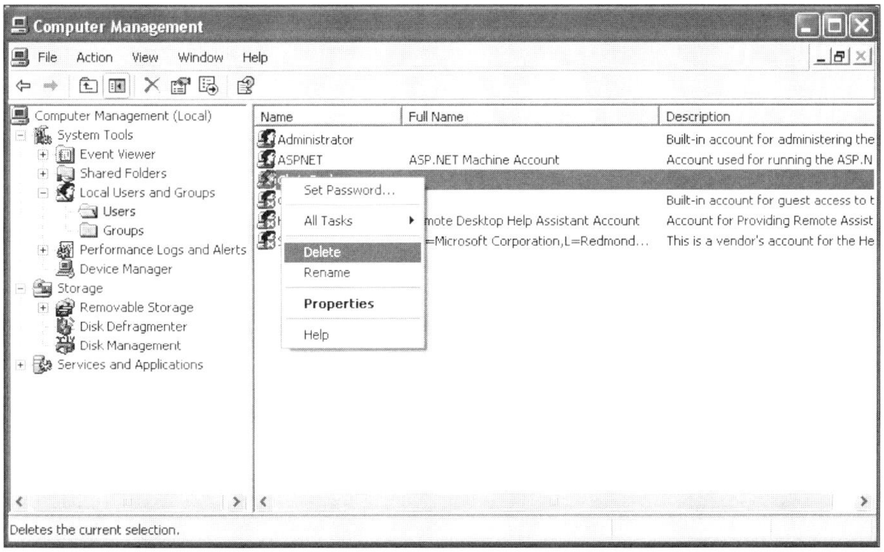

project 12.5

Configuring and Troubleshooting Local Group Accounts

exam objective

Configure and troubleshoot local user and group accounts. Answer end-user questions related to user accounts. Configure and troubleshoot local user accounts.

overview

On one of your visits to a branch office, you discover that users have been installing software that is not on the hospital's list of approved applications. When you investigate the Users and Groups settings on the database workstation computer, you discover that all users are assigned to the Administrators group. You decide to create a new group called Field Services, add multiple users to the group, and remove users from the Administrators group.

learning objective

After completing this project, you will be more familiar with editing group members.

specific requirements

See General Requirements.

estimated completion time

15 minutes

project steps

1. Click **Start**, right-click **My Computer** and click **Manage** to open the **Computer Management** console.
2. Double-click **Local Users and Groups**.
3. Select the **Groups** folder, open the **Action** menu, and click **New Group** to open the **New Group** dialog box.
4. Type **Field Service** in the **Group name** text box.
5. Type **Database Users** in the **Description** text box.
6. Click the **Add** button to open the **Select Users** dialog box.
7. Click the **Advanced** button to expand the dialog box.
8. Click the **Find Now** button to search for all users on the local computer (**Figure 12-18**).
9. In the **Name** (**RDN**) column, select **Test User**. To add more than one user, press [**Ctrl**] and select each username.
10. Click **OK** to add the users to the **Enter the object names to select** box.
11. Click **OK** to close the Select Users dialog box.
12. Click **Create** to create the group.
13. Click **Close** to close the New Group dialog box. The new local group appears in the **Groups** folder in the **Computer Management** console.
14. To remove users from the **Administrators** group, select the **Groups** folder in the scope pane, if necessary.
15. Right-click the **Administrators** group and click **Properties** to open the **Administrators Properties** dialog box.
16. Select the users you want to delete on the **Members** list and click the **Remove** button (**Figure 12-19**).
17. Click **OK** to close the Administrators Properties dialog box.
18. Close the Computer Management console.

Figure 12-18 Finding users to add to a group

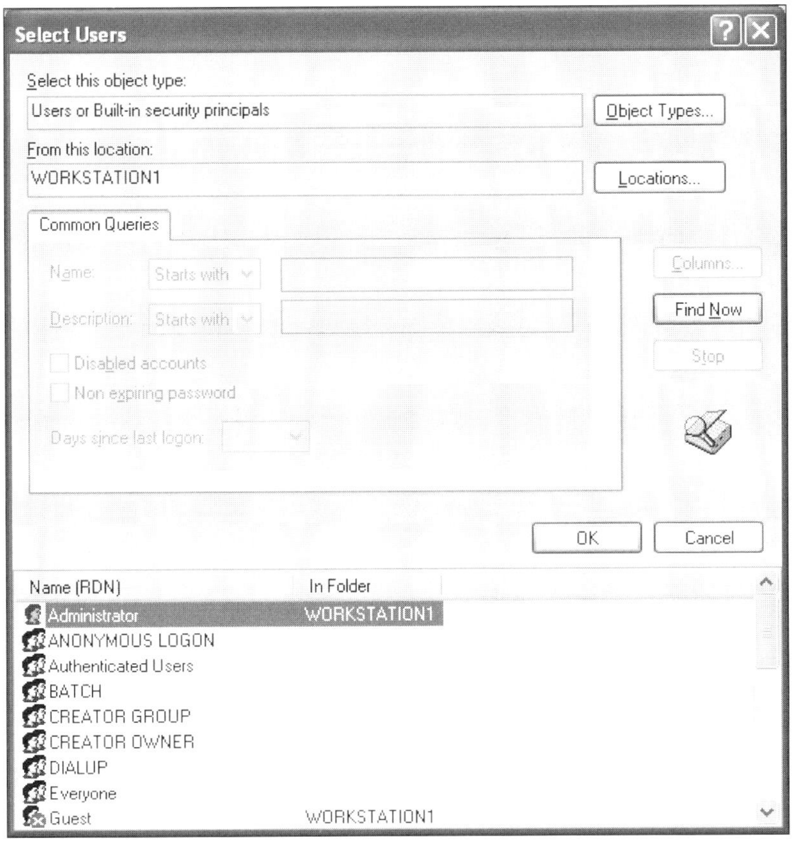

Figure 12-19 Removing a member from a group

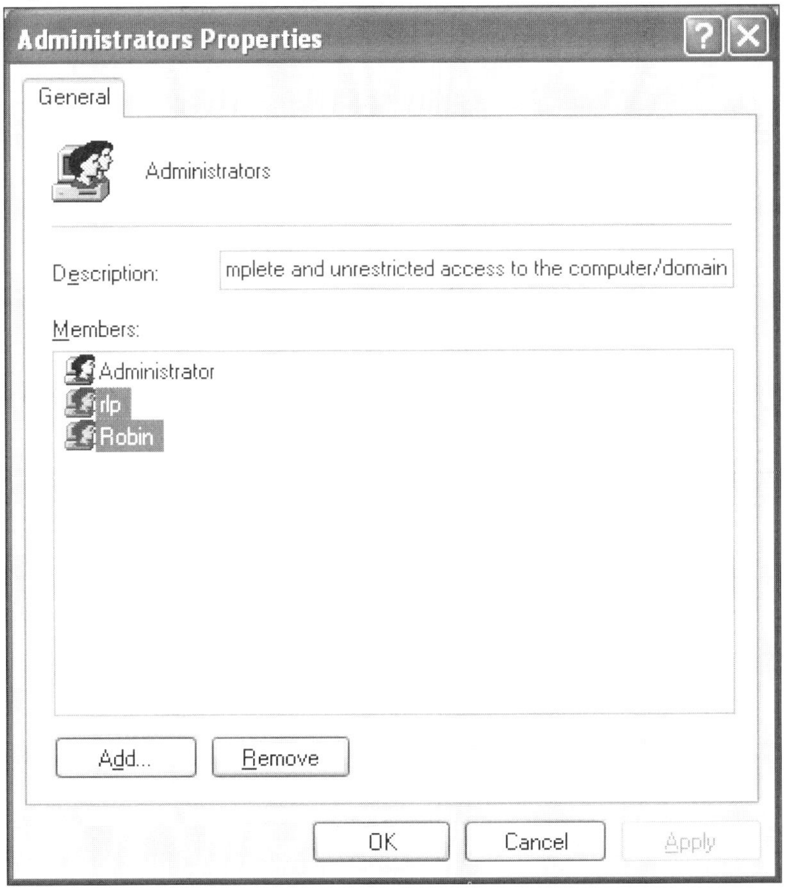

project 12.6

Troubleshooting System Startup Problems

exam objective

Troubleshoot system startup and user logon problems. Answer end-user questions related to system startup issues. Troubleshoot system startup problems.

overview

You receive a distress call from the hospital's art director, who tells you that she is unable to access the network. Another administrator recently worked at the computer. You decide to use the Last Known Good Configuration to return the computer to its previous working state.

learning objective

After completing this project, you will know how to start up a computer using the Last Known Good Configuration.

specific requirements

See General Requirements. To complete this project, you will also need a network card.

estimated completion time

15 minutes

project steps

You can verify how the Last Known Good Configuration works by opening the Device Manager and turning off a network adapter. After you complete the exercise, you will see that the adapter has been turned back on. To disable the adapter, follow these steps:

1. Click **Start**, right-click **My Computer**, and select **Manage** to open the **Computer Management** console.
2. Click the **Device Manager** node.
3. Double-click **Network adapters** to view the network adapter cards on the computer.
4. Right-click the **NIC** icon and select **Disable**.
5. A warning message appears, notifying you that the device will stop functioning. Click **Yes**.
6. Close the Computer Management console.

To start the computer using the Last Known Good Configuration, follow these steps:

1. Click **Start** and select **Turn Off Computer** or **Shut Down**, depending on whether the computer is a standalone computer or a member of a network (**Figure 12-20**).
2. In the **Turn Off Computer** (**Shut Down Windows**) dialog box, select **Restart** in the **What do you want the computer to do** list box and click **OK**.
3. When the computer boots, press [**F8**] to view the **Windows Advanced Options Menu** screen (**Figure 12-21**).
4. Use the down arrow key to scroll down and select **Last Known Good Configuration (your most recent settings that worked)**.
5. Press [**Enter**].
6. When the computer reboots, log on and open the **Computer Management** console.
7. Double-click **Device Manager**.
8. Double-click **Network adapters** to view the network adapter cards in the computer.
9. Note that the NIC is no longer disabled (**Figure 12-22**).

Figure 12-20 Restarting the computer

Figure 12-21 The Windows Advanced Options Menu screen

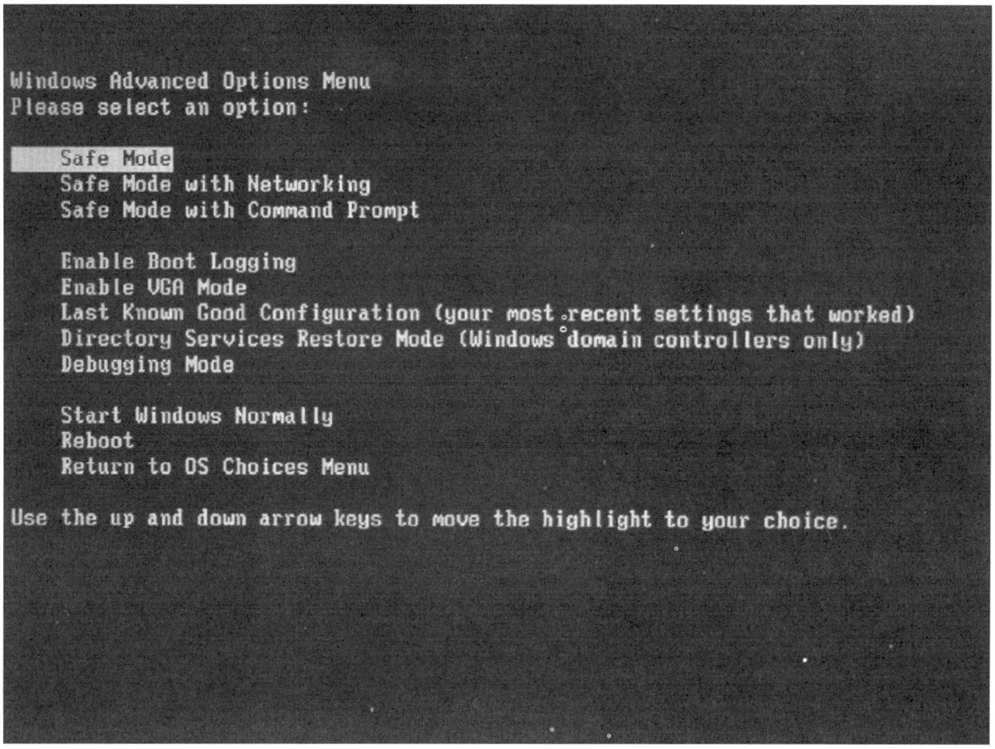

Figure 12-22 Functional network adapter in the Device Manager

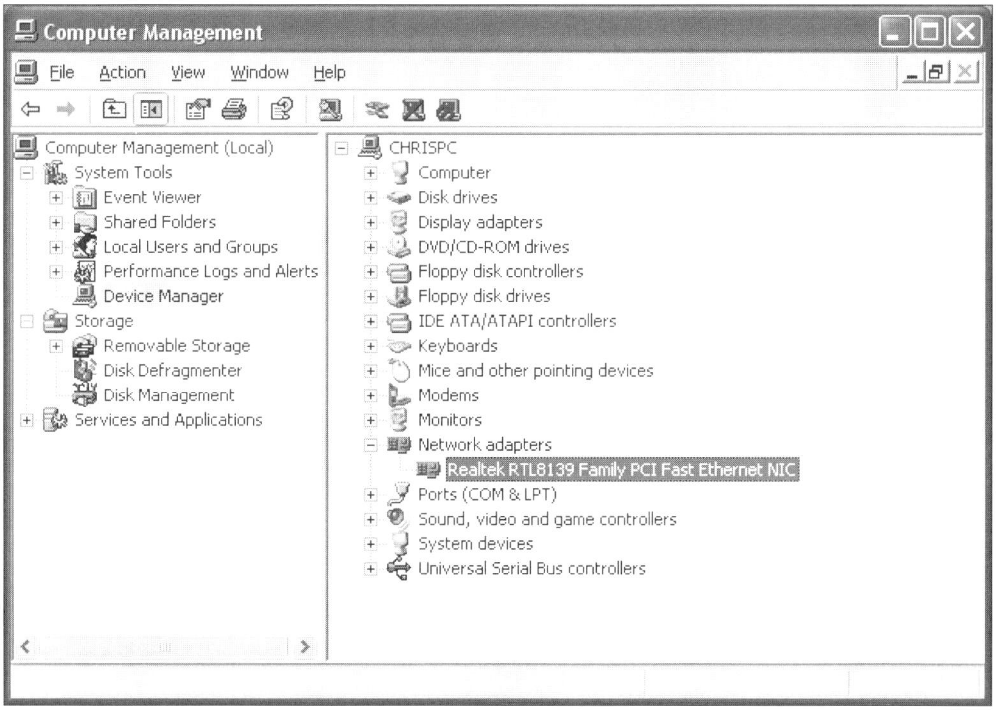

project 12.7

Troubleshooting Local User Logon Issues

exam objective

Troubleshoot system startup and user logon problems. Answer end-user questions related to user logon issues. Troubleshoot local user logon issues.

overview

A temporary employee at your office site logs on with the correct password but receives the error, "The local policy of this system does not permit you to log on interactively." You must log on to the computer and change the local security policy to allow the user to log on.

learning objective

After completing this project, you will know how to change the local security policy of a compute to allow a user to log on locally.

specific requirements

See General Requirements.

estimated completion time

15 minutes

project steps

1. Click **Start** and then **Run** to open the **Run** dialog box.
2. In the **Open** text box, type **gpedit.msc** and press **Enter** to open the **Group Policy** console.
3. In the **Computer Configuration** node, double-click **Windows Settings** to expand the node.
4. In the scope pane, double-click **Security Settings**.
5. Double-click **Local Policies**.
6. Click the **User Rights Assignment** node (**Figure 12-23**).
7. Double-click **Deny logon locally** to open the **Deny logon locally Properties** dialog box.
8. Select the **Guest** account and click the **Remove** button to remove the Guest account from the policy (**Figure 12-24**).
9. Click **OK** to close the Deny logon locally Properties dialog box.
10. Double-click **Log on locally** to open the **Log on locally Properties** dialog box.
11. Check to make sure that the Guest account is on the list of users who can log on (**Figure 12-25**).
12. If not, click the **Add User or Group** button to open the **Select Users or Groups** dialog box.
13. Type **Guest** in the **Enter the object names to select** box and click **OK** to close the dialog box and add the user to the Logon locally list.
14. Click **OK** to close the Log on locally Properties dialog box.
15. Close the Group Policy console.

Figure 12-23 User Rights Assignments node

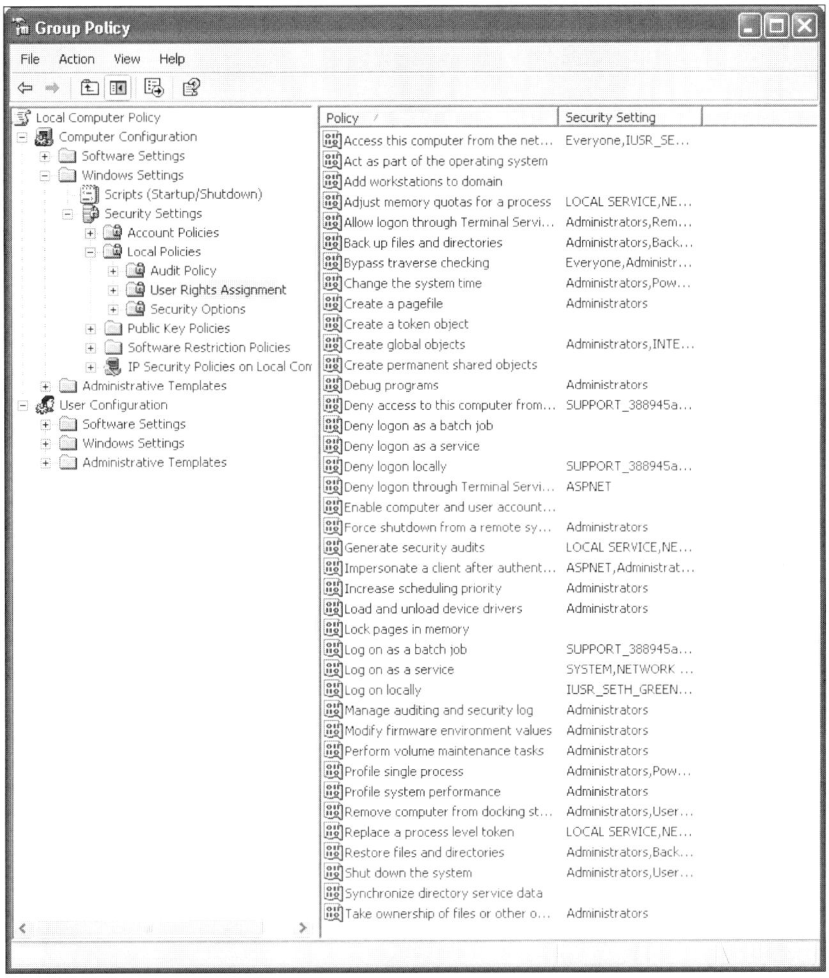

Figure 12-25 Log on locally Properties dialog box

Figure 12-24 Deny logon locally Properties dialog box

project 12.8 Troubleshooting Startup Issues

exam objective

Troubleshoot system startup and user logon problems. Answer end-user questions related to system startup issues. Troubleshoot system startup problems.

overview

You have been trying to troubleshoot a computer that does not always boot up. The computer presently will not boot to the Last Known Good Configuration. Luckily, the user created an ASR backup set last week. After you get the computer to start in Safe Mode, you run the Automated System Recovery utility.

learning objective

After completing this project, you will know how to run the Automated System Recovery utility.

specific requirements

See General Requirements. To perform an automated recovery backup, you also will need one floppy disk and a backup storage medium sufficient to store the backup files.

estimated completion time

30 minutes

project steps

1. Click **Start**, point to **All Programs**, point to **Accessories**, point to **System Tools**, and select **Backup** to open the **Backup or Restore Wizard** (**Figure 12-26**).
2. Click the **Advanced Mode** link to open the **Backup Utility** window (**Figure 12-27**).
3. Click the **Automated System Recovery Wizard** button to start the **Automated System Recovery Preparation Wizard**.
4. Click **Next** to view the **Backup Destination** screen.
5. Enter the path to the media and a name for the backup in the **Backup media or file name** text box. Alternatively, click the **Browse** button and navigate to the removable storage drive on which you are going to save the backup of your system files, and name and save the file in the **Save As** dialog box.
6. Click **Next** to open the **Completing the Automated System Recovery Preparation Wizard** screen.
7. Click **Finish** to create the backup of the system files.
8. The **Backup Progress** dialog box displays the progress of the ASR backup process and the **Selection Information** dialog box displays the file and byte estimates (**Figure 12-28**).
9. The entire process can take quite some time (**Figure 12-29**).
10. When it is complete, a **Backup Utility** dialog box prompts you to insert a floppy disk to create the ASR floppy disk (**Figure 12-30**).
11. Insert a blank formatted floppy disk in the floppy disk drive and click **OK** to close the dialog box.
12. After the files are copied to the floppy disk, another Backup Utility dialog box opens to prompt you to label and safely store the disk (**Figure 12-31**).
13. Click **OK** to close the dialog box, and remove and label the disk. The backup set and the floppy disk will be used to restore the system.

Figure 12-26 The Advanced Mode link in the Welcome to the Backup or Restore Wizard

Figure 12-27 The Backup Utility window

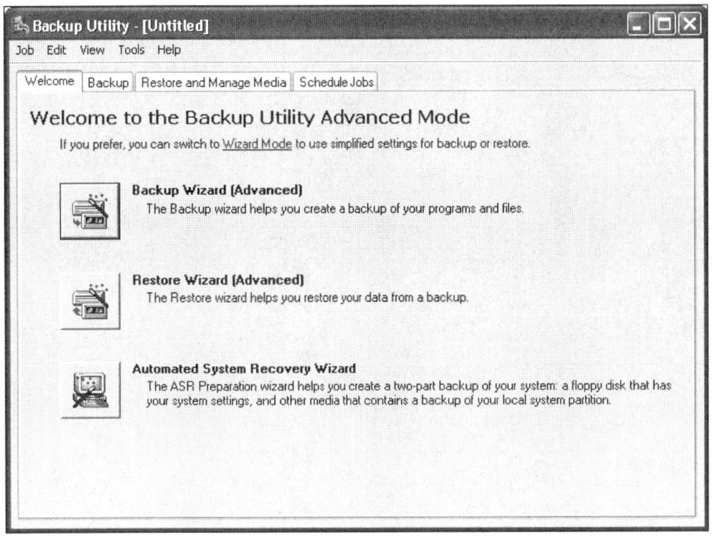

Figure 12-28 The Selection Information dialog box

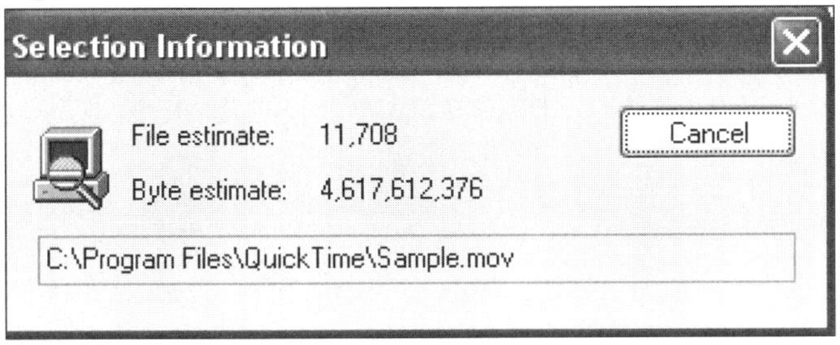

Figure 12-29 The Backup Progress dialog box

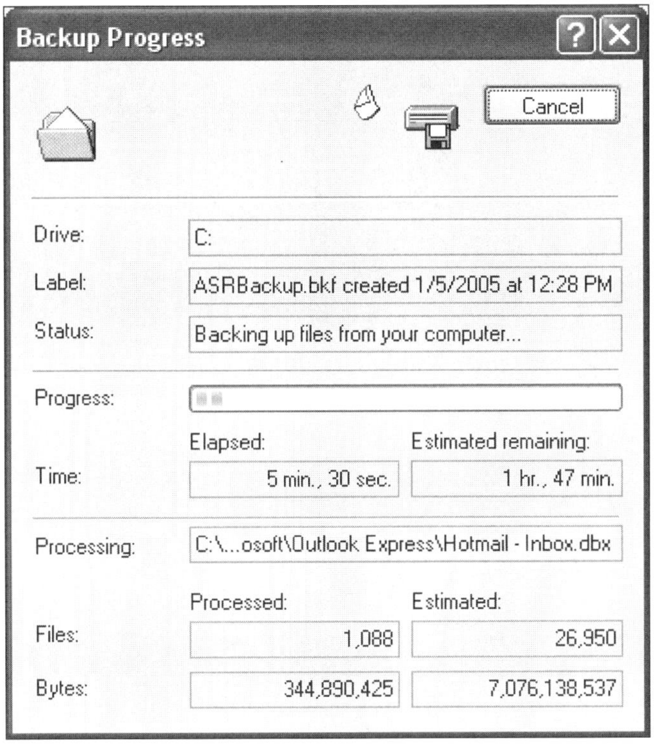

Figure 12-30 Creating the ASR floppy disk

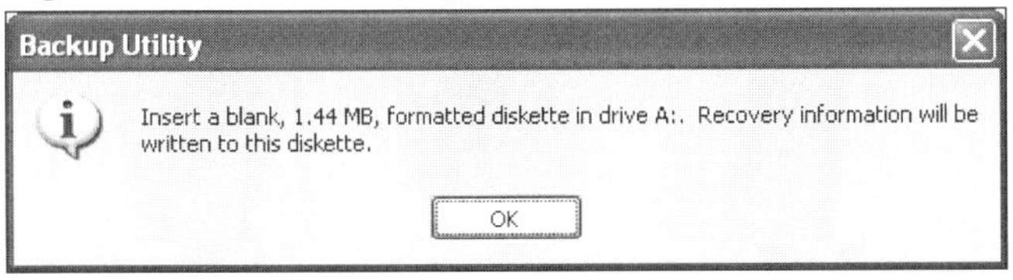

Figure 12-31 Labeling the Windows Automated System Recovery disk

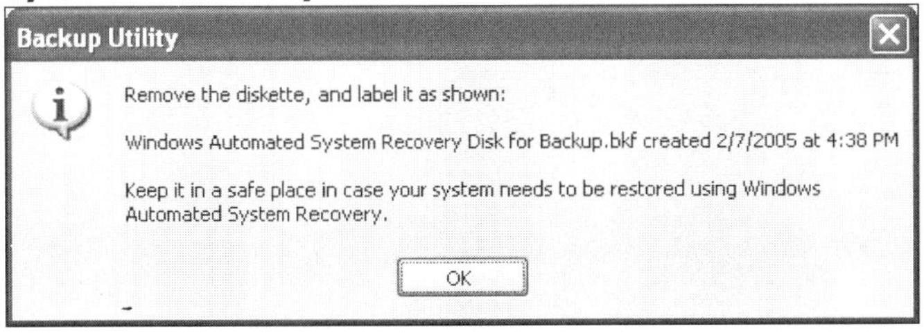

LESSON

13 Monitoring and Analyzing System Performance

In today's digital world, high productivity often depends on office computers running at peak performance. Poorly maintained computers can result in frustrating work delays and downtime. Windows XP provides numerous tools to manage performance and prevent digital bottlenecks.

Poor computer performance can be the result of hardware problems or startup and background applications To determine which startup and background applications are running, you can use the System Configuration Utility. To help improve performance, you can also use the Performance Options dialog box, which is accessed from the Advanced tab on the System Properties dialog box. Here, you can adjust Windows XP for best performance or best appearance. You can also control processor scheduling, memory usage, and virtual memory in the Performance Options dialog box.

You can also use the Task Manager and the Performance console to analyze computer performance. Using the Performance console, you can establish performance baselines and diagnose performance bottlenecks. The Performance console houses the System Monitor and Performance Logs and Alerts tools. The System Monitor provides a graphical representation of the performance of computer resources. Using Performance Logs and Alerts and the System Monitor, you can monitor numerous computer and network functions such as processor, disk, and network activity. The Alerts utility can be used to monitor performance and send an alert when performance surpasses a threshold value.

You can use alerts to monitor system performance by:

- Sending a message to another computer on the network
- Running a program
- Starting a new log
- Creating an entry in the Application log

This lesson provides practice monitoring system performance using the Performance console and the Task Manager. It also provides practice using the Performance and Monitoring section in the Windows Help and Support Center.

Scenario

It is holiday season at City Hospital, and many users are putting new computers on their holiday wish list. These users complain that their current computers are running slowly and that it takes too long to complete certain tasks. The head of the IT department asks you to start evaluating computer performance to find out if bottlenecks exist on individual computers.

Lesson 13 Monitoring and Analyzing System Performance

Project	Exam 70-271 Objective
13.1 Monitoring System Performance	**Monitor and analyze system performance**. Answer end-user questions related to system performance.
13.2 Configuring Alerts	**Monitor and analyze system performance**. Answer end-user questions related to system performance.
13.3 Using Help and Support to Troubleshoot System Performance	**Monitor and analyze system performance**. Use Help and Support to view and troubleshoot system performance.
13.4 Using Task Manager to Troubleshoot System Performance	**Monitor and analyze system performance**. Use Task Manager to view and troubleshoot system performance.
13.5 Using the Performance Console	**Monitor and analyze system performance**. Use the Performance tool to capture system performance information.

General Requirements

To complete the projects in this lesson, you will need administrative rights on a Windows XP Professional computer. To view changes in networking activity in Project 13.4, your Windows XP Professional computer must be a member of a network, either a workgroup or a domain. You may also find it helpful to refer to Lesson 13 in your Prentice Hall Certification Series Exam 70-271 textbook for further information about the topics covered by the projects in this lesson.

project 13.1

Monitoring System Performance

exam objective

Monitor and analyze system performance. Answer end-user questions related to system performance.

overview

One of the users in the medical education department has sent an e-mail complaining that his computer is running slowly. The user mainly works with a database, so you decide to adjust the visual effects so that it is set to Best Performance. You also want to do further tests on the computer, but during testing you want ensure that it boots with only Microsoft services, so you use msconfig to stop all startup services except those provided by Microsoft.

learning objective

After completing this project, you will know how to use the Performance Options dialog box and Msconfig.exe to start up a computer using only Microsoft services.

specific requirements

See General Requirements.

estimated completion time

15 minutes

project steps

1. Click **Start**, right-click **My Computer**, and click **Properties** to open the **System Properties** dialog box.
2. Click the **Advanced** tab **(Figure 13-1)**.
3. In the **Performance** section, click the **Settings** button to open the **Performance Options** dialog box.
4. On the **Visual Effects** tab, select the **Adjust for best performance** option button **(Figure 13-2)**.
5. Click **OK** to close the **Performance Options** dialog box.
6. Click **OK** to close the **System Properties** dialog box.
7. Click **Start** and then **Run** to open the **Run** dialog box.
8. Type **msconfig** in the **Open** text box and press **[Enter]** to open the **System Configuration Utility**.
9. Click the **Services** tab **(Figure 13-3)**.
10. Select the **Hide All Microsoft Services** check box.
11. Click the **Disable All** button (at this point, you might want to reenable any virus protection services).
12. Click **OK** to close the **System Configuration** Utility.
13. A **System Configuration** message box prompts you to restart the computer. Click the **Restart** button **(Figure 13-4)**.
14. When the computer restarts, log on and follow steps 1 through 3 to reopen the **Performance Options** dialog box.
15. Select the **Let Windows choose what's best for my computer** option button.
16. Click **OK** to close the **Performance Options** dialog box.
17. Click **OK** to close the **System Properties** dialog box.
18. Follow Steps 7 and 8 to reopen the **System Configuration Utility** and reenable the services you turned off in Step 11.

Figure 13-1 The System Properties dialog box - Advanced tab

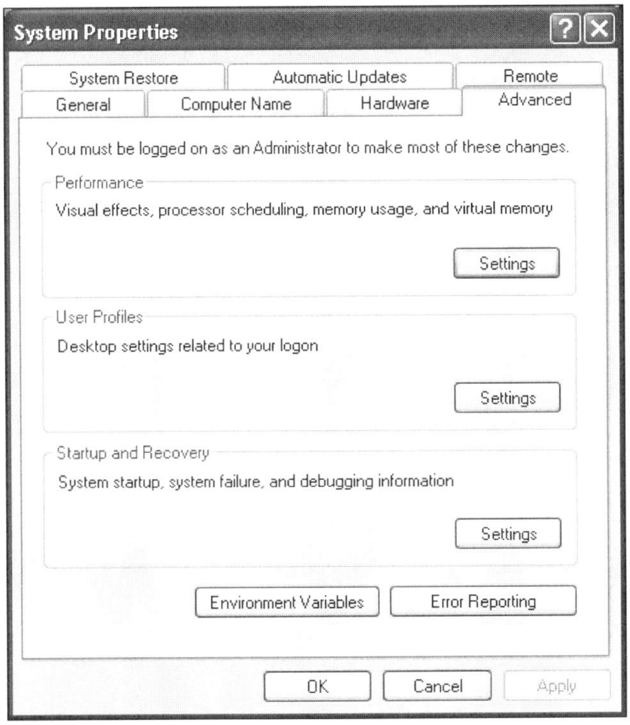

Figure 13-2 The Performance Options dialog box–Visual Effects tab

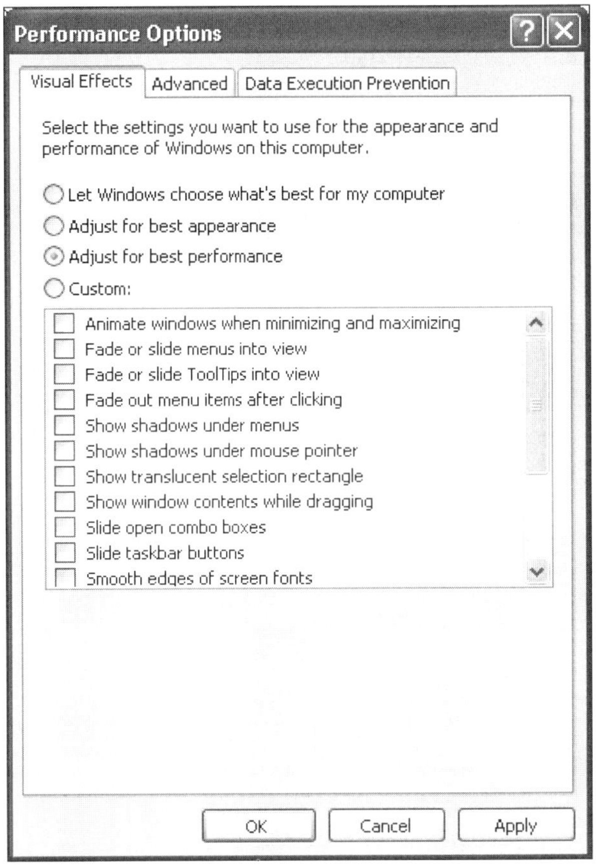

Figure 13-3 System Configuration Utility–Services tab

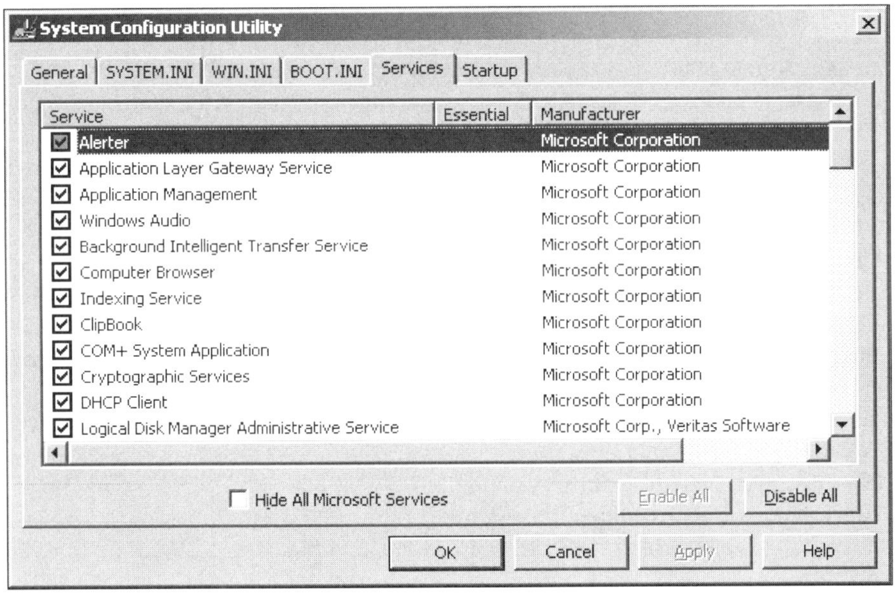

Figure 13-4 The System Configuration message box

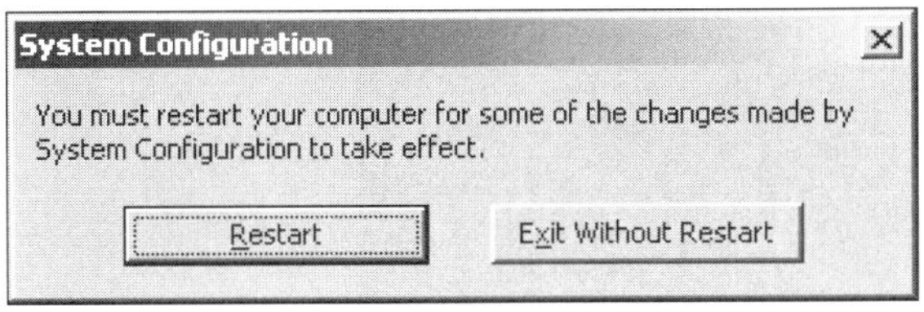

project 13.2

Configuring Alerts

exam objective

Monitor and analyze system performance. Answer end-user questions related to system performance.

overview

You are evaluating one of the computers in the City Hospital medical education department. This computer runs a database that tracks thousands of medical education meetings. Periodically, you need to run a utility that deletes records and compresses the database file; otherwise, the application tends to run very slowly. You want to create an alert that warns you when the hard drive is low on disk space.

learning objective

After completing this project, you will know how to create a low disk space alert.

specific requirements

See General Requirements.

estimated completion time

30 minutes

project steps

1. Click **Start** and then **Control Panel** to open the **Control Panel**.
2. In **Category view**, click the **Performance and Maintenance** link to open the **Performance and Maintenance** window.
3. Click the **Administrative Tools** link to open the **Administrative Tools** window.
4. Double-click the **Performance** icon to open the **Performance** console.
5. Click the plus sign (+) button to expand the **Performance Logs and Alerts** node.
6. Right-click **Alerts** and select **New Alert Settings** to open the **New Alert Settings** dialog box.
7. Enter a **name** for the new alert in the Name text box. For example, type **Disk Free Space Alert (Figure 13-5)**.
8. Click **OK** to open the **Disk Free Space Alert** dialog box.
9. In the **Comment** text box, type **Monitor hard disk space**.
10. Click the **Add** button to open the **Add Counters** dialog box.
11. In the **Performance object** list box, select **LogicalDisk**.
12. Make sure that the **Select counters from list** option button is selected and select **%FreeSpace (Figure 13-6)**.
13. Click the **Add** button to add the counter to the **Counters** box in the **Disk Space Free Space Alert** dialog box.
14. Click **Close** to close the **Add Counters** dialog box.
15. In the **Alert when value is** list box, select **Under**.
16. In the **Limit** text box, enter the threshold value **524288** (for 512MB or 0.5GB) **(Figure 13-7)**.
17. In the **Sample data every Interval** spin box, enter **1**.
18. In the **Units** list box, select **days.**
19. Click the **Action** tab.
20. Select the **Send a network message to** check box.

Figure 13-5 Creating a new alert

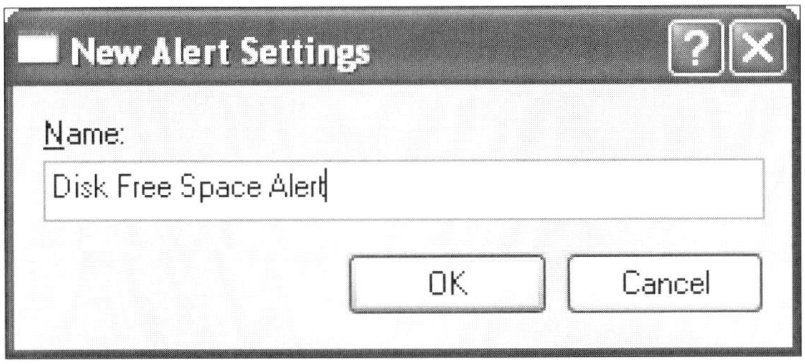

Figure 13-6 Selecting a counter

Figure 13-7 Setting a threshold value

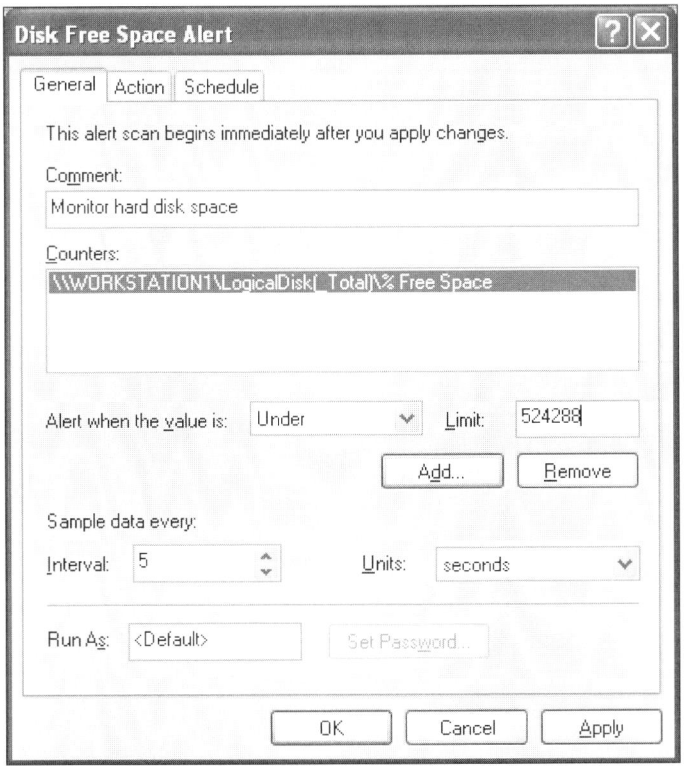

project 13.2

Configuring Alerts *(cont'd)*

exam objective

Monitor and analyze system performance. Answer end-user questions related to system performance.

project steps

21. Enter the name of the computer to which you want the alert sent. For example, type **\\servera (Figure 13-8)**.
22. Click the **Schedule** tab.
23. In the **Start scan** section, select the **Manually (using the shortcut menu)** option button if you want to manually start the alert.
24. If you want to set a time for the alert to begin, select the **At** option button and set a time and date in the spin boxes.
25. In the Stop Scan section, click the **After** option button and enter **365** in the spin box.
26. In the **Units** list box, select **days (Figure 13-9)**.
27. In the **When an alert scan finishes** section, add a check mark to the **Start a new scan** check box.
28. Click **OK** to save the alert settings and close the dialog box.
29. Click **Alerts** in the Performance console.
30. Right-click the **Disk Free Space Alert** in the right pane and select **Start** to manually start the alert.
31. Close the Performance console and the Administrative Tools window.

Figure 13-8 Setting an action

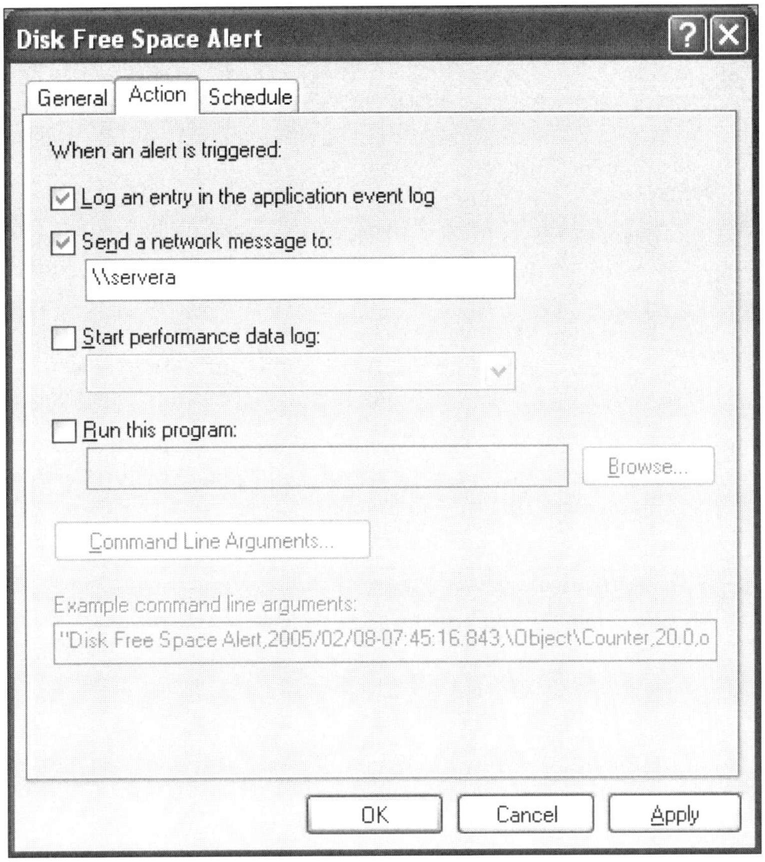

Figure 13-9 Scheduling the alert

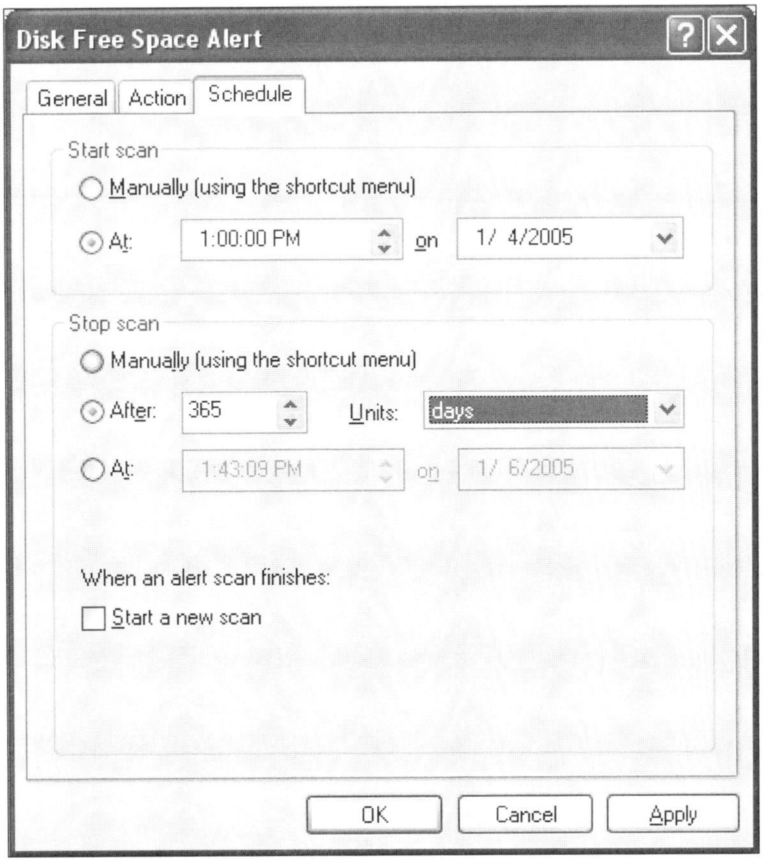

project 13.3

Using Help and Support to Troubleshoot System Performance

exam objective

Monitor and analyze system performance. Use Help and Support to view and troubleshoot system performance.

overview

One of the users in the City Hospital medical education unit is complaining of errors after she runs a scan disk. She reports that the errors indicate the inability to read certain sectors and that there were also some "found bad sectors" messages. You must troubleshoot. To prepare for the job, you decide to check the model number and other manufacturing information for the disk in the System Information utility in case you need to replace the hard disk. You then research disk troubleshooting tips in the Microsoft Help and Support center.

learning objective

After completing this project, you will be more familiar with using the System Support Utility and the Performance and Maintenance section of the Help and Support Center.

specific requirements

See General Requirements.

estimated completion time

30 minutes

project steps

1. Click **Start** and then **Run** to open the **Run** dialog box.
2. Type **msinfo32** in the **Open** text box and press **[Enter]** to open the **System Information** console.
3. Click the plus sign **(+)** button to expand the **Components** node.
4. Click the plus sign **(+)** button to expand the **Storage** node.
5. Select **Disks** to view information about the disk size, partition, and manufacturer and model number **(Figure 13-10)**.
6. Open the **File** menu and select **Exit** to close the System Information console.
7. Click **Start** and then **Help and Support** to open the **Help and Support Center**.
8. Under **Pick a Help topic**, click the **Performance and maintenance** link.
9. In the **Performance and maintenance** list in the left pane of the window, select **Fixing performance and maintenance problems**.
10. In the right pane, in the **Overviews, Articles and Tutorials** section, select **Detecting and repairing disk errors (Figure 13-11)**.
11. Follow the instructions to check for disk errors. If necessary, schedule the disk check to occur the next time you restart the computer.
12. Close the Properties dialog box for the disk, the My Computer window, and the Help and Support Center.

Figure 13-10 The System Information console - viewing disk information

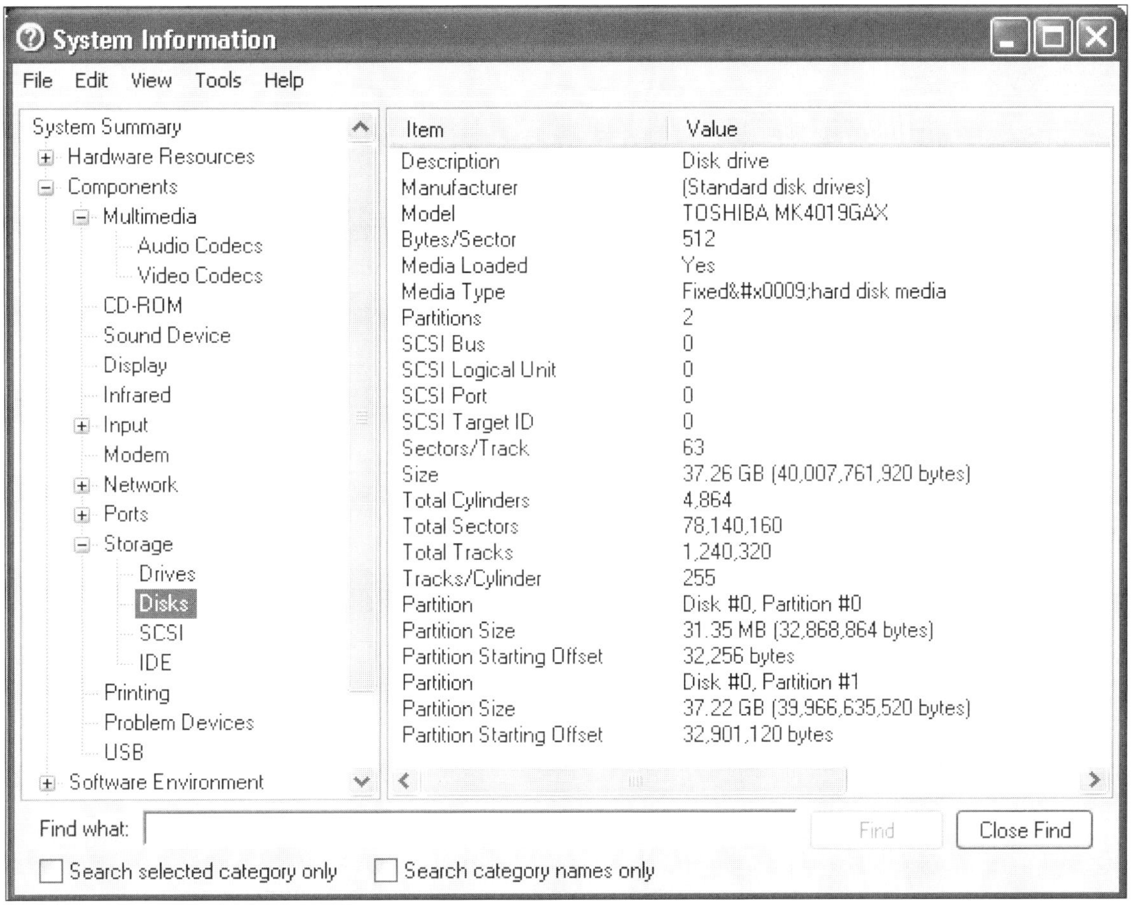

Figure 13-11 Fixing performance and maintenance problems

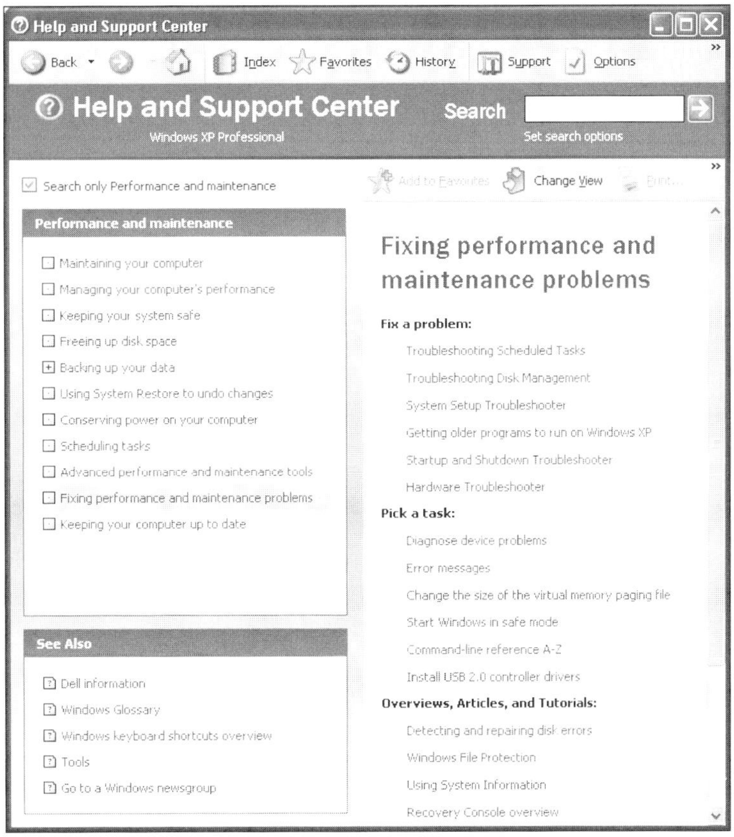

project 13.4

Using Task Manager to Troubleshoot System Performance

exam objective

Monitor and analyze system performance. Use Task Manager to view and troubleshoot system performance.

overview

Several users of a multiuser database at City Hospital are complaining of sluggish performance when they search for hospital records. You suspect that the database application might be low on virtual memory when users keep many applications open. You decide to use the Task Manager to monitor virtual memory, I/O disk reads and writes, and bytes sent and received on the network. If the applications users are working with are using too much virtual memory and creating too much network traffic, you will need to instruct them to keep these closed when the database is in use.

learning objective

After completing this project, you will be more familiar with using the Task Manager.

specific requirements

See General Requirements. To view changes in networking activity, your Windows XP Professional computer must be a member of a network, either a workgroup or a domain.

estimated completion time

15 minutes

project steps

1. Press **[Ctrl]**+**[Alt]**+**[Delete]** to open the **Windows Security** dialog box.
2. Click the **Task Manager** button to open the **Task Manager**.
3. Click the **Processes** tab.
4. Open the **View** menu and select **Select Columns** to open the **Select Columns** dialog box.
5. Select the **Virtual Memory Size**, **I/0 Reads**, and **I/0 Writes** check boxes in addition to those already selected **(Figure 13-12)**.
6. Click **OK** to close the **Select Columns** dialog box.
7. Launch several applications to view the changes in the **Virtual memory**, **I/O Reads**, and **I/O Writes** columns.
8. Click the **Networking** tab.
9. Open the **View** menu and select **Select Columns** to open the **Select Columns** dialog box.
10. Select the **Bytes Sent** and **Bytes Received** check boxes in addition to those already selected **(Figure 13-13)**.
11. Click **OK** to close the **Select Columns** dialog box.
12. View the changes on the **Networking** tab as you access files over the network **(Figure 13-14)**.
13. Close the Task Manager.

Figure 13-12 Adding more columns to the Process tab

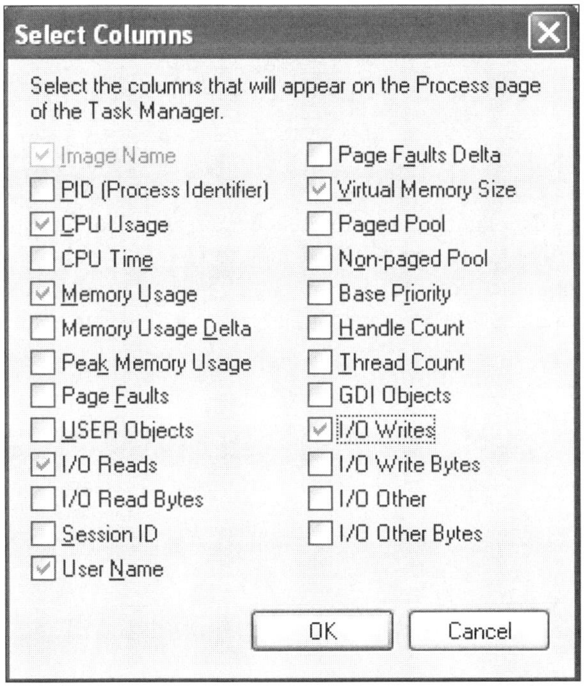

Figure 13-13 Adding more columns to the Networking tab

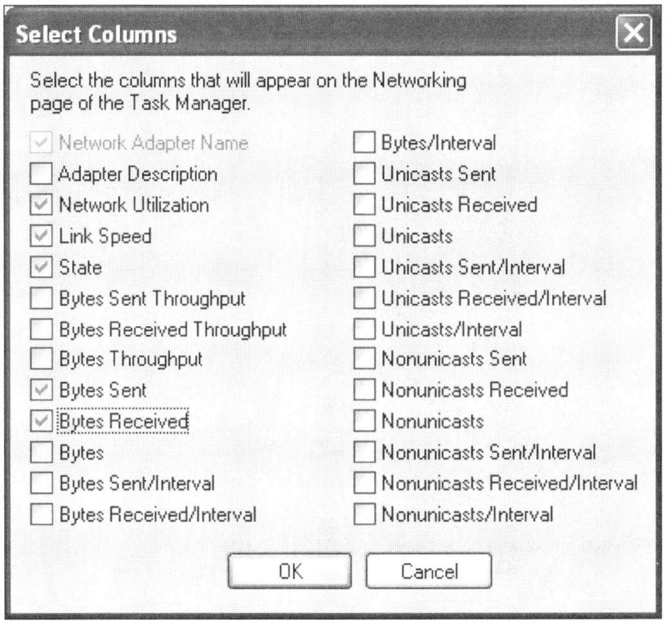

Figure 13-14 Viewing bytes sent and bytes received

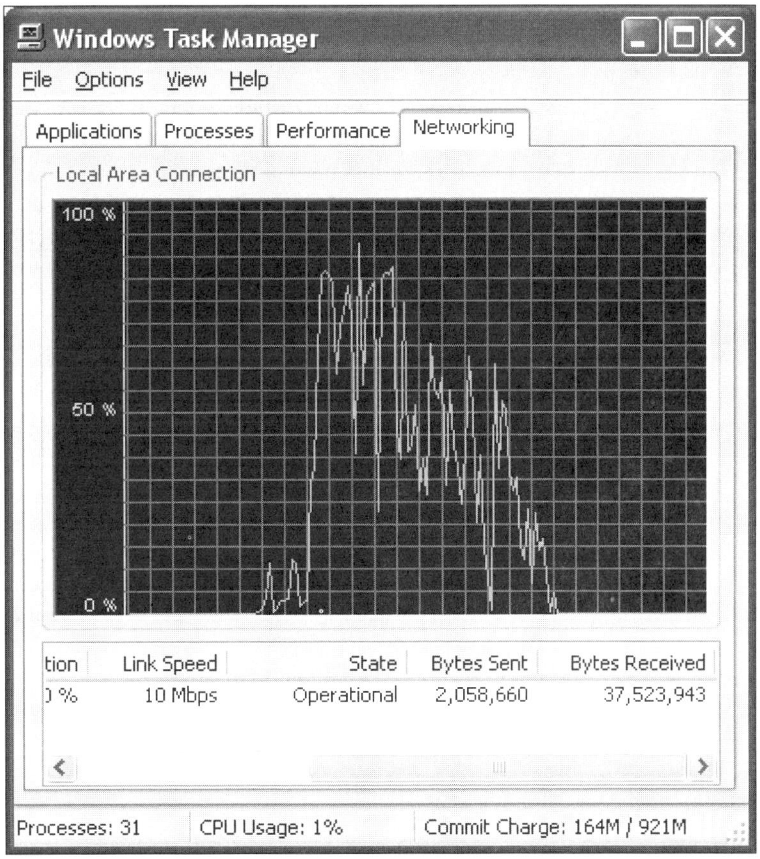

project 13.5 Using the Performance Console

exam objective

Monitor and analyze system performance. Use the Performance tool to capture system performance information.

overview

One of the multimedia producers at City Hospital is developing a complex presentation that requires digital video and sound editing. Excellent disk performance is essential so that this project can be created efficiently and without data errors. You decide to test the multimedia disk to see whether it still meets the manufacturer's read/write specifications. You use the Performance console to monitor disk usage as you test viewing, copying, and saving sound and video files.

learning objective

After completing this project, you will know how to use the Performance console to view a histogram of data.

specific requirements

See General Requirements.

estimated completion time

15 minutes

project steps

1. Click **Start** and then **Control Panel t**o open the **Control Panel**.
2. In **Category view**, click the **Performance and Maintenance** link to open the **Performance and Maintenance** window.
3. Click the **Administrative Tools** link to open the **Administrative Tools** window.
4. Double-click the **Performance** icon to open the **Performance** console.
5. On the **System Monitor** toolbar, click the plus sign button **(+)** to open the **Add Counters** dialog box.
6. Select the **Use local computer counters** option button.
7. In the **Performance object** list box, select **Physical Disk**.
8. Press **[Ctrl]** and select the **Disk Reads/sec** and **Disk Writes/sec** counters in the **Select counters from list** box **(Figure 13-15)**.
9. Click the **Add** button to add the counters to the System Monitor.
10. Click **Close** to close the **Add Counters** dialog box.
11. On the **System Monitor** toolbar, click the **View Histogram** button to display the data as a histogram **(Figure 13-16)**. Note how the color legend at the bottom of the Performance console designates the color used to display data for each counter in the histogram.
12. On the **System Monitor** toolbar, click the **Clear Display** button to clear the display so you can see new data in the graph.
13. To simulate testing, open an application, save and load files, and view the changes in the histogram.
14. Close the Performance console and the Administrative Tools window.

Figure 13-15 Adding the Disk Read/sec and Disk Writes/sec counters

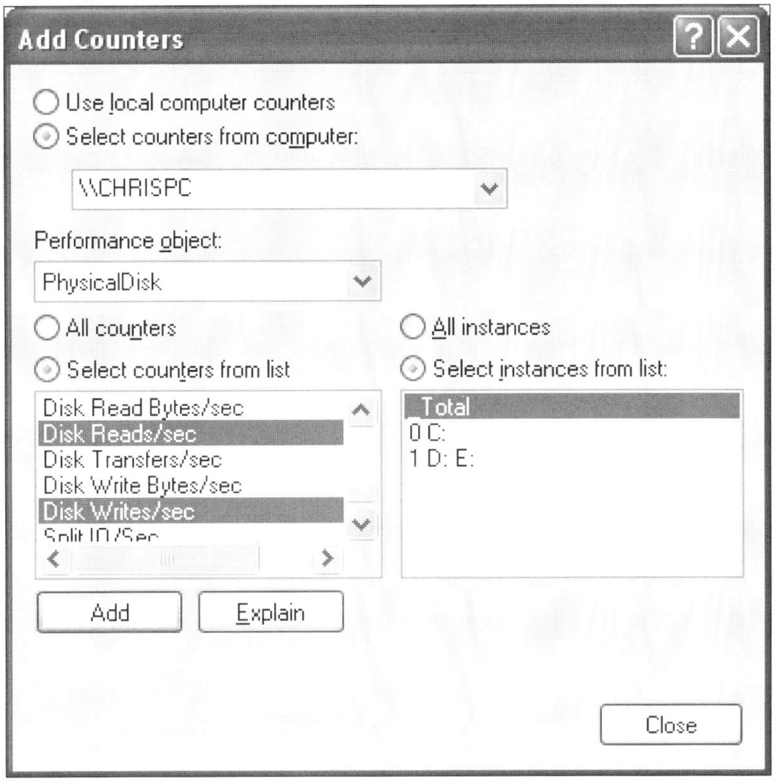

Figure 13-16 Viewing a histogram

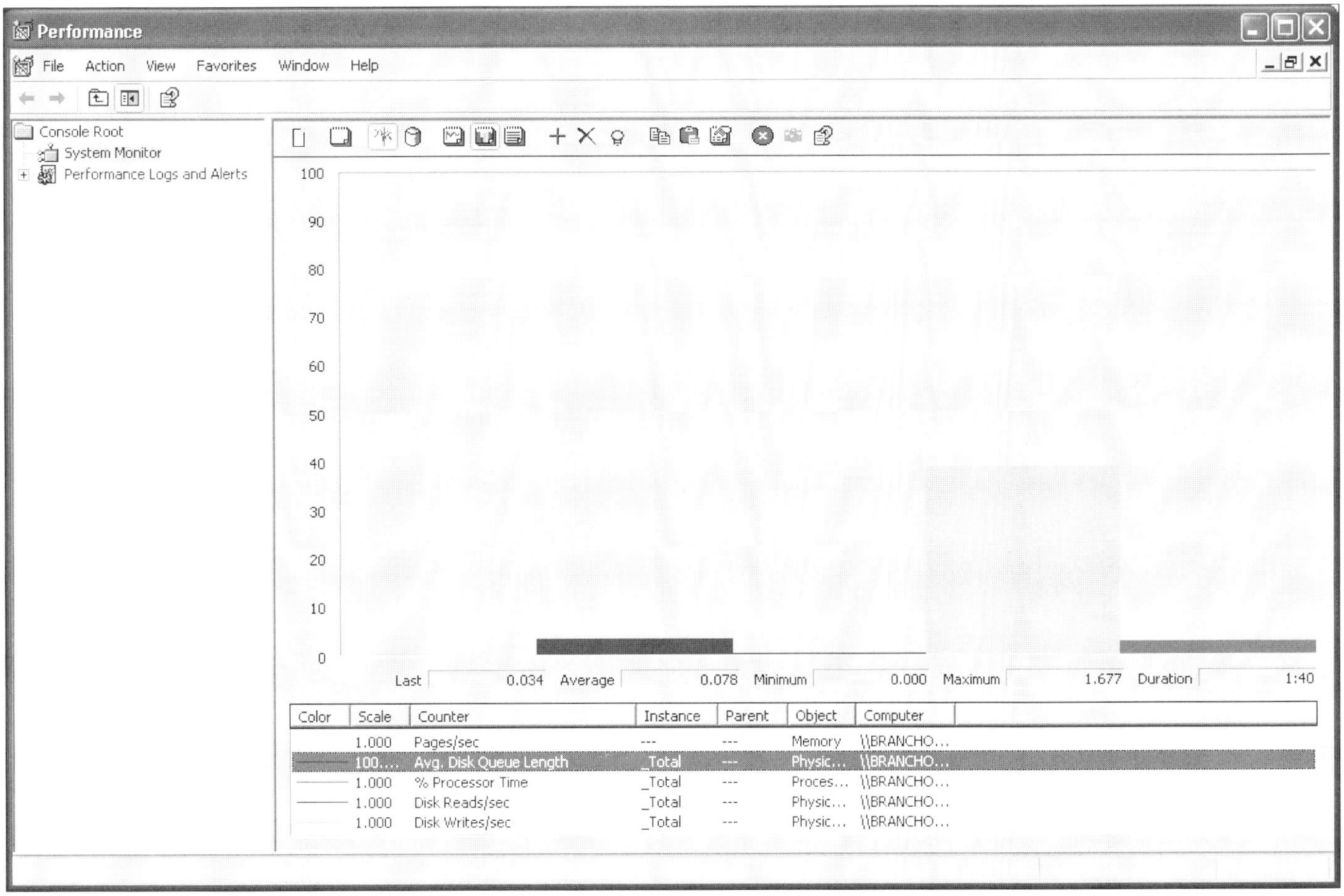

LESSON

14 Troubleshooting TCP/IP and Name Resolution

The network is the lifeblood of most medium and large businesses. If a network is not operating efficiently, productivity suffers. Network problems can cause communication interruptions, data corruption, and printing problems. A properly configured and smooth-running network is essential for the day-to-day operation of a trouble-free and efficient business.

Fortunately, most modern networks use the Transmission Control Protocol/Internet Protocol (TCP/IP) protocol suite, which provides efficient communication among computers on most networks, even if they include diverse hardware architecture and operating systems. Computers using TCP/IP are assigned a unique IP address, which identifies the device on the network. Many networks use Dynamic Host Configuration Protocol (DHCP) to automatically assign IP addresses, but IP addresses can also be assigned manually.

The process of translating a host name (such as a printer name or Web site domain name) into an IP address is called name resolution. For Windows XP clients, Domain Name System (DNS) is the primary name resolution service provided by servers running Windows 2000 Server and Windows Server 2003.

Older Windows networks use Network Basic Input/Output System (NetBIOS). In this system, network resources are identified by a NetBIOS name. In order for TCP/IP hosts to communicate on a NetBIOS network, host names must be resolved to IP addresses. Windows 2000 Server and Windows Server 2003 provide backward compatibility for NetBIOS clients.

Windows 2000 and Windows Server 2003 use WINS (Windows Internet Naming Service) server(s) to resolve NetBIOS names. When a NetBIOS client logs on to a TCP/IP network, the following methods are used, in the order listed, to resolve NetBIOS names:

- NetBIOS names cache
- WINS
- Broadcast (a request sent to all network hosts on the same subnet as the sender)
- LMHOSTS file

Windows XP provides several utilities that you can use to automatically configure networks, manually assign IP addresses, and troubleshoot network problems. You can access several of these utilities in the Network Connections applet in the Control Panel. You can run other utilities from a command prompt. These utilities include Ping, Pathping, Ipconfig, Tracert, Arp, and Route.

This lesson contains projects that will help you become familiar with a variety of TCP/IP troubleshooting utilities. You will practice configuring an alternative IP address, as well as use the Ping and Ipconfig utilities to troubleshoot TCP/IP problems. You will also practice configuring Windows Firewall.

Scenario

You are the network administrator for Big State University Teaching Hospital. As part of your support work, you must help troubleshoot installations for staff and physicians at the hospital, as well as at several branch offices.

Lesson 14 Troubleshooting TCP/IP and Name Resolution	
Project	**Exam 70-271 Objective**
14.1 Troubleshooting TCP/IP	**Troubleshoot TCP/IP. Tools include ARP; the Repair utility; connection properties; and the ping, ipconfig, pathping, and nslookup commands**. Answer end-user questions related to configuring TCP/IP settings.
14.2 Configuring and Troubleshooting Manual TCP/IP Configurations	**Troubleshoot TCP/IP. Tools include ARP; the Repair utility; connection properties; and the ping, ipconfig, pathping, and nslookup commands.** Configure and troubleshoot manual TCP/IP configuration. Answer end-user questions related to configuring TCP/IP settings.
14.3 Configuring and Troubleshooting Automated TCP/IP Configurations	**Troubleshoot TCP/IP. Tools include ARP; the Repair utility; connection properties; and the ping, ipconfig, pathping, and nslookup commands**. Configure and troubleshoot automated TCP/IP address configuration. Answer end-user questions related to configuring TCP/IP settings.
14.4 Configuring and Troubleshooting Internet Connection Firewall (ICF)	**Troubleshoot TCP/IP. Tools include ARP; the Repair utility; connection properties; and the ping, ipconfig, pathping, and nslookup commands**. Configure and troubleshoot Internet Connection Firewall (ICF) settings such as enable and disable. Considerations include indications of issues related to enabling or disabling ICF.
14.5 Troubleshooting ICF	**Troubleshoot TCP/IP. Tools include ARP; the Repair utility; connection properties; and the ping, ipconfig, pathping, and nslookup commands**. Configure and troubleshoot Internet Connection Firewall (ICF) settings such as enable and disable. Considerations include indications of issues related to enabling or disabling ICF.
14.6 Troubleshooting Name Resolution	**Troubleshoot name resolution issues**. Configure and troubleshoot host name resolution issues on a client computer. Considerations include HOSTS files and DNS.

General Requirements

To complete the projects in this lesson, you will need administrative rights on a Windows XP Professional computer that is on a network. You may also find it helpful to refer to Lesson 14 in your Prentice Hall Certification Series Exam 70-271 textbook for further information about the topics covered by the projects in this lesson.

project 14.1

Troubleshooting TCP/IP

exam objective

Troubleshoot TCP/IP. Tools include ARP; the Repair utility; connection properties; and the ping, ipconfig, pathping, and nslookup commands. Answer end-user questions related to configuring TCP/IP settings.

overview

As an IT professional, you realize that despite your best efforts, communications problems can arise on the network. You decide to organize a training session for non-technical office staff so that they can perform the initial troubleshooting process when they cannot reach the Internet. During the session, you will present handouts and slides and perform a hands-on demonstration of the TCP/IP troubleshooting utilities.

learning objective

After completing this project, you will better understand the process of checking network connections and the functions of the TCP/IP troubleshooting utilities.

specific requirements

See General Requirements.

estimated completion time

45 minutes

project steps

1. Check the physical connection at the computer. Make sure that the network cable is securely attached to the network card in the computer. Unplug and re-plug to make sure it is connected properly. If the computer has several network cards, make sure that all are securely connected and that the correct network cable is plugged into the correct network card.
2. Look for cable that appears to be damaged and/or plugs that appear to be damaged, either on the cable or the plug on the network card. Also look for pins that might be bent or broken off. Try a new Ethernet cable.
3. Look at the physical connection to the hub, modem, or wall jack as appropriate. If the cable is connected to a hub or switch, make sure the link light is on. If the light is not on, check a different port on the hub or switch. If the hub or switch attaches to a gateway device such as a cable or DSL modem, check that connection as well. Make sure the link light connections between the two devices are lit. In some of the offices, there are several ports, one for data and one for voice. Call the IT department and make sure the data jack is on and connected to the LAN.
4. Make sure that the network cards are installed in the correct slots if they are external cards and that they are pushed all the way in. For cards that are installed in the motherboard, the IT department can make sure that they are properly installed if all else fails. Check the Device Manager to make sure the network card is recognized by the operating system and that there are no conflicts or errors recorded. Update the driver if necessary.
5. Click **Start** and then **Control Panel** to open the **Control Panel**.
6. In **Category View**, click **Network and Internet Connections** to open the **Network and Internet Connections** window.
7. Click **Network Connections** to open the **Network Connections** window.
8. Right-click **Local Area Connection** and select **Properties** to open the **Local Area Connection Properties** dialog box.
9. Select **Internet Protocol (TCP/IP)** and click the **Properties** button to open the **Internet Protocol (TCP/IP) Properties** dialog box. Check to see if you have a dynamic or static configuration. If it is a static configuration, record the IP address, subnet mask, default gateway, and preferred DNS server **(Figure 14-1)**.

Figure 14-1 Checking the TCP/IP configuration

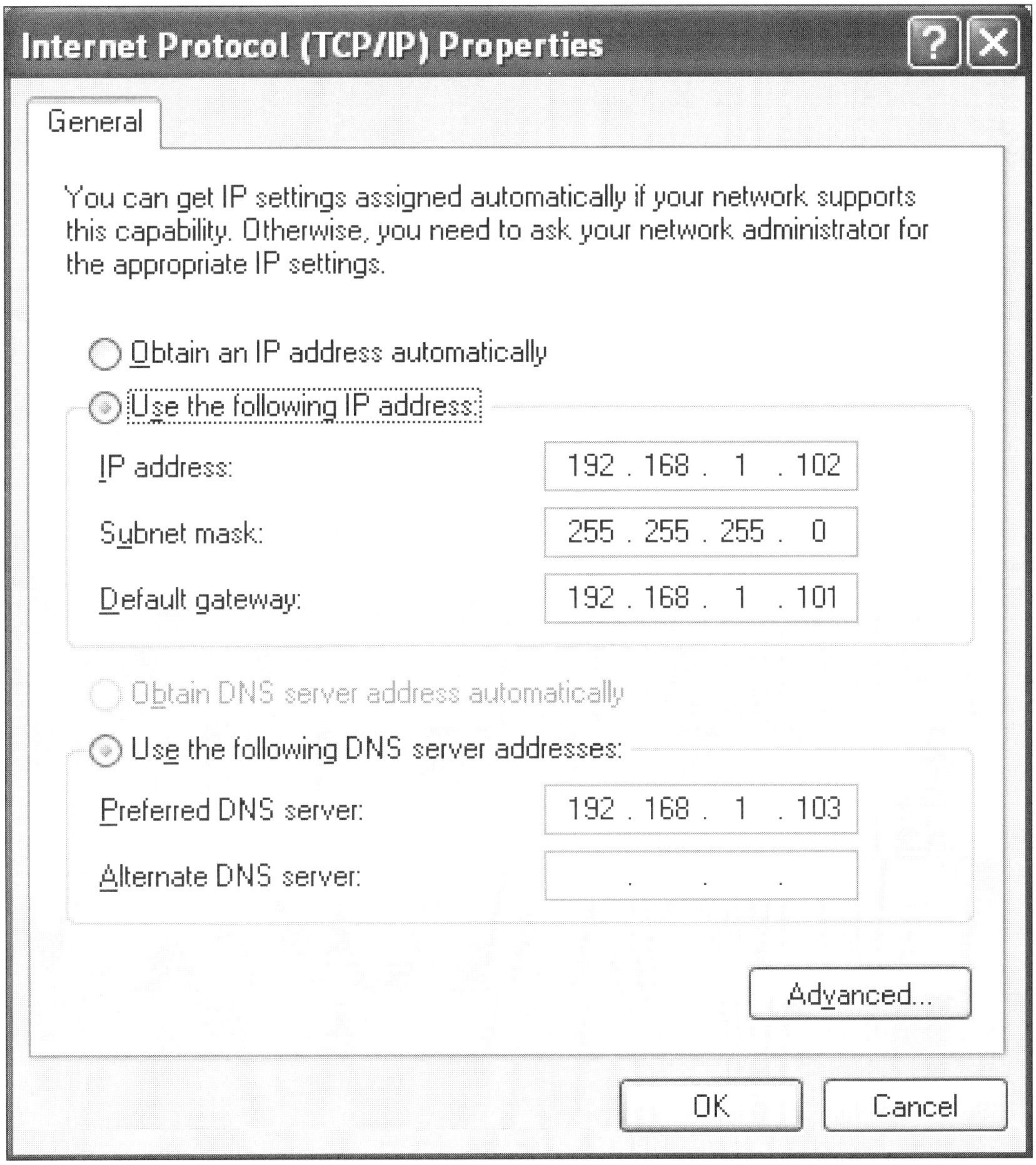

project 14.1

Troubleshooting TCP/IP *(cont'd)*

exam objective

Troubleshoot TCP/IP. Tools include ARP; the Repair utility; connection properties; and the ping, ipconfig, pathping, and nslookup commands. Answer end-user questions related to configuring TCP/IP settings.

project steps

10. Close the two dialog boxes and leave the Network Connections window open.
11. To make sure that the computer is receiving the correct IP configuration information, click **Start** and then click **Run** to open the Run dialog box.
12. Type **cmd** in the **Open** text box and click **OK** to open the command prompt.
13. At the command prompt, type **ipconfig /all** and press **[Enter]** to display the host name, description of your network adapter, physical address, information about DNS and WINS servers, and details about how your IP address is configured. Record the information if necessary.
14. Close the command prompt.
15. In the **Network Connections** window, double-click **Local Area Connection** to open the **Local Area Connection Status** dialog box.
16. Click the **Support** tab **(Figure 14-3)**.
17. To view the IP addresses, click the **Details** button to open the **Network Connection Details** dialog box **(Figure 14-4)**.
18. Click **Close** to exit the Network Connection Details dialog box.
19. Click **Close** to exit the Local Area Connection Status dialog box.
20. Close the Network Connections window.
21. Reopen the command prompt, type **ping 127.0.0.1**, and then press [**Enter**] to test if TCP/IP is installed and properly configured on your computer This is the loopback address that instructs the computer to send a packet to itself. If the ping command succeeds, then the TCP/IP stack is working properly. If it fails, reinstall TCP/IP.
22. Type **ping** ***<IP address>*** (the IP address you recorded in either step 9 or step 13). This test ensures that the network card is working properly. If this fails, remove the network card drivers and reinstall them.
23. Type **ping** ***<default gateway address>*** to see if the problem is at the router (**Figure 14-5).**
24. Review the results from ipconfig/all in step 13. Is there at least one DNS server listed? If not, type **ipconfig/renew** to renew the IP address lease. If you cannot get the proper information and your network uses a DHCP server **(Obtain IP address automatically** is selected in the Internet Protocol (TCP/IP) Properties dialog box), the DNS server should have been provided by the DHCP server along with the IP address and the default gateway. The problem may be with improperly configured DNS and name resolution that does not function.
25. Type **nslookup** ***<hostname>*** and press **Enter** to verify that your DNS server is resolving host names **(Figure 14-6)**.
26. Close the command prompt.

Figure 14-2 Using ipconfig/all to check IP configuration

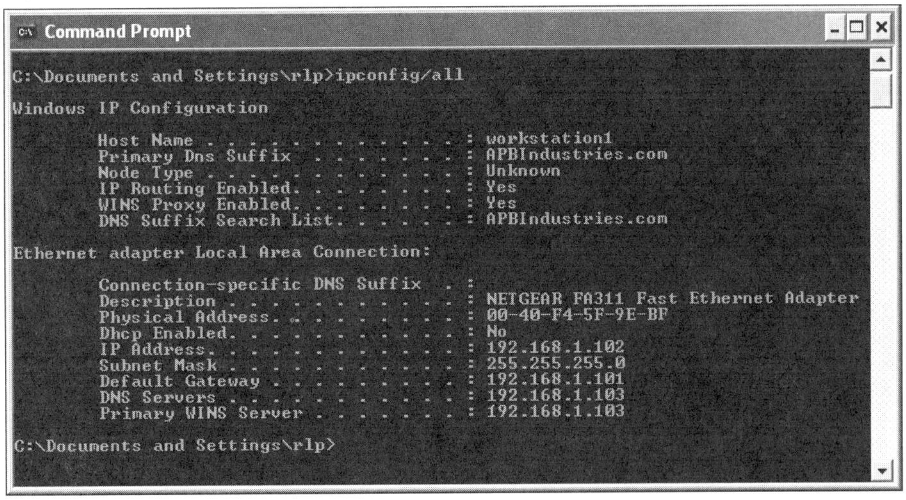

Figure 14-3 The Local Area Connection Status dialog box

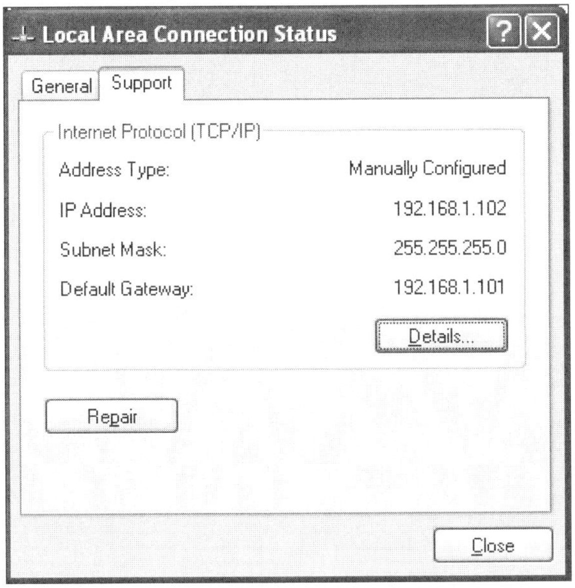

Figure 14-4 The Network Connection Details dialog box

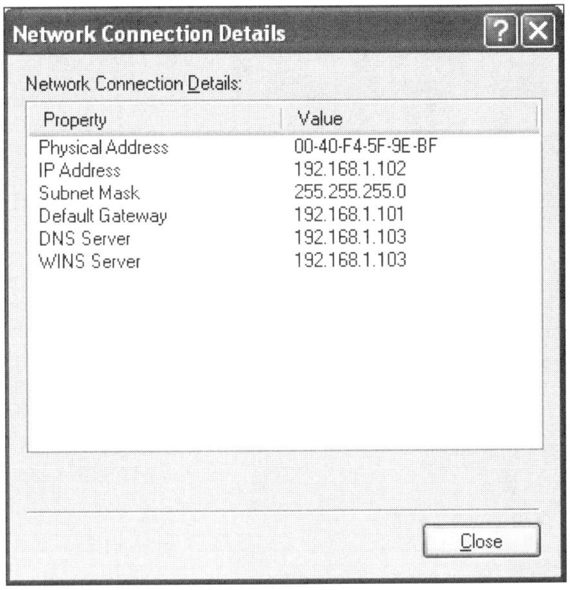

Figure 14-5 Checking TCP/IP, the network card, and the router

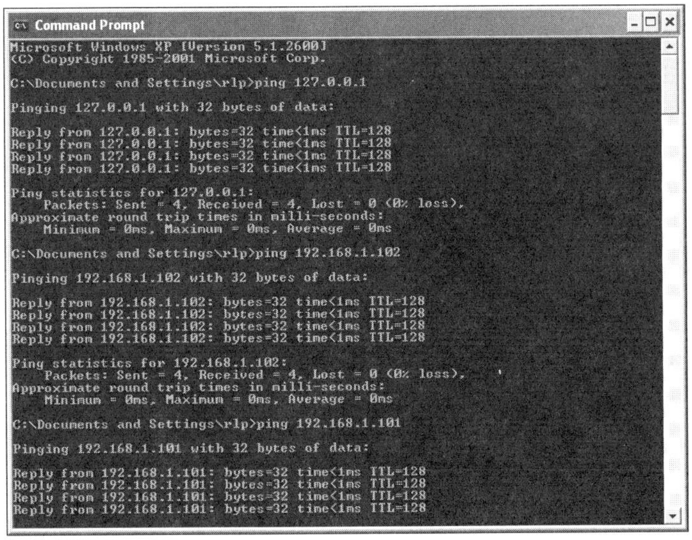

Figure 14-6 Nslookup

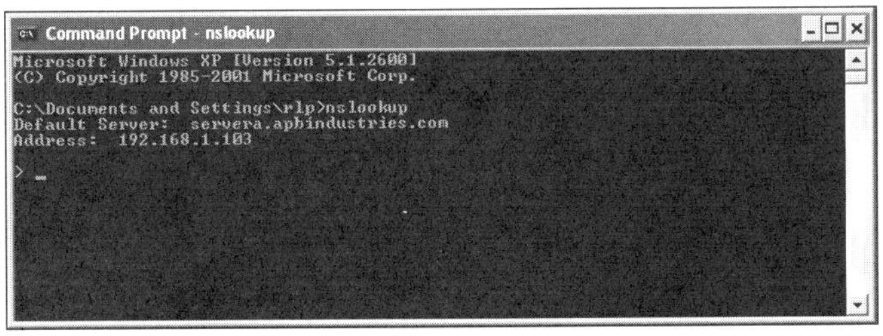

project 14.2

Configuring and Troubleshooting Manual TCP/IP Configurations

exam objective

Troubleshoot TCP/IP. Tools include ARP; the Repair utility; connection properties; and the ping, ipconfig, pathping, and nslookup commands. Configure and troubleshoot manual TCP/IP configuration. Answer end-user questions related to configuring TCP/IP settings.

overview

One of the professors who works at the hospital shuttles his laptop between the hospital and his office. He needs to be able to plug in to both the hospital network and his own office network, which requires a static IP address. The professor doesn't want to reconfigure his laptop each time he connects to either network. You solve the problem by setting up an alternate IP address.

learning objective

After completing this project, you will know how to configure a static IP address and how to create an alternate IP configuration.

specific requirements

See General Requirements.

estimated completion time

15 minutes

project steps

1. Click **Start** and then **Control Panel** to open the **Control Panel**.
2. Click **Switch** to **Classic View**, if necessary.
3. Double-click the **Network Connections** icon to open the **Network Connections** window.
4. Right-click the **Local Area Connection** icon and select **Properties** to open the **Local Area Connections Properties** dialog box.
5. In the **This connection uses the following items** list box, select **Internet Protocol (TCP/IP) (Figure 14-7)**.
6. Click the **Properties** button to open the **Internet Protocol (TCP/IP) Properties** dialog box.
7. Click the **Alternate Configuration** tab.
8. Click the **User Configured** option button.
9. In the **IP address** text box, type **192.168.1.204**.
10. Click the **Subnet mask** text box. Windows XP Professional automatically assigns a subnet mask according to the given IP address **(Figure 14-8)**.
11. Click **OK** to confirm the settings and close the Internet Protocol (TCP/IP) Properties dialog box.
12. Click **OK** to close the Local Area Connection Properties dialog box.
13. Close the Network Connections window.

Figure 14-7 The Local Area Connection Properties dialog box

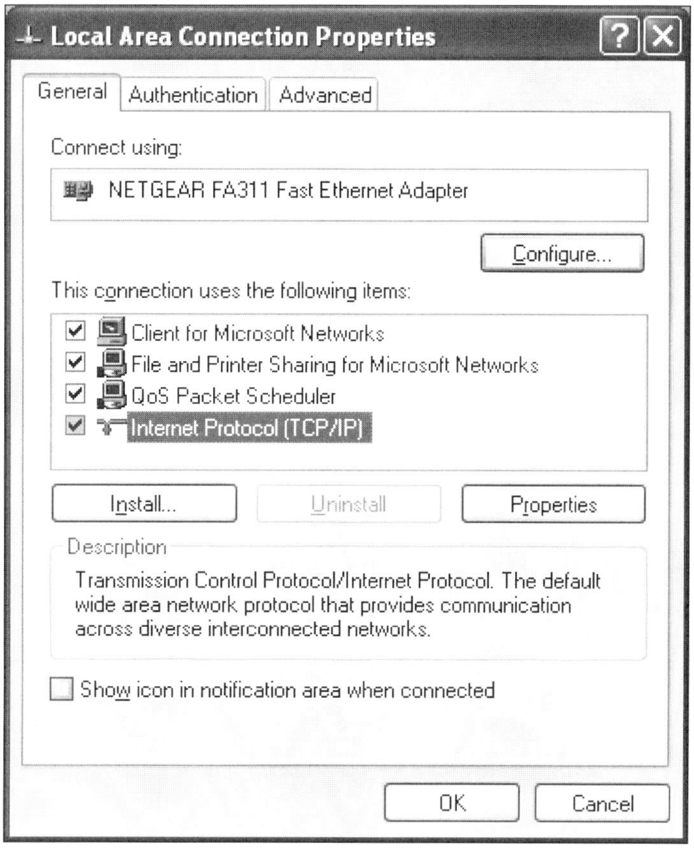

Figure 14-8 The Alternate Configuration tab

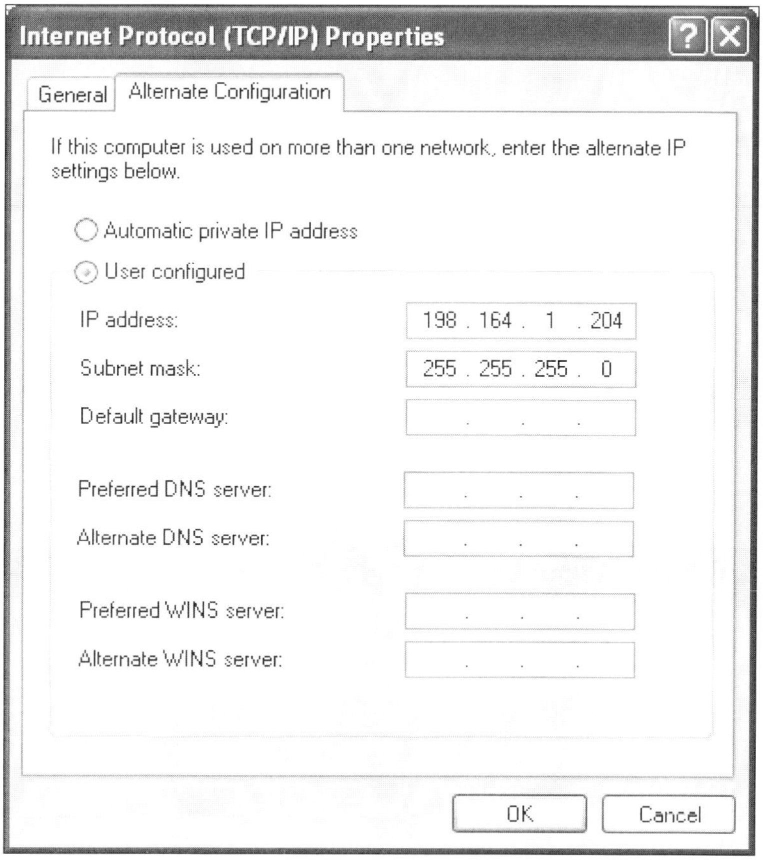

project 14.3

Configuring and Troubleshooting Automated TCP/IP Configurations

exam objective

Troubleshoot TCP/IP. Tools include ARP; the Repair utility; connection properties; and the ping, ipconfig, pathping, and nslookup commands. Configure and troubleshoot automated TCP/IP address configuration. Answer end-user questions related to configuring TCP/IP settings.

overview

You are working in an office that has installed a new network and switched from static to dynamic IP addressing. Use the Internet Protocol (TCP/IP) Properties dialog box to change the settings.

learning objective

After completing this project, you will be familiar with configuring automatic IP addressing and the IP address release and renewal process.

specific requirements

See General Requirements.

estimated completion time

15 minutes

project steps

1. Click **Start** and then **Control Panel** to open the **Control Panel**.
2. Click **Switch** to **Classic View**, if necessary.
3. Double-click the **Network Connections** icon to open the **Network Connections** window.
4. Right-click the **Local Area Connection** icon and select **Properties** to open the **Local Area Connections Properties** dialog box.
5. In the **This connection uses the following items** list box, select **Internet Protocol (TCP/IP)**.
6. Click the **Properties** button to open the **Internet Protocol (TCP/IP) Properties** dialog box.
7. Select the **Obtain an IP address automatically** option button **(Figure 14-9)**.
8. Click **OK** to close the Internet Protocol (TCP/IP) Properties dialog box.
9. Click **Close** to exit the Local Area Connections dialog box.
10. Close the Network Connections window.

To use the **ipconfig** command to release and renew the IP address:

1. Click **Start** and then **Run** to open the **Run** dialog box.
2. Type **cmd** in the **Open** text box and click **OK** to open the command prompt.
3. At the command prompt, type **ipconfig /release** and press [**Enter**].
4. Type **ipconfig /renew** and press [**Enter**] **(Figure 14-10)**.
5. Close the command prompt.

Figure 14-9 Configuring automatic IP addressing

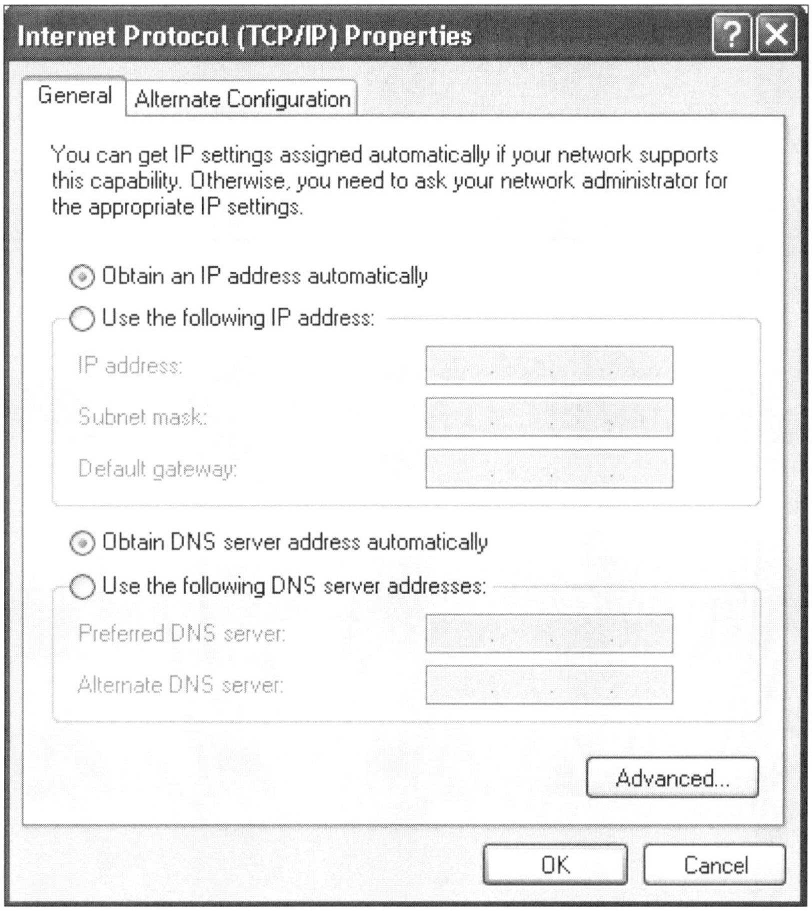

Figure 14-10 Releasing and renewing an IP address

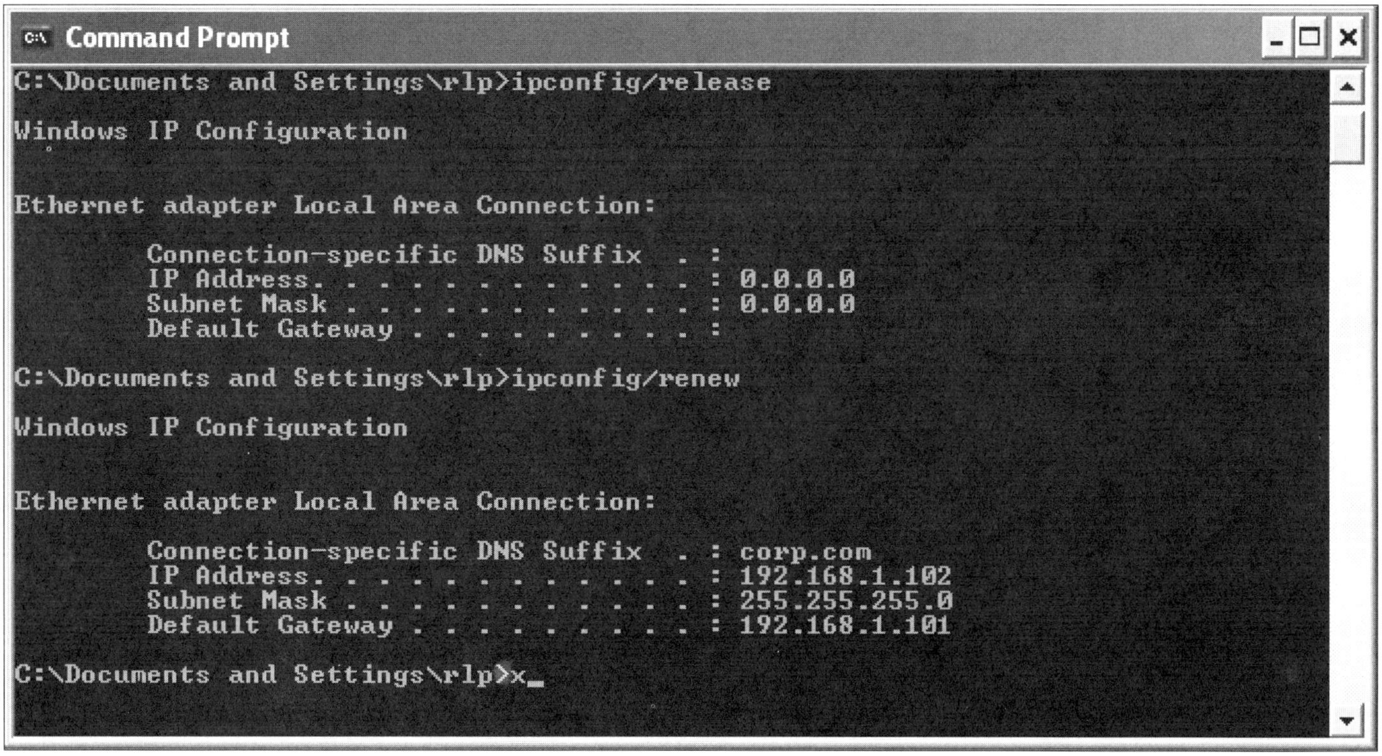

project 14.4

Configuring and Troubleshooting Windows Firewall

exam objective

Troubleshoot TCP/IP. Tools include ARP; the Repair utility; connection properties; and the ping, ipconfig, pathping, and nslookup commands. Configure and troubleshoot Internet Connection Firewall (ICF) settings such as enable and disable. Considerations include indications of issues related to enabling or disabling ICF.

overview

You decide to configure Windows Firewall at a small network at a physician's office that recently upgraded to Service Pack 2. (Windows Firewall is the Service Pack 2 version of Internet Connection Firewall in Service Pack 1.) You decide that you want to create a log file to monitor potential security threats. You want the log file to list dropped packets. You also want to allow incoming Internet Control Message Protocol (ICMP) echo requests.

learning objective

After completing this project, you will know how to create a log file in Windows Firewall.

specific requirements

See General Requirements. In addition, Service Pack 2 must be installed in order to access Windows Firewall.

estimated completion time

15 minutes

project steps

1. Click **Start** and then **Control Panel** to open the **Control Panel**.
2. Click **Switch** to **Classic View**, if necessary.
3. Double-click the **Network Connections** icon to open the **Network Connections** window.
4. Right-click the **Local Area Connection** icon and select **Properties** to open the **Local Area Connections Properties** dialog box.
5. Click the **Advanced** tab to view the **Windows Firewall** section **(Figure 14-11)**.
6. Click the **Settings** button to open the **Windows Firewall** dialog box.
7. On the **General** tab, select the **On (recommended)** option button to turn on Windows Firewall **(Figure 14-12)**.
8. Click the **Advanced** tab.
9. In the **Security Logging** section, click the **Settings** button to open the **Log Settings** dialog box.
10. Select the **Log dropped packets** check box **(Figure 14-13)**.
11. Click the **Save As** button to open the **Save As** dialog box.
12. Save the log file as **pfirewall.log** in a new folder on the **C** drive named **Logs**.
13. Click **OK** to close the Log Settings dialog box.
14. In the **ICMP** section, click the **Settings** button to open the **ICMP Settings** dialog box.
15. Select the **Allow incoming echo request** check box, if necessary. Echo requests are automatically allowed if TCP port 445 is enabled **(Figure 14-14)**.
16. Click **OK** to close the ICMP Settings dialog box.
17. Click **OK** to close the Windows Firewall dialog box.
18. Click **OK** to close the Local Area Connections Properties dialog box.
19. Close the Network Connections window.

Figure 14-11 The Local Area Connections Properties dialog box - Advanced tab

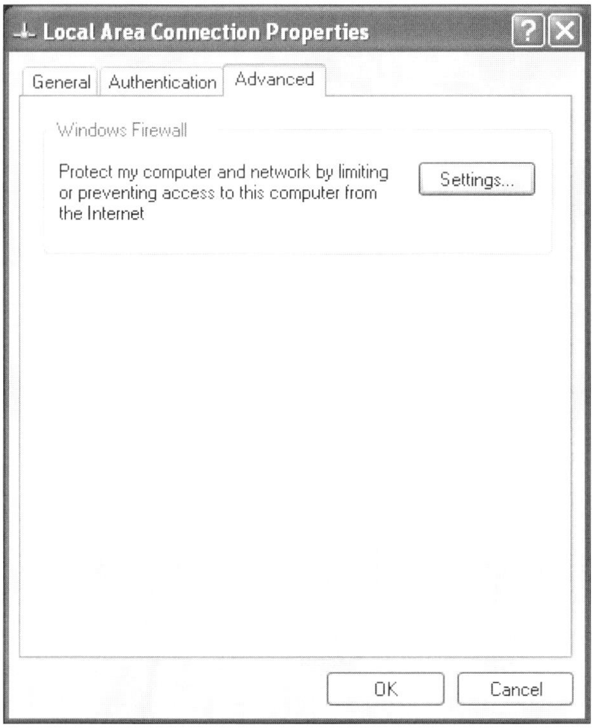

Figure 14-12 The Windows Firewall dialog box

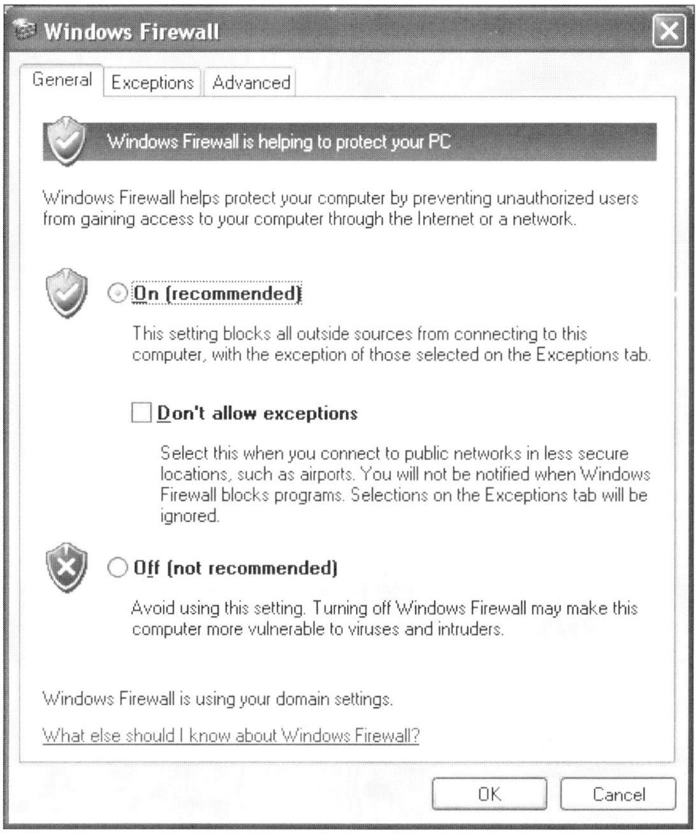

Figure 14-13 The Log Settings dialog box

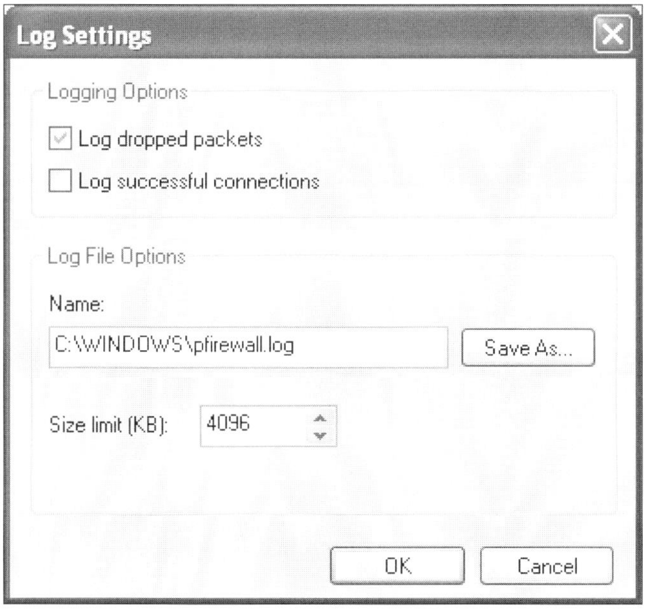

Figure 14-14 The ICMP Settings dialog box

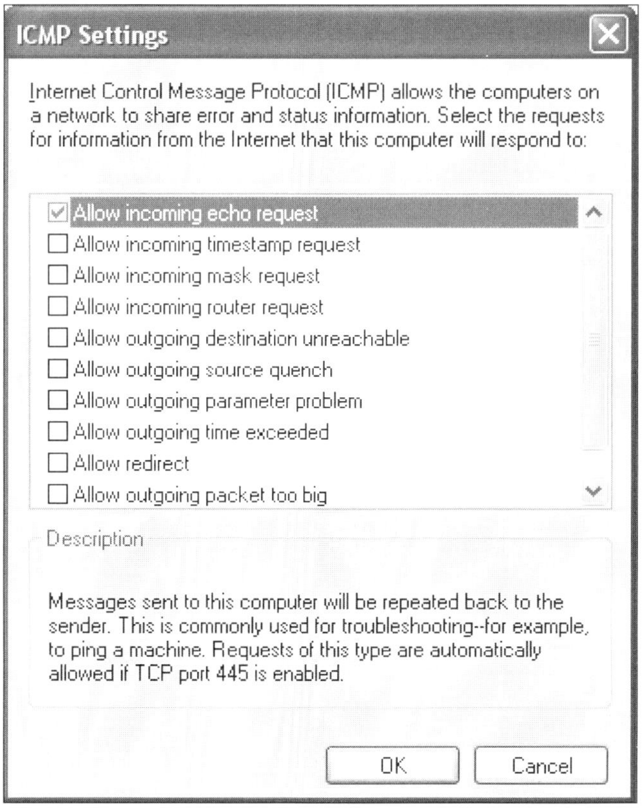

project 14.5 Troubleshooting Windows Firewall

exam objective

Troubleshoot TCP/IP. Tools include ARP; the Repair utility; connection properties; and the ping, ipconfig, pathping, and nslookup commands. Configure and troubleshoot Internet Connection Firewall (ICF) settings such as enable and disable. Considerations include indications of issues related to enabling or disabling ICF.

overview

After you enable Windows Firewall, you find that you are unable to install antivirus software over the small office network. You check the software vendor's Web site and learn that you must change the Windows Firewall settings to enable File and Printer Sharing. This opens the ports necessary for the installation.

learning objective

After completing this project, you will know how to change Windows Firewall settings.

specific requirements

See General Requirements. You also must have successfully completed Project 14.4, which requires a computer running Service Pack 2.

estimated completion time

15 minutes

project steps

1. Click **Start** and then **Control Panel** to open the **Control Panel**.
2. Click **Switch** to **Classic View**, if necessary.
3. Double-click the **Network Connections** icon to open the **Network Connections** window.
4. Right-click the **Local Area Connection** icon and select **Properties** to open the **Local Area Connections Properties** dialog box.
5. Click the **Advanced** tab to view the Windows Firewall section.
6. Click the **Settings** button to open the **Windows Firewall** dialog box.
7. On the **General** tab, select the **On** [**recommended**] option button to turn on Windows Firewall, if necessary.
8. Make sure that the **Don't allow exceptions** check box is not selected **(Figure 14-15)**.
9. Click the **Exceptions** tab.
10. Click **File and Printer Sharing (Figure 14-16)**.
11. Click **OK** to close the Windows Firewall dialog box.
12. Click **OK** to close the Local Area Connection Properties dialog box.
13. Install the antivirus software.
14. After the antivirus software is installed, repeat steps 1 through 11, but turn off exceptions and File and Printer Sharing.

Figure 14-15 The Windows Firewall dialog box - General tab

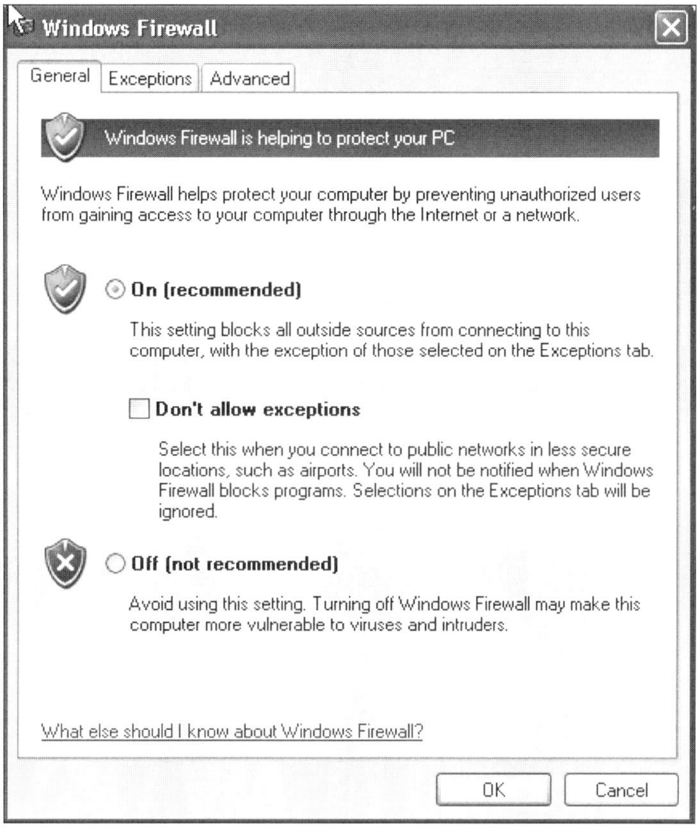

Figure 14-16 The Windows Firewall dialog box - Exceptions tab

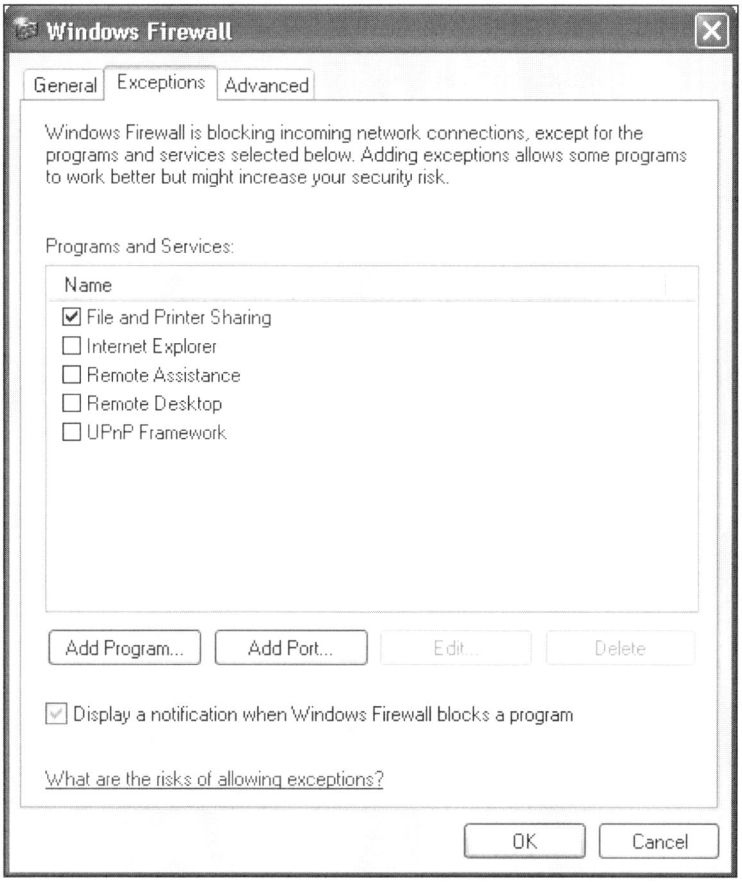

project 14.6

Troubleshooting Name Resolution

exam objective

Troubleshoot name resolution issues. Configure and troubleshoot host name resolution issues on a client computer. Considerations include Hosts files and DNS.

overview

One of the computers at the office is not connecting to a particular Web site. You have already checked the TCP/IP configuration and determined that TCP/IP is not the cause. You decide to flush the DNS cache and block negative DNS entries in the Registry so that the user will not have this problem in the future.

learning objective

After completing this project, you will be more familiar with flushing the DNS cache, using the HOSTS file, and the differences between DNS and WINS servers.

specific requirements

See General Requirements.

estimated completion time

15 minutes

project steps

1. Click **Start** and then **Run** to open the **Run** dialog box.
2. Type **cmd** in the **Open** text box and click **OK** to open the command prompt.
3. At the command prompt, type **ipconfig /flushdns** and press [**Enter**] **(Figure 14-17)**. The Windows XP DNS cache stores both successful and unsuccessful entries. If the DNS cache holds a negative entry and the Web site the user wants to use is now up and running, the user may still get a DNS error. Unsuccessful entries are stored for five minutes by default. However, most ISPs and DNS registrars now have a four-hour TTL (Time to Live). This is the amount of time that must pass before DNS information is updated.
4. Close the command prompt.
5. Click **Start** and then **Run** to open the **Run** dialog box.
6. Type **regedit** in the **Open** text box and press [**Enter**] to open the Registry Editor.
7. Expand the **HKEY_LOCAL_MACHINE** node.
8. Expand the **SYSTEM** node.
9. Expand **CurrentControlSet\Services\DNScache\Parameters (Figure 14-18)**.
10. Right-click **Parameters**, point to **New**, and select **DWORD value** to create a new Registry value.
11. Type **MaxNegativeCacheTTL** and press [**Enter**].
12. Right-click **MaxNegativeCacheTTL**, and click **Modify** to open the **Edit DWORD Value** dialog box.
13. Type **0** in the **Value data** text box **(Figure 14-19)**.
14. Click **OK** to close the dialog box. Now no unsuccessful DNS entries will be stored in the DNS cache.
15. Close the Registry Editor.

tip

Before you make Registry changes, you should always back up the Registry.

Figure 14-17 Ipconfig /flushdns

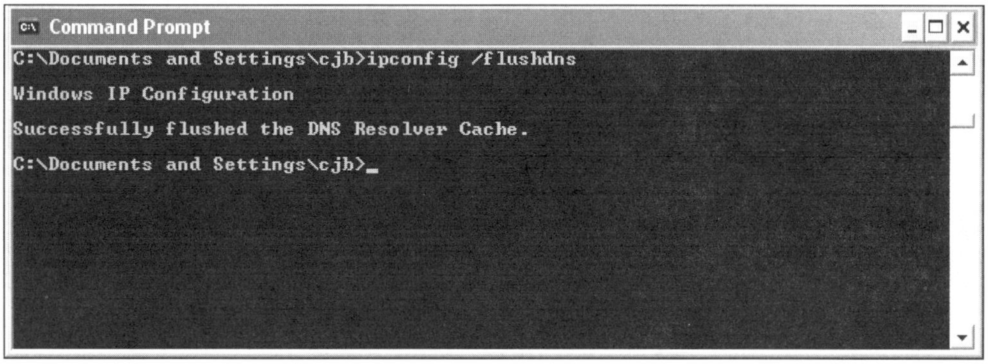

Figure 14-18 HKEY_LOCAL_MACHINE\SYSTEM\CurrentControlSet\Services\DNScache\Parameters

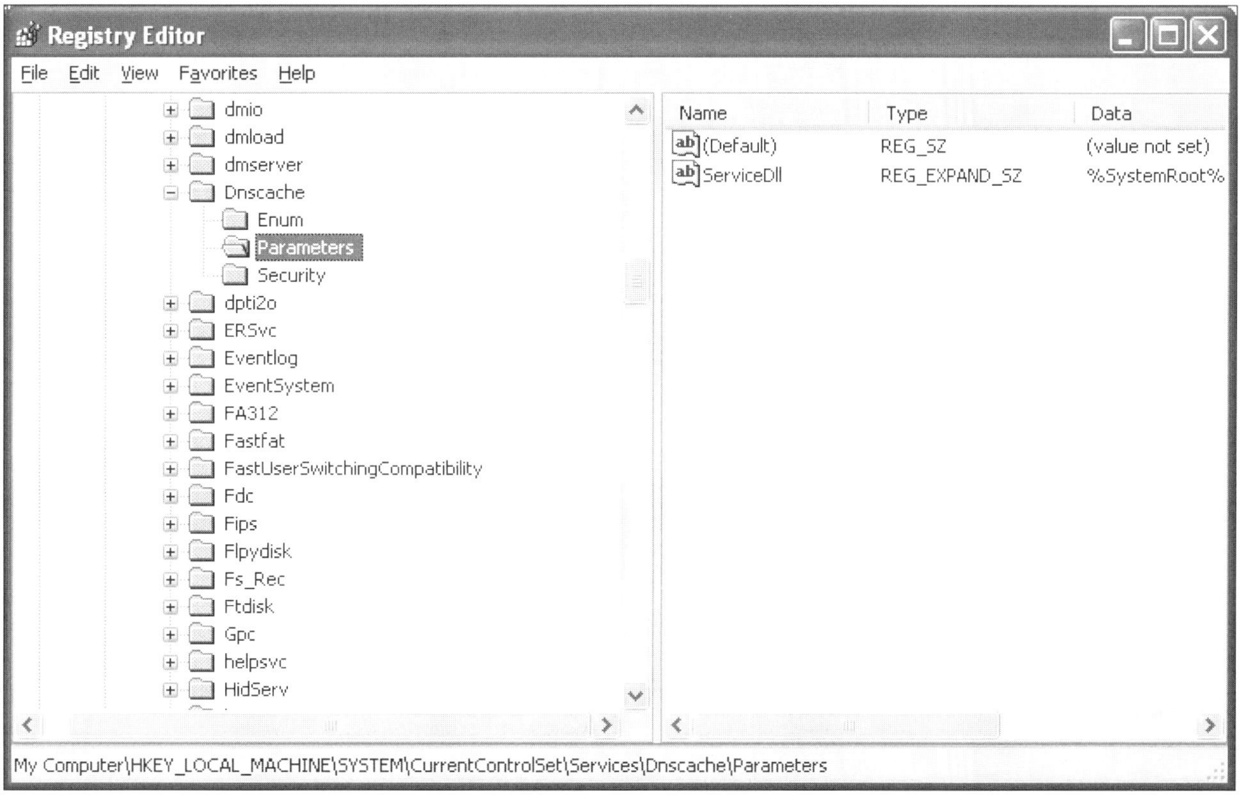

Figure 14-19 The Edit DWORD Value dialog box

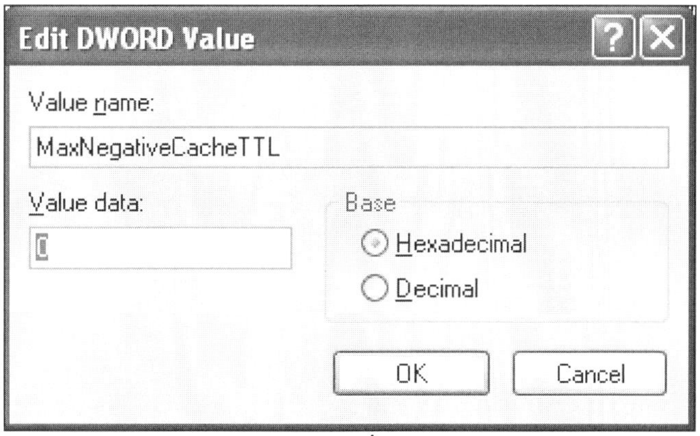

LESSON

15 Configuring and Troubleshooting Remote Connections

Windows XP allows users to connect remotely to network resources using dial-up networking, Remote Access Service (RAS), and virtual private networks (VPNs).

These services allow telecommuters, on-the-road employees, and others to connect to networks and share resources such as databases, e-mail, and other applications. In a RAS setup, a RAS server uses a modem or a modem pool to allow users to dial in from remote computers using modems. The RAS server and the RAS client must use the same connection medium. For example, if the RAS server uses an Integrated Services Digital Network (ISDN) modem, the RAS client must also use one. Using RAS, you connect to the local area network (LAN) by dialing the phone number of the RAS server. When you dial in to the RAS server, it receives the data from the modem and sends it to the LAN through the network interface card (NIC).

A VPN is a secure point-to-point connection established via a private network or a public network such as the Internet. Secure connections in VPNs are created using either Point-to-Point Tunneling Protocol (PPTP) or Layer Two Tunneling Protocol (L2TP). PPTP uses Microsoft Point-to-Point Encryption (MPPE) to provide encryption. If you use L2TP, a "tunnel" is created but data is not encrypted. To provide data encryption, L2TP must be used with IP Security (IPSec).

You use the New Connection Wizard to configure a Windows XP computer for remote access connections. To troubleshoot a remote connection, you can start by examining the configuration settings, but you may also need to physically examine a modem connection. You can also use Device Manager to examine the hardware devices on the computer. The Windows Help and Support Center also includes troubleshooting wizards.

When troubleshooting a VPN you might also need to utilize network analysis utilities such as Ping, Arp, Tracert, and Netstart. This lesson provides practice installing and troubleshooting remote connections.

Scenario

As an IT administrator at City Hospital, you have set up a new VPN for remote offices and employees who want to work at home. The hospital also maintains a RAS server that you will phase out in the next few years. Thus, for the next few years you will be configuring and troubleshooting both RAS client connections and VPN connections.

Lesson 15 Configuring and Troubleshooting Remote Connections

Project	Exam 70-271 Objective
15.1 Configuring an Inbound Connection	**Configure and troubleshoot remote connections.**
15.2 Configuring a Dial-up Connection	**Configure and troubleshoot remote connections.** Configure and troubleshoot a remote dialup connection. Tasks include client-side configuration.
15.3 Troubleshooting Dial-up Connections	**Configure and troubleshoot remote connections.** Configure and troubleshoot a remote dialup connection. Tasks include client-side configuration.
15.4 Configuring a VPN Connection	**Configure and troubleshoot remote connections.** Configure and troubleshoot a remote connection across the Internet. Tasks include client-side configuration.
15.5 Configuring a VPN Host	**Configure and troubleshoot remote connections.** Configure and troubleshoot a remote connection across the Internet. Tasks include client-side configuration.

General Requirements

To complete the projects in this lesson, you will need administrative rights on two Windows XP Professional computers with a standard 56.6 Kbs modem, a network adapter, and the TCP/IP protocol installed. You also may find it helpful to refer to Lesson 15 in your Prentice Hall Certification Series Exam 70-271 textbook for additional information about the topics covered by the projects in this lesson.

project 15.1

Configuring an Inbound Connection

exam objective

Configure and troubleshoot remote connections.

overview

Before leaving the office to work on site, you want to copy files directly from your computer to a laptop that you will be taking on the road. You need to create a direct connection between the computers so you can copy the files.

learning objective

After completing this project, you will know how to create a direct connection with another computer in which your Window XP Professional computer will be the guest.

specific requirements

See General Requirements.

estimated completion time

15 minutes

project steps

1. Click **Start** and then **Control Panel** to open the **Control Panel**.
2. In **Category View,** click **Network and Internet Connections** to open the **Network and Internet Connections** window.
3. Under **or pick a Control Panel icon**, click **Network Connections** to open the **Network Connections** dialog box.
4. Under **Network tasks** in the left pane, click the **Create a connection** link to start the **New Connection Wizard**.
5. Click **Next** to open the **Network Connection Type** screen.
6. Select the **Set up an advanced connection** option button **(Figure 15-1).**
7. Click **Next** to open the **Advanced Connection Options** screen.
8. Select the **Connect directly to another computer** option button **(Figure 15-2).**
9. Click **Next** to open the **Host or Guest**? screen.
10. Select the **Host** option button **(Figure 15-3)**.
11. Click **Next** to open the **Connection Device** screen.
12. Select the device that will be used for the connection. Select **Communications Port (COM1)** to connect with a null modem cable **(Figure 15-4)**.
13. Click **Next** to open the **User Permissions** screen.
14. Select your user name in the list.
15. Click **Next** to open the **Completing the New Connection Wizard** screen.
16. Click **Finish** to complete the wizard.
17. Close the Network Connections window.

Figure 15-1 Setting up an advanced connection

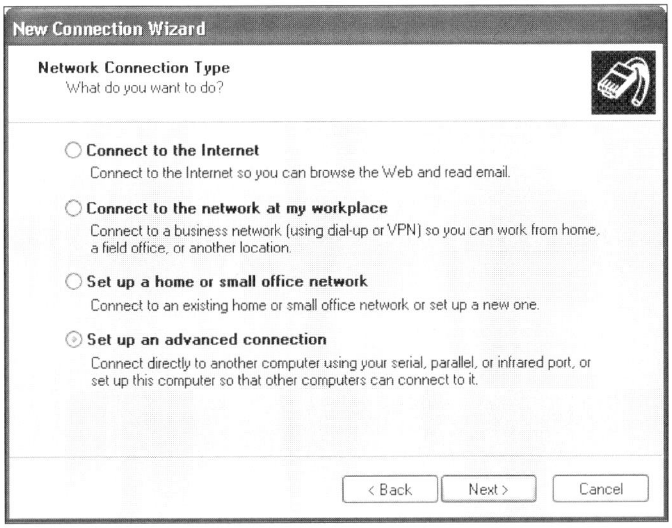

Figure 15-2 The Advanced Connection Options screen

Figure 15-3 The Host or Guest? screen

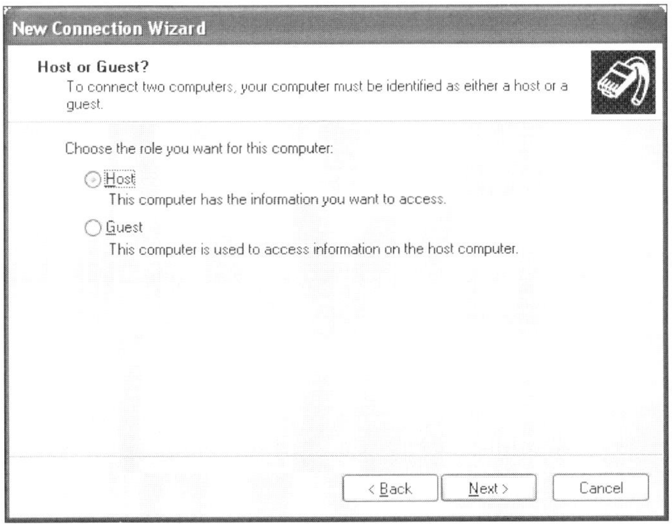

Figure 15-4 Selecting the communications port

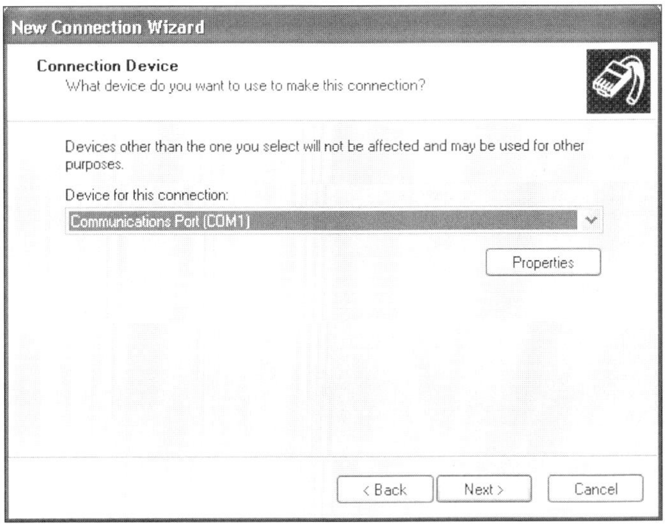

project 15.2 Configuring a Dial-up Connection

exam objective

Configure and troubleshoot remote connections. Configure and troubleshoot a remote dialup connection. Tasks include client-side configuration.

overview

You are working at Willows Medical Office, a remote office where you must configure RAS clients. For security purposes, you want to set up the configuration so that the client automatically logs off after 30 minutes. Because you have had problems with the phone connection dropping, you also want the RAS client to automatically redial if the line is dropped. Finally, you want to change the default security setting to require a secure password.

learning objective

After completing this project, you will know how to set up a dial-up connection and how to change RAS property settings.

specific requirements

See General Requirements.

estimated completion time

15 minutes

project steps

1. Click **Start** and then **Control Panel** to open the **Control Panel**.
2. Click the **Switch to Classic View** link.
3. Double-click the **Network Connections** icon to open the **Network Connections** window.
4. Under **Network Tasks**, click the **Create a new connection** link to start the **New Connection Wizard**.
5. Click **Next** to open the **Network Connection Type** screen.
6. Select the **Connect to the network at my workplace** option button.
7. Click **Next** to open the **Network Connection** screen.
8. Select the **Dial-up connection** option button **(Figure 15-5)**.
9. Click **Next** to open the **Connection Name** screen.
10. Enter a name for the connection in the **Company Name** text box (for example, **Willows Medical Office**).
11. Click **Next** to open the **Phone Number to Dial** screen.
12. Enter the telephone number you will use to dial in to the RAS server in the **Phone number** text box.
13. Click **Next** to open the **Connection Availability** screen. (Note: This step is applicable only if the computer is a domain member.)
14. Select the **Anyone's use** option button, if necessary.
15. Click **Next** to open the **Completing the New Connection Wizard** screen.
16. Click **Finish** to complete the New Connection Wizard.
17. The **Connect** dialog box opens **(Figure 15-6)**.
18. Click the **Properties** button to open the **Properties** dialog box for the connection.
19. Click the **Options** tab.
20. In the **Redialing options** section, select **30 minutes** in the **Idle time before hanging up** list box **(Figure 15-7)**.
21. Select the **Redial if the line is dropped** check box.
22. Click the **Security** tab.
23. In the **Validate my identity as follows** list box, select **Require secured password**.
24. Click **OK** to close the Properties dialog box for the connection and to return to the Connect dialog box.
25. You can now click the **Dial** button to dial in to the RAS server.

Figure 15-5 Creating a dial-up connection

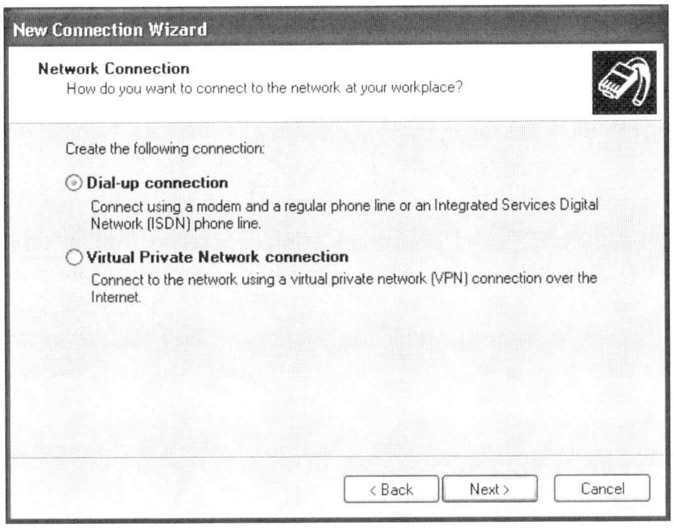

Figure 15-6 The Connect dialog box

Figure 15-7 The Properties dialog box for a connection-Options tab

project 15.3

Troubleshooting Dial-up Connections

exam objective

Configure and troubleshoot remote connections. Configure and troubleshoot a remote dialup connection. Tasks include client-side configuration.

overview

A user at a medical field office is having problems connecting to the RAS server. You visit the site to troubleshoot the connection. You start by double-checking that the connection from the computer to the modem is correct. You check the connection from the phone jack to the computer. As an additional check, you connect a telephone to the jack and call the server to make sure that the line to the home office is working. To complete your diagnosis, you use Windows XP utilities to troubleshoot the modem.

learning objective

After completing this project, you will know how to troubleshoot a modem connection.

specific requirements

See General Requirements.

estimated completion time

15 minutes

project steps

1. Click **Start** and then **Control Panel** to open the **Control Panel**.
2. Click the **Switch to Classic View** link, if necessary.
3. Double-click the **Phone and Modem Options** icon. If no area code has yet been recorded for the computer, the **Location Information** dialog box opens.
4. Enter your area code in the **What area code (or city code) are you in now**? text box **(Figure 15-8)**.
5. Click **OK** to close the dialog box.
6. Double-click the **Phone and Modem Options** icon to open the **Phone and Modem Options** dialog box.
7. Click the **Modems** tab, select the modem, and click the **Properties** button to open the **Properties** dialog box for the modem **(Figure 15-9)**.
8. Click the **Diagnostics** tab.
9. To test the modem, click the **Query Modem** button.
10. Scroll through the responses to see whether the queries are successful **(Figure 15-10)**.
11. Click the **General** tab.
12. If you need to continue troubleshooting, click the **Troubleshoot** button to open the **Modem Troubleshooter** in the **Help and Support Center (Figure 15-11)**.
13. Follow the step-by-step instructions to troubleshoot the modem.
14. Click **OK** to close the Properties dialog box for the modem.
15. Click **OK** to close the Phone and Modem Options dialog box, if necessary.
16. Close the Control Panel.

tip

If the area code has already been entered, when you click the Phone and Modem Options icon, the Phone and Modem Options dialog box opens.

Figure 15-8 The Location Information dialog box

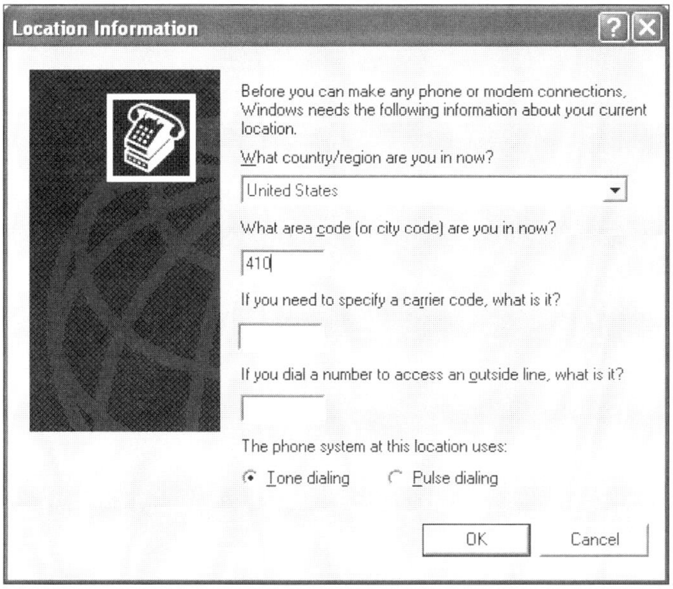

Figure 15-9 Modem Properties dialog box - General tab

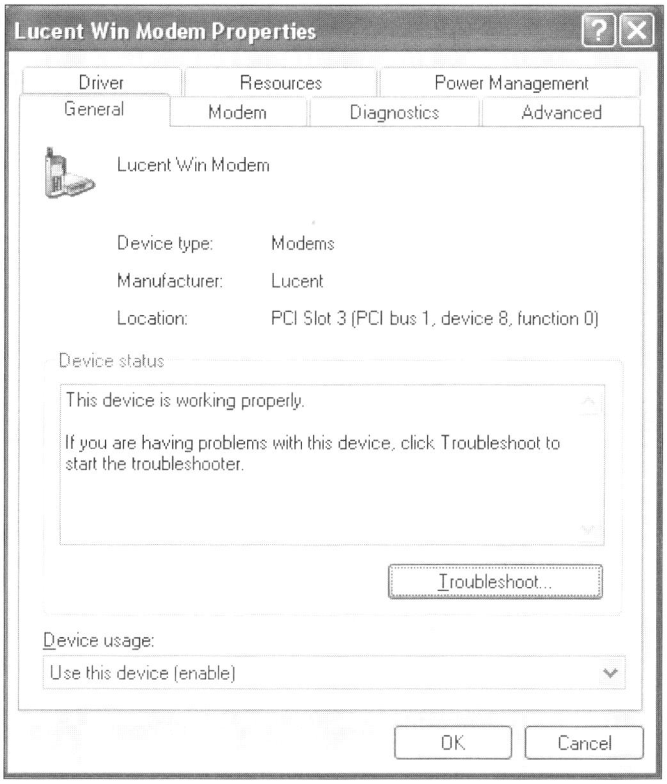

Figure 15-10 Modem Properties dialog box- Diagnostics tab

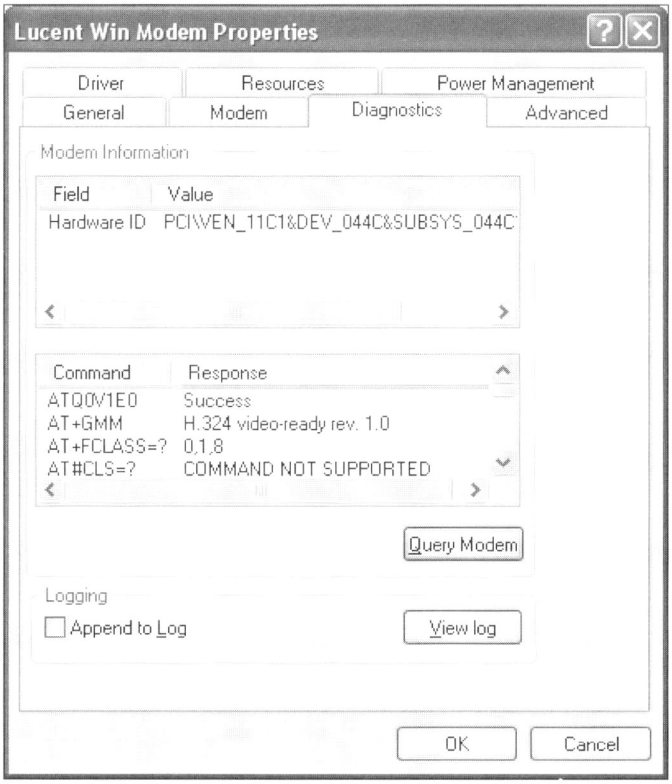

Figure 15-11 Modem Troubleshooter page in the Help and Support Center

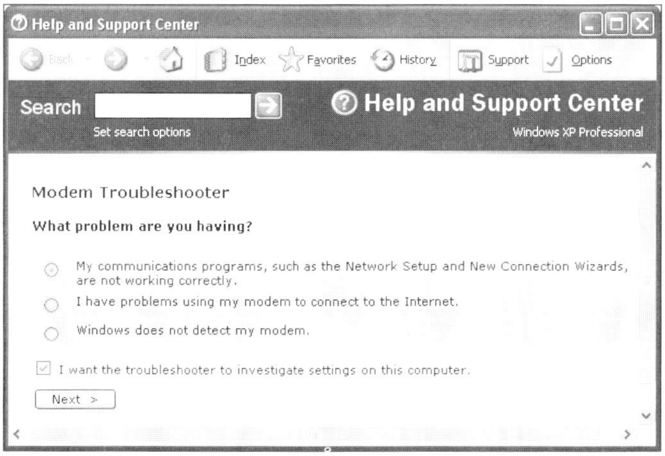

project 15.4 Configuring a VPN Connection

exam objective

Configure and troubleshoot remote connections. Configure and troubleshoot a remote connection across the Internet. Tasks include client-side configuration.

overview

Several of your co-workers have configured Windows XP computers as VPN clients. After querying users, you decide that you would like to have the VPN client automatically log on with the user's Windows name and password. You must create the VPN connection and configure it appropriately.

learning objective

After completing this project, you will know how to set up a VPN connection and set VPN properties.

specific requirements

None

estimated completion time

15 minutes

project steps

1. Click **Start** and then **Control Panel** to open the **Control Panel**.
2. Click the **Switch to Classic View** link.
3. Double-click the **Network Connections** icon to open the **Network Connections** window.
4. Click the **Create a new connection** link to start the **New Connection Wizard**.
5. Click **Next** to open the **Network Connection Type** screen.
6. Select the **Connect to the network at my workplace** option button.
7. Click **Next** to open the **Network Connection** screen.
8. Select the **Virtual Private Network connection** option button **(Figure 15-12)**.
9. Click **Next** to open the **Connection Name** screen.
10. Enter a name for the VPN connection in the **Company Name** text box. You can use the name of your organization or the name of the server to which you will be dialing in.
11. Click **Next** to open the **Public Network** screen. Select the **Automatically dial this initial connection** option button and select the name for your Internet connection in the list box.
12. Click **Next** to open the **VPN Server Selection** screen. Enter the host name or IP address for the VPN server to which you want to connect in the **Host name or IP address** text box **(Figure 15-13)**.
13. Click **Next** to open the **Connection Availability** screen. Select the **My use only** option button. (Note: This step is applicable only if the computer is a domain member.)
14. Click **Next** to open the **Completing the New Connection Wizard** screen. If desired, select the **Add a shortcut to this connection to my desktop** check box.
15. Click **Finish** to exit the wizard.
16. The **Connect** dialog box opens **(Figure 15-14)**.
17. Click the **Properties** button to open the **Properties** dialog box for the connection.
18. Click the **Security** tab and select the **Automatically use my Windows logon name and password** check box **(Figure 15-15)**.
19. Click **OK** to close the Properties dialog box for the connection.
20. The connection is dialed.

Figure 15-12 Creating a VPN connection

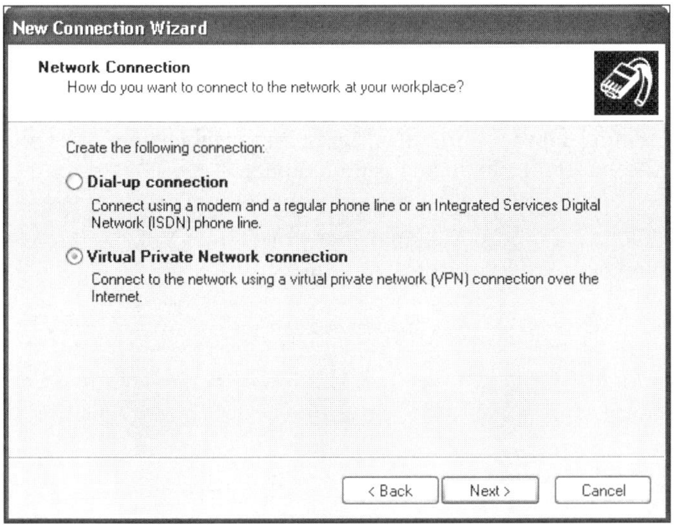

Figure 15-13 The VPN Server Selection screen

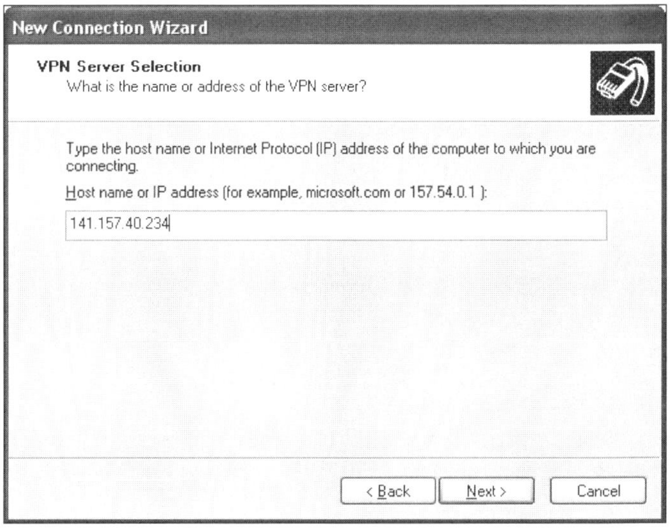

Figure 15-14 Connecting to a VPN

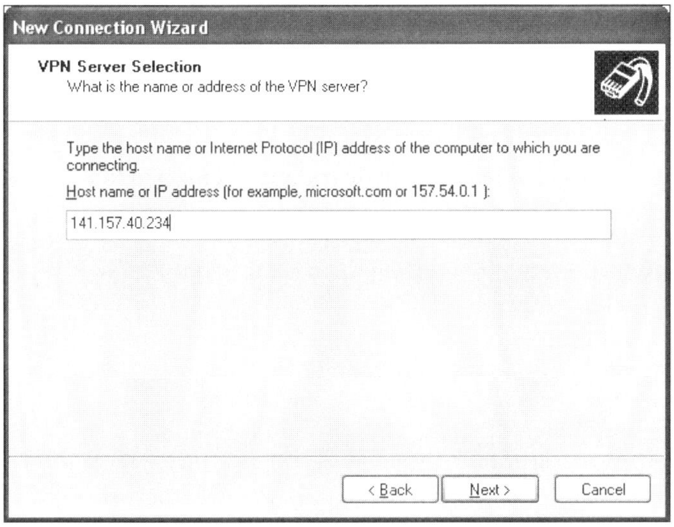

Figure 15-15 Changing VPN security properties

project 15.5

Configuring a VPN Host

exam objective

Configure and troubleshoot remote connections. Configure and troubleshoot a remote connection across the Internet. Tasks include client-side configuration.

overview

You have a request at a branch office to set up a VPN. To demonstrate how a VPN works, you need to set up a Windows XP computer to receive VPN connections.

learning objective

After completing this project, you will know how to set up a Windows XP computer to accept VPN connections.

specific requirements

See General Requirements. In addition, in order for a remote client to dial in, it must have a local user account on the Windows XP computer on which the incoming VPN connection is created.

estimated completion time

15 minutes

project steps

1. Click **Start** and then **Control Panel** to open the **Control Panel**.
2. Double-click **Network Connections** to open the **Network Connections** window.
3. Click the **Create a new connection** link to start the **New Connection Wizard**.
4. Click **Next** to open the **Network Connection Type** screen.
5. Select the **Setup an advanced connection** option button.
6. Click **Next** to open the **Advanced Connection Options** screen.
7. Select the **Accept incoming connections** option button **(Figure 15-16)**.
8. Click **Next** to open the **Devices for Incoming Connections** screen. Select the device, such as the modem, that you want to use for the incoming connection.
9. Click **Next** to open the **Incoming Virtual Private Network (VPN) Connection** screen.
10. Select the **Allow virtual private connections** option button **(Figure 15-17)**.
11. Click **Next** to open the **User Permissions** screen. Select the users that you will allow to connect.
12. Click **Next** to open the **Networking Software** screen.
13. Select **Internet Protocol (TCP/IP),** if necessary, and click the **Properties** button to open the **Incoming TCP/IP Properties** dialog box.
14. Make sure that the **Allow callers to access my local area network** check box is selected **(Figure 15-18)**.
15. Click **OK** to close the Incoming TCP/IP Properties dialog box.
16. Click **Next** to open the **Completing the Network Connection Wizard** screen.
17. Click **Finish** to exit the wizard.

Figure 15-16 Accepting incoming connections

Figure 15-17 Allowing VPN connections

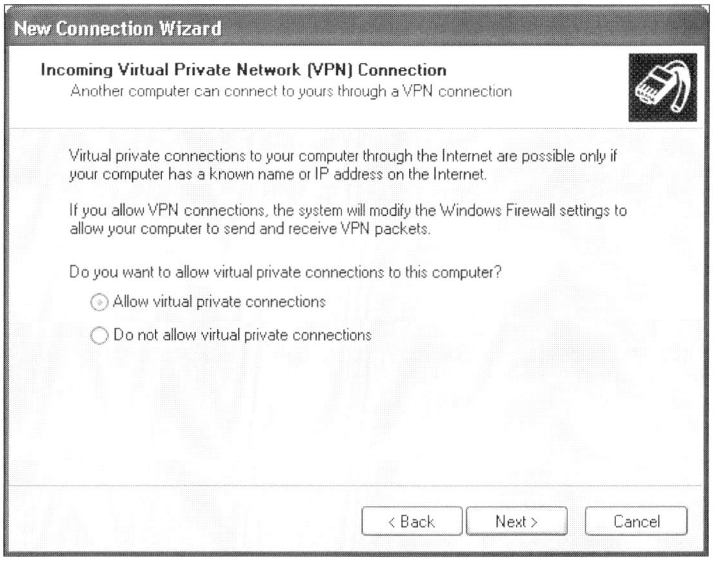

Figure 15-18 The Incoming TCP/IP Properties dialog box

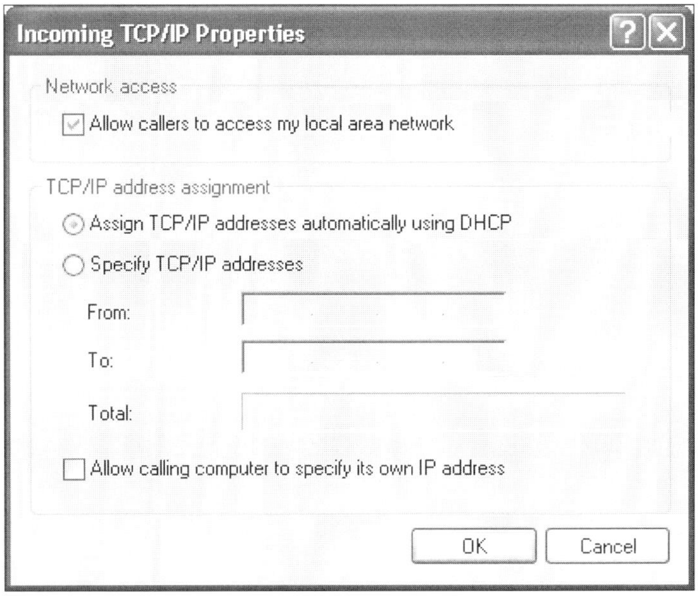

LESSON

16 Configuring and Troubleshooting Internet Explorer

Internet Explorer is the Internet browsing application that is automatically installed with Windows XP. Internet Explorer can display Internet pages, load Hypertext Markup Language (HTML) files saved to disk, and display Hypertext Transfer Protocol (HTTP) database applications such as library catalogs.

You can configure Internet Explorer to establish a dial-up or network-based Internet connection. You can also set a default home page, manage temporary Internet files, and cache settings. Most importantly, you can customize privacy and security settings that can help ensure that your computer is protected from harmful software and undesirable Web content. Internet Explorer also allows you to import and export favorite sites, enlarge text (for the visually impaired), and even control the colors used for Internet links.

Since many companies rely on the Internet for research, communication, and e-commerce, it is essential that Internet Explorer is installed properly and securely.

This lesson provides projects designed to familiarize you with setting up Internet connections, changing security settings, and customizing Internet Explorer.

Scenario

You work in the education department of a large hospital. Your department creates medical education Web sites for both doctors and patients. As part of your support work, you must help troubleshoot installations for users at the hospital as well as onsite at physicians' offices.

Lesson 16 Configuring and Troubleshooting Internet Explorer

Project	*Exam 70-271 Objective*
16.1. Configuring Internet Explorer Connection Properties	**Configure and troubleshoot Internet Explorer**. Configure and troubleshoot Internet Explorer connections properties.
16.2. Configuring and Troubleshooting Internet Explorer Security Settings - I	**Configure and troubleshoot Internet Explorer**. Configure and troubleshoot Internet Explorer security properties.
16.3. Configuring and Troubleshooting Internet Explorer Security Settings - II	**Configure and troubleshoot Internet Explorer**. Configure and troubleshoot Internet Explorer security properties.
16.4. Configuring Internet Explorer General Properties - I	**Configure and troubleshoot Internet Explorer**. Configure and troubleshoot Internet Explorer general properties.
16.5. Configuring Internet Explorer General Properties - II	**Configure and troubleshoot Internet Explorer**. Configure and troubleshoot Internet Explorer general properties.

General Requirements

To complete the projects in this lesson, you will need administrative rights on a Windows XP Professional computer that can be connected to the Internet via a local area network (LAN), DSL, or cable modem, using Internet Explorer. You may also find it helpful to refer to Lesson 16 in your Prentice Hall Certification Series Exam 70-271 textbook for additional information about the topics covered by the projects in this lesson.

project 16.1

Configuring Internet Explorer Connection Properties

exam objective

Configure and troubleshoot Internet Explorer. Configure and troubleshoot Internet Explorer connections properties.

overview

Your hospital provides a Litigation database that can be accessed over its network or offsite by a select group of hospital staff. Some users connect using a broadband connection, whereas others connect via a dial-up modem. You must configure Internet Explorer to connect to the Litigation database for both broadband and dial-up modem users.

Learning objective

After completing this project, you will know how to use Internet Explorer to set up a remote access connection to the Internet through a local area network, DSL, or cable modem.

specific requirements

See General Requirements.

estimated completion time

15 minutes

project steps

Set up the connection using a local area network:

1. Open **Internet Explorer**.
2. Open the **Tools** menu and click **Internet Options** to open the **Internet Options** dialog box.
3. Click the **Connections** tab **(Figure 16-1).**
4. Click the **LAN Settings** button to open the **Local Area Network (LAN) Settings** dialog box.
5. Select the **Automatically detect settings** check box.
6. Select the **Use automatic configuration script** check box.
7. In the **Address** text box, type the address **http://litigation.hosplib.org:8080/proxy.pac (Figure 16-2)**.
8. Click **OK** to close the Local Area Network (LAN) Settings dialog box.
9. Click **OK** to close the Internet Options dialog box.

Set up an Internet connection using a modem:

1. Open **Internet Explorer.**
2. Open the **Tools** menu and click **Internet Options** to open the **Internet Options** dialog box.
3. Click the **Connections** tab.
4. In the **Dial-up and Virtual Private Network settings** list box, select **Dial-up Connection (Default) (Figure 16-3).**
5. Click the **Settings** button to open the **Dial-up Connection Settings** dialog box.
6. Select the **Automatically detect settings** check box.
7. Select the **Use automatic configuration script** check box.
8. In the **Address** text box, type: **http://litigation.hosplib.org:8080/proxy.pac (Figure 16-4).**
9. Click **OK** to close the Dial-up Connection Settings dialog box.
10. Click **OK** to close the Internet Options dialog box.

tip

Some Internet service providers (ISPs) may not allow this type of proxy connection.

Figure 16-1 The Connections tab in the Internet Options dialog box

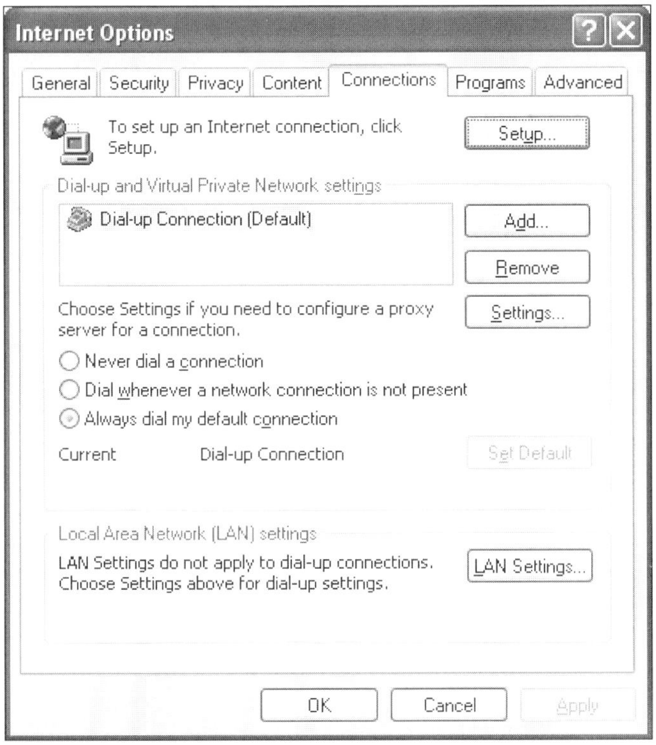

Figure 16-2 Setting a connection address

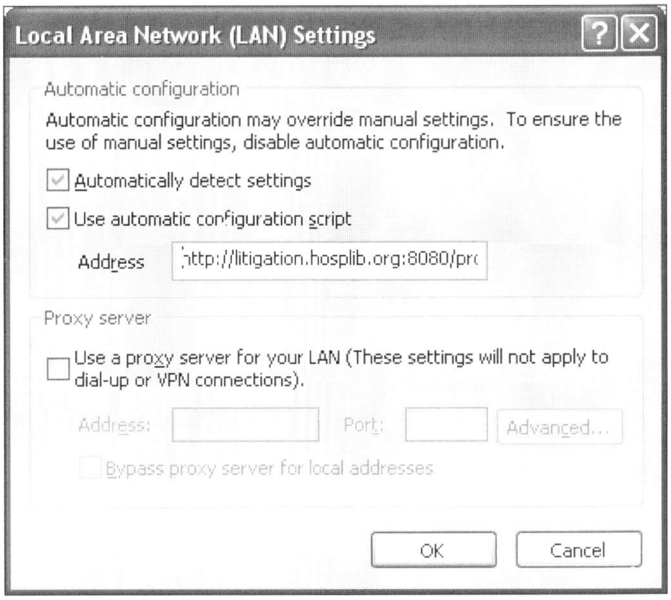

Figure 16-3 Selecting the default dial-up connection

Figure 16-4 The Dial-up Connection Settings dialog box

project 16.2

Configuring and Troubleshooting Internet Explorer Security Settings - I

exam objective

Configure and troubleshoot Internet Explorer. Configure and troubleshoot Internet Explorer security properties.

overview

You have been called to troubleshoot for a group of users who can no longer connect to one of the hospital's Web sites. You have been told that an administrator changed the Internet Explorer privacy settings on all of the computers. You have also been told that users cannot log on to the hospital's Web site, and that they were never able to view the site's educational Flash animated sequences.

After analyzing the Internet Explorer settings, you discover that the privacy setting has been set to High and that Web site logons use a type of cookie that is blocked by this setting. You also realize that the Flash animation does not work because the administrator disabled ActiveX controls and plug-ins in Internet Explorer. You ask the administrator why she set the security to High and whether you should set up a trusted Web site for the hospital. She advises you that it will be acceptable to lower the Internet privacy settings and enable ActiveX controls.

learning objective

After completing this project, you will know how to change the privacy and ActiveX controls settings in Internet Explorer.

specific requirements

See General Requirements.

estimated completion time

15 minutes

project steps

Change the privacy settings:

1. Open **Internet Explorer.**
2. Open the **Tools** menu and click **Internet Options** to open the **Internet Options** dialog box.
3. Click the **Privacy** tab.
4. Click and drag the slider in the **Settings** section to Medium High **(Figure 16-5).**

Activate ActiveX controls:

1. In the **Internet Options** dialog box, click the **Security** tab.
2. Click the **Internet** icon.
3. Click the **Custom Level** button to open the **Security Settings** dialog box.
4. Scroll down to the **Run ActiveX controls and plug-ins** section and click the **Enable** option button **(Figure 16-6).**
5. Click **OK** to close the **Security Settings** dialog box.
6. A **Warning** dialog box prompts you to confirm that you want to change the security settings for the zone. Click **Yes** (**Figure 16-7**).
7. Click **OK** to close the Internet Options dialog box.

Figure 16-5 Internet Options dialog box-Privacy tab

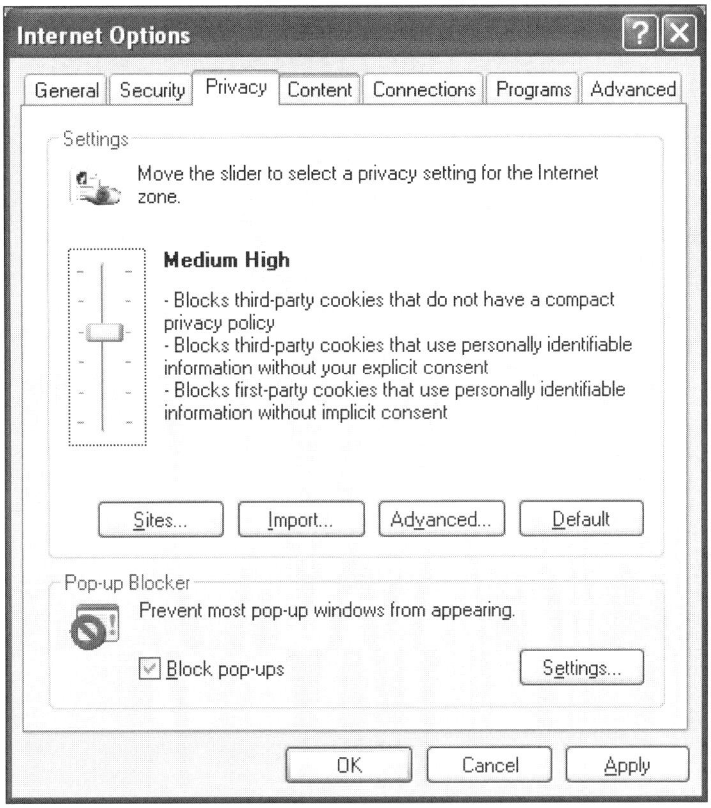

Figure 16-6 Enabling ActiveX controls and plug-ins

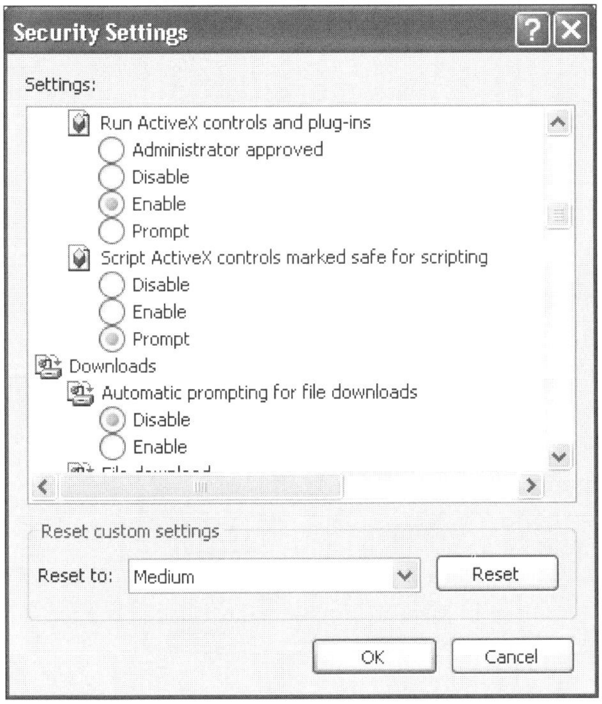

Figure 16-7 Confirming security settings changes

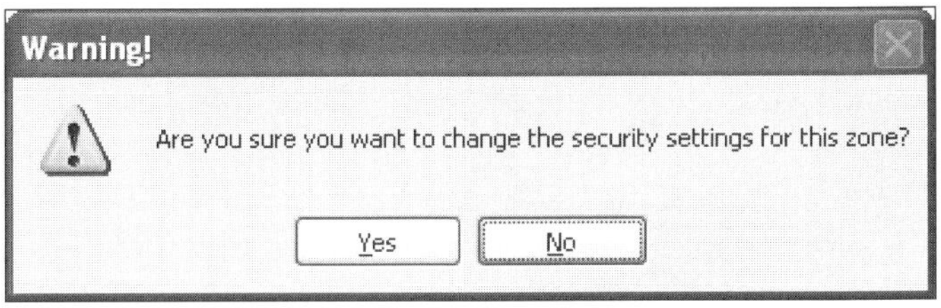

project 16.3

Configuring and Troubleshooting Internet Explorer Security Settings - II

exam objective

Configure and troubleshoot Internet Explorer. Configure and troubleshoot Internet Explorer security properties.

overview

You have been asked to configure Internet use security guidelines for the hospital staff. You must decide how Internet Explorer will be set up to ensure that users cannot download viruses and other harmful files. However, all users must be able to log on and download files from the hospital education Web sites. **Figure 16-8** and **Figure 16-9** show how to set up a trusted site.

learning objective

After completing this project, you will be more familiar with the privacy settings in Internet Explorer.

specific requirements

See General Requirements.

estimated completion time

15 minutes

project steps

Users at your hospital cannot log on to hospital Web sites when the privacy setting in Internet Explorer is set to **High**. You want to set up a privacy setting of **High** for all sites except hospital Web sites. Describe how you would do this in Internet Explorer.

Figure 16-8 Configuring security settings for a Web content zone

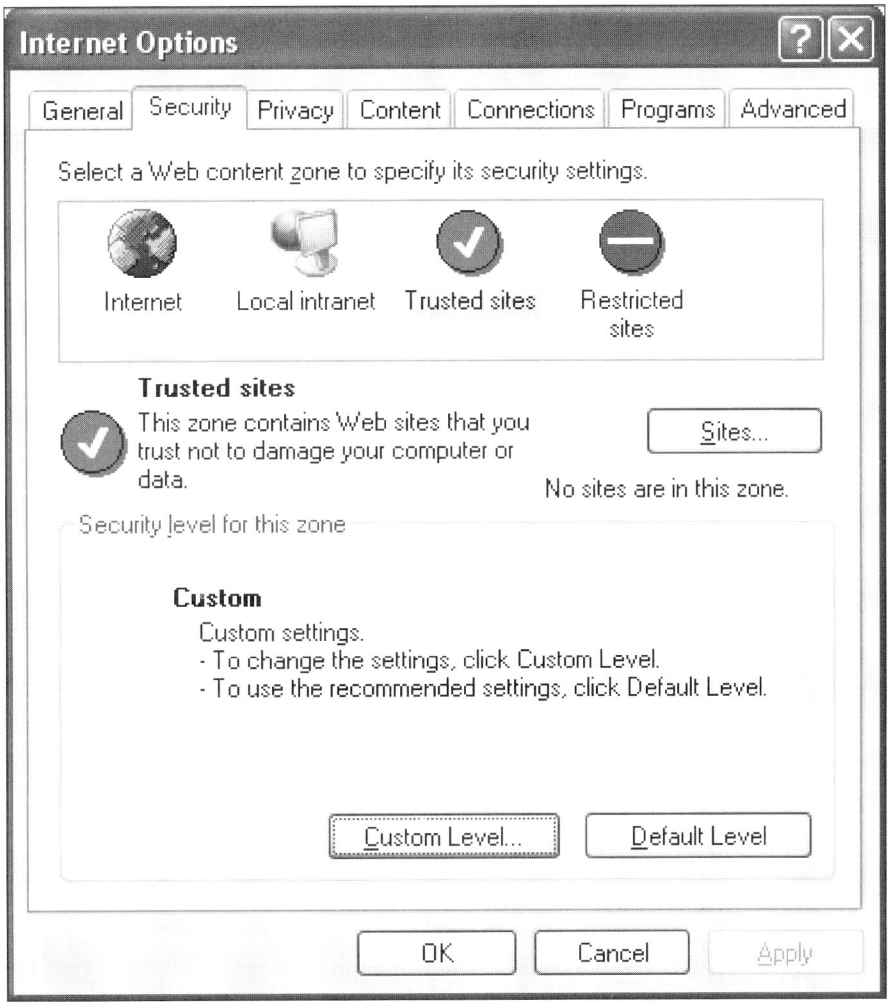

Figure 16-9 The Trusted sites dialog box

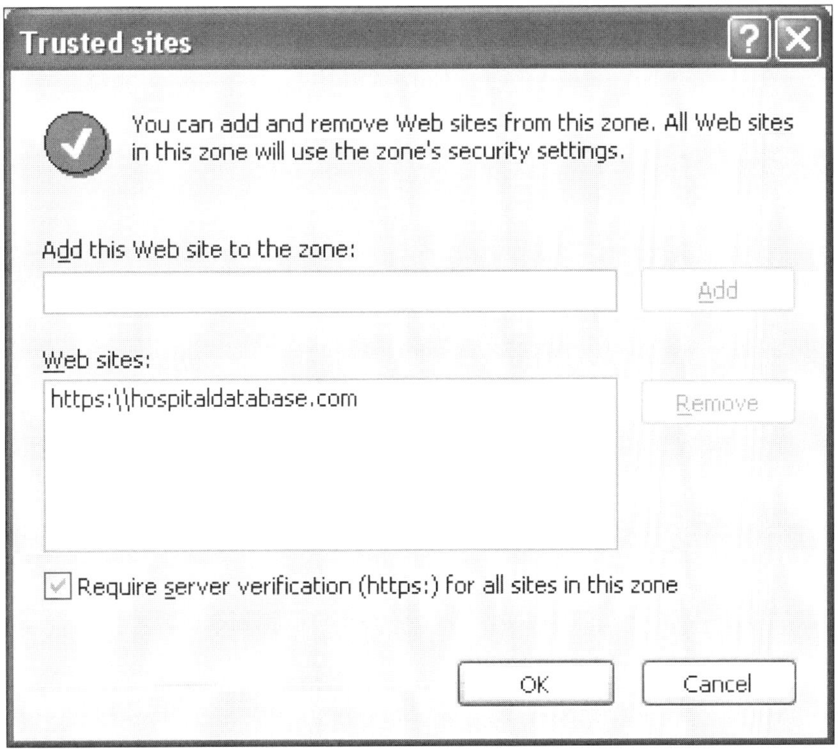

project 16.4

Configuring Internet Explorer General Properties - I

exam objective

Configure and troubleshoot Internet Explorer. Configure and troubleshoot Internet Explorer general properties.

overview

The hospital has compiled a list of recommended favorite medical and health Web sites. When you install Internet Explorer at a small medical office with a few physicians, you must add these favorite sites to users' browsers. To do this, you can export the Internet Favorites folder from your computer and import it into Internet Explorer on the users' computers.

learning objective

After completing this project, you will know how to export and import the Internet Explorer Favorites folder.

specific requirements

A Windows XP Professional computer connected to the Internet

estimated completion time

15 minutes

project steps

1. If you do not have any favorite Web sites designated in Internet Explorer, browse to a Web site, open the **Favorites** menu, and select **Add to Favorites** to open the **Add Favorite** dialog box.
2. Click **OK** to add the site to your **Favorites** list.
3. To export the Favorites list, open the **File** menu and click **Import and Export** to start the **Import/Export Wizard (Figure 16-10)**.
4. Click **Next** to view the **Import/Export Selection** screen.
5. In the **Choose an action to perform** box, select **Export Favorites.**
6. Click **Next** to view the **Export Favorites Source Folder** screen. The **Favorites** folder is selected by default **(Figure 16-11)**.
7. Click **Next** to view the **Export Favorites Destination** screen. By default, the **Import/Export Wizard** saves the list to your **My Documents** folder and names the export file **bookmark.htm**. If you want to change the destination, click the **Browse** button and choose a different destination location. For example, you can save the file to a disk in your **A:** drive. Do not change the file name.
8. Click **Next** to view the **Completing the Import/Export Wizard** screen.
9. Click **Finish**. An **Export Favorites** alert notifies you that the file has been successfully exported **(Figure 16-12).**
10. Click **OK**.
11. To import the bookmark file to another computer, open **Internet Explorer** on the other computer.
12. Open the **File** menu and click **Import and Export** to start the **Import/Export Wizard**.
13. Click **Next** to view the **Import/Export Selection** screen.
14. In the **Choose an action to perform** box, select **Import Favorites (Figure 16-13)**.
15. Click **Next** to view the **Import Favorites Source** screen.
16. To select the file to import, click the **Browse** button to open the **Select Bookmark File** dialog box.
17. To load the file from the A: drive, select **3 ½ Floppy (A:)** in the **Save in** list box.

Figure 16-10 The Import/Export Wizard

Figure 16-11 Exporting Favorites

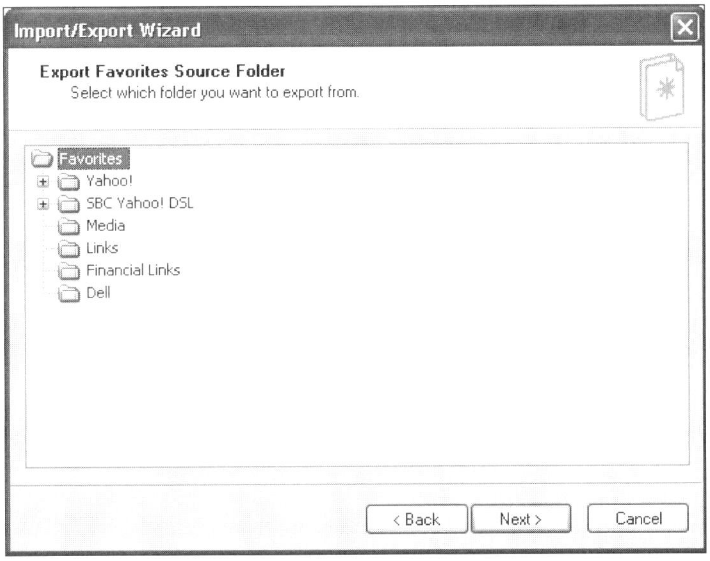

Figure 16-12 The Export Favorites confirmation message box

Figure 16-13 Importing Favorites

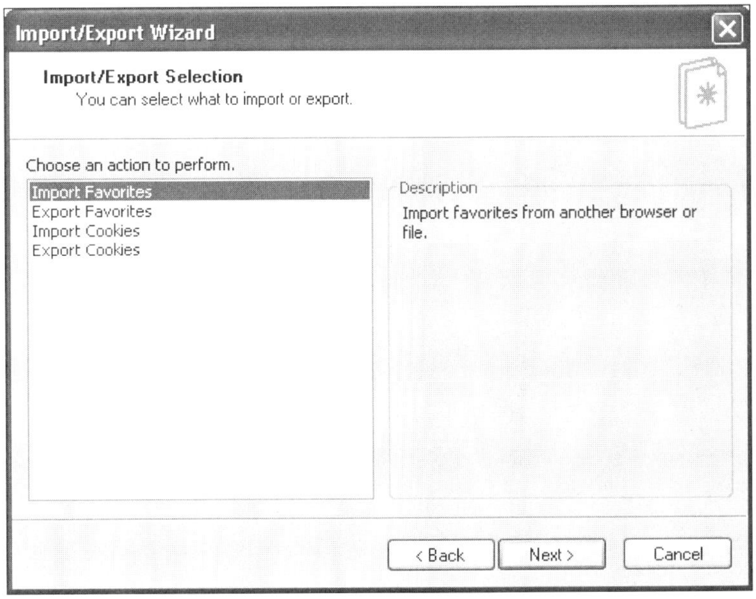

project 16.4

Configuring Internet Explorer General Properties - I (cont'd)

exam objective

Configure and troubleshoot Internet Explorer. Configure and troubleshoot Internet Explorer general properties.

project steps

18. Select the **bookmark.htm** file and click the **Save** button **(Figure 16-14)**.
19. Click **Next** to view the **Import Favorites Destination Folder** screen. The **Favorites** folder is selected by default.
20. Click **Next** to view the **Completing the Import/Export Wizard** screen.
21. Click **Finish**. An **Import Favorites** alert notifies you that the file has been successfully imported.
22. Click **OK**.
23. Close Internet Explorer.

Figure 16-14 The Select Bookmark File dialog box

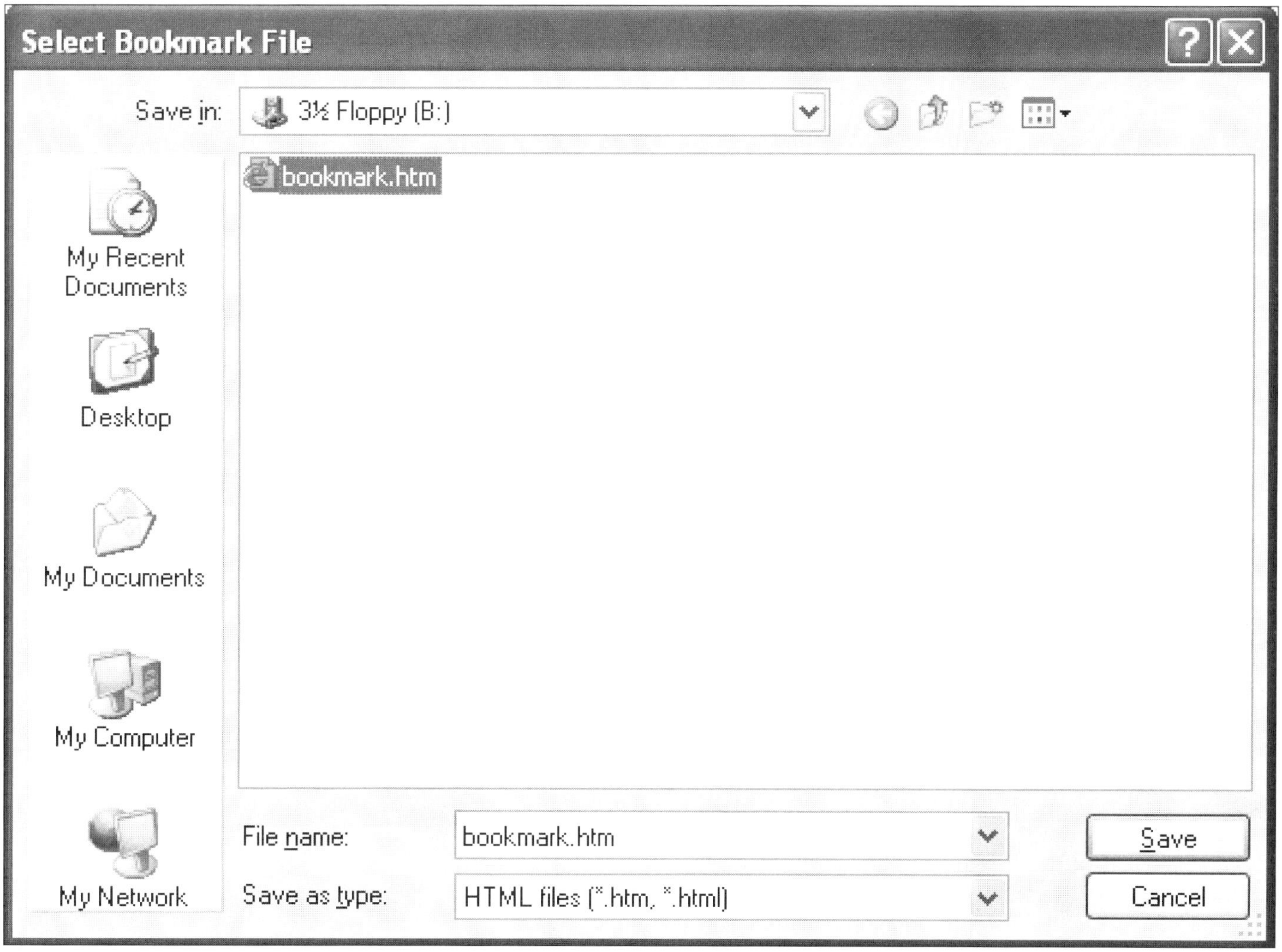

project 16.5

Configuring Internet Explorer General Properties - II

exam objective

Configure and troubleshoot Internet Explorer. Configure and troubleshoot Internet Explorer general properties.

overview

You have been asked to help an employee who is visually impaired. She is having problems seeing text on the screen and returning to Web links that she needs for research. You have also been told by the employee's supervisor that she has been downloading music from the Internet, which is in violation of the company's security policy. You decide to help the employee by enlarging the screen fonts in Internet Explorer and changing the visited link colors to red. You decide to set up a restricted site so she can no longer download music and files from a site that can potentially harm her computer.

learning objective

After completing this project, you will know how to change text size, change link colors, and add a restricted site.

specific requirements

A Windows XP Professional computer connected to the Internet

estimated completion time

15 minutes

project steps

1. Open **Internet Explorer**.
2. To increase the text size, open the **View** menu, point to **Text Size,** and click **Largest (Figure 16-15).**
3. To change the link color for visited sites, open the **Tools** menu and click **Internet Options** to open the **Internet Options** dialog box.
4. Click the **Colors** button to open the **Colors** dialog box **(Figure 16-16)**.
5. Click the **Visited color** button to open the **Color** dialog box, which contains a color palette.
6. Click the bright red color in the **Color** dialog box **(Figure 16-17)**.
7. Click **OK** to close the **Color** dialog box.
8. Click **OK** to close the **Colors** dialog box.
9. To set up a restricted site, in the **Internet Options** dialog box, click the **Security** tab.
10. Click the **Restricted Sites** icon.
11. Click the **Sites** button to open the **Restricted sites** dialog box.
12. In the **Add this Web site to the zone** text box, type the Uniform Resource Locator (URL) of the restricted site: **http://downloadmoremusic.com (Figure 16-18)**.
13. Click the **Add** button to add the site to the **Web sites** list box.
14. Click **OK** to close the **Restricted sites** dialog box.
15. Click **OK** to close the Internet Options dialog box.
16. Close Internet Explorer.

Figure 16-15 Changing Internet Explorer text size

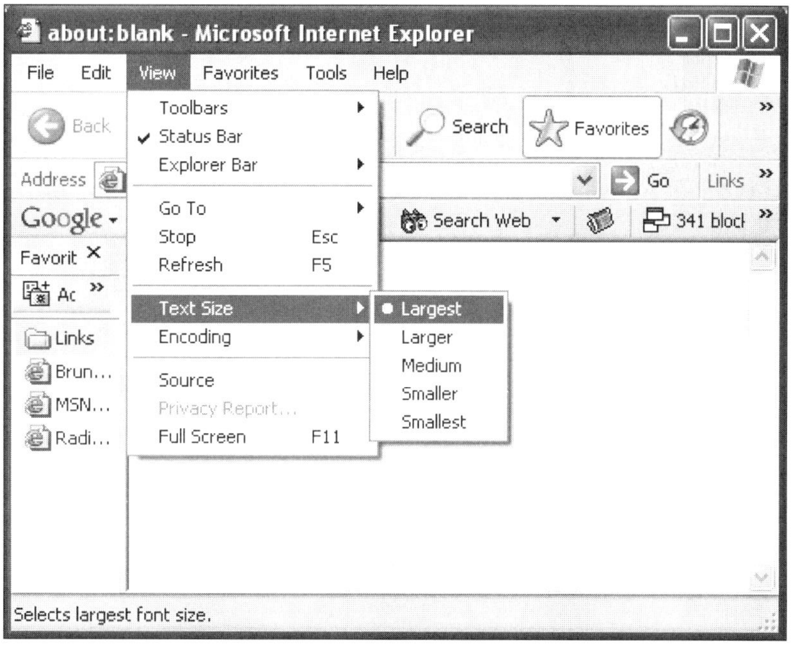

Figure 16-16 The Colors dialog box

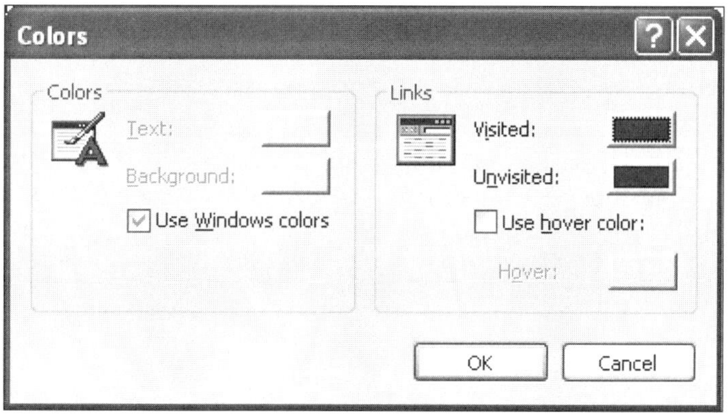

Figure 16-17 The Color dialog box

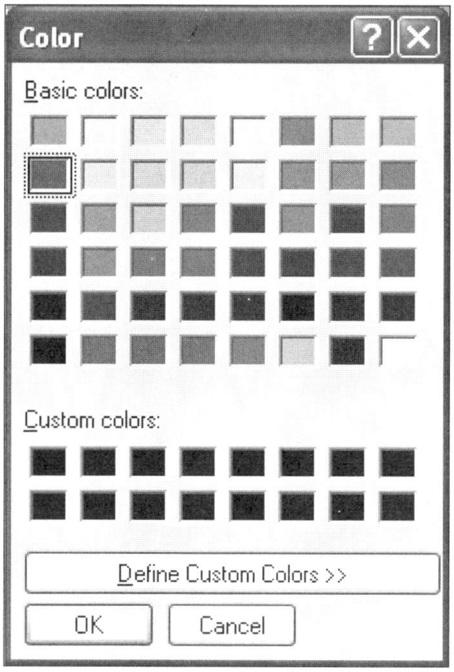

Figure 16-18 Adding a restricted Web site

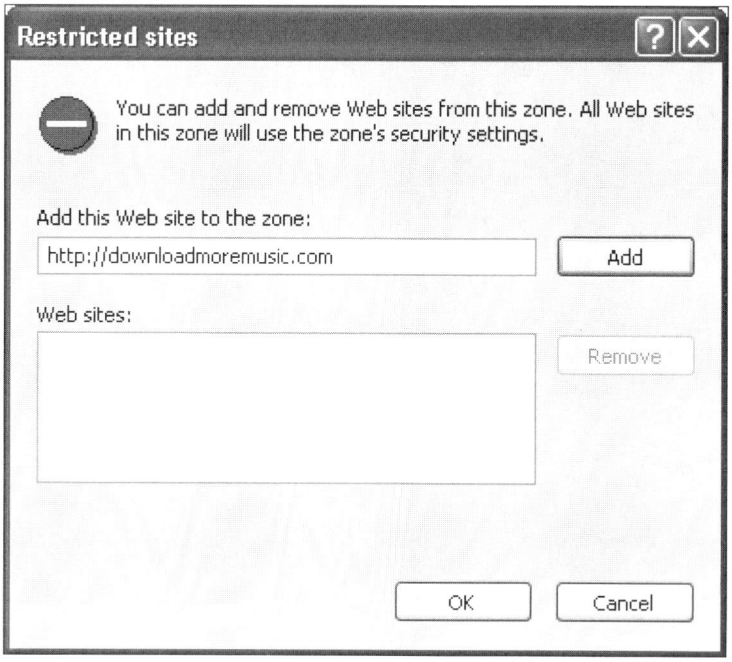

LESSON

17 Configuring and Troubleshooting End-User Systems Remote Tools

The Windows XP Remote Desktop and Remote Assistance utilities allow you to remotely control another computer in order to perform remote troubleshooting and configuration. IT staff members can use Remote Desktop to help users who need troubleshooting assistance or to access their own computers from another location. Using Remote Desktop you can access files, run applications, and access network resources.

Remote Assistance allows users to quickly create and send a help request to another computer using either e-mail or Windows Messenger. If you receive a Remote Assistance invitation, you can respond by initiating a Remote Desktop session with the user who needs help. After you access the remote computer, you can work on it just as if you were using the mouse and keyboard attached to it.

To initiate and run a Windows XP Remote Desktop or Remote Assistance session, you must be on a local area network (LAN) or the Internet. The remote computers must be able to send e-mail or communicate through Windows Messenger. If both users have public IP addresses assigned by an Internet service provider (ISP), the connection is established through TCP port 3389. If Internet Connection Firewall is enabled, port 3389 is opened automatically.

When a user sends an e-mail Remote Assistance request, Windows XP creates an XML attachment file. This XML file includes an RCTicket attribute, which specifies the IP address of the sender, and the computer's remote communications port, typically 3389. If a connection is made via digital subscriber line (DSL) or a cable modem with a home router using Network Address Translation (NAT) addressing, the RCTicket attribute is written as a private IP address. In order to communicate, you must substitute this private IP address for the public IP address, which can be obtained at **http://ip.nefsc.noaa.gov/**.

This lesson features projects that will show you how to configure and use Remote Desktop to help end users. You will also learn how to configure Remote Assistance to request help from another user.

Scenario

You are working at Covault Bank in the software development division. Your programming team is testing custom banking software at bank branches and small offices. In order to troubleshoot software and operating system installations, you are going to set up Remote Desktop and Remote Assistance on the computers at different test sites.

Lesson 17 Configuring and Troubleshooting End-User Systems Remote Tools

Project	*Exam 70-271 Objective*
17.1. Understanding Remote Desktop and Remote Assistance	**Configure and troubleshoot end-user systems by using remote connectivity tools**. Use Remote Desktop to configure and troubleshoot an end user's desktop. Use Remote Assistance to configure and troubleshoot an end user's desktop.
17.2. Using Remote Desktop	**Configure and troubleshoot end-user systems by using remote connectivity tools**. Use Remote Desktop to configure and troubleshoot an end user's desktop.
17.3. Using Remote Assistance - I	**Configure and troubleshoot end-user systems by using remote connectivity tools**. Use Remote Assistance to configure and troubleshoot an end user's desktop.
17.4. Using Remote Assistance - II	**Basic knowledge**

General Requirements

To complete the projects in this lesson, you will need administrative rights on two Windows XP Professional computers on a domain that is connected to the Internet. Each Windows XP computer must have Outlook Express configured as its default e-mail program. You may also find it helpful to refer to Lesson 17 in your Prentice Hall Certification Series Exam 70-271 textbook for additional information about the topics covered by the projects in this lesson.

project 17.1

Understanding Remote Desktop and Remote Assistance

exam objective

Configure and troubleshoot end-user systems by using remote connectivity tools. Use Remote Desktop to configure and troubleshoot an end user's desktop. Use Remote Assistance to configure and troubleshoot an end user's desktop.

overview

First, you must train the programming team. You decide to prepare a handout describing the benefits of using Remote Desktop and Remote Assistance. Your handout must include step-by-step instructions and screen shots showing how to set up Remote Desktop and Remote Assistance.

learning objective

After completing this project, you will be more familiar with configuring Remote Desktop and Remote Assistance.

specific requirements

See General Requirements.

estimated completion time

30 minutes

project steps

Create a handout explaining how people can use Remote Desktop and Remote Assistance for troubleshooting and what system requirements must be met. Follow the steps below and capture screenshots for the handout. You will be working on the computer with which you want to establish a remote connection.

1. Click **Start** and then **Control Panel** to open the **Control Panel**.
2. Double-click **System** to open the **System Properties** dialog box.
3. Click the **Remote** tab.
4. In the **Remote Assistance** section, make sure that the **Allow Remote Assistance invitations to be sent from this computer** check box is selected.
5. In the **Remote Desktop** section, make sure that the **Allow users to connect remotely to this computer** check box is selected.
6. Click the **Advanced** button to open the **Remote Assistance Settings** dialog box.
7. Make sure that the **Allow this computer to be controlled remotely** check box is selected (**Figure 17-1**).
8. Click **OK** to close the Remote Assistance Settings dialog box.
9. Click the **Select Remote Users** button to open the **Remote Desktop Users** dialog box (**Figure 17-2**).
10. Click **Add** to open the **Select Users** dialog box.
11. Click the **Locations** button to open the **Locations** dialog box.
12. Expand the **Entire Directory** node and select your domain (**Figure 17-3**).
13. Click **OK** to close the Locations dialog box.
14. Click the **Advanced** button to open the **Select Users or Groups** dialog box.
15. Click the **Find Now** button to list the user accounts in the domain in the search results list at the bottom of the dialog box.
16. Hold down the [**Ctrl**] key and select the users who will be allowed to access the computer remotely (**Figure 17-4**).
17. Click **OK** to close the Select Users or Groups dialog box.
18. Click **OK** to close the Remote Desktop Users dialog box.
19. Click **OK** to close the System Properties dialog box.

Figure 17-1 The Remote Assistance Settings dialog box

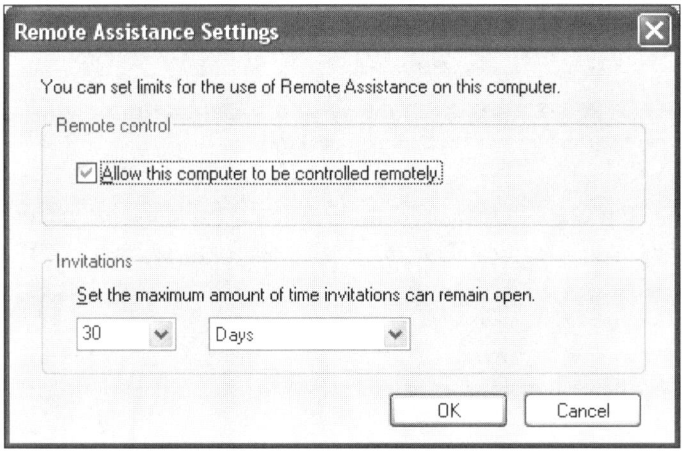

Figure 17-2 The Remote Desktop Users dialog box

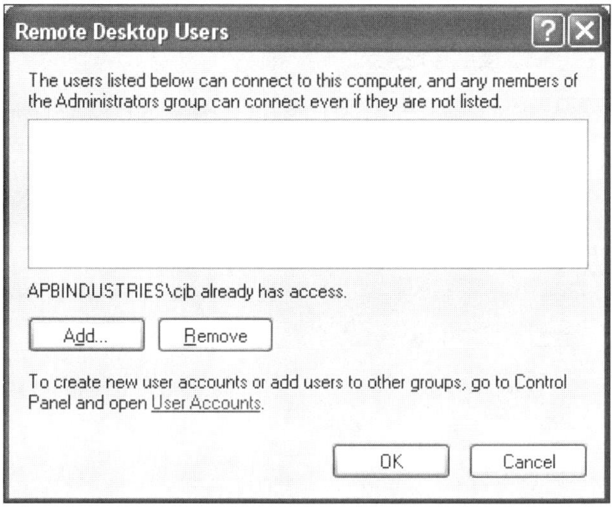

Figure 17-3 The Locations dialog box

Figure 17-4 The Select Users or Groups dialog box

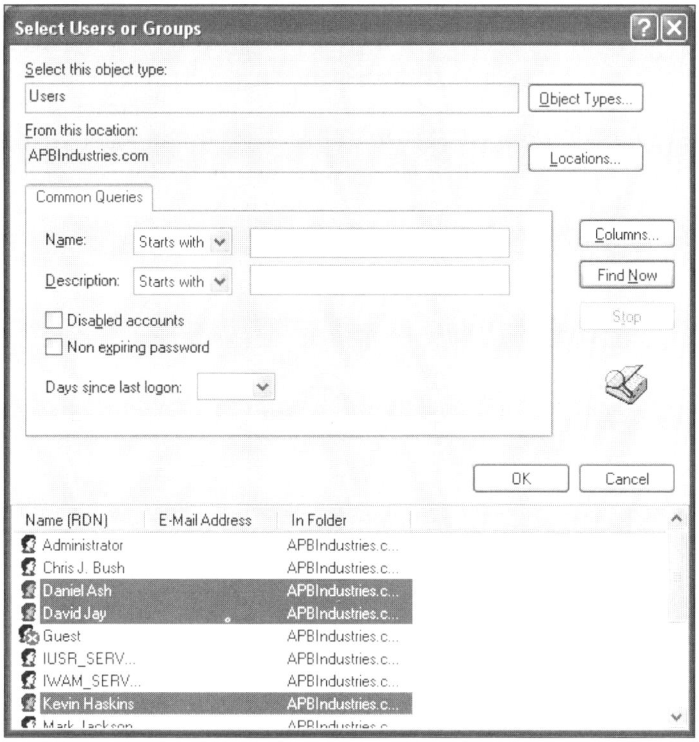

project 17.2

Using Remote Desktop

exam objective

Configure and troubleshoot end-user systems by using remote connectivity tools. Use Remote Desktop to configure and troubleshoot an end user's desktop.

overview

You need to set up a Remote Desktop connection in order to run banking software on a remote computer. You set up Remote Desktop so it can access local serial devices.

learning objective

After completing this project, you will know how to log on using a Remote Desktop connection and how to change connection options.

specific requirements

See General Requirements.

estimated completion time

15 minutes

project steps

1. Click, **Start**, point to **All Programs**, point to **Accessories**, point to **Communications**, and click **Remote Desktop Connection** to open the **Remote Desktop Connection** dialog box.
2. Enter the name of the computer to which you want to connect in the **Computer** text box (**Figure 17-5**).
3. Click the **Options** button to expand the dialog box.
4. Click the **Local Resources** tab, and then click the **Serial ports** check box (**Figure 17-6**).
5. Click the **Connect** button. The **Remote Desktop Connection Security Warning** dialog box opens to caution you that allowing serial ports to be made available to the remote computer is potentially unsafe **(Figure 17-7)**.
6. Click **OK** to close the warning dialog box and connect to the remote computer.
7. In the **Log on to Windows** dialog box for the remote computer, enter your user name and password and click **OK** to log on.
8. When you want to log off, click **Start** and then click either **Log Off** or **Disconnect** to end the session. Log Off provides options to close your programs and log off or to leave programs running and log on as another user. The Disconnect option disconnects the session. You can log on again later to reconnect to the session.

Figure 17-5 The Remote Desktop Connection dialog box

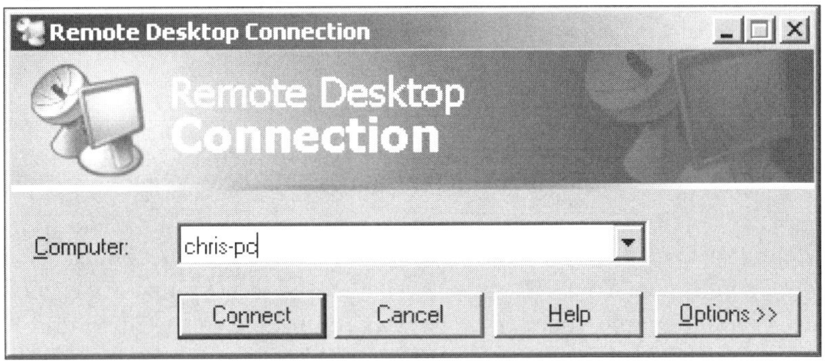

Figure 17-6 The Remote Desktop Connection dialog box-Local Resources tab

Figure 17-7 The Remote Desktop Connection Security Warning

project 17.3

Using Remote Assistance – I

exam objective

Configure and troubleshoot end-user systems by using remote connectivity tools. Use Remote Assistance to configure and troubleshoot an end user's desktop.

overview

You need to test banking software at a location connected to the Internet via a DSL connection. To use Remote Assistance, you must obtain the public IP address for the user's computer and change the RCTicket attribute in the invitation file. When you use Remote Assistance utilities, you decide to save the invitation file to your desktop so that you can easily access and edit it.

learning objective

After completing this project, you will be more familiar with Remote Assistance, and you will know how to edit the RCTicket attribute.

specific requirements

See General Requirements.

estimated completion time

30 minutes

project steps

1. Find the public IP address of the computer that you need to set up for Remote Assistance by opening this URL: **http://ip.nefsc.noaa.gov/**.
2. Click **Start** and then **Help and Support** to open the **Help and Support Center**.
3. Under **Ask for Assistance,** click the **Invite a friend to connect to your computer with Remote Assistance** link.
4. On the **Remote Assistance** screen, click the **Invite someone to help you** link.
5. Scroll down and select the **Save invitation as a file (Advanced)** link **(Figure 17-8).**
6. On the **Remote Assistance - Save Invitation** screen, enter the name that you would like to appear on the invitation and the expiration time **(Figure 17-9)**.
7. Click the **Continue** button.
8. Enter a password and confirm the password in the appropriate fields.
9. Click the **Save Invitation** button to open the **Save As** dialog box. Save the **RAInvitation.msrcincident** file on the desktop **(Figure 17-10).**
10. Close the Help and Support Center.
11. On the desktop, right-click the **RAInvitation.msrcincident** icon and click **Open With** to open the **Open With** dialog box.
12. Select **Notepad** in the **Programs** list and click **OK**.
13. Find the **RCTICKET** attribute and change the IP address to the public IP address **(Figure 17-11).**
14. Open the **File** menu and click **Save**. Close Notepad.
15. Double-click the invitation file. When the file opens, a dialog box allows to you connect to the user's computer that requested assistance.

Figure 17-8 Saving a Remote Assistance invitation as a file

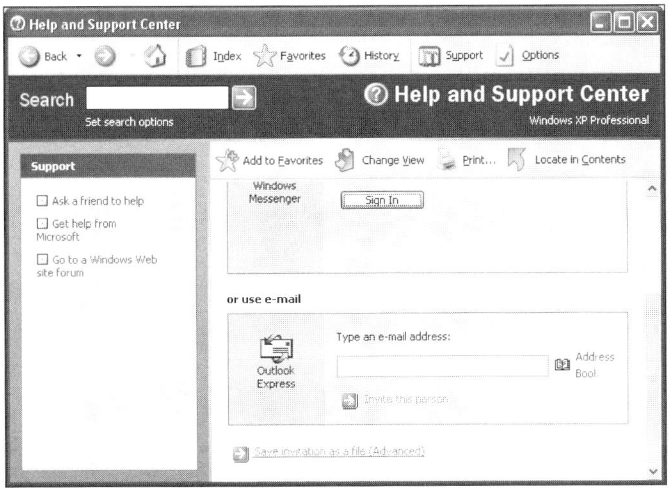

Figure 17-9 Entering the name and expiration time for the invitation

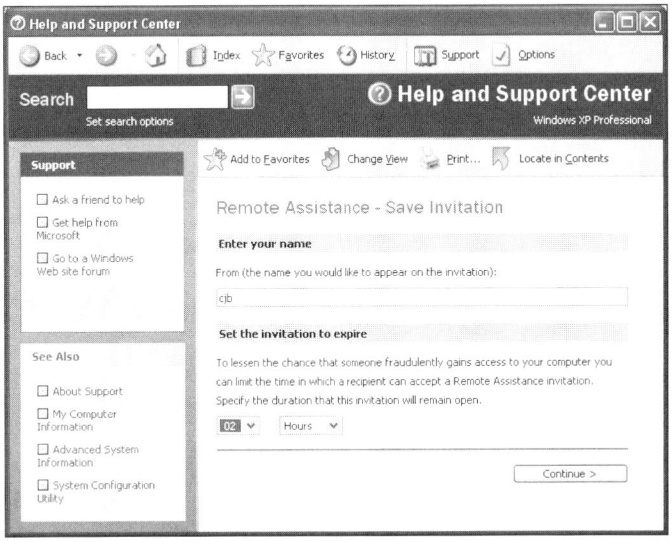

Figure 17-10 Saving the RAInvitation file

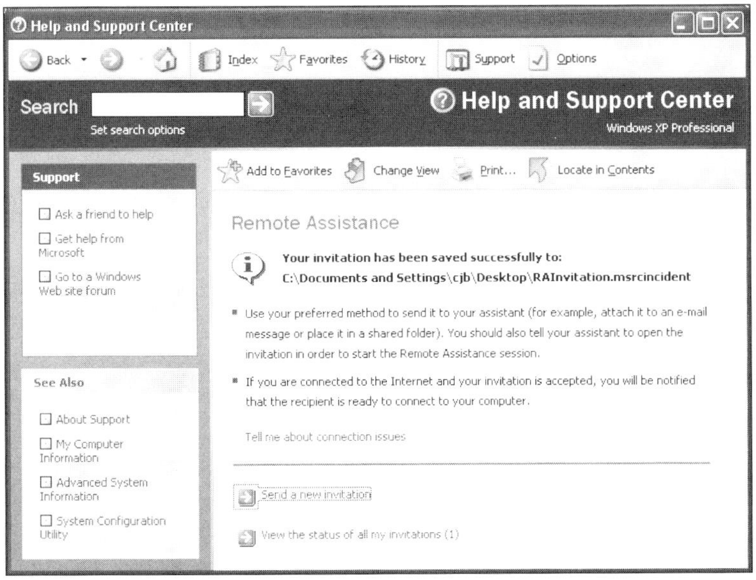

Figure 17-11 The RCTICKET attribute in XML invitation file

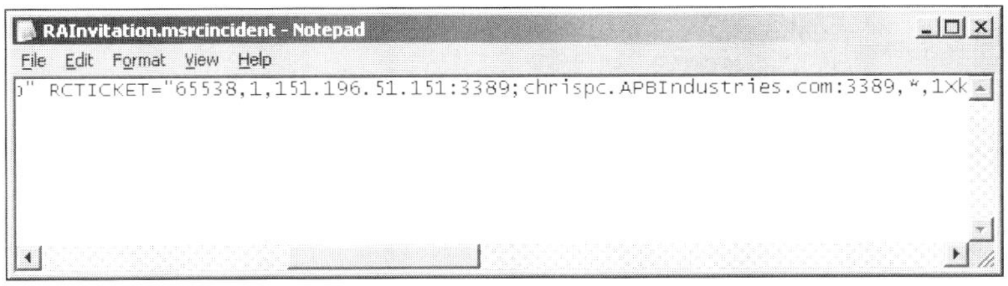

project 17.4

Using Remote Assistance – II

exam objective

Basic knowledge

overview

You receive a phone call (rather than an e-mail message) from a user at the bank who needs remote assistance. You have administrative privileges on your computer and you know the computer name of the end user's computer. You use the Help and Support Center to initiate a Remote Assistance session.

learning objective

After completing this project, you will know how to offer remote assistance.

specific requirements

See General Requirements.

estimated completion time

15 minutes

project steps

1. Click **Start** and then **Help and Support** to open the **Help and Support Center**.
2. In the Help and Support **Search** field, type **Offer Remote Assistance** and click the green arrow button to start the search **(Figure 17-12).**
3. In the search results column, click **Offer Remote Assistance**.
4. On the **Offer Remote Assistance** screen, enter the computer name or IP address of the computer to which you want to connect **(Figure 17-13)**.
5. Click the **Connect** button.
6. You can now log on to the remote computer and begin your Remote Desktop session.

Figure 17-12 Help and Support Center

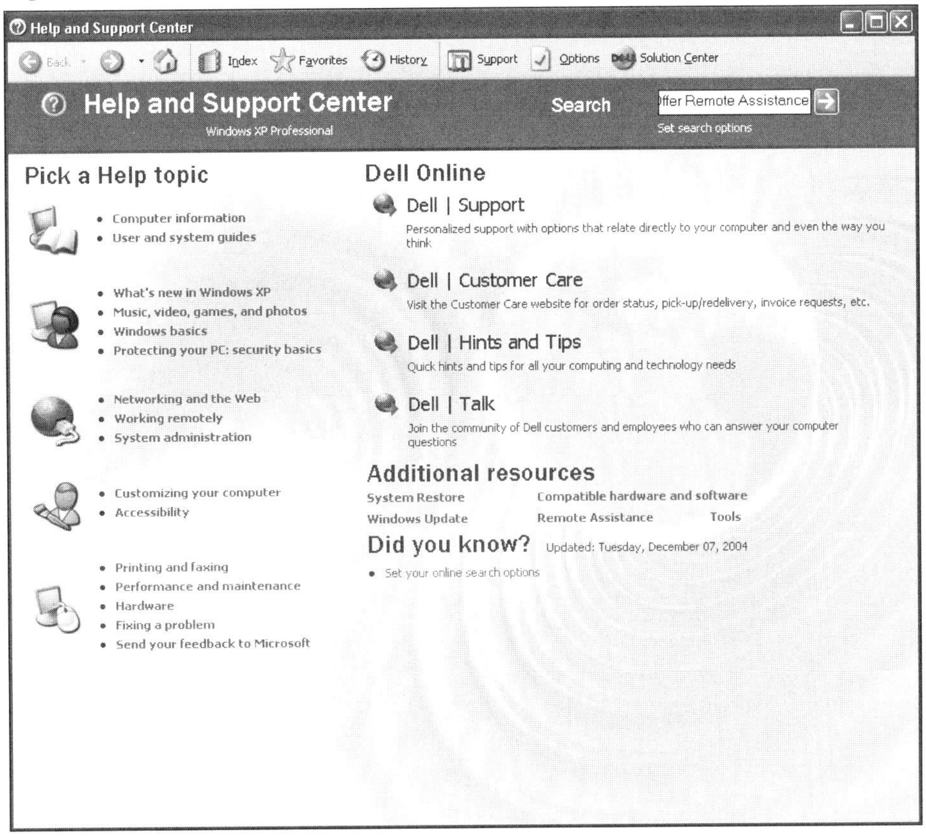

Figure 17-13 Offer Remote Assistance page in the Help and Support Center

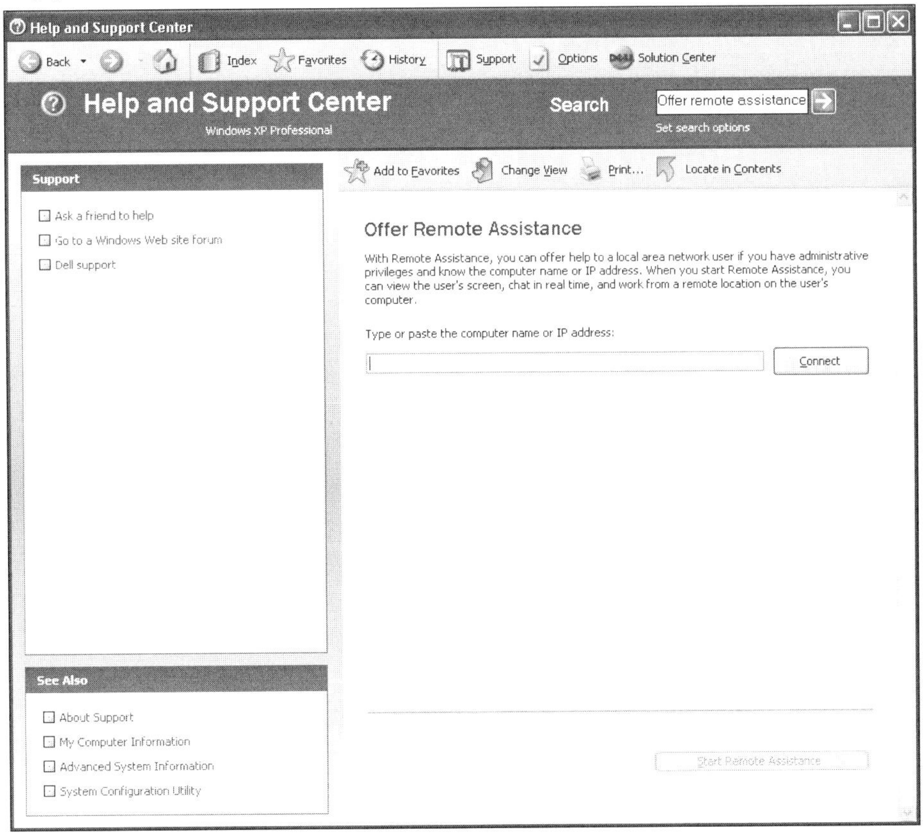

Glossary

Access Denied A type of message that informs a user that he or she has been refused access to a resource.

Accessibility Options Options that enable you to configure the Windows XP user environment to meet special visual, auditory, or mobility needs. Examples include FilterKeys, MouseKeys, StickyKeys, ToggleKeys, and SoundSentry.

ACPI See Advanced Configuration and Power Interface.

Action log See Setupact.log.

Active Directory The database segment of the Windows directory service. Active Directory stores information about network objects such as users and groups, printers, and computers. Users access Active Directory to locate resources on the network.

Active partition When basic storage is used, the partition where the boot files that are required for starting the computer are stored. Also referred to as the system partition.

Active volume When dynamic storage is used, the volume where the boot files that are required for starting the computer are stored. Also referred to as the system volume.

Add Printer Wizard The wizard used to add and share a local or network printer on a computer.

Add/Remove Programs Wizard The utility used to safely and completely remove applications including Registry files. The Add/Remove Programs Wizard now includes Windows Installer, which is useful for its diagnostic capabilities for malfunctioning applications.

Address Resolution Protocol (ARP) A protocol used to map an IP address to a media access control (MAC) address.

**ADMIN$** The shared folder used by administrators to administer Windows XP Professional. By default, C:\Windows, the system root folder, is shared as ADMIN$.

Administrative shares Folders that are automatically shared whose contents are available only to administrators. Administrative shares are appended with a dollar sign ($) to hide them from other users on the network. For example, the *%Systemroot%* folder, the root of each volume, and the location of the printer drivers are hidden administrative shares.

Advanced Configuration and Power Interface (ACPI) Power management standard that enables the operating system to control and manage power consumption.

Advanced Power Management (APM) BIOS-controlled method of power management. Uses activity timeouts to determine when to transition devices to low power states.

Alert Generated when a specific counter exceeds or falls below a specified value.

Answer file A script that is used to automate the installation process for unattended installations. It supplies the answers that would normally have to be entered during the Setup process, such as accepting the license agreement, the workgroup and computer name, network details, and so on. The script can fully automate or only partially automate the Setup process.

APIPA See Automatic Private IP Addressing.

APM See Advanced Power Management.

Appearance Settings for Internet Explorer that include the colors, fonts, languages, and accessibility features that you see on the Web pages you view.

Application Compatibility Toolkit A compatibility tool designed primarily for application developers, it provides a great deal of information valuable for troubleshooting, investigating, and resolving application compatibility issues with Windows XP. It contains various documents and tools such as the Application Verifier (AppVerifier), Application Compatibility Analyzer, and the Compatibility Administrator.

Application log Records events that occur when an application is run.

Application Verifier (AppVerifier) Allows you to configure a comprehensive series of tests to run in the background so you can monitor your applications' interactions with the Windows XP operating system.

ARP See Address Resolution Protocol.

Arp A command that displays and modifies the IP address-to-physical address (MAC address) translation tables used by the Address Resolution Protocol (ARP).

Automated System Recovery (ASR) A utility that is used to create an Automated System Recovery backup. The ASR backup is used to restore the system state and all files stored on the system volume.

Automatic Private IP Addressing (APIPA) A feature that you can use to automatically assign addresses to hosts on a network.

Automatic Updates A Windows XP utility that facilitates the downloading and installation of service packs and hotfixes.

Backup utility Used to create backup copies of data files and crucial operating system files to prevent the accidental loss of data due to hardware or software failure or user error. It can also be used to schedule system and data backups at regular intervals

Bare bones installation An installation in which you temporarily remove all nonessential hardware (sound cards, network cards, modems, etc.) and then reinstall each component after the installation is complete. This is done after you receive STOP errors during an installation so that you can install the operating system and identify the hardware, software, or device driver that is causing the problem.

Baseline data System configuration and performance data taken at various times to mark hardware and software changes. You compare current performance parameters to the baseline information to determine the effects of recent changes on system performance.

Basic Input/Output System (BIOS) Built-in computer software that determines what a computer can do without accessing any programs from a disk. The BIOS on a PC contains all of the code required to control the keyboard, display screen, disk drives, serial communications, and other miscellaneous functions. See also Firmware.

Basic storage A type of storage that divides a hard disk into primary and extended partitions. A basic disk can have up to four partitions. Basic disks are compatible with MS-DOS, Windows 3x, Windows 9x, Windows NT, Windows 2000, and Windows Server 2003.

BIOS See Basic Input/Output System.

Blue Screen of Death See STOP error.

Boot partition When basic storage is used, the partition where the Windows XP operating system files (*%Systemroot%* folder) are stored.

Boot volume When dynamic storage is used, the volume where the Windows XP operating system files (*%Systemroot%* folder) are stored.

Bottleneck A system resource that slows down the performance of a computer.

Broadcast A method for sending data simultaneously to all network hosts. Broadcasts can be used as a method of NetBIOS name resolution, but is inefficient because it generates a substantial amount of network traffic. It will not work on large networks that contain subnets connected by routers, because routers generally block broadcasts.

Cache A reserved portion of disk space in which recently accessed data is stored.

Caching The process in which data is copied from a server to a local workstation. Network files that are stored locally are called offline files. Caching reduces network traffic because data does not have to be accessed across the network more than once unless the copy on the server has changed.

Challenge Handshake Authentication Protocol (CHAP) Provides authentication when a user attempts to establish a connection based on values calculated using an algorithm.

Change permission A share permission that enables users to create folders, add files to folders, modify data in files, add data to files, modify file attributes, and delete files and folders, in addition to actions permitted by the Read permission.

CHAP See Challenge Handshake Authentication Protocol.

Checkupgradeonly switch The switch used to run the Windows XP Compatibility tool, which is included on the Windows XP Professional CD-ROM. You use this switch to generate a hardware compatibility report.

Chkdsk A utility used to check a hard disk for file system errors and bad sectors.

Cipher command The command issued at a command prompt that encrypts and decrypts files and folders.

CIW See Client Installation Wizard.

Client Installation Wizard (CIW) The wizard provided by RIS that prompts users through a remote installation of the operating system. CIW is used on client computers by end users who have been granted the right to create computer objects in the domain to select the RIS image to install.

Cmd.exe The command interpreter used by the Windows XP command shell. Cmd.exe is used to start programs and to send commands between applications. It translates the commands a user inputs into a form that the operating system understands.

Combination installation A type of installation in which you install the slipstreamed operating system as well as any additional application software that you want to include in the installation.

Command shell The program used instead of the graphical interface so that a user can interact directly with the operating system. Rather than clicking buttons and choosing commands from menus, users type commands and view text-based output.

Command.com The DOS file in which the DOS command processor, which receives and executes operating system commands, is stored.

Computer name (NetBIOS name) A unique name for a computer that can contain no more than 15 characters. The same name cannot be given to another computer, workgroup, or domain. On a domain-based network, the NetBIOS name appears in Active Directory as an object. It is used in the UNC path you use to create connections to shared resources.

Counter log Uses GUI data from System Monitor to create a log file.

Counter A performance measure for an object that can be quantified, such as the percentage of time the processor is busy (%Processor Time).

Default gateway Acts as an intermediate device between hosts on different network segments.

Defragmentation The process that rearranges files, programs, and unused space to ensure that all related components of the files and programs are placed in contiguous locations on the disk, enabling files to be located and opened more quickly.

Detect model A six-step troubleshooting model developed by Microsoft for addressing operating system problems.

Driver Rollback The tool used to reverse driver changes.

Device driver Software that enables a specific device—such as a printer, modem, or network card—to communicate with an operating system.

Device Manager A utility in Windows XP used to view and change device properties, update device drivers, configure device settings, and uninstall devices.

Digital certificate Digital data that contains the user's public key, identifies the Certification Authority (CA) that issued the data, names or identifies the subscriber, identifies the period of time the certificate is valid, and is digitally signed by the CA that issued it.

Directory database The database in which all user accounts for a domain are stored as well as all security configurations for the domain. The Directory database is the database segment of the Windows directory service, Active Directory.

Disk access time The amount of time it takes for the disk subsystem on a computer to access and display data that is requested by the operating system.

Disk Cleanup A utility used to locate files you are likely to want to delete such as Temporary Internet files, so that you can free space on a hard drive. It also selects files that you have not accessed for some time to target them for compression.

Disk Defragmenter A utility that rearranges files and unused space on a hard disk so that related data is placed in contiguous sectors on the hard disk.

Disk Management snap-in A utility used to view disk properties and perform disk management functions such as creating new partitions or volumes, setting an active partition, formatting drives, changing drive letters, and upgrading a disk from a conventional basic disk to a dynamic disk.

Disk space error The "Not enough disk space for installation" message during Setup indicates that you must use the Setup program to create a partition using the existing free space on the hard disk.

Distribution server A network file server that contains the Windows XP installation files.

DNS See Domain Name System.

Domain A group of networked computers that access a central directory database to log on to the network and access shared resources. All user accounts and security configurations for a domain are stored in the directory database. In Active Directory, a domain represents a single administrative entity.

Domain controller A server on which Active Directory is stored. Domain controllers manage security-related aspects of user/domain interactions. In a Windows domain, all domain controllers are, for the most part, equals, doing away with the concept of primary and backup domain controllers used in Windows NT.

Domain Name System (DNS) The main name resolution service for Windows. Correlates host names and fully qualified domain names (FQDNs) to IP addresses.

Dynamic Host Configuration Protocol (DHCP) A protocol that automatically assigns IP addresses.

Dynamic storage A storage method that uses volumes rather than partitions. On a dynamic disk, you can create an unlimited number of volumes, and you can extend volumes onto additional physical disks.

EAP See Extensible Authentication Protocol.

Effective permissions The actual permissions for a user or group when the cumulative effect of all of the shared folder permissions and NTFS permissions are considered. First, calculate the NTFS permissions for files and folders. The effect of NTFS permissions is cumulative, or least restrictive. Then calculate the shared folder permissions. When you combine the two, the most restrictive permission level is applied.

EFI See Extensible Firmware Interface.

EFS See Encrypting File System.

Empty recovery policy A recovery agent policy that remains on the computer after the recovery agent certificates are deleted.

Encrypting File System (EFS) A feature used to encrypt files and folders. Data is scrambled so that no one can access the file or folder unless they have a file encryption certificate and a private key.

Error log See Setuperr.log.

Event Viewer A console that contains the Application, Security, and System logs. These logs may contain information that can be helpful for determining the cause of a problem.

Extended partition A partition that is created by combining unpartitioned free space on a hard disk and linked to a primary partition to increase the available disk space.

Extensible Authentication Protocol (EAP) Used to extend the logon security process using smart cards or certificates.

Extensible Firmware Interface (EFI) Firmware is known as the Basic Input/Output System (BIOS) on x86-based computers and internal adapters, and as Extensible Firmware Interface (EFI) on Itanium-based computers. EFI is an updated BIOS model, developed by Intel for Itanium based computers. The EFI interface is designed to be independent of any specific operating system platform so that it can concentrate on support for feature functionality rather than operating system compatibility.

Fast User Switching feature that enables multiple users with local user accounts to be logged on to the same computer at the same time.

FAT See File Allocation Table.

FAT32 file system The 32-bit version of the FAT file system. It keeps track of the status of various segments of disk space used for file storage.

File Allocation Table (FAT) A list maintained by the operating system that keeps track of the status of various segments of disk space used for file storage. Also referred to as FAT16.

File Signature Verification utility A utility that is part of the Windows File Protection file-checking process. It can be run to identify and view information about unsigned files on a computer.

Files and Settings Transfer Wizard Used to transfer the files and settings of a user's old computer to a Windows XP computer provided that the two computers are connected by a direct cable or a network connection.

FilterKeys An accessibility option that programs the system to ignore repeated keystrokes.

Firmware Programming instructions, or code, contained in the motherboard. Firmware contains operating system-independent code necessary for the operating system to perform low-level functions such as startup self-tests and the initialization of the devices required to start Windows XP. Firmware is also known as the Basic Input/Output System (BIOS) on x86-based computers and internal adapters, and as Extensible Firmware Interface (EFI) on Itanium-based computers.

Forward lookup query Resolves a name to an IP address.

Full Control permission An NTFS permission for files and folders; also a share permission. The NTFS Full Control permission for files allows users to change permissions, take ownership, and perform all actions permitted by the other NTFS file permissions. The NTFS Full Control permission for folders allows users to change permissions and take ownership of folders. This permission includes all actions that are permitted by all other NTFS folder permissions. The Full Control share permission allows users full access to a shared folder, including all actions permitted by the Read and Change permissions; users can also change permission to the share.

Gpresult.exe A tool that simply displays which policies are applying to the computer and user account.

Group Policy Settings that are used to enhance and secure the working environment for users. Most Group Policy settings are associated with the Registry.

Group Policy Management Console (GPMC) A tool that performs many of the same functions as RSoP; however, GPMC does so in a more user-friendly environment and also adds group policy linking, creation, deletion, import/export, and modification functionality.

Group Policy Object (GPO) See Network policies.

Handle Any resource, such as a file, that is used by an application that has its own identification so that the program can access it.

Hardware profiles Contains information about the devices that need to be started when you boot the computer and the settings with which the devices should be started.

Help and Support Center Provides a user-friendly starting point for accessing system information that might be difficult to find otherwise. From the home page of the Help and Support Center, you can run troubleshooting wizards that seek to fix a particular performance issue. You can also use tools to view detailed information about the components of a system and how they are operating.

HelpAssistant account A built-in account that is activated when you send a remote assistance invitation.

Helper Console During a Remote Assistance session, the participants conduct their work through consoles that contain controls. The person providing assistance works with the Helper Console.

Hibernate A power management option used to save the contents of a computer's memory before a user shuts down the system. When the system is restarted, the files and documents that the user had open will be open on the desktop just as they were before hibernation was activated.

History A list of links to pages you have previously visited, stored in Internet Explorer's History bar and in the Address bar drop-down list.

Home folder A private network location used to store user data.

Home page The Web page that loads into a browser window by default when you first launch the browser or click the Home button on the toolbar.

Host name Name of a specific computer on a given network.

Hostname A utility that displays the host name for the local computer.

HOSTS file A text file stored on the local computer that contains the static mappings of host names to IP addresses and is used by Transmission Control Protocol/Internet Protocol (TCP/IP) utilities to resolve host names to their IP addresses.

Hot swapping The ability to add and remove devices without shutting down and restarting the system. Also called hot plugging.

Hotfix A software update package that includes one or more files that are used to address a problem.

ICF See Internet Connection Firewall.

Installation script A customized script that is created using Windows XP Setup Manager to specify variations in the software configurations of the computers on which Windows XP is being installed.

Integrated installation A type of installation in which you update the original Windows XP installation files on a shared distribution folder on a network with the files from the service pack. Also referred to as a slipstreamed installation.

Internet Connection Firewall (ICF) A stateful firewall for Windows XP clients that is intended to protect shared disks and folders from Internet attacks. It is a basic, not overly sophisticated firewall that monitors all traffic, checking both the source and the destination addresses.

Internet Explorer An Web browser program included and installed with Windows XP. It is used primarily to access Hypertext Markup Language (HTML) and File Transfer Protocol (FTP) resources, but also can be used to access resources stored locally and on your local area network (LAN).

Internet Protocol Security (IPSec) A set of security protocols and cryptographic protection that are used to encrypt TCP/IP traffic to ensure that communications within an intranet or the Internet are more secure. Typically used to support VPNs, IPSec provides the highest level of Internet security currently possible.

I/O (input/output) devices Include many familiar pieces of hardware that add functionality to a computer. Common input devices that users might need help with are mice, keyboards, scanners, and cameras. Common output devices include monitors, printers, speakers, and headphones.

IPC$ (Interprocess Communications) The administrative share used to facilitate IPC communication between systems.

Ipconfig The command used to confirm TCP/IP configuration parameter.

IPSec See Internet Protocol Security.

Kerberos V5 The primary authentication protocol for domains in Windows XP.

L2TP See Layer Two Tunneling Protocol.

Last Known Good Configuration (LKGC) A startup option used to start a computer using the information that was saved in the Registry after the last successful log on.

Layer Two Tunneling Protocol (L2TP) A tunneling protocol that creates a secure tunnel across an untrusted communication channel. L2TP must be used in connection with IPSec if you want to provide for data encryption.

List Folder Contents permission Allows users to view only the names of subfolders and files in a folder.

LKGC See Last Known Good Configuration.

LMHOSTS file A text file, stored on the local computer, that contains the static mappings of NetBIOS names to IP addresses for computers on remote networks only.

Local policy The base group policy for a computer. Contains settings that apply only to that computer. These settings are used to configure individual aspects of the system security that are not configured by Active Directory group policies, or apply security settings in cases in which the computer is not part of Active Directory (such as a workgroup computer, or a computer connected to a Windows NT domain).

Local print device Any device for which the spooling is done locally. The printer (software) is loaded locally on the computer, and all print functions are handled by the local computer.

Local security database A database that lists user accounts and resource security information for the local computer. Each computer user can share resources such as printers and folders with other users on the network. Users set access permissions for groups or other individual users to control access to resources stored on their computer.

Local security database The local accounts database responsible for storing local user and group accounts.

Local security policy The security settings component of the local policy.

Local user account An account that allows a user to log on only to a local computer and access only the resources on that computer.

Log files Files saved by the operating system or an application typically in a text format. You can use Notepad or an equivalent text editor to view the contents of a text log file to determine if it contains information useful for troubleshooting a problem.

Logged boot Enabled any time you choose a Safe Mode boot or when you choose the Enable Boot Logging option in the Advanced Boot Options menu. A logged boot creates a log file named Ntbtlog.txt in the *%Systemroot%* directory. This log file can be read with any text editor, and can be used to determine drivers that are causing the boot process to fail.

Logical drive When dynamic storage is used, refers to disk space set aside for storage within an extended volume

Logical partition When basic storage is used, refers to disk space set aside for storage within an extended partition.

Logical printer The software interface installed on a computer that delivers the requests for service from the operating system to the physical print device. When you make a request for a print job, the document is spooled (or stored) on the logical printer before it is sent to the actual print device. The logical printer represents a set of printer and print job capabilities including the types of document formats and the media types that are supported.

Logon script A script that runs each time a user logs on to a system.

Manage Documents permission The printer permission that allows the user to pause, resume, restart, and cancel all other users' printing jobs, but does not allow the user to send documents to the printer or control the status of the printer.

Manage Printers permission A printer permission that grants administrative control over a printer. Users can pause and restart the printer and change printer properties.

Master boot record (MBR) Located in the first sector of the hard drive. A program stored in this location begins the boot process by reading the partition table to determine which partition to boot from.

Master disk image In a Sysprep installation, you must first prepare a distribution model computer by performing a clean installation of Windows XP, installing all of the applications you will use on the network, and installing all necessary update service packs. You use this installation to create the master disk image with a third-party imaging tool. The master disk image will be transferred to the hard disks of the target computers.

Master file table (MFT) Contains information regarding in which cluster or clusters a file is stored.

MBR See Master boot record.

Member server A computer that is not a domain controller but is running the Windows 2000 Server or Windows Server 2003 operating system. Member servers participate in a domain, but they do not store a copy of the Active Directory database. They do not authenticate users, but they do use Kerberos to validate users' credentials with a domain controller. Shared resources, such as printers and folders, are stored on member servers.

MFT See Master file table.

Microsoft CHAP (MS-CHAP) Microsoft version of CHAP.

Mini-Setup Wizard An abbreviated version of the Setup Wizard, which is installed by the Sysprep tool on the distribution model computer so that, when a clone computer is booted up for the first time, the user will be prompted to accept the licensing contract and enter the product ID, regional settings, user name, company name, network configuration, workgroup or domain, and time zone. The Mini-Setup program also includes Plug and Play detection.

Mirrored volume Also known as RAID Level 1, this type of volume provides fault tolerance by duplicating data on two hard disks. Not supported by Windows XP.

Modem A device used to communicate between two computers over a telephone line.

Modify permission An NTFS permission for files and folders. The NTFS Modify permission for files allows users to modify and delete the file, run applications, change attributes, and perform all other actions permitted by the Write and Read & Execute permissions. The NTFS Modify permission for folders allows users to view, create, delete, and modify the content of folders, and to change attributes. It includes all tasks permitted by the Read, Write, and Read & Execute permissions.

MouseKeys An accessibility option that enables users to perform mouse functions using the numeric keyboard.

MS-CHAP See Microsoft CHAP.

Multiple booting Enables you to choose between one or more operating systems when you turn the computer on. The operating systems are saved in different folders (typically named Windows or Winnt), which can be on the same partition or on different partitions.

Multiple displays Enables you to expand the size of your desktop across more than one monitor.

My Computer Information A utility used to check what programs and hardware are installed on a computer, check the amount of available memory, or review diagnostic information about the health of this computer system.

Name resolution A process that resolves names into IP addresses and vice versa.

NBNS See NetBIOS name server.

Nbstat A command that displays protocol statistics and current TCP/IP connections using NetBIOS over TCP/IP (NBT).

Net Share A command-line utility used to create a shared folder using the syntax: net share *sharename=drive: path*, where *sharename* is the network name for the shared resource, *drive* designates the drive it is stored on, and *path* is the complete path to its location.

Net use A command-line utility used to create shortcuts to shared folders using the syntax: net use *driveletter: \\computername\sharename*.

NetBIOS name cache Stores information about the most recently resolved NetBIOS names in client memory.

NetBIOS name resolution The process of mapping a NetBIOS name to an IP address.

NetBIOS name See Computer name.

NetBIOS name server (NBNS) An application responsible for mapping NetBIOS names to IP addresses.

Netstat A command that displays TCP/IP protocol statistics and its network connections.

Network client A software application that enables a target computer without an operating system installed to connect to a distribution server.

Network Diagnostics utility Used to gather information about a computer to help users to troubleshoot network-related problems. A variety of tests can be run to scan a system to see whether network connectivity has been established and whether network-related programs and services are running.

Network polices Similar to local policies, network policies also apply Registry changes and configure the operating system. However, unlike local policies, more than one network policy may be applied to the computer or user account. Network policies are also known as Group Policy Objects (GPOs).

Network printer A device for which the spooling is done remotely. Workstations connect to these printers over the network, and all print jobs are sent from the workstation to the print server, which controls all printing to the print device.

Network Setup Wizard When you share a folder in Windows XP for the first time, you are prompted to use the Network Setup Wizard to ensure security for the computer or workgroup. The Network Setup Wizard sorts through the various configuration possibilities and offers you options.

New Connection Wizard Used to select the networking components required to establish connections with different kinds of computers.

No recovery policy The result of removing the recovery policy from a computer to disable EFS. Either a no recovery policy or an empty recovery policy disables EFS on a stand-alone computer. A no recovery policy at a higher level in a domain disables EFS at that level only; lower-level computers use their own local policies.

Notification area The area on the right end of the Windows taskbar that includes the clock, volume control, and other icons.

Nslookup A command for diagnosing problems with DNS name servers on your network by making DNS queries to these DNS servers.

NTFS file system An advanced file system that supports file system recovery, large storage media, long file names, file encryption, and disk quotas.

NTFS permissions Used to control access to objects on an NTFS volume, such as files and folders, and to ensure the security of data on an NTFS volume. They determine the tasks that users can perform to the content of files and folders.

Object A system resource, such as a processor, disk, network interface card (NIC), or memory, whose performance can be monitored.

Offline Files A Windows XP Professional feature that enables users to work on network files whether or not they are connected to the network. If granted permission to do so, administrators and users can select certain network files and folders to be cached, so that they are copied to the local workstation.

Optional Component Manager A Setup component that allows the integration of external components into the Setup process, such as IIS and COM+, which have their own setup routines.

Organizational unit (OU) A component of Active Directory representing a portion of a domain that can be administered separately.

PAP See Password Authentication Protocol.

Partition Part of a hard disk drive that has been configured to act as a logically separate unit of storage. Acts a logical division for storing data in an organized manner .

Password Authentication Protocol (PAP) Protocol that uses plaintext passwords for authentication.

Pathping The utility that combines the ping and tracert commands. It provides a statistical analysis of results over a period of time, which can vary depending on how many jumps must be analyzed. It displays the computer name and IP address for each jump and also calculates the percentage of lost/sent packets to each router or link.

Peer-to-peer network Another name for a workgroup network. All computers share resources as equals without a dedicated server.

Performance console A Microsoft Management Console that includes System Monitor and the Performance Logs and Alerts tool. System Monitor is used to view a graphical presentation of the performance of the resources on a computer system and the Performance Logs and Alerts toll is used to record the performance of resources in logs and to configure alerts to tell you when certain thresholds have been passed.

Performance Logs and Alerts Used to record the performance of resources in logs and to configure alerts which are activated based on threshold values that you set to perform specific actions.

Peripheral firmware Device-specific instructions that enable a device—such as an adapter card, CD-ROM drive, or audio device—to perform specific functions, but are independent of the operating system.

PHO The initial troubleshooting hierarchy (Physical, Hardware, Operating System), which guides you to check all of the physical issues first, the hardware issues second and the operating System issues last. This strategy follows the most generic to the most complex troubleshooting strategy recommended by the majority of professionals in the IT field.

Ping A utility used to test TCP/IP configurations and identify connection failures.

Plug and Play A standard developed by Intel that enables the operating system to recognize automatically a device when that device is connected to a computer.

Point-to-Point Tunneling Protocol (PPTP) A tunneling protocol that creates secure connections between VPN nodes, such as to corporate networks over the Internet.

Port mapping Created by setting a particular port number for a particular type of traffic when configuring Internet Connection Sharing (ICS). For example, you can forward inbound HTTP traffic to a Web server on your LAN by mapping port 80 on the computer, which is designated as the port for the HTTP service, to the NetBIOS name or IP address for the Web.

Power options Enable Windows XP to control and manage all of the power requirements of a system in order to manage power consumption.

Power schemes Enable Windows XP to automatically switch off a monitor and hard disk when the user is not working on the system.

PPTP See Point-to-Point Tunneling Protocol.

Primary partition A physical unit of storage created on a basic disk. You can create up to four partitions, or three primary partitions and one extended partition, on a basic disk using the MBR partition style.

Print device The physical hardware that actually prints the data.

Print permission A printer permission that allows users to connect to a network printer and print documents.

Print queue A list of print jobs from different workstations that is stored on the spool of the print server.

Print server A computer that is connected to and sharing one or more print devices. It is used to print documents and manage printers on the network.

Print spooling Refers to the process of caching print requests to a hard disk or memory, where it is held until the printer is ready for it.

Printer The software interface that delivers the request for service from the operating system to the physical print device.

Printer driver The software that contains the information used by the operating system to convert the print commands for a particular model of print device into a printer language such as Printer Control Language (PCL) or PostScript.

Printer permissions Permissions that you can assign to different types of users to control access to a printer and printer usage. There are three levels of printer permissions: Print, Manage Printers, and Manage Documents.

Printer pool A single printer that can queue print jobs to multiple ports and their associated print devices.

Printer port The software interface that a computer uses to communicate with a printer. The printer port does not refer to the physical hardware port, but rather to the software that communicates with it.

Private key An encryption key that a server or client keeps secret. It is the key used to decrypt data that is encrypted with its matching public (published) key.

Process In Task Manager, refers to an executable program or an application running as a component of the primary application.

Program Compatibility Wizard Enables you to test your program in different operating system modes (such as the operating system recommended for the program or that previously ran the program correctly) and with different settings (such as screen resolution and color display settings) to determine whether your software can work in another environment. After you determine the required mode and settings, you can permanently apply the changes to enable you to run the program successfully in the future.

Proxy server Provides a connection to the Internet for computers on a LAN, and a means of controlling incoming and outgoing requests for service.

Public key A key published by a server or client for other servers or clients to use. The public key is used to encrypt data that is sent to the owner of the key, but it cannot be used to decrypt the data.

Public key infrastructure (PKI) Defines the rules, policies, standards, and software that regulate certificates and public and private keys. It is the system of digital certificates, CAs, and other registration authorities that validates the authenticity of the parties in a digital transaction.

Quick Launch toolbar Contains shortcuts for frequently used items, giving the user quick, one-click access to them. It is located just to the right of the Start button.

RAID Level 0 See Striped volume.

RAID Level 1 See Mirrored volume.

RAID-5 volume A fault-tolerant, striped volume on which data is written across three to 32 hard disks, and parity information is stored across all of the disks so that data can be reconstructed in the event of a disk failure. RAID-5 is the best fault-tolerant solution for most companies, but it is more expensive to implement than mirroring. Not supported by Windows XP.

RAS connection See Remote Access Service connection.

Rbfg.exe See Remote Boot Floppy Generator utility.

Read & Execute permission An NTFS permission for files and folders. The NTFS Read & Execute permission for a file allows users to view the contents of files and run program applications. The NTFS Read & Execute permission for folders includes the tasks permitted by the Read and List Folder Contents permissions and gives users the ability to navigate, or traverse, through folders for which they do not have permission, to get to files and folders for which they do have permissions. Users can also run program files.

Read permission An NTFS permission for files and folders; also a share permission. The NTFS Read permission for files allows users to read the file and view the file attributes, file ownership, and permissions. The NTFS Read permission for folders allows users to open and view the content of files, folders, and subfolders. Users can also view the ownership of objects, permissions assigned to objects, and folder attributes such as Read-Only, Hidden, Archive, and System.

Recovery agent An account that is configured with a recovery agent certificate and a private key that can be used to open and use an encrypted file.

Recovery Console A command-line tool that you can start from Setup. You can use the Recovery Console to start and stop services, format drives, read and write data on a local drive (including drives formatted to use NTFS), and perform many other administrative tasks.

Regional and Language Options Enables the user to display the operating system in multiple languages and control the formatting of items such as numbers, currencies, time, and dates.

Remote Access Service (RAS) connection A connection that enables you to share and access resources on a computer or network from remote locations.

Remote Assistance Used to request help from an expert, help desk support personnel, a network technician, or someone who simply knows more about a particular problem than the person requesting assistance. The person providing assistance must be at another Windows XP computer, and the person requesting help must not be behind a firewall.

Remote Boot Floppy Generator utility (Rbfg.exe) Used to create a RIS bootable floppy disk that is required to install RIS-based operating systems on client computers that do not have a PXE-enabled boot ROM.

Remote Desktop Enables a user to access a remote computer from a local computer to run applications, open files, and access network resources.

Remote Desktop Connection Client software used to connect to a server using Remote Desktop for Administration and Terminal Services. The Remote Desktop client software is included in the default installation of Windows XP Professional.

Remote installation An installation in which the administrator connects to a Windows 2000 Server or Windows Server 2003 RIS server, which stores RIS images. RIS images are copies of the Windows XP Professional installation files. An installation of Windows XP Professional, without user interaction, can then be performed from a central location.

Remote Installation Preparation Wizard (Riprep.exe) Creates an operating system image and installs it on the RIS server. Can also be used to create an image that contains additional applications to be installed with the operating system and customized configuration settings.

Remote Installation Services (RIS) Enables administrators to create an image of the operating system that can be downloaded and installed automatically by client computers on a network.

Remote Installation Services server (RIS server) A Windows 2000 Server or Windows Server 2003 server on which RIS images are stored.

Remote Installation Services Setup Wizard (Risetup.exe) Creates an image of the Windows XP Professional installation files that can be used for an attended installation.

Repair installation An installation that deletes the files normally installed by Windows XP and then reinstalls them from the disk. A repair installation will not rebuild the Registry, delete applications and user settings, or fix problems caused by a program.

Repair utility Helps resolve several common network connectivity issues at once. The utility can renew an IP address lease that was assigned by a DHCP server, register with the DNS and WINS services, and clear out the name caches for ARP, DNS, and NetBIOS.

Resolver A host or library that can perform a recursive search and can issue iterative queries. A resolver queries other DNS name servers, including the root servers, to look up DNS records on behalf of the client. If the local DNS server cannot resolve the host name to its IP address, it sends an iterative query on behalf of the client to assist in answering the recursive query.

Restore point A saved "snapshot" of the data on a computer and the system state at a particular point in time. System restore points are created by default every 24 hours if the computer is left on. If the computer is shut down, a new restore point is created if the previous restore point is more than 24 hours old. If an unsigned driver is installed, a restore point will also be created.

Resultant Set of Policy (RSoP) A tool that enables you to visually examine the application of Group Policy.

Reverse lookup query Resolves an IP address to a name.

Riprep.exe See Remote Installation Preparation tool.

RIS See Remote Installation Services.

RIS boot disk The bootable floppy disk that is required to install RIS-based operating systems on client computers that do not have a PXE-enabled boot ROM. The Rbfg.exe floppy disk generator is used to create the RIS boot disk, which can be used with a variety of supported a Peripheral Component Interconnect (PCI)-compliant network adapters.

RIS image A copy of the Windows XP Professional installation files. Usually referred to simply as an image.

RIS server See Remote Installation Services server.

Risetup.exe See Remote Installation Services Setup Wizard.

Root-cause analysis The practice of searching for the source of problems to prevent them from recurring.

Route A command that displays and modifies the local routing table.

Routing table Used to provide routers with directions they will use to forward data packets to locations on other networks.

RSoP See Resultant Set of Policy.

Safe Mode Upon startup, loads a very basic set of drivers and services to allow for basic operating system functionality, disabling all others. Particularly useful in resolving problems related to a newly installed driver or application that crashes the system on a normal boot. Comes in three versions: Safe Mode, Safe Mode with Networking, and Safe Mode with Command Prompt.

Sector An organizational unit on a FAT16 or FAT32 partition. It is the smallest unit used to transfer data to and from the disk. It can contain 512 bytes of data.

Security and Configuration Analysis snap-in Uses databases to import a security template and compares the template to the currently configured computer settings. This functionality allows for "what-if" scenarios, enabling you to see the changes that will occur if you apply a particular template. In addition, you can use the Security Configuration and Analysis snap-in to compare current security settings to predefined security settings listed in a template.

Security settings Segments of Group Policy that are used to configure computers on your network to use IP security and to specify settings for everything from user rights to system services.

Security template A group of security settings that can be used to implement security in Windows 2000, Windows XP, or Windows Server 2003.

Security zone An Internet Explorer concept that groups Web sites based on the level of security required by their content. There are four zones: Internet, Local intranet, Trusted sites, and Restricted sites. Each zone has a default security level (such as low, medium or high), which you can customize if the default setting does not suit your precise needs.

Separator page A file, also referred to as a banner page, that identifies a printed document, usually with the name of the user who requested it, and the date and time. It is printed between documents so that you can easily identify the start and end of each print job.

Service pack A tested, cumulative set of all hotfixes, security updates, critical updates, and updates issued over a period of time for an operating system. Service packs may also contain additional fixes for problems discovered by the manufacturer since the product release and design changes requested by customer.

Setup Wizard The graphical phase of an installation, in which the Setup Wizard prompts you to provide information that is required to complete the installation.

Setupact.log Contains information about the events that transpired during Setup, including file copying, the creation of Registry entries, and any errors that may have occurred. Each event is recorded as it happened. Log files are created during the GUI phase of setup. Also referred to as the action log.

Setupapi.log A plaintext log file that provides a record of device and driver changes as well as major system changes, such as service pack and hotfix installations.

Setuperr.log Stores a description of the errors that have occurred and an entry indicating the magnitude of each error. Also referred to as the error log.

Setuplog.txt A hidden ASCII text file that is stored in the root directory, which contains data that is collected during Setup. This file is most often useful for installations that are hanging. It contains all of the installation options that are chosen during Setup.

Shared Documents folder Created and shared in the C:\Documents and Settings\All Users folder when Simple File Sharing is enabled. Two shared subfolders are automatically created: Shared Pictures and Shared Music. Any subfolder created in the Shared Documents folder is also shared.

Shiva Password Authentication Protocol (SPAP) An authentication protocol used when connecting to a Shiva server.

Simple File Sharing A feature exclusive to Windows XP used for file sharing in Windows XP Home Edition, where it is enabled by default. Simple File Sharing is also available in Windows XP Professional. It is enabled by default on stand-alone computers running Windows XP Professional and on XP Professional computers that are members of a workgroup. Simple File Sharing is disabled on computers running Windows XP Professional that are members of a domain.

Simple volume A type of volume on a dynamic disk that consists of disk space from only a single hard drive.

Site A component of Active Directory representing a single physical location.

Slipstreamed installation See Integrated installation.

Smart card A credit card-sized device used to store passwords, public and private keys, and other types of identifying information. A smart card reader can be attached to a Windows XP computer and used to make certificate-based authentication possible.

SoundSentry An accessibility function that programs Windows XP to generate visual warnings when the system's built-in speaker plays a sound.

Spanned volume A type of volume that consists of disk space from two to 32 disks that are combined to appear as one disk. Spanned volumes do not provide fault tolerance. When writing data to a spanned volume, Windows XP uses the disk space on the first available disk, and then continues to write data on other disks.

SPAP See Shiva Password Authentication Protocol.

Spool A folder where print jobs are stored before they are printed.

Standby A power management option used to shut off power to hardware components that are not in use, such as the monitor or hard drive, while maintaining power to the computer's memory so that users' work is not lost.

Start button The button on the Windows taskbar that opens the Windows XP Start menu.

Start menu Enables user to access resources available on the computer, such as programs, files, Control Panel, Help and Support, Search, etc.

Stateful firewall A system that prevents access to or from a network by adhering to a security policy that allows for forwarding of data packets that already correspond to an existing connection flow. Packets that are sent from behind the firewall that do not correspond to an existing connection flow are forwarded only after an entry is recorded in the ICF connection flow table. Packets that are received externally that do not correspond to an existing connection flow or port mapping are dropped.

StickyKeys An accessibility option that configures the system so that users do not have to hold down multiple keys simultaneously.

STOP error Can occur during an installation, generally when there are problems with incompatible software, device drivers, or hardware. The STOP error code provides valuable information to determine the source of the problem. Also referred to as the Blue Screen of Death.

Striped volume Also known as RAID Level 0. A type of volume that consists of two or more dynamic disks (up to 32) on which data is written in stripes across the disks, increasing disk performance. However, if one disk in a striped volume fails, you generally lose all of your data.

Subnet mask A 32-bit, four-part number used to break up an IP address into the network ID and host ID.

Support Tools A collection of tools included on the Windows installation CD, but not installed with the operating system. You must install them separately using the Support Tools Setup program. These tools assist Microsoft support personnel and network administrators to diagnose and resolve computer problems.

Symmetric key encryption An encryption system which uses a single, common key to encrypt and decrypt data.

Synchronization The process by which changes to offline files are updated to network files.

Sysprep.exe See System Preparation tool.

System Configuration Utility Used for a number of tasks, including stopping services. It is used to temporarily disable startup programs to alter how Windows XP Professional starts up. To use the System Configuration Utility, you must be logged on as an administrator or a member of the Administrators group.

System File Checker Used to scan and verify the version of all protected system files. If a protected file has been overwritten, the correct version of the file is retrieved from the *%Systemroot%*\system32\dllcache folder.

System Information console Stores information about a computer such as what devices are installed and loaded and the history of the drivers that have been installed on the machine. You can look here to find out if a new driver has recently been installed. You can also access other troubleshooting tools in the System Information console.

System Monitor Used to view a graphical representation of the performance of resources on your computer.

System partition See Active partition.

System Preparation tool (Sysprep.exe) Utility that is used to prepare a computer's hard disk for disk imaging. Sysprep works in conjunction with a third-party, disk-imaging application. It removes computer-specific information, such as the computer name, so that the image that is created can be transferred to the other computers.

System Restore A tool used to save or restore system states. The System Restore tool can be used to "roll back" operating system changes that may have made a system unstable, including Registry changes. It works by creating backup copies of configuration information before the change has occurred. These backup copies are made based on predefined trigger events (System restore points), which include activities such as installing an unsigned driver, installing applications, and auto-update installations.

System state A collection of system-specific data maintained by the operating system that must be backed up as a unit. The System State data includes the Registry, COM+ Class Registration database, system files, boot files, and files under Windows File Protection.

System volume See Active volume.

Task Manager A tool used to monitor and manage programs and processes running on a computer.

Taskbar Consists of several components, such as the Start button, the Quick Launch toolbar, program buttons (when programs are running), and the notification area. The default location for the taskbar is at the bottom of the desktop.

Temporary Internet files Copies of the Web pages you visit and the secondary files that are associated with the pages, such as images, cookies, audio, and scripts.

Thread A block of program code that is being executed.

Time to Live (TTL) The time during which the DNS server keeps a history of query results received from other name servers in its cache memory.

ToggleKeys An accessibility option that causes the computer to generate sounds when certain locking keys are pressed.

Trace log Surveys events that take place on the system.

Tracert A command that checks the route a packet follows to reach its destination.

Troubleshooting The process of isolating the source of a problem and then fixing it.

TTL See Time to Live.

UNC See Universal Naming Convention.

Uninstall The program that is used to uninstall the operating system. If hardware or software does not function as expected after you install Windows XP, Uninstall can be used to remove all Setup files from a computer and restore the previous operating system. Uninstall is available if you upgrade to Windows XP from Microsoft Windows 98, Microsoft Windows 98 Second Edition, and Microsoft Windows Me.

Uninterruptible power supply (UPS) Supplies backup battery power to a system during a sudden loss of electrical power.

Universal Naming Convention (UNC) The naming convention used to connect to any resource on a network for which the user has permission. The syntax for the UNC path is: *computername**sharename*.

Universal Serial Bus (USB) An external bus device (communication line) used to transfer data among the components in a computer system.

Untrusted network An open public network that can be accessed by anyone.

Update installation A type of installation in which the service pack is installed on a computer that already has Windows XP running on it, thus "updating" the operating system with new files.

Upgrade Advisor Tool that enables users to test their system's hardware and software compatibility before they purchase Windows XP.

UPS See Uninterruptible Power Supply.

USB See Universal Serial Bus.

User Console During a Remote Assistance session, the participants conduct their work through consoles that contain controls. The user requesting help works with the User Console.

VGA Mode Similar to Safe Mode, except it configures only the current video driver to display a resolution of 640 x 480. No other drivers or services are affected. Useful in situations where the display resolution was set too high and needs to be reverted.

Video adapter An expansion card that plugs into the motherboard of a computer to give it more display capabilities.

Virtual private network (VPN) A secure connection established using tunneling and encryption to transfer data securely over the Internet.

Volume Logical division of a dynamic disk. Can consist of portions of a single hard disk or several hard disks.

WDM See Win32 Driver Model.

WHQL See Windows Hardware Quality Lab.

Win32 Driver Model (WDM) A common model for device drivers supported across the Windows 98, Windows 2000, and Windows XP operating systems platforms. WDM supplies a cohesive architecture for device drivers that provides for cross-platform power management and supports Plug and Play capabilities.

Windows application compatibility mode Used to test programs running on Windows XP and make changes to the operating system to accommodate the programs. Instead of using the Program Compatibility Wizard, you can make changes manually using Windows application compatibility mode.

Windows Catalog Web-based Microsoft catalog that lists hardware devices that have been certified by Microsoft as compatible with Windows XP.

Windows File Protection A utility that prevents the replacement of system files in protected folders, some of which end in .sys, .dll, .ocx, .fon, and .exe. It detects any attempt by other programs to replace or move a protected system file and looks up the file signature in a catalog file (.cat) to determine if the correct Microsoft version is being installed.

Windows File Signature A verification utility used to identify unsigned files on your computer and display the related information such as the file's name, location, last modification date, file type, and the file's version number.

Windows Hardware Quality Lab (WHQL) A testing agency that qualifies hardware so that it can carry a "Designed for Windows" logo and be listed in the Windows Catalog.

Windows Installer An application installation technology that now augments the Add/Remove Programs Wizard. It helps network administrators with application deployment by providing an organized file format (.msi) that lists program functions so that they can manage user installation options. It also ensures the complete and safe removal of applications, including Registry files, and is useful for its diagnostic capabilities for malfunctioning applications.

Windows Internet Naming Service (WINS) Used to map IP addresses to NetBIOS or computer names.

Windows Update A Microsoft Web site that contains catalog of the latest updates available for your computer's operating system, software, and hardware. The list is ranked to let you know if the update is critical or just recommended, and may also include security updates and Internet and multimedia updates. The Web site is primarily intended for operating system service packs, but you can also update some drivers using this method.

Windows XP Compatibility tool A utility used to generate a hardware compatibility report. When you use the Windows XP Compatibility tool, you start the Setup program and check for compatible hardware and software. Then Setup stops and produces the report.

WINS See Windows Internet Naming Service.

WINS client A client on a network that has been configured to use WINS.

WINS database A database that holds NetBIOS name-to-IP address mappings.

WINS server The computer that runs WINS.

Workgroup A group of computers that are connected, most often through a LAN, enableing users to share information and resources. A workgroup is also referred to as a peer-to-peer network.

Write permission NTFS permission for files and folders. The NTFS Write permission for a folder allows users to create new files and subfolders in the folder, to view folder ownership and the assigned permissions, and to use the Properties dialog box to change folder attributes. The NTFS Write permission for a file allows users to change the file, change file attributes, and view file ownerships and permissions.

Exam 70-271 Objectives

INSTALLING A WINDOWS DESKTOP OPERATING SYSTEM

1.01 Perform and troubleshoot an attended installation of a Windows XP operating system.
- 1.01 (a) Answer end-user questions related to performing an attended installation of a Windows XP operating system.
- 1.01 (b) Troubleshoot and complete installations in which an installation does not start. Tasks include configuring the device boot order and ascertaining probable cause of the failure to start.
- 1.01 (c) Troubleshoot and complete installations in which an installation fails to complete. Tasks include reviewing setup log files and providing needed files.
- 1.01 (d) Perform post-installation configuration. Tasks include customizing installations for individual users and applying service packs.

1.02 Perform and troubleshoot an unattended installation of a Windows desktop operating system.
- 1.02 (a) Answer end-user questions related to performing an unattended installation of a Windows XP operating system. Tasks include starting an installation, answering questions asked by an end user during an installation, and performing post-installation tasks.
- 1.02 (b) Configure a PC to boot to a network device and start installation of a Windows XP operating system. Tasks include configuring PXE compliant network cards.
- 1.02 (c) Perform an installation by using unattended installation files.

1.03 Upgrade from a previous version of Windows.
- 1.03 (a) Answer end-user questions related to upgrading from a previous version of Windows. Considerations include available upgrade paths and methods for transferring user state data.
- 1.03 (b) Verify hardware compatibility for upgrade. Considerations include minimum hardware and system resource requirements.
- 1.03 (c) Verify application compatibility for upgrade. Tasks include ascertaining which applications can and cannot run, and using the application compatibility tools.
- 1.03 (d) Migrate user state data from an existing PC to a new PC.
- 1.03 (e) Install a second instance of an operating system on a computer.

MANAGING AND TROUBLESHOOTING ACCESS TO RESOURCES

2.01 Monitor, manage, and troubleshoot access to files and folders.
- 2.01 (a) Answer end-user questions related to managing and troubleshooting access to files and folders.
- 2.01 (b) Monitor, manage, and troubleshoot NTFS file permissions.
- 2.01 (c) Manage and troubleshoot simple file sharing.
- 2.01 (d) Manage and troubleshoot file encryption.

2.02 Manage and troubleshoot access to shared folders.
- 2.02 (a) Answer end-user questions related to managing and troubleshooting access to shared folders.
- 2.02 (b) Create shared folders.
- 2.02 (c) Configure access permission for shared folders on NTFS partitions.
- 2.02 (d) Troubleshoot and interpret Access Denied messages.

2.03 Connect to local and network print devices.
- 2.03 (a) Answer end-user questions related to printing locally.
- 2.03 (b) Configure and manage local printing.
- 2.03 (c) Answer end-user questions related to network-based printing.
- 2.03 (d) Connect to and manage printing to a network-based printer.

2.04 Manage and troubleshoot access to and synchronization of offline files.
- 2.04 (a) Answer end-user questions related to configuring and synchronizing offline files.
- 2.04 (b) Configure and troubleshoot offline files.
- 2.04 (c) Configure and troubleshoot offline file synchronization.

CONFIGURING AND TROUBLESHOOTING HARDWARE DEVICES AND DRIVERS

3.01 Configure and troubleshoot storage devices.
- 3.01 (a) Answer end-user questions related to configuring hard disks and partitions or volumes.
- 3.02 (b) Manage and troubleshoot disk partitioning.
- 3.03 (c) Answer end-user questions related to optical drives such as CD-ROM, CD-RW, DVD, and DVD-R.
- 3.04 (d) Configure and troubleshoot removable storage devices such as pen drives, flash drives, and memory cards.

3.02 Configure and troubleshoot display devices.
- 3.02 (a) Answer end-user questions related to configuring desktop display settings.
- 3.02 (b) Configure display devices and display settings.
- 3.02 (c) Troubleshoot display device settings.

3.03 Configure and troubleshoot Advanced Configuration and Power Interface (ACPI).
- 3.03 (a) Answer end-user questions related to configuring ACPI settings.
- 3.03 (b) Configure and troubleshoot operating system power settings.
- 3.03 (c) Configure and troubleshoot system standby and hibernate settings.

3.04 Configure and troubleshoot I/O devices.
- 3.04 (a) Answer end-user questions related to configuring I/O devices.
- 3.04 (b) Configure and troubleshoot device settings.
- 3.04 (c) Configure and troubleshoot device drivers for I/O devices.
- 3.04 (d) Configure and troubleshoot hardware profiles.

CONFIGURING AND TROUBLESHOOTING THE DESKTOP AND USER ENVIRONMENTS

4.01 Configure the user environment.
- 4.01 (a) Answer end-user questions related to configuring the desktop and user environment.
- 4.01 (b) Configure and troubleshoot task and toolbar settings.
- 4.01 (c) Configure and troubleshoot accessibility options.
- 4.01 (d) Configure and troubleshoot pointing device settings.
- 4.01 (e) Configure and troubleshoot fast-use switching.

4.02 Configure support for multiple languages or multiple locations.
- 4.02 (a) Answer end-user questions related to regional settings.
- 4.02 (b) Configure and troubleshoot regional settings.
- 4.02 (c) Answer end-user questions related to language settings.
- 4.02 (d) Configure and troubleshoot language settings.

4.03 Troubleshoot security settings and local security policy.
- 4.03 (a) Answer end-user questions related to security settings.
- 4.03 (b) Identify end-user issues caused by local security policies such as Local Security Settings and Security Configuration and Analysis.
- 4.03 (c) Identify end-user issues caused by network security policies such as Resultant Set of Policy (RSoP) and Group Policy.

4.04 Configure and troubleshoot local user and group accounts.
- 4.04 (a) Answer end-user questions related to user accounts.
- 4.04 (b) Configure and troubleshoot local user accounts.
- 4.04 (c) Answer end-user questions related to local group accounts.
- 4.04 (d) Configure and troubleshoot local group accounts. Considerations include rights and permissions.

4.05 Troubleshoot system startup and user logon problems.
- 4.05 (a) Answer end-user questions related to system startup issues.
- 4.05 (b) Troubleshoot system startup problems.
- 4.05 (c) Answer end-user questions related to user logon issues.
- 4.05 (d) Troubleshoot local user logon issues.
- 4.05 (e) Troubleshoot domain user logon issues.

4.06 Monitor and analyze system performance.
- 4.06 (a) Answer end-user questions related to system performance.
- 4.06 (b) Use Help and Support to view and troubleshoot system performance.
- 4.06 (c) Use Task Manager to view and troubleshoot system performance.
- 4.06 (d) Use the Performance tool to capture system performance information.

TROUBLESHOOTING NETWORK PROTOCOLS AND SERVICES

5.01 Troubleshoot TCP/IP. Tools include ARP; the Repair utility; connection properties; and the ping, ipconfig, pathping, and nslookup commands.
- 5.01 (a) Answer end-user questions related to configuring TCP/IP settings.
- 5.01 (b) Configure and troubleshoot manual TCP/IP configuration.
- 5.01 (c) Configure and troubleshoot automated TCP/IP address configuration.
- 5.01 (d) Configure and troubleshoot Internet Connection Firewall (ICF) settings such as enable and disable. Considerations include indications of issues related to enabling or disabling ICF.

5.02 Troubleshoot name resolution issues.
- 5.02 (a) Configure and troubleshoot host name resolution issues on a client computer. Considerations include Hosts files and DNS.
- 5.02 (b) Configure and troubleshoot NetBIOS name resolution issues on a client computer. Considerations include Lmhosts files and WINS.

5.03 Configure and troubleshoot remote connections.
- 5.03 (a) Configure and troubleshoot a remote dialup connection. Tasks include client-side configuration.
- 5.03 (b) Configure and troubleshoot a remote connection across the Internet. Tasks include client-side configuration.

5.04 Configure and troubleshoot Internet Explorer.
- 5.04 (a) Configure and troubleshoot Internet Explorer connections properties.
- 5.04 (b) Configure and troubleshoot Internet Explorer security properties.
- 5.04 (c) Configure and troubleshoot Internet Explorer general properties.

5.05 Configure and troubleshoot end-user systems by using remote connectivity tools.
- 5.05 (a) Use Remote Desktop to configure and troubleshoot an end user's desktop.
- 5.05 (b) Use Remote Assistance to configure and troubleshoot an end user's desktop.

Notes

Notes

Notes

Notes

Notes